Standard Catalogue of British Coins

Volume I

COINS OF ENGLAND AND THE UNITED KINGDOM

18th Edition

Edited by

Peter Seaby & P. Frank Purvey

adapted, with additional material, from the catalogue originally compiled by

H. A. Seaby

Seaby

London

A Catalogue of the Coins of Great Britain
and Ireland
first published 1929

Standard Catalogue of the Coins of Great
Britain and Ireland
first published 1945

Standard Catalogue of British Coins:
Parts 1 & 2. Coins of England and the United Kingdom
published annually 1962-1976
Volume 1 Revised, 16*th edition*, 1978
17*th edition*, 1980
18*th edition*, 1981

Photography by P. Frank Purvey

Distributed by B. A. Seaby Ltd.
11 Margaret Street, London W1N 8AT.

also

M. R. Roberts, Wynyard Coin Centre,
7, Hunter Arcade, Sydney, N.S.W., 2000
Australia.

Numismatic Fine Arts, P.O.B. 3788,
342 North Rodeo Drive, Beverly Hills,
California, 90212, U.S.A.

Sequoia Numismatics Inc.,
P. O. Box 401, Clementon, N. J., 08021
U.S.A.

ISBN 0 900652 58 6

Printed in England by ROBERT STOCKWELL LTD., London SE1 1YP

CONTENTS

PREFACE

It is just twenty years since we prepared the first issue of *Coins of England and the United Kingdom* as the first volume of Seaby's "Standard Catalogue of British Coins", which itself had been an adaptation and improvement upon our *Standard Catalogue of the Coins of Great Britain and Ireland*, first published in 1945.

In this new edition valuations have been revised to accord with current market prices and there have been minor revisions to the text. There has also been the addition of a number of recently-discovered new types, such as the new silver coins of Verica and the new silver penny type of the 'Empress' Matilda. If comparisons are made with values given in early editions it should be borne in mind that in this edition the values of Ancient British gold and silver are now stated for coins in "Very fine" condition, though base metal coins remain as "Fine". Values of Roman coins are all for "Very fine" pieces unless otherwise stated. This change reflects the average condition of pieces available to collectors.

This volume, though intended primarily for the collector, will also be found to be a compact general handbook for the archaeologist, museum curator and amateur coin finder, and for that matter, any person who has a coin to identify and who wishes to know its approximate value. Its format corresponds with that of our *Roman Coins and their Values*, *Byzantine Coins and their Values*, and the two-volume *Greek Coins and their Values.*

We would like to acknowledge the help we have received from a number of collectors and specialists in certain series, and we have particularly valued the comments and suggestions of those who have used previous editions of the catalogue.

Those who have been engaged in the revision of this edition, apart from the editors, are Stephen Mitchell (gold coins), David Sear (Roman), Robert Sharman (hammered coins), Donna Hills and Brian Reeds (milled coins).

P. J. SEABY
P. F. PURVEY

January 1981

VIEW AND REVIEW

The numismatic event of the year has to be the issue by the Royal Mint of a complete set of proof gold coins from the five pounds down to the half sovereign. It had been a great disappointment to collectors of British gold coins that proofs had not been made available in 1953 to maintain the continuity of jubilee and coronation gold sets. It is a pity that the Royal Mint authorities have such a poor sense of timing; the obvious occasion for the issue would have been the Silver Jubilee year, but we remember that the Mint was a couple of years late with the 'Last Sterling' proof set. However, we have to record that the Queen Mother's 80th Birthday crown did arrive on time!

Your editors are also pleased to note that their suggestion that a half-sovereign issue might be 'a real money spinner and a foreign currency earner' (View and Review, 17th Ed.) has been taken seriously by the Mint. Although a proof issue was not exactly what we had in mind we wonder whether this may be a forerunner to a non-proof issue?

While on the subject of the Royal Mint, there have been a number of comments made on the removal of the Mint's collection of coins, medals, dies and coining tools from their former Tower Hill home to the new mint at Llantrisant in South Wales. It may not seem unreasonable for them to want their reference collection to be held adjacent to their manufactory, but a very strong case could be made out, not only for retaining the collection in London, but also for amalgamating it with the National Collection held at the British Museum in Bloomsbury. From a purely numismatic point of view there could be many advantages in moving the entire Department of Coins and Medals to Tower Hill. With more room available for both staff and students the Department could function more efficiently and give a better service.

A world record price of one million dollars for a coin was established in 1980 and we are pleased to note that it was not a modern rarity which brought this figure but a true numismatic work of art—the celebrated silver dekadrachm of Akragas in Sicily struck *c.* 412 B.C. This magnificent Greek coin is one of a very few known specimens, the majority of which are in museums. The highest price for a British coin (and a new record) in 1980 was £45,000 for a gold triple unite of Charles I of the Shrewsbury mint.

The English series continues to be a leader in collecting interest throughout the English speaking world. Early portrait pieces, Royal Maundy money and Royal Mint proof sets have all shown major gains over the past year. A marked increase in both interest and value is also noted in the field of commemorative medals, particularly of the Georgian period, for which a guide now exists with the publication of the first volume of *British Historical Medals* by Laurence Brown.

Some series of English coins have presented great difficulty in re-pricing this year. Contrary to popular belief, not all coins have risen substantially in value this last year, or indeed by the same percentage. Many coins in fine and very fine condition show little movement in value over the last year while a few in this condition have risen by 50% or more. The tendency has been for the differential between coins in very fine and extremely fine condition to increase substantially, reflecting the continuing desire of collectors for superb examples. Despite the interest shown in coins by the investor in recent years this is still very much a collector-orientated hobby and, in fact, many who began as investors have become so fascinated by the history and lore of coins that they are now avid collectors. Long may this continue.

THIS CATALOGUE

Arrangement

The arrangement of this catalogue is not completely uniform, but generally it is divided into metals (gold, silver, copper, etc.) under each reign, then into coinages, denominations and varieties. In the Celtic section the uninscribed coins are listed before the dynastic coins; under Charles II all the hammered coins precede the milled coinage; the reign of George III is divided into coins issued up to 1816 and the new coinage from 1816 to the end of the reign; and under Elizabeth II the decimal issues are separated from the *£.s.d.* coinages.

Every major coin type is listed though not every variety. We have endeavoured to give rather more coverage to the varieties of relatively common coins, such as the pence of Edward I, II and III, than to the very much rarer coins of, for instance, King Offa of Mercia.

Values

The values given represent the scale of **retail prices** at which Seaby's are offering coins **for sale** at the time of going to press, and *not* the price that Seaby's pay. These prices are based on our knowledge of the numismatic market, the current demand for particular coins, recent auction sale prices and, in those cases where certain coins have not appeared for sale for some years, our estimation of what they would be likely to sell at today, bearing in mind their rarity and appeal in relation to somewhat similar coins where a current value *is* known. Values are given for two grades of preservation from the end of the 10th century and for three grades of preservation for most coins of the 19th and early 20th centuries.

Seaby's endeavour to be reasonably conservative in grading the state of preservation of coins, as our clients well know. Collectors normally require coins in the best condition they can afford and, except in the case of a really rare coin, a piece that is considerably worn is not wanted and has little value. The values given in the catalogue are for the exact state of preservation stated at the head of each column; and bearing in mind that a score of identical coins in varying states of wear could be lined up in descending order from mint condition (FDC, *fleur de coin*), through *very fine* (VF) to *poor* state, it will be realized that only in certain instances will the values given apply to particular coins. A 'fine' (F) coin may be worth anything between one quarter and a half of the price quoted for a 'very fine' (VF), on the other hand a piece in really mint condition will be valued substantially higher than the price quoted for 'extremely fine' (EF).

We emphasize again that the purpose of this catalogue is to give a general value for a particular class of coin in a specified state of preservation, and also to give the collector an idea of the range and value of coins in the English series. The value of any particular piece depends on three things:

Its exact design, legend, mintmark or date.

Its exact state of preservation; this is of prime importance.

The demand for it in the market at any given time.

Some minor varieties are much scarcer than others, and, as the number of coins issued varies considerably from year to year, coins of certain dates and mintmarks are rarer and of more value than other pieces of similar type. The prices given for any type are for the commonest variety, mintmark or date of that type.

Ordering coins from this catalogue

We do not have every coin in stock that is listed in this catalogue. A large selection is, however, always available for viewing by personal callers and coins may be ordered by post on seven days approval from time of delivery by known clients who have a credit account with us.

When making enquiries please ensure that the number of the coin is quoted correctly and that the reference is to the 18th edition.

A BEGINNER'S GUIDE TO COIN COLLECTING

The Scope

Coin collecting is a fascinating recreation. It requires little physical exertion and only as much mental effort as one wishes to give at any one time. Numismatics has vast scope and boundless ramifications and byways, and it encompasses not only things historical and geographical, but it also touches on economics, metallurgy, heraldry, literature, the fine arts, politics, military history and many other disciplines. This catalogue is solely concerned with British coinage, but from the start the beginner should appreciate that the coinage of our own nation may be seen as a small, but important part of the whole gamut of world currency.

The first coins, made of electrum, a natural alloy of gold and silver, were issued in western Asia Minor about the middle of the seventh century B.C. Over the next century or so coinage of gold and silver spread across the Aegean to mainland Greece, southwards to the eastern Mediterranean lands and eventually westward to the Adriatic cities and the Greek colonies in southern Italy, Sicily and beyond. The coins of the Greeks are noted for their beautiful, sometimes exquisite craftsmanship, with many of the coin types depicting the patron deities of their cities. Coins of Philip II of Macedon (359-336 B.C.), father of Alexander the Great, circulated amongst the Celtic peoples of the Danubian basin and were widely copied through central Europe and by the Gauls in France. Gold Gaulish staters were reaching Britain around the beginning of the first century B.C. and the earliest gold to be struck in the island must have been produced shortly afterwards.

The coins of the Romans cover some seven centuries and comprise an enormous number of different types current throughout a major part of the civilized world from Spain to further Syria and from the Rhine in the north to the Sudan in the south. The Roman province of Britain was part of this vast empire for four hundred years and innumerable Roman coins have been recovered from sites in this country, most being made of brass or bronze and many being quite inexpensive.

Following the revival of commerce after the Dark Ages coinage in Western Europe was virtually restricted to silver until the thirteenth century, though gold was still being minted at Byzantium and in the Islamic world. In the Middle Ages many European cities had their own distinctive coinage, and money was issued not only by kings, but also by many lesser nobles, bishops and abbots. From the time of the later Crusades gold returned to the west; and the artistic developments of the Renaissance brought improved portraiture and new minting techniques.

Large silver crown-size thalers were first minted at Joachimsthal in Bohemia early in the sixteenth century. With substantial shipments of silver coming to Europe from the mines of Spanish America over the next couple of centuries a fine series of larger coins were issued by the European states and cities.

Both Germany and Italy became unified nation states during the nineteenth century but balancing the reduction in European minting authorities were the new coins of the independent states of South and Central America. Over the past quarter century many new nations have established their independence and their coinage provides a large field for the collector of modern coins.

It can be seen that the scope for the collector is truly vast, but besides the general run of official coinage there is also the large series of token coins—small change unofficially produced to supplement the inadequate supply of authorised currency. These tokens were issued by merchants, innkeepers and manufacturers in many towns and villages in the 17th, 18th and 19th centuries and many collectors specialise in their local issues.

Some coins have designs of a commemorative nature; an example being the recent Silver Jubilee crown, but there are also large numbers of commemorative medals which, though never intended for use as coinage, are sometimes confused with coins, being metal objects of a similar shape and sometimes a similar size to coins. This is another interesting field for collectors as these medals may have excellent portraits of famous men or women, or they may commemorate important events or scientific discoveries. Other metallic objects of coin-like appearance may be reckoning counters, advertising tickets, various other tickets and passes, and items such as brass coin weights.

Minting processes

From the time of the earliest Greek coins to about the middle of the 16th century coins were made by hand.

The method of manufacture was simple. The obverse and reverse designs were engraved or punched into the prepared ends of two bars of iron, shaped or tapered to the diameter of the required coin. The obverse die, known as the *pile*, was usually spiked to facilitate its being anchored firmly into a block of wood or metal. The reverse die, the *trussel*, was held by hand or grasped by tongs.

The coin was struck by placing a metal blank between the two dies and striking the trussel with a hammer. Thus, all coinage struck by this method is known as 'hammered' money. Some dies are known to have been hinged to ensure exact register between the upper and lower die. Usually a 'pair of dies' consisted of one obverse die (normally the more difficult to make) and two reverse dies. This was because the shaft of iron bearing the reverse design eventually split under the constant hammering; two reverse dies usually being needed to last out the life of the obverse die.

Sometime towards the middle of the 16th century experiments, first in Germany and later in France, resulted in the manufacture of coins by machinery.

The term 'milled' which is applied to all machine-made coins comes from the type of machinery used, the mill and screw press. With this machinery the obverse die was fixed and the reverse die brought into contact with the blank by heavy vertical pressure applied by a screw or worm-drive connected to a cross bar with heavy weights at each end. These weights usually had long leather thongs attached which allowed a more powerful force to be applied by the operators who revolved the arms of the press. New blanks were placed on the lower die and struck coins were removed by hand. The screw press brought more pressure to bear on the blanks and this pressure was evenly applied.

Various attempts were made during the reigns of Elizabeth I and Charles I to introduce this type of machinery with its vastly superior products. Opposition from the moneyers who feared the new press would destroy their livelihood prevailed until the restoration, when Charles II brought to London from Holland the Roettiers brothers and their improved screw press.

The first English coins made for circulation by this new method were the silver crowns of 1662, which bore an inscription on the edge, DECVS ET TVTAMEN, "an ornament and a safeguard", a reference to the fact that the new coins could not be clipped; a crime made easier by the thin and often badly struck hammered coins.

The mill and screw press was used until new steam powered machinery made by Boulton and Watt was installed in the new mint on Tower Hill. This machinery had been used most successfully by Boulton to strike the 'cartwheel' two- and one-penny pieces of 1797 and many other coins, including 'overstriking' Spanish eight real pieces into Bank of England 'dollars', the old Mint presses not being able to exert sufficient power to do this. This new machinery was first used at the Mint to strike the 'new coinage' halfcrowns of 1816, and it operated at a far greater speed than the old type of mill and screw presses and achieved a greater sharpness of design.

The modern coining presses by Hordern, Mason and Edwards, now operating at the new mint at Llantrisant are capable of striking at a rate of up to 300 coins a minute.

Condition

One of the more difficult problems for the beginner is accurately to assess the condition of a coin. A common fault among collectors is to overgrade and, consequently, to overvalue their coins.

Most dealers will gladly spare a few minutes to help new collectors. Dealers, such as ourselves, who issue price lists with illustrations enable collectors to see exactly what the coins look like and how they have been graded.

Coins cannot always be graded according to precise rules. Hammered coins often look weak or worn on the high parts of the portrait and the tops of the letters; this can be due to weak striking or worn dies and is not always attributable to wear through long use in circulation. Milled coins usually leave the mint sharply struck so that genuine wear is easier to detect. However a $\times 8$ or $\times 16$ magnifying glass is essential, especially when grading coins of Edward VII and George V where the relief is very low on the portraits and some skill is required to distinguish between an uncirculated or FDC coin and one in EF condition.

The condition or grade of preservation of a coin is usually of greater importance than its rarity. By this we mean that a common coin in superb condition is often more desirable and more highly priced than a rarity in poor condition. Few coins that have been pierced or mounted as a piece of jewellery have any interest to collectors.

One must be also on the lookout for coins that have been 'plugged', i.e., that have been pierced at some time and have had the hole filled in, sometimes with the missing design or letters re-engraved.

Badly cleaned coins will often display a complexity of fine interlaced lines and such coins have a greatly reduced value. It is also known for coins to be tooled or re-engraved on the high parts of the hair, in order to 'increase' the grade of the coin and its value.

Cleaning coins

Speaking generally, *don't* clean coins. More coins are ruined by injudicious cleaning than through any other cause, and a badly cleaned coin loses much of its value. A nicely toned piece is usually considered desirable. Really dirty gold and silver can, however, be carefully washed in soap and water. Copper coins should never be cleaned or washed, they may be lightly brushed with a brush that is not too harsh.

Buying and selling coins

Swopping coins at school or with other collectors, searching around the antique shops, telling your relatives and friends that you are interested in coins, or even trying to find your own with a metal detector, are all ways of adding to your collection. However, the time will come for the serious collector when he wants to acquire specific coins or requires advice on the authenticity or value of a coin.

At this point an expert is needed, and generally the services of a reputable coin dealer will be sought. There are now a large number of coin dealers in the U.K., many of whom belong to the B.N.T.A. or the I.A.P.N. (the national and international trade associations) and a glance through the 'yellow pages' under 'coin dealer' or 'numismatist' will often provide local information.

We at Seaby's have been buying and selling coins for over fifty years, and have been publishing a priced catalogue since 1929. In addition to our books on English, Greek, Roman and Byzantine coins and on British tokens, we also publish "Seaby's Monthly Coin and Medal Bulletin", a magazine containing articles, and lists of coins for sale.

Our stock of coins for sale represent every period from Greek and Roman times to the present day, and individual prices of coins range from a pound or so to several thousands. Callers at our premises are always made very welcome and in addition to the coins our ground floor bookshop carries a stock of almost two thousand titles on coins and allied subjects.

When buying coins Seaby's reckon to pay a fair proportion of the retail value; this ranges from a half or less for inexpensive common coins to three quarters or more for particularly choice and expensive items.

Useful suggestions

Security and insurance. The careful collector should not keep valuable coins at home unless they are insured and have adequate protection. Local police and insurance companies will give advice on what precautions may be necessary.

Most insurance companies will accept a valuation based on the Standard Catalogue. It is usually possible to have the amount added to a householders' contents policy. A 'Fire, Burglary and Theft' policy will only cover loss from the assured's address, but an 'All Risks' policy will usually cover accidental damage and loss anywhere within the U.K. We can recommend a Lloyds broker, if requested.

Coins deposited with a bank or placed in a safe-deposit box will usually attract a lower insurance premium.

Keeping a record. All collectors are advised to have an up-to-date record of their collection, and, if possible, photographs of the more important and more easily identifiable coins. This should be kept in a separate place from the collection, so that a list and photographs can be given to the police should loss occur. Note the price paid, from whom purchased, the date of acquisition and the condition.

Storage and handling. New collectors should get into the habit of handling coins by the edge. This is especially important as far as highly polished proof coins are concerned.

Collectors may initially keep their coins in paper or plastic envelopes housed in boxes, albums or special containers. Many collectors will eventually wish to own a hardwood coin cabinet in which the collection can be properly arranged and displayed. If a home-made cabinet is being constructed avoid oak and cedar wood; mahogany, walnut and rosewood are ideal. It is important that coins are not kept in a humid atmosphere; especial care must be taken with copper and bronze coins which are very susceptible to damp or condensation which may result in a green verdigris forming on the coins.

From beginner to numismatist

The new collector will feel that he has much to learn. He can best advance from tyro to experienced numismatist by examining as many coins as possible, noting their distinctive features and by learning to use the many books of reference that are available. It will be an advantage if there is a local numismatic society to join as this will provide an opportunity for meeting other enthusiasts and obtaining advice from more knowledgeable collectors. Most societies have a varied programme of lectures, exhibitions and occasional auctions of members' duplicates (see pp. 310-11).

Those who become members of one or both of the national societies, the Royal Numismatic Society and the British Numismatic Society, can be sure of receiving an annual journal containing authoritative papers.

Many museums have coin collections available for study and a number of museum curators are qualified numismatists.

COIN DENOMINATIONS

Gold	
Angel	Eighty pence (6s. 8d.) from 1464; later 7s. 6d., 10s. and 11s.
Aureus	Roman currency unit (originally $\frac{1}{60}$th lb), discontinued A.D. 324.
Britain Crown	Five shillings, 1604-12; 5s. 6d. (66d.) 1612-19.
Broad	Twenty shillings, Cromwell, 1656.
Crown	Five shillings, from 1544 (and see below and Britain crown above).
Crown of the Rose	Four shillings and 6 pence, 1526.
Crown of the Double Rose	Five shillings, 1526-44.
Florin (Double Leopard)	Six shillings, Edward III.
George Noble	Eighty pence (6s. 8d.) 1526.
Gold 'Penny'	Twenty to twenty-four pence, Henry III.
Guinea	Pound (20s.) in 1663, then rising to 30s. in 1694 before falling to 21s. 6d., 1698-1717; 21s., 1717-1813.
Halfcrown	Thirty pence, 1526 intermittently to 1612; 2s. 9d. (33d.), 1612-19.
Helm (Quarter Florin)	Eighteen pence, Edward III.
Laurel	Twenty shillings, 1619-25.
Leopard (Half florin)	Three shillings, Edward III.
Noble	Eighty pence (6s. 8d., or half mark), 1344-1464.
Pound	Twenty shillings, 1592-1600 (see also Unite, Laurel, Broad, Guinea and Sovereign).
Quarter Angel	1s. 10½d., 1544-7 and 1558-1600.
Rose-Noble (or Ryal)	Ten shillings, 1464-70.
Rose-Ryal	Thirty shillings, 1604-24.
Ryal	Ten shillings, Edward IV and Henry VII; fifteen shillings under Mary and Elizabeth I (see also Spur Ryal).
Solidus	Roman currency unit ($\frac{1}{72}$nd lb) from A.D. 312: the 's' of the £. *s. d.*

Sovereign	Twenty shillings or pound, 1489-1526 (22s. 6d. 1526-44), 1544-53, 1603-04 and from 1817 (see also Pound, Unite, Laurel, Broad and Guinea, and Fine Sovereign below).
'Fine' Sovereign	Thirty shillings, 1550-96 (see also Rose-Ryal)
Spur-Ryal	Fifteen shillings, 1605-12; 16s. 6d., 1612-25.
Stater	Name commonly given to the standard Celtic gold coin.
Third guinea	Seven shillings, 1797-1813.
Thistle Crown	Four shillings, 1604-12; 4s. 5d., 1612-19.
Thrymsa	Early Anglo Saxon version of the late Roman tremissis (one-third solidus).
Triple Unite	Three pounds, Charles I (Shrewsbury and Oxford only, 1642-4).
Unite	Twenty shillings, 1604-12 and 1625-62; 22s., 1612-19.

Silver (and Cupro-Nickel)

Antoninianus	Roman, originally $1\frac{1}{2}$ denarii in A.D. 214 (later debased to bronze).
Argenteus	Roman, a revived denarius.
Crown	Five shillings, 1551-1965.
Denarius	Roman, originally 10 then 16 asses (25 to the aureus), later debased: the 'd' of the *£.s.d.*
Farthing	Quarter penny, 1279-1544.
Florin	Two shillings, from 1849.
Groat	Four pence, 1279-*c.* 1305 and 1351-1561 (Halfgroat from 1351). 'Britannia' groat, 1836-55 (and 1888 for Colonial use only. See also Maundy).
Halfcrown	Thirty pence (2s. 6d.), 1551-1967.
Halfpenny	Intermittently, *c.* 890-*c.* 970, *c.* 1108 and, more generally, 1279-1660.
Maundy money	Four, three, two and one penny, from 1660.
New pence	Decimal coinage: 50p. from 1969, 25p. (crown) 1972 and 1977, 10p. and 5p. from 1968.
Quinarius	Roman, half denarius or 8 asses; later debased.
Penny (*pl.* pence)	Standard unit of currency from *c.* 775/780 A.D.
Sceat	Early Anglo-Saxon, small, thick penny.
Shilling	Twelve pence, 1548-1966.
Siliqua	Roman, $\frac{1}{24}$th solidus.
Sixpence	From 1551.
Testern (Portcullis money)	One, two, four and eight testerns for use in the Indies (and equal to the Spanish 1, 2, 4 and 8 reales); 1600 only.
Testoon	Shilling, Henry VII and VIII.
Threefarthings	Elizabeth I, 1561-82.
Threehalfpence	Elizabeth I, 1561-82, and for Colonial use, 1834-62
Threepence	From 1551.

Copper, Bronze, Tin, Nickle-Brass, etc.

As	Roman, an early unit of currency; reduced in size and equal to $\frac{1}{16}$th denarius in Imperial times.
Centenionalis	Roman, replaced the depleted follis in A.D. 346.
Dupondius	Roman, brass two asses or one-eighth of a denarius.
Farthing	Quarter penny: Harrington, Lennox, Richmond, Maltravers and 'rose' farthings, 1613-49; regal issues, 1672-1956 (tin, 1648-92).
Follis	Roman, silver-washed bronze coin, $\frac{1}{5}$th argenteus, introduced *c.* A.D. 290, later debased.
Half Farthing	Victoria, 1839-56 (and for Colonial use 1828-37).
Halfpenny	From 1672 to 1967 (tin, 1685-92).
Penny	From 1797 to 1967 (previously a silver coin).
Quadrans	Roman, quarter as or $\frac{1}{64}$th denarius.
Quarter Farthing	For Colonial use only, 1839-53
Semis	Roman, half as or $\frac{1}{32}$nd denarius.
Sestertius	Roman, brass four asses or quarter denarius.
Third Farthing	For Colonial use only, 1827-1913.
Threepence	Nickle-brass, 1937-67.
Twopence	George III, 'Cartwheel' issue, 1797 only.

SOME NUMISMATIC TERMS EXPLAINED

Obverse	That side of the coin which normally shows the monarch's head.
Reverse	The side opposite to the obverse.
Blank	The coin as a blank piece of metal, i.e., before it is struck.
Flan	The whole piece of metal after striking.
Type	The main, central design.
Legend	The inscription.
Field	That flat part of the coin between the main design and the inscription or edge.
Exergue	That part of the coin below the main design, usually separated by a horizontal line, and normally occupied by the date.
Die	The block of metal, with design cut into it, which actually impresses the coin blank with the design.
Die variety	Coin showing slight variation of design.
Mule	A coin with the current type on one side and the previous (and usually obsolete) type on the other side, or a piece struck from two dies that are not normally used together.
Graining	The crenellations around the edge of the coin, commonly known as 'milling'.
Proof	Carefully struck coin from special dies with a mirror-like or matt surface. (In this country 'Proof' is *not* a term used to describe the state of preservation).
Hammered	Refers to the old craft method of striking a coin between dies hammered by hand.
Milled	Coins struck by dies worked in a coining press.

ABBREVIATIONS

Archb.	Archbishop	*mm.*	mintmark
Bp.	Bishop	mon.	monogram
cuir.	cuirassed	*O., obv.*	obverse
d.	penny, pence	p.	new penny, pence
diad.	diademed	pl.	plume
dr.	draped	quat.	quatrefoil
ex.	exergue	qtr.	quarter
grs.	grains	rad.	radiate
hd.	head	℞., *rev.*	reverse
i.c.	inner circle	s.	shillings
illus.	illustration	var.	variety
l.	left	wt.	weight
laur.	laureate		

CONDITIONS OF A COIN

(i.e. grade of preservation) in order of merit as generally used in England.

Proof. See above.

FDC = *Fleur-de-coin.* Mint state, unused, flawless, without any wear, scratches or marks.

Unc. = *Uncirculated.* A coin in new condition as issued by the Royal Mint, but, owing to modern mass-production methods of manufacture, not necessarily perfect.

EF = *Extremely Fine.* A coin that shows little sign of having been in circulation, but which may exhibit slight surface marks on very close inspection.

VF = *Very Fine.* Only slight traces of wear on the raised surfaces; a coin that has had only slight circulation.

F = *Fine.* Considerable signs of wear on the raised surfaces, or design weak through faulty striking.

Fair. A coin that is worn, but which has the inscriptions and main features of the design still distinguishable, or a piece that is very weakly struck.

Poor. A very worn coin, of no value as a collector's piece unless extremely rare.

EXAMPLES OF CONDITION GRADING

EXTREMELY FINE

VERY FINE

FINE

FAIR

Edward III groat | *George II halfcrown* | *Victoria halfcrown*

LEGEND

Anglo Saxon and Norman, including Angevin mints. (to 1279) ●

Edwardian and later mints. (after 1279) ○

Mints operating in both periods. ◉

Charles 1st. and Civil War mints. *

CELTIC COINAGE

PERIOD OF BELGIC MIGRATION

The earliest uninscribed coins found in Britain were made in Gaul and brought to this country by trade and by the migration of Belgic peoples from the continent (Gallo-Belgic issues A to F). The earliest may date from sometime late in the second century B.C., coinciding with Germanic tribes pushing westward across the Rhine and ending with refugees fleeing from the Roman legions of Julius Caesar. Certain of these coins became the prototypes for the first gold staters struck in Britain, their designs being ultimately derived from the gold staters (M) of Philip II, King of Macedonia (359-336 B.C.).

The following list is based on the 1975 edition of R. P. Mack, *The Coinage of Ancient Britain*, which now incorporates the classification for the uninscribed coins published by D. F. Allen, *The Origins of Coinage in Britain; A Reappraisal*, and from information kindly supplied by H. R. Mossop, Esq.

M 1 3 5 7

Gold Gallo-Belgic Issues

1	Gallo-Belgic A. (Ambiani), *c.* 125-100 B.C. *Stater.* Good copy of Macedonian stater, large flan. Laureate hd. of Apollo to l. or r. ℞. Horse to l. or r. *M.* 1, 3	£1250
2	— *Quarter stater.* As last. *M.* 2, 4	£650
3	— B. (Ambiani), *c.* 115 B.C. *Stater.* Somewhat similar to 1, but small flan and "defaced" *obv.* die, some with lyre shape between horse's legs on *rev.* *M.* 5, 7	£1000
4	— — *Quarter stater.* As last. *M.* 6, 8	£475
5	— C. (Ambiani), *c.* 100-70 B.C. *Stater.* Disintegrated face and horse. *M.* 26	£600
6	— D. *c.* 80 B.C. *Quarter stater.* Portions of Apollo head. ℞. Unintelligible mixture of stars, crescents, pellets, zig-zag lines; often referred to as "Geometric" types. (See also British 'O', *S.* 49). *M.* 37, 39, 41, 41a, 42	£200
7	— E. (Ambiani), *c.* 57-45 B.C. *Stater.* Blank *obv.* ℞. Disjointed curved horse, pellet below. *M.* 27	£325
8	— F. (Suessiones), *c.* 50 B.C. *Stater.* Disintegrated head and horse to r. *M.* 34a	£600
9	— Xc. *c.* 80 B.C. *Stater.* Blank except for VE monogram at edge of coin. ℞. S below horse to r. *M.* 82a	£900
10	— — *Quarter stater.* Similar, but horse to l. *M.* 83	£450
11	— Xd. *c.* 50 B.C. *Quarter stater.* Head l. of good style, horned serpent behind ear. ℞. Horse l. *M.*—	£1250

Note. Prices quoted in this section are for gold and silver coins in VF (very fine) and base metal coins in F (fine) condition.

13 18

Billon Gallo-Belgic Issues

Armorican (Channel Isles and N.W. Gaul), *c.* 75-50 B.C.

12 *Stater*. Class I. Head r. ℞. Horse, boar below, remains of driver with Victory above, lash ends in one or two loops, or "gate" £30

13 Class II. Head r. ℞. Horse, boar below, remains of Victory only, lash ends in small cross of four pellets £28

14 Class III. Head r., anchor-shaped nose. ℞. Somewhat similar to Class I £30

15 Class IV. Head r. ℞. Horse with reins, lyre shape below, driver holds vertical pole, lash ends in three prongs £35

16 Class V. Head r. ℞. Similar to last, lash ends in long cross with four pellets £35

17 Class VI. Head r. ℞. Horse, boar below, lash ends in "ladder" £40

18 *Quarter stater*. Similar types to above .. .. *from* £60

Celtic Coins Struck In Britain

Uninscribed gold staters

19 20 21 22

19 A. Westerham type, *c.* 95-65 B.C. As 5, but horse more disjointed. *M.* 28, 29 £475

20 B. Chute type, *c.* 85-55 B.C. Similar but crab-like figure below horse. *M.* 32 £450

21 C. Yarmouth (I.O.W.) type, *c.* 80-70 B.C. Crude variety of 5. *M.* 31 .. £850

22 D. Cheriton type, *c.* 80-70 B.C. Variety of 20 with large crescent face. *M.* 33 £1500

23 E. Waldingfield type, *c.* 90-70 B.C. Annulet and pellet below horse. *M.* 48 *Extremely rare*

24 F. Clacton type 1. *c.* 90-70 B.C. Similar to Westerham type but rosette below horse to l. *M.* 47 .. .. £950

25

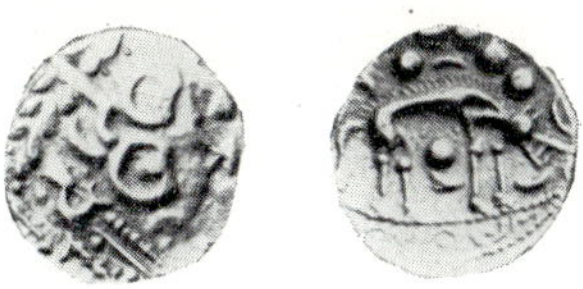

28

25 G. Clacton type 2. Similar, but horse r., with pellet, or pellet with two curved lines below. *M.* 46, 46a £475

26 H. North East Coast type, *c.* 75-30 B.C. Variety of 5, pellet or rosette below horse to r. *M.* 50, 50a, 51, 51a £800

27 I. — — Similar, horse l., pellet, rosette or star with curved rays below. *M.*52-57 .. .. £950

28 J. Norfolk wolf type, *c.* 65-45 B.C. ℞. Crude wolf to r. or l. *M.* 49, 49a, 49b £1750

30

31

29 Ka. Coritani, South Ferriby type, *c.* 30 B.C.-A.D. 10. Crude wreath. ℞. Disjointed horse l., rectangular compartment enclosing four pellets above. *M.* 447-8 .. .. *Extremely rare*

30 Kb. — — Similar, but star or rosette below horse. *M.* 449-450a £850

30A — — — Trefoil with central rosette of seven pellets. ℞. Similar to last. *M.* 450a .. .. *Unique*

31 L. Whaddon Chase type, *c.* 45-20 B.C. ℞. Spirited horse r. of new style, various symbols below. *M.* 133-138A, 139a £450

32 — — *O.* Plain. ℞. Horse r., with ring ornament below or behind. *M.* 140-43 .. .. £500

33 Lx. North Thames group, *c.* 40-20 B.C. *O.* Blank apart from reversed SS. ℞. Similar to last. *M.* 146 .. .. *Extremely rare*

34 Ly. North Kent group, *c.* 45-20 B.C. *O.* Blank. ℞. Horse l. or r., numerous ring ornaments in field. *M.* 293, 4 .. .. £950

35

35 Lz. Weald group *c.* 35-20 B.C. *O.* Blank. ℞. Horse l., panel below. *M.* 84, 292 .. .. £1100

Note. Prices quoted in this section are for gold and silver coins in VF (very fine) and base metal coins in F (fine) condition.

Uninscribed gold staters *continued*

36 Lz. *O.* Blank with some traces of Apollo head. ℞. Horse r., large wheel ornament below. *M.* 144-5 .. .. £1000

37 M. Wonersh type, *c.* 35-20 B.C. Crossed wreath design with crescents back to back in centre. ℞. Spiral above horse, wheel below. *M.* 148 .. .. £900

38

38 NA. Iceni, *c.* 30 B.C.-A.D. 10. Double crescent design. ℞. Horse r. *M.* 397, 399 .. .. £1150

39 NB. — Trefoil on cross design. ℞. Similar to last. *M.* 401-3a £1150

40 NC. — Cross of pellets. ℞. Similar to last. *M.* 400.. .. .. .. £1250

41

43

41 QA. British "Remic" type, *c.* 45-25 B.C. Crude laureate head. ℞. Triple-tailed horse, wheel below. *M.* 58, 60, 61 .. .. £450

42 QB. — Similar, but *obv.* blank. *M.* 59, 62 .. .. £400

43 R. Dobunni, *c.* 30 B.C.-A.D. 10. Similar, but branch emblem or ear of corn on *obv.* *M.* 374 .. .. £1250

Uninscribed Quarter Staters

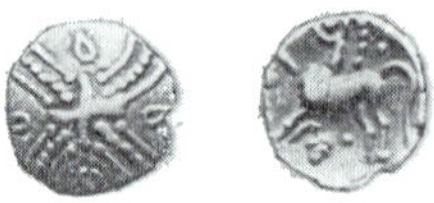

44

45

46

44 LX. N. Thames group, *c.* 40-20 B.C. Floral pattern on wreath. ℞. Horse l. or r. *M.* 76, 151, 270-1 .. .. £450

45 LY. N. Kent group, *c.* 45-20 B.C. *O.* Blank. ℞. Horse r. *M.* 78, 284-5 £450

46 LZ. Weald group, *c.* 35-20 B.C. Spiral design on wreath. ℞. Horse l. or r. *M.* 77, 80-1 .. .. £450

47 — — *O.* Blank. ℞. Horse l., panel below. *M.* 85 .. .. .. £500

48 N. Iceni, *c.* 30 B.C.-A.D. 10. Floral pattern. ℞. Horse r. *M.* 404.. .. £1750

49

50

51

49 O. Geometric type, Sussex group, *c.* 80-60 B.C. Unintelligible patterns (some blank on *obv.*). *M.* 40, 43-45 .. .. £250

50 P. — Kentish group, *c.* 65-45 B.C. *O.* Blank. ℞. Trophy design. *M.* 36, 38 .. .. £450

51 Qc. British "Remic" type, *c.* 40-20 B.C. Head or wreath pattern. ℞. Triple-tailed horse, l. or r. *M.* 63-67, 69-75 .. .. £300

52 R. Dobunni, *c.* 30 B.C.-A.D. 10. *O.* Blank. ℞. Somewhat as last. *M.* 68 £700

Uninscribed Silver

53

55

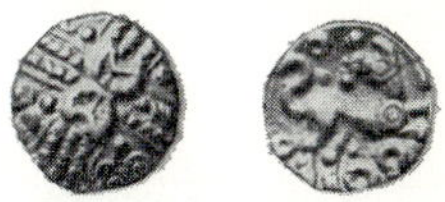
56

52A (L) North Thames group. Head r. with headband (or diadem) and flowing hair. ℞. New style horse of Whaddon Chase type (See *S.* 31A). *M.*— .. *Unique*

53 Lx. Head l. or r. ℞. Horse l. or r. *M.* 280, 435, 436, 438, 441 .. .. £450

54 — — Head l. ℞. Goat r., with long horns. *M.* 437 .. .. .. £450

55 — — Two horses or two beasts. *M.* 442, 443, 445 .. .. £450

56 — — Star of four rays or wreath pattern. ℞. Horse or uncertain animal r. *M.* 67, 272a, 414, 439, 440 .. .. £450

56A — — Hd. r. with corded hair and headband. ℞. Horse l., leaf (?) below, ornaments in field. (Somewhat similar to *S.* 77) *M.*— *Extremely rare*

56E — — *Half unit.* Cruciform pattern with ornaments in angles. ℞. Horse l., ear of corn between legs, crescent and pellets above. *M.*— *Extremely rare*

57 Lz. South Thames group. Wreath or head of serpent. ℞. Horse. *M.*— (*Allen* L 28-10) £650

58 — — Helmeted head r. ℞. Horse. *M.* 89 .. .. £600

59 — — *Quarter unit* ($3\frac{1}{2}$-4 grains). Similar. *M.* 90-1 .. .. £450

60

64

60 Durotriges, *c.* 60 B.C.-A.D. 20. Size and type of Westerham staters (no. 19 above). *M.* 317 .. .. £250

61 — Size and type of Sussex Geometric type (no. 49 above). *M.* 319 .. .. £275

62 — Very thin flans, *c.* 55 B.C. *M.* 320-1 .. .. £650

63 Dobunni, *c.* 30 B.C.-A.D. 10. Head r., with recognisable face. ℞. Triple-tailed horse l. or r. *M.* 374a, b, 375, 376, 378 .. .. £350

64 — Very crude head. ℞. Similar to last. *M.* 378a-384d £200

65 — *Quarter unit.* As last. *M.* 384c .. .. *Extremely rare*

Note. Prices quoted in this section are for gold and silver coins in VF (very fine) and base metal coins in F (fine) condition.

Uninscribed silver *continued*

66 72

66 Coritani, *c.* 50 B.C.-A.D. 10. I. Prototype issue of good style and execution. Boar r., with rosette and ring ornaments. ℞. Horse. *M.* 405, 405a, b, 406, 451 .. £500

67 — — *Half unit.* Similar. *M.* 406a, 451a £250

68 — II. South Ferriby type. Vestiges of boar on *obv.* ℞. Horse. *M.* 410, 452, 453 .. .. £350

69 — — *O.* Plain. ℞. Horse. *M.* 453a, 454 .. .. £350

70 — — *Half unit.* Similar. *M.* 455-6 .. .. £275

71 — — *Quarter unit.* Similar. *M.* 456a £275

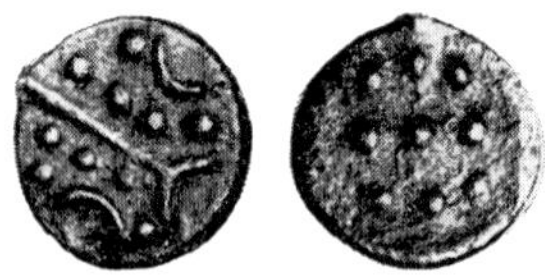

74 77 82

72 Iceni, *c.* 10 B.C.-A.D. 60. Boar r. ℞. Horse r. *M.* 407–9 .. .. .. £150

73 — *Half unit.* Similar. *M.* 411 .. .. £200

74 — Head r. ℞. Horse. *M.* 412-413e £120

74A — Similar, but inverted ear of corn between legs of horse on *rev.* *M.*—(413 *variety*). .. .. *Extremely rare*

75 — Double crescent and wreath pattern. ℞. Horse. *M.* 414-5, 440 .. £85

76 — *Half unit.* Similar. *M.* 417, 417a £250

Uninscribed Bronze

77 Lx. North Thames group. Head l. with braided hair. ℞. Horse l. *M.* 273, 274, 281 .. .. £65

78 — — Horned pegasus l. ℞. Pegasus l. *M.* 446 .. .. .. *Extremely rare*

79 — — Other types .. .. *from* £180

80 Ly. North Kent group. Boar. ℞. Horse. *M.* 295-6 .. .. .. £120

81 Durotriges, *c.* A.D. 20-50. Debased form of Æ stater (no. 60). *M.* 318.. .. £55

82 — Cast coins, *c.* A.D. 50-70. As illustration. *M.* 322-70 .. .. .. £50

83 84

Potin (bronze with a high tin content)

83 Thames and South, *c.* 1st century B.C. Cast. Class I. Crude head. ℞. Lines representing bull. (*Allen*, types A-L). *M.* 1-22a £25

84 Kent and N. Thames, *c.* mid. 1st century A.D. Cast. Class II. Smaller flan, large central pellet. (*Allen*, types M-P). *M.* 23-25 .. .. £100

CELTIC DYNASTIC ISSUES

The Celtic dynastic issues are among the most interesting and varied of all British coins. A great deal is known about some of the issuers from Julius Caesar's *Commentaries* and other sources—chiefly the kings of the Attrebates, Regni and Catuvellauni—while many are issues of kings quite unknown to history bearing legends which defy interpretation.

Roman influence in coinage design is particularly noticeable in the reign of Cunobelin (*c.* A.D. 10-40), but the Icenian revolt of A.D. 61 in which Colchester and London were sacked with the massacre of over 70,000 Romans, resulted in the termination of British Celtic coinage which previously had been allowed to circulate along with Roman coins.

The dates given for the various rulers are, in most cases, very approximate. Staters and quarter staters are gold coins of varying quality.

N.B. Bronze coins in poor condition are worth very much less than the values given for 'Fine' coins.

SOUTHERN BRITAIN

Atrebates and Regni. *Berks., Hants., Surrey and Sussex*

85 **Commius,** *c.* 35-20 B.C. *Stater.* Portions of laureate hd. r. ℞. COMMIOS around triple tailed horse r. *M.* 92 .. .. £3500

Copied from the "Remic" type QA (no. 41), this is the first inscribed British coin.

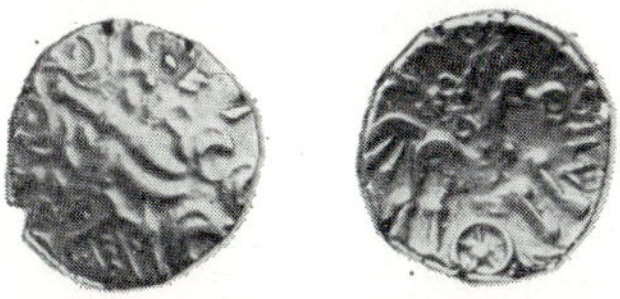

85

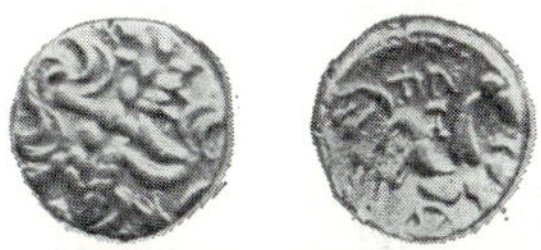

86

86 **Tincommius,** *c.* 20 B.C.-A.D. 5. Celtic style. *Stater.* Similar, but TINC COMMI F, or TIN DV around horse. *M.* 93, 94 .. .. £2250

87 — *Quarter stater.* TINCOM, zig-zag ornament below ℞. Horse l. *M.* 95 £1750

88 Classical style. *Stater.* TINC or COM · F on tablet. ℞. Horseman with javelin. *M.* 96, 98, 100 .. .. £2000

89 — *Quarter stater.* TINC on a tablet, C above, A or B below. ℞. Medusa hd. facing. *M.* 97 .. .. £1000

90 — — *O.* As 88. ℞. Horse l. or r. *M.* 99, 101-4 .. .. £800

91 — *Silver.* Head r., TINCOM. ℞. Eagle facing. *M.* 105 .. .. .. £1100

92 — — Head l. ℞. Bull charging l., TINC. *M.* 106 .. .. £1000

92A — — — TINCOMMIVS. ℞. Horse l. *M.* 131b. (Listed in Mack under Verica) .. .. *Extremely rare*

93 — — TINC. ℞. Animal prancing l. *M.* 106a.. .. .. .. *Extremely rare*

94 — *Silver quarter unit.* C F within two interlinked squares. ℞. Dog to r., TINC. *M.* 118 .. .. *Extremely rare*

88

95

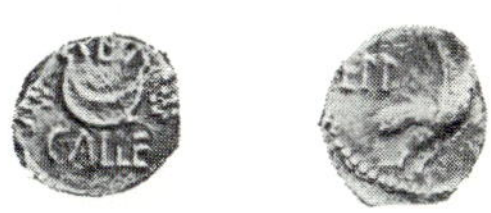

96

95 **Eppillus,** *c.* A.D. 5-10 (see also under Cantii). *Quarter stater.* Star over CALLEV (*Silchester*). ℞. EPPI over horse r. *M.* 107 .. .. .. *Extremely rare*

95A — EPPILLV · COMM · F · around crescent. ℞. Horse r., star above and below. *M.*— .. .. *Unique*

96 *Silver.* EPP over eagle. ℞. REX crescent CALLE. *M.* 108 .. .. *Extremely rare*

96A *Bronze.* Floral design of 8 petals surrounded by 4 crescents and 4 annulets. ℞. Hound r., EPPI above, COM F below .. .. *Extremely rare*

Note. Prices quoted in this section are for gold and silver coins in VF (very fine) and base metal coins in F (fine) condition.

Attrebates and Regni *continued*

99

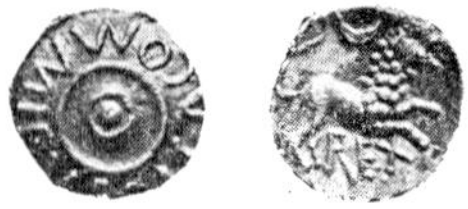

105

110

97 **Verica,** *c.* A.D. 10-40. *Stater.* Group I. COM · F on tablet. ℞. VIR below horseman r. *M.* 109, 110 £1150

98 — II. Similar but title REX added. *M.* 121 £1000

99 — III. Vineleaf between VI — RI. ℞. Horseman r. *M.* 125 £1200

100 *Quarter stater.* I. COM · F etc. ℞. Horse VIR etc. *M.* 111-114 £750

101 — II. VERIC COM · F in two lines. ℞. Horse r., REX below. *M.* 122 £750

102 — III. Vineleaf, VERI below. ℞. Horseman as no. 97. *M.* 124 £750

103 — — Head or seated figure. ℞. Horseman r. *M.* 126-7 £1000

104 *Silver.* I. Crescents, COM · F. ℞. Boar. *M.* 115 £550

104A — — VIRIC across field, ornaments above and below. ℞. Pegasus r., star design below (12.2 grs.) *Extremely rare*

105 — II. Name around circles. ℞. Lion r. *M.* 123 £650

106 — III. Horseman with spear. ℞. Horseman with shield. *M.* 128 £600

107 — — Seated figure. ℞. Two cornucopiae. *M.* 129 £650

107A — — Bird l. ℞. As last. *M.*— *Extremely rare*

108 — — Head r. ℞. Seated or standing figure. *M.* 130-31 £750

108A — — Head r. ℞. Eagle. *M.* 131a *Extremely rare*

109 *Silver quarter unit.* I. *O.* Various. ℞. Animal. *M.* 116-117; 119-120e £500

109A — — Eagle l., VIR. ℞. Lion's hd. with mane r. *M.* — *Extremely rare*

110 — III. C · F in wreath. ℞. Head r., VERI. *M.* 132 £550

111A — IV. VIR/VAR on tablet. ℞. Pegasus r., CO below *M.* — *Extremely rare*

111B — — VERICA around bucranium. ℞. Tomb, or altar, C.F. *M.* — *Extremely rare*

113

117

117A

112 **Epaticcus,** *c.* A.D. 25-35. *Stater.* TASCI · F, ear of wheat ℞. EPATICCV, horseman r. *M.* 262 £2000

113 *Silver.* Head of Hercules r., EPATI. ℞. Eagle stg. on snake. *M.* 263 £300

114 — Victory seated r. ℞. Boar. *M.* 263a £375

115 *Silver quarter unit.* *O.* EPATI. ℞. Lion's head (?), TA below. *M.* 264 £750

116 *Bronze.* Head r. ℞. Horseman charging r., EPA. *M.*— *? Unique*
Only known from P. W. P. Carlyon-Britton, sale, 1913, lot 65.

117 **Caratacus,** *c.* A.D. 35-40. *Silver.* As 113, CARA. *M.* 265 £3500
The above two rulers were brother and son of Cunoblin, (see Catuvellauni), but their coins appear in the same area as Verica's.

117A *Silver quarter unit.* CARA around pellet in circle. ℞. Pegasos r., no legend. *M.*— *Extremely rare*

Cantii *Kent*

118 **Dubnovellaunus,** *c.* 15-1 B.C. (*See also under Trinovantes*). *Stater.* *O.* Blank. ℞. Horse r., DVBNOVELLAVNOS or DVBNOVI. *M.* 282-3 .. .. £1000

119 *Silver.* Griffin r. or horned animal. ℞. Horse l. or seated figure. *M.* 286-7 £550

120 — Head l. ℞. Pegasus. *M.* 288 .. .. £550

121 *Bronze.* Boar. ℞. Eagle, horseman or horse. *M.* 289, 291, 291a .. £150

122 — Animal. ℞. Horse or lion l., DVBN on tablet below. *M.* 290 .. .. £150

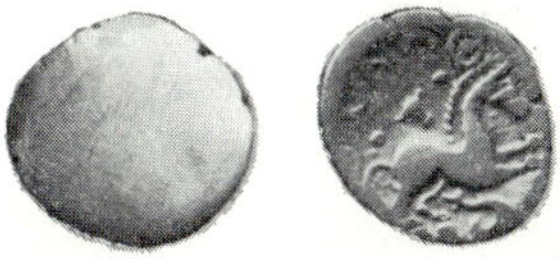
118

124

123 **Vosenios,** *c.* A.D. 5. *Stater.* *O.* Blank. ℞. Serpent below horse. *M.* 297 .. .. *Extremely rare*

124 *Quarter stater.* Similar, VOSII below horse. *M.* 298 .. .. £1000

125 *Silver.* Griffin and horse. ℞. Horse, retrograde legend. *M.* 299a .. £750

126 *Bronze.* Boar l. ℞. Horse l., SA below. *M.* 299 .. .. £250

128

130

131

127 **Eppillus,** *c.* A.D. 10-25. (*See also under Atrebates*). *Stater.* COM · F in wreath. ℞. Horseman l., EPPILLVS. *M.* 300 .. .. £1500

128 — Victory in wreath. ℞. Horseman r. Illustrated above. *M.* 301 .. £2500

129 *Quarter stater.* EPPIL / COM · F. ℞. Pegasus. *M.* 302 .. .. .. £750

130 — EPPI around wreath, or COM · F. ℞. Horse. *M.* 303-4 .. .. .. £750

131 *Silver.* Head r. or l. ℞. Lion or horseman. *M.* 305-6 .. .. .. £600

132 — Diademed head l. or r., IOVIR. ℞. Victory or capricorn. *M.* 307-308a £600

133 *Bronze.* Head l. ℞. Victory holding wreath. *M.* 311 .. .. .. £250

134 — Cruciform ornament or bull. ℞. Eagle. *M.* 309-10 .. .. .. £250

135 — Bearded head l. ℞. Horse r. *M.* 312 .. .. £250

136

136 **Amminus,** *c.* A.D. 15? *Silver.* Plant. ℞. Pegasus r. *M.* 313 .. .. £1250

137 — A within wreath. ℞. Capricorn r. *M.* 314 .. .. £1000

138 *Silver quarter unit.* A within curved lines. ℞. Bird. *M* 316 .. .. £450

139 *Bronze.* Head r. ℞. Capricorn r. *M.* 315 .. .. £200

Note. Prices quoted in this section are for gold and silver coins in VF (very fine) and base metal coins in F (fine) condition.

Unattributed coins of the Cantii

140 *Silver quarter unit.* Horseman. ℞. Seated figure wearing belt and holding spear or staff. *M.* 316e .. .. *Extremely rare*

141 *Bronze.* Boar or head. ℞. Lion to r. or l. *M.* 316a, c £200

142 — Animal r. ℞. Horse l. *M.* 316b £200

143 — *O.* Uncertain. ℞. Ring ornaments. *M.* 316d .. .. .. *Extremely rare*

144 *Bronze quarter unit.* Quatrefoil pattern. ℞. Horse r. *M.* 316f £300

145

Durotriges *W. Hants., Dorset, Somerset and S. Wilts*

145 **Crab.** *Silver.* CRAB in angles of cross. ℞. Eagle. *M.* 371 .. .. £1250

146 *Silver quarter unit.* CRAB on tablet. ℞. Star shape. *M.* 372 .. .. £750

147 **Uncertain.** Silver. Two boars back to back. ℞. Ring ornaments etc. in field. *M.* 373 .. .. *Unique*

NORTH THAMES

Trinovantes *Essex and counties to the West*

150

152

148 **Addedomaros,** *c.* 15-1 B.C. *Stater.* Crossed wreath or spiral. ℞. Horse, wheel or cornucopiae below. *M.* 266-7 .. .. £850

149 — Double crescent ornament. ℞. Horse, branch below. *M.* 268 .. £1000

150 *Quarter stater.* Similar, but rectangle or wheel below horse. *M.* 269 .. £600

[Note. For uninscribed bronze, sometimes attributed to Addedomaros, see *S.* 77 (*M.* 273/4)].

151 **Diras?,** *c.* A.D. 1 ? *Stater.* *O.* Blank. ℞. DIRAS and snake (?) over horse, wheel below. *M.* 279 .. .. *Extremely rare*

152 **Dubnovellaunus,** *c.* A.D. 1-10. (*See also under Cantii*). *Stater.* Wreath design. ℞. Horse l., branch below. *M.* 275 .. .. £900

153 *Quarter stater.* Similar. *M.* 276 .. .. £500

154 *Bronze.* Head r. or l. ℞. Horse l. or r. *M.* 277-8 .. .. .. £100

155 — Without legend but associated with the Trinovantes. Head or boar. ℞. Horse or horseman. *M.* 280a, b, d.. .. .. £125

Catuvellauni *N. Thames, Herts., Beds., spreading East and South*

157

163

Tasciovanus, *c.* 20 B.C.-A.D. 10, and associated coins

157 *Stater.* Crescents in wreath. ℞. TASCIAV and bucranium over horse. *M.* 149-50 £950

158 — Similar, sometimes with VER (*Verulamium*). ℞. Horseman r., TASC. *M.* 154-6 £950

159 — Similar, but T, or V and T. ℞. Similar to last. *M.* 157 *Extremely rare*

160 — As 157. ℞. Horse, CAMV monogram (*Camulodunum*). *M.* 186 £1200

161 — TASCIOV / RICON in panel. ℞. Horseman l. *M.* 184 £2000

162 — TASCIO in panel. ℞. Horseman r., SEGO. *M.* 194 £2000

163 *Quarter stater.* Wreath, TASCI or VERO. ℞. Horse, TAS or TASC. *M.* 152-3 £700

164 — *O.* As 160. ℞. CAMVL mon. over horse. *M.* 187 £750

165 — *O.* As 161, omitting RICON. ℞. Pegasus l. *M.* 185 £700

166 — *O.* As 162. ℞. Horse l. omitting SEGO. *M.* 195 £700

167 *Silver.* Bearded head l. ℞. Horseman r., TASCIO. *M.* 158 £650

168 — Pegasus l., TAS. ℞. Griffin r., within circle of pellets. *M.* 159 £650

169 — Eagle stg. l., TASCIA. ℞. Griffin r. *M.* 160 £650

170 — VER in beaded circle. ℞. Horse r., TASCIA. *M.* 161 £600

171 — — ℞. Naked horseman, no legend. *M.* 162 £600

172

175

178

172 — Laureate hd. r., TASCIA. ℞. Bull butting l. *M.* 163 £650

173 — Cruciform ornament, VERL. ℞. Boar, r. TAS. *M.* 164 £650

174 — TASC in panel. ℞. Pegasus l. *M.* 165 £600

175 — — ℞. Horseman l. carrying a long shield. *M.* 166 £600

176 — SEGO on panel. ℞. Horseman. *M.* 196 £1000

177 — DIAS / C / O. ℞. Horse, VIR (?) below. *M.* 188 £850

178 *Bronze.* Two heads in profile, one bearded. ℞. Ram l., TASC. *M.* 167 £90

179 — Bearded head r. ℞. Horse l., VIIR, VER or TAS. *M.* 168-9 £90

180 — Head r., TASC. ℞. Pegasus l., VER. *M.* 170 £90

181 — — TAS ANDO. ℞. Horse r. *M.* 170a *Unique*

182 — Head r., TAS. ℞. Horseman r., VER. *M.* 171 £90

183 — VERLAMIO between rays of star-shaped ornament. ℞. Bull l. *M.* 172 £80

Note. Prices quoted in this section are for gold and silver coins in VF (very fine) and base metal coins in F (fine) conditions.

Tasciovanus *continued*

190 191

184 *Bronze.* Similar, without legend. ℞. Sphinx l., legend SEGO? *M.* 173 .. £80
185 — Similar. ℞. Bull r. *M.* 174 .. .. £80
186 — Similar. ℞. Horse l., TASCI. *M.* 175 .. .. £80
187 — Head r., TASC . . . ℞. Horse r. in double circle. *M.* 175a .. *Extremely rare*
188 — Laureate hd. r., TASCIO. ℞. Lion r., TASCIO. *M.* 176 .. .. .. £90
189 — Head r. ℞. Figure std. l., VER below. *M.* 177 .. .. £90
190 — — TASCIAVA. ℞. Pegasus l., TAS. *M.* 178 (*double bronze denomination*) *Extremely rare*
191 — Cruciform ornament of crescents and scrolls. ℞. Boar r., VER. *M.* 179 £110
192 — Laureate head r. ℞. Horse l., VIR. *M.* 180 .. .. £90
193 — Raised band across centre, VER or VERL below, uncertain objects above. ℞. Horse grazing r. *M.* 183a £85
194 — RVII above lion r. within wide beaded circle. ℞. Eagle looking l., sometimes reading RVE. *M.* 189 .. .. £110
195 — Bearded head r., RVIIS. ℞. Horseman r., VIR. *M.* 190 .. .. .. £95
196 — RVIIS on panel. ℞. Animal l. *M.* 191 .. .. £110
197 — Head r., TASC DIAS. ℞. Centaur r. playing double pipe, or sometimes horses, *M.* 192 .. .. £100
198 *Bronze half denomination.* Lion ? r. ℞. Sphinx l. *M.* 181 .. *Extremely rare*
199 — Bearded head l. or r., VER. ℞. Goat or boar r. *M.* 182-3 .. .. £150
200 — Head l. ℞. Animal l. with curved tail. *M.* 183b, c £150
201 — Annulet within square with curved sides. ℞. Eagle l., RVII. *M.* 193 .. £150

202 203 205

202 **Andoco,** *c.* A.D. 5-15. *Stater.* Crossed wreath design. ℞. Horse r., AND. *M.* 197 .. .. £1250
203 *Quarter stater.* Crossed wreaths, ANDO. ℞. Horse l. *M.* 198 .. .. £650
204 *Silver.* Bearded head l. in looped circle. ℞. Pegasus l., ANDOC. *M.* 199 £800
205 *Bronze.* Head r., ANDOCO. ℞. Horse r., AND. *M.* 200 .. .. .. £135
206 *Bronze half denomination.* Head l. ℞. Horse r., A between legs, branch in exergue. *M.*— £175

207

208

207 **Cunobelin** (*Shakespeare's Cymbeline*), *c.* A.D. 10-40. *Stater.* CAMVL on panel. R. Leaf above two horses galloping l., CVNOBELIN on curved panel below. *M.* 201 .. .. £2000

208 — Ear of corn dividing CA MV. R. Horse prancing r., CVNO below. *M.* 203, 206, 210-13 .. .. £1250

209 — Similar, but horse l. *M.* 208 .. .. *Extremely rare*

210 *Quarter stater.* Similar to 207. *M.* 202 .. .. £850

211 — Similar to 208. *M.* 204, 209 .. .. £850

212 — Similar to 208 but CAM CVN on *obv.* *M.* 205 .. .. .. *Extremely rare*

Fine

213 *Silver.* Two bull headed snakes intertwined. R. Horse l., CVNO. *M.* 214 £1000

214 — Head l., CAMVL before. R. CVNO beneath Victory std. r. *M.* 215 .. £750

215 — CVNO BELI in two panels. R. CVN below horseman galloping r. (legends sometimes retrograde). *M.* 216, 7 .. .. £650

216 — Two leaves dividing CVNO. R. CAM below horseman galloping r. *M.* 218 £800

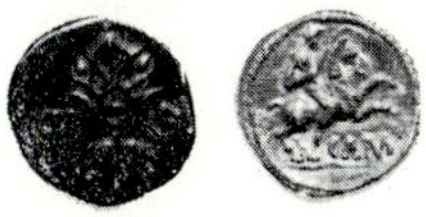

216

221

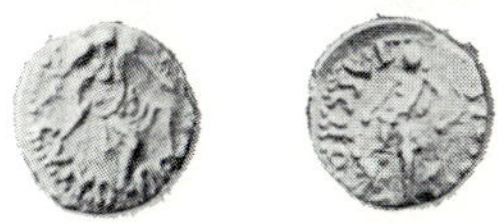

225

217 — Flower dividing CA MV. R. CVNO below horse r. *M.* 219 .. .. £800

218 — CVNO on panel. R. CAMV on panel below griffin. *M.* 234 .. .. £650

219 — CAMVL on panel. R. CVNO below centaur l. carrying palm. *M.* 234a .. £650

220 — CVNO on panel. R. TASC F below Pegasus r. *M.* 235 .. .. .. £650

221 — Head r., CVNOBELINI. R. TASCIO below horse r. *M.* 236 .. .. £700

222 — Winged bust r., CVNO. R. Sphinx std. l., TASCIO. *M.* 237 .. .. £700

223 — Draped female figure r., TASCIIOVAN. R. Figure std. r. playing lyre, tree behind. *M.* 238 .. .. £700

224 — Male figure stg. diving CV NO. R. Female std. side saddle on animal, TASCIIOVA. *M.* 239 .. .. £750

225 — Figure r. carrying dead animal, CVNOBELINVS. R. Figure stg. holding bow, dog at side, TASCIIOVANI. *M.* 240 .. .. £750

226 — CVNO on panel, horn above, two birds below. R. Figure stg. r., altar behind. *M.* 241a £1000

Note. Prices quoted in this section are for gold and silver coins in VF (very fine) and base metal coins in F (fine) condition.

Cunobelin *continued*

227 *Silver.* CVNO on panel. ℞. Fig. walking r., CV N. *M.* 254 .. .. £650

228 — — ℞. Animal springing l. *M.* 255 .. .. £750

229 — CVN in centre of wreath. ℞. CAM below dog or she-wolf stg. r. *M.* 256 £650

230 — CVNO, animal l. ℞. CA below figure std. r. holding caduceus. *M.* 258 £900

231 — SOLIDV in centre of looped circle. ℞. Standing figure l., CVNO. *M.* 259 £1000

232 *Bronze.* Head l., CVNO. ℞. Boar l., branch above. *M.* 220 .. .. £65

233 — CVNOB ELINI in two panels. ℞. Victory std. l., TASC · F. *M.* 221 .. £65

234 — Winged animal l., CAM below. ℞. CVN before Victory stg. l. *M.* 222a £65

235 — Bearded head facing. ℞. Similar to no. 232. *M.* 223 .. .. .. £100

236 — Ram-headed animal coiled up within double ornamental circle. ℞. CAM below animal l. *M.* 224 .. .. £120

237 — Winged animal r., CAMV. ℞. CVN below horse galloping r. *M.* 225 .. £90

238 — Bearded head l., CAMV. ℞. CVN or CVNO below horse l. *M.* 226, 229 .. £70

239 — Laureate head r., CVNO. ℞. CVN below bull butting l. *M.* 227 .. £100

240 — Crude head r., CVN. ℞. Figure stg. l., CVN. *M.* 228 .. .. .. £70

241 — CAMVL / ODVNO in two panels. ℞. CVNO beneath sphinx crouching l. *M.* 230 .. .. £75

242

247

251

242 — Winged beast springing l., CAMV. ℞. Victory stg. r. divides CV NO. *M.* 231 .. .. £90

243 — Victory walking r. ℞. CVN below, horseman r. *M.* 232 .. .. £90

244 — Beardless head l., CAM. ℞. CVNO below eagle. *M.* 233 .. .. .. £75

245 — Laureate head l., CVNOBELINI. ℞. Centaur r., TASCIOVANI . F. *M.* 242 £75

246 — Helmeted bust r. ℞. TASCIIOVANII above, sow stg. r., F below. *M.* 243 £75

247 — Horseman galloping r. holding dart and shield, CVNOB. ℞. Warrior stg. l., TASCIIOVANTIS. *M.* 244 .. .. £65

248 — Helmeted bust l., CVNOBII. ℞. TASC . FIL below boar l. std. on haunches. *M.* 245 .. .. £120

249 — Bare head r., CVNOBELINVS REX. ℞. TASC below bull butting r. *M.* 246 £70

250 — Bare head l., CVNO. ℞. TASC below bull stg. r. *M.* 247 .. .. £90

251 — Winged head l., CVNOBELIN. ℞. Metal worker std. r. holding hammer, working on a vase, TASCIO behind. *M.* 248 .. .. £70

252 — Pegasus springing r., CVNO. ℞. Victory r., sacrificing bull, TASCI. *M.* 249 .. .. £65

253 — CVNO on panel within wreath. ℞. CAMV below horse, full faced, prancing r. *M.* 250 .. .. £80

Note. Prices quoted in this section are for gold and silver coins in VF (very fine) and base metal coins in F (fine) condition.

254

254 *Bronze.* Bearded head of Jupiter Ammon l., CVNOBELIN. ℞. CAM below horseman galloping r. *M.* 251 .. .. £90

255 — Janus head, CVNO below. ℞. CAMV on panel below, sow std. r. beneath a tree. *M.* 252 .. .. £120

256 — Bearded head of Jupiter Ammon r., CVNOB. ℞. CAM on panel below lion crouched r. *M.* 253 .. .. £90

257 — Sphinx r., CVNO. ℞. Fig. stg. l. divides CA M. *M.* 260 .. .. .. £150

258 — Animal stg. r. ℞. CVN below horseman r. *M.* 261 .. .. .. £150

259 *Half bronze denomination.* Animal l. looking back. ℞. CVN below horse l. *M.* 233a £175

S.W. MIDLANDS

Dobunni *Glos., Here., Mon., Oxon., Som., Wilts. and Worcs.*

260

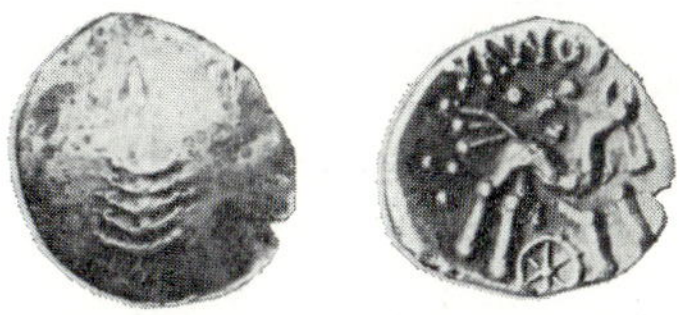

266

260 **Anted.** *Stater.* Ear of corn. ℞. ANTED or ANTEDRIG over triple tailed horse r. *M.* 385-6 .. .. £1850

261 *Silver.* Crude head r., as 64. ℞. AN TED over horse l. *M.* 387 .. .. £500

262 **Eisu.** *Stater.* Similar to 260 but EISV or EISVRIG. *M.* 388 .. .. .. £3000

263 *Silver.* Similar to 261 but EISV. *M.* 389 .. .. £1750

264 **Inam.** (or Inara). *Stater.* Similar to 260 but INAM (or INARA). *M.* 390 *Extremely rare*

265 **Catti.** *Stater.* Similar to 260 but CATTI. *M.* 391 .. .. £2250

266 **Comux.** *Stater.* Similar to 260 but COMVX outwardly. *M.* 392 .. .. £3000

267 **Corio.** *Stater.* Similar to 260 but CORIO. *M.* 393 .. .. £2000

268 *Quarter stater.* COR in centre. ℞. Horse r. without legend. *M.* 394 .. *Unique*

269

270

269 **Bodvoc.** *Stater.* BODVOC across field. ℞. As last. *M.* 395 .. .. £2500

270 *Silver.* Head l., BODVOC. ℞. As last. *M.* 396 .. .. .. *Extremely rare*

EASTERN ENGLAND

Iceni *Cambs., Norfolk and Suffolk* *c.* A.D. 10-61

272

273

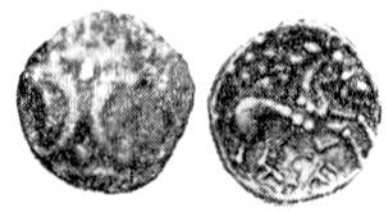

279

271 **Duro.** *Silver.* Boar. ℞. Horse r., CAN(S) above, DVRO below. *M.* 434 £850

272 **Anted.** *Stater.* Triple crescent design. ℞. ANTED in two monograms below horse. *M.* 418 .. .. *Extremely rare*

273 *Silver.* Two crescents back to back. ℞. ANTED as last. *M.* 419-21 .. £135

274 *Silver half unit.* Similar to last. *M.* 422 .. .. £250

275 **Ecen.** *Silver.* As 273. ℞. Open headed horse r., ECEN below. *M.* 424 £125

276 *Silver half unit.* Similar, but legends read ECE, EC, or ECN. *M.* 431 .. £250

277 **Ed.** *Silver.* Similar to 275 but ED (also E, EI and EDN) below horse. *M.* 423, 425b £135

278 **Ece.** *Silver.* As 273. ℞. Stepping horse r., ECE below. *M.* 425a .. £135

279 — Similar, but "Y" headed horse r., ECE below. *M.* 426-7 .. .. .. £125

280 — Similar, but horse l. *M.* 428 .. .. £175

281 **Saemu.** *Silver.* As 273. ℞. "Y" headed horse r., SAEMV below. *M.* 433 £375

282 **Aesu.** *Silver.* As 273. ℞. As last, AESV. *M.* 432 .. .. .. £375

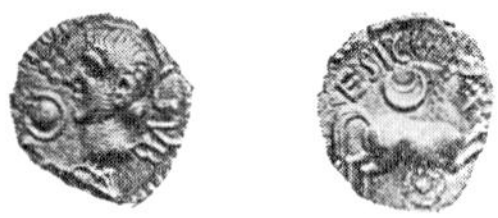

283

283 **Prasutagus,** Client King of the Iceni under Claudius; husband of Boudicca. *Silver.* Head of good style l. SUB RI PRASTO. ℞. Rearing horse r., ESICO FECIT. *M.* 434a £3500

The attribution by H. Mossop of these rare coins to King Prasutagus has been made after a study of the legends on the ten known specimens and will be published in a forthcoming issue of "Britannia."

284 **Iat Iso.** *Silver.* (I)AT / ISO in two lines above wreath of pellets. ℞. Horse r., E above. *M.* 416 .. .. £1000

285 **Ale Sca.** *Silver.* Boar r., ALE below. ℞. Horse, SCA below. *M.* 469 *Extremely rare*

Note. Prices quoted in this section are for gold and silver coins in VF (very fine) and base metal coins in F (fine) condition.

Coritani *Lincs., Yorks. and E. Midlands* *c.* A.D. 10-61

291

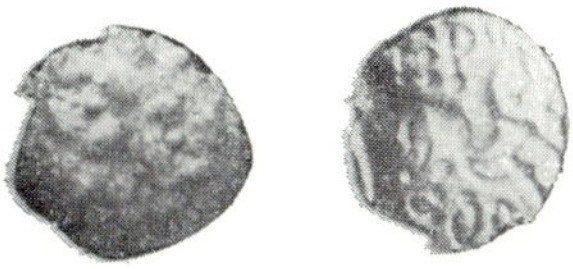

292

298

286 **Aun Cost.** *Stater.* Crude wreath type. ℞. Disjointed horse l., AVN COST. *M.* 457 .. £1850

287 *Silver.* *O.* Blank. ℞. AVN above horse l. *M.* 458 .. £600

288 *Silver half unit.* Similar. *Vide M. p.* 166 .. *Extremely rare*

289 **Esup Asu.** *Stater.* As 286 but IISVP ASV. *M.* 456b .. £2500

290 *Silver.* Similar. *M.* 456c .. *Extremely rare*

291 **Vep Corf.** *Stater.* As 286. ℞. Disjointed horse, VEP CORF. *M.* 460 .. £1350

292 *Silver.* Similar. *M.* 460b, 464 .. £400

293 *Silver half unit.* Similar. *M.* 464a .. *Extremely rare*

294 **Vepos Comes** (?). *Silver.* Similar but VEPOC (M)ES, pellets below horse. *M.*— .. *Extremely rare*

295 *Silver half unit.* Similar. *M.*— .. *Extremely rare*

296 **Vep.** *Stater.* *O.* Blank. ℞. VEP. (Only plated coins are known). *M.* 460a .. *Extremely rare*

297 *Silver.* As 286. ℞. VEP only. *M.*— .. *Unique*

298 *Silver half unit.* Similar. *M.* 464b .. £500

299 **Dumno Tigir Seno.** *Stater.* DVMN across wreath. ℞. Horse l., TIGIR SENO. *M.* 461 .. £2250

300 *Silver.* *O.* DVMNO. ℞. As last. *M.* 462 .. £650

301

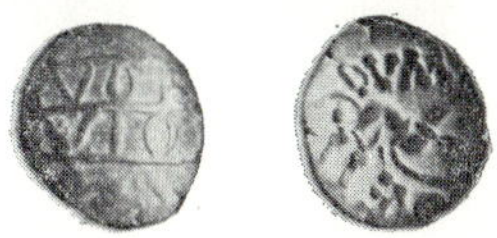

305

301 **Volisios Dumnocoveros.** *Stater.* VOLI / SIOS in two lines. ℞. Horse, DVMNOCOVEROS across crude wreath. *M.* 463 .. £1500

302 *Silver.* As last. *M.* 463a .. £750

303 *Silver half unit.* As last but DVMNOCO. *M.* 465 .. £750

304 **Volisios Dumnovellaunos.** *Stater.* As 301 ℞. Horse, DVMNOVELLAVNOS. *M.* 466 .. £1750

305 *Silver half unit.* As last but DVMNOVE. *M.* 467 .. £500

306 **Volisios Cartivel.** *Silver half unit.* As 301. ℞. Horse, CARTIVEL. *M.* 468 .. *Extremely rare*

ROMAN BRITAIN

From the middle of the first century A.D. until the early part of the fifth century, Britannia was a province of the vast Roman Empire—a single state encompassing the whole of the Mediterranean basin. In common with other western provinces, no local coinage was officially produced in Britain during this period (unlike the Eastern part of the Empire where hundreds of towns were permitted to issue municipal currency) until the latter part of the third century. It was, therefore, the regular Imperial coinage produced mainly at Rome until the mid-third century, that supplied the currency requirements of the province, and no representative collection of British coins is complete without some examples of these important issues.

Although Britain was on the fringe of the Roman World, and never entirely subdued by the legions, a surprisingly large number of coin types allude to events in the province—usually frontier wars in the north. In the closing years of the third century, the usurper Carausius established two mints in Britain; one in London, the other not yet certainly identified (either Camulodunum: Colchester or Clausentum: Bitterne, Southampton). After the defeat of the rebellion London became an official Roman mint, with a substantial output of bronze coinage until its closure, by Constantine the Great, in A.D. 325. Other coins were produced unofficially in Britain at various times: soon after the conquest (copies of bronze coins of Claudius, etc.), in the troubled times of the early 270's (copies of Claudius II and the Tetrici, i.e., "Barbarous radiates") and in the final years of the occupation (mostly imitated from the bronze coinage of Constantius II—"soldier spearing fallen horseman" type).

The Roman legions were withdrawn to the continent by Honorius in A.D. 411, but a Romano-British civil administration continued to operate for some time afterward until disrupted by the Teutonic invasions.

For general information on Roman coinage see *Roman Coins and their Values* by D. R. Sear and *Roman Coins* by J. P. C. Kent; For more detailed works consult *Roman Imperial Coinage*, the British Museum Catalogues of Roman coins and *Roman Silver Coins* (4 vols.) by H. A. Seaby.

An invaluable companion volume for anyone studying Roman coinage is S. W. Stevenson's *A Dictionary of Roman Coins*.

THE REPUBLIC

Only a few representative examples are listed. Many Republican coins circulated well into the Imperial period and found their way to Britain.

451 C. Naevius Balbus, moneyer, 79 B.C. AR *denarius*. Diad. hd. of Juno r. ℞. Victory in triga r. £12

452

454

452 C. Calpurnius Piso, moneyer, 67 B.C. AR *denarius*. Head of Apollo r. ℞. Horseman galloping r. £35

453 **Julius Caesar,** dictator, †44 B.C. Made two expeditions to Britain in 55 and 54 B.C. AR *denarius*. ℞. Venus stg. l. £300

454 AR *denarius*. Laur. head r. Elephant stg. r. ℞. Sacrificial implements .. £80

455 **Mark Antony,** triumvir, † 30 B.C. AR *denarius*. Galley r. ℞. Legionary eagle between two standards .. .. *from* £65

Known for all Legions from I (PRI*mus*) to XXIII, though only the following are known to have served in Britain during the Roman occupation—II Augusta, VI Victrix, IX Hispana, XIV Gemina Martia Victrix and XX Valeria Victrix.

Note. Prices in this section are for VF (very fine) examples except those marked F (fine).

THE EMPIRE

456

461

456 **Augustus,** 27 B.C.-A.D. 14. AR *denarius.* ℞. Caius and Lucius Caesars .. £65

457 Æ *as.* ℞. The Altar of Lugdunum .. .. *F* £30

458 **Divus Augustus Pater,** commemorative issue. Æ *as.* ℞. PROVIDENT S . C. Altar .. .. *F* £30

459 **Livia,** wife of Augustus. Æ *dupondius.* ℞. Legend around S . C. *F* £80

460 **Agrippa,** general and statesman, † 12 B.C. Æ *as.* ℞. Neptune stg. l. *F* £35

461 **Tiberius,** A.D. 14-37. AR *denarius.* ℞. Livia seated r. £120
This coin is often referred to as the "Tribute Penny" of the Bible.

462 **Drusus,** son of Tiberius, † A.D. 23. Æ *as.* ℞. Legend around S . C. *F* £45

463 **Nero Claudius Drusus,** father of Claudius, † 9 B.C. Æ *sestertius.* ℞. Claudius seated amidst arms .. .. *F* £140

464 **Antonia,** mother of Claudius, † A.D. 37. Æ *dupondius.* ℞. Claudius stg. l. .. .. *F* £65

465 **Germanicus,** father of Caligula, † A.D. 19. Æ *as.* ℞. Legend around S . C. .. .. *F* £40

466 **Agrippina Senior,** wife of Germanicus, † A.D. 33. Æ *sestertius.* ℞. Two mules drawing covered carriage .. .. *F* £250

467 **Caligula,** 37-41. Æ *as.* ℞. VESTA. Vesta seated l. .. .. *F* £45

468

474

468 **Claudius,** 41-54. Invaded Britain A.D. 43. AV *aureus.* ℞. DE BRITANN on triumphal arch £1800

469 AR *denarius.* Similar £350

470 AR *didrachm* of Caesarea. ℞. DE BRITANNIS below Emperor in quadriga r. £300

471 Æ *sestertius.* ℞. SPES AVGVSTA S . C. Spes walking l., of barbarous style, struck in Britain .. .. *F* £90

472 Æ *dupondius.* ℞. CERES AVGVSTA S . C. Ceres seated l., of barbarous style, struck in Britain .. .. *F* £40

473 Æ *as.* ℞. S . C. Minerva brandishing javelin .. .. .. *F* £30

474 **Nero,** 54-68. AR *denarius.* ℞. SALVS. Salus seated l. £150

475 Æ *as.* ℞. S . C. Victory flying l. .. .. *F* £30

476 **Galba,** 68-69. AR *denarius.* ℞. DIVA AVGVSTA. Livia stg. l. £175

477 **Otho,** 69. AR *denarius.* ℞. SECVRITAS P . R. Securitas stg. l. £300

478 **Vitellius,** 69. AR *denarius.* ℞. XV . VIR SACR . FAC. Tripod with dolphin £150

479 483

479 **Vespasian,** 69-79. Commanded one of the legions in the Claudian invasion of Britain. Æ *denarius.* ℞. ANNONA AVG. Annona seated l. £40

480 Æ *as.* ℞. PROVIDENT. S. C. Large altar .. .. *F* £24

481 **Titus,** 79-81. Æ *denarius.* ℞. FORTVNA AVGVST. Fortuna stg. l. £75

482 **Domitian,** 81-96. Æ *denarius.* ℞. IMP . XI . COS . XI . CENS . P . P . P. Minerva fighting £35

483 Æ *dupondius.* ℞. VIRTVTI AVGVSTI. S. C. Virtus stg. r. .. .. *F* £18

484 **Nerva,** 96-98. Æ *denarius.* ℞. CONCORDIA EXERCITVVM. Clasped hands £75

485 489

485 **Trajan,** 98-117. Æ *denarius.* ℞. P . M . TR . P . COS . IIII . P . P. Victory standing r. on prow £35

486 Æ *sestertius.* ℞. S . P . Q . R . OPTIMO PRINCIPI. S . C. Fortuna stg. l. *F* £40

487 **Hadrian,** 117-138. Visited Britain *c.* A.D. 122 and constructed his famous wall from the Tyne to the Solway. Æ *denarius.* ℞. FIDES PVBLICA. Fides stg. r. £35

488 Æ *sestertius.* ℞. ADVENTVI AVG . BRITANNIAE. S . C. Emperor and Britannia sacrificing over altar .. .. *Extremely rare*

489 — ℞. BRITANNIA. S . C. Britannia seated l. .. .. *Extremely rare*

490 — ℞. EXERC . BRITANNI. S.C Emperor on horseback addressing soldiers *Extremely rare*

491 Æ *as.* ℞. PONT . MAX . TR . POT . COS . III . BRITANNIA. S . C. Britannia seated l. .. .. *F* £100

492 **Sabina,** wife of Hadrian, Æ *denarius.* ℞. CONCORDIA AVG. Concordia seated l. £55

493 **Aelius Caesar,** 136-138. Æ *as.* ℞. TR . POT . COS . II . S . C. Fortuna stg. l. .. .. *F* £30

494 **Antoninus Pius,** 138-161. His generals in Britain pushed the Roman frontier forward to the Forth-Clyde line (the Antonine Wall). *N aureus.* ℞. IMPERATOR II . BRITAN. Victory stg. on globe £1200

495 Æ *denarius.* ℞. AEQVITAS AVG. Aequitas stg. l. £30

496

499

496 Æ *sestertius.* ℞. BRITANNIA. S . C. Britannia seated l. on rocks .. *F* £350

497 — ℞. IMPERATOR II . BRITAN. S . C. Victory stg. on globe .. .. *F* £150

498 Æ *as.* ℞. Victory l. holding shield inscribed BRI · TAN .. .. *F* £75

499 — ℞. BRITANNIA COS . IIII. S . C. Britannia seated l. in attitude of sadness *F* £45
This coin was very possibly struck at a temporary travelling mint in Britain.

500 **Faustina Senior,** wife of Antoninus Pius, AR *denarius.* ℞. AVGVSTA. Ceres stg. r. £30

501 Æ *sestertius.* ℞. IVNO S . C. Juno stg. l. .. .. *F* £32

502 **Marcus Aurelius,** 161-180. AR *denarius.* ℞. COS III. Jupiter seated l... £35

503 Æ *sestertius.* ℞. IMP . VI . COS . III. S . C. Roma seated l. .. *F* £35

504

510

515

504 **Faustina Junior,** wife of Marcus Aurelius. AR *denarius.* ℞. IVNONI REGINAE. Juno and peacock £35

505 Æ *as.* ℞. DIANA LVCIF . S . C. Diana stg. l. .. .. *F* £12

506 **Lucius Verus,** 161-169. AR *denarius.* ℞. CONCORD . AVG . COS . II. Concordia seated l. £45

507 **Lucilla,** wife of Lucius Verus. Æ *dupondius.* ℞. SALVS S . C. Salus stg. l. *F* £15

508 **Commodus,** 177-192. There was considerable military activity in northern Britain in the early part of his reign. AR *denarius.* ℞. MARTI VLTORI AVG. Mars stg. l. £45

509 Æ *sestertius.* ℞. BRITT . etc. Britannia stg., holding sword and wreath *Extremely rare*

510 — ℞. VICT . BRIT . etc. Victory seated r., inscribing shield .. *F* £75

511 **Crispina,** wife of Commodus, Æ *as.* ℞. IVNO LVCINA S . C. Juno stg. l. *F* £22

512 **Pertinax,** 193. One time governor of Britain, under Commodus. AR *denarius.* ℞. LAETITIA TEMPOR COS . II. Laetitia stg. l. £500

513 **Didius Julianus,** 193. Æ *sestertius.* ℞. CONCORD MILIT S . C. Concordia stg. l. .. .. *F* £200

514 **Clodius Albinus,** 195-197. Proclaimed emperor while governor of Britain. AR *denarius.* ℞. MINER . PACIF . COS . II. Minerva stg. l. £120

515 **Septimius Severus,** 193-211. Campaigned in Britain with his sons Caracalla and Geta; died at York. AV *aureus.* ℞. VICTORIAE BRIT. Victory l., holding wreath and palm £2500

516 AR *denarius.* ℞. Similar £60

517 — ℞. Similar, but Victory seated l. £65

518 — ℞. Similar, but Victory stg. beside palm tree £70

519 — ℞. VIRT . AVG. Roma stg. l. £25

520

528

520 Æ *sestertius.* ℞. VICTORIAE BRITANNICAE S.C. Two Victories affixing shield to palm tree, two captives below .. .. *F* £175

521 Æ *dupondius.* ℞. Similar, but Victory inscribing shield on palm tree *F* £85

522 Æ *as.* ℞. Similar, Victory stg. r. holding vexillum .. .. .. *F* £85

524 **Julia Domna,** wife of Septimius Severus. AR *denarius.* ℞. PIETAS PVBLICA. Pietas stg. l. £25

525 **Caracalla,** 198-217. Personally led the campaign of A.D. 210. AV *aureus.* ℞. VICTORIAE BRIT. Victory seated l., holding shield £2500

526 AV *quinarius.* ℞. VICTORIAE BRIT. Victory advancing l., holding wreath and palm £3000

527 AR *denarius.* ℞. MARTI PACATORI. Mars stg. l. £25

528 — ℞. VICTORIAE BRIT. Victory advancing l., holding wreath and palm .. £65

529 — ℞. VICTORIAE BRIT. Victory advancing r., holding trophy £65

530 Æ *sestertius.* ℞. VICT . BRIT . P . M . TR . P . XIIII . COS . III . P . P . S . C. Victory stg. r., erecting trophy .. .. *F* £175

531 — ℞. VICT . BRIT . etc. Victory inscribing shield on tree .. .. *F* £150

532 — ℞. VICTORIAE BRITANNICAE. S . C. Two Victories erecting shield on tree *F* £200

533 Æ *dupondius.* ℞. VICTORIAE BRITANNICAE. S . C. Victory seated l., on shields £80

534 **Plautilla,** wife of Caracalla. AR *denarius.* ℞. PIETAS AVGG. Pietas stg. r. £45

535 **Geta,** 209-212. AR *denarius.* ℞. PONTIF . COS . II. Genius stg. l. .. £50

536 — ℞. VICTORIAE BRIT. Victory advancing r., holding wreath and palm .. £75

537 Æ *sestertius.* ℞. VICTORIAE BRITANNICAE. S . C. Victory seated r., inscribing shield .. .. *F* £200

537

541

538 — ℞. VICTORIAE BRITANNICAE. S . C. Victory standing r., erecting trophy; Britannia stg. facing with hands tied .. .. *F* £200

538A **Geta,** 209-12. Billon *tetradrachm* of Alexandria, Egypt. ℞. NEIKH . KATA . BPET. Victory flying l. .. .. *F* £250

539 **Macrinus,** 217-218. AR *denarius.* ℞. SALVS PVBLICA. Salus seated l., feeding snake £80

540 **Diadumenian Caesar,** 217-218. AR *denarius.* ℞. PRINC IVVENTVTIS. Diadumenian holding sceptre £200

541 **Elagabalus,** 218-222, AR *denarius.* ℞. FIDES MILITVM. Fides stg. r., holding standards £60

542 **Julia Paula,** wife of Elagabalus. AR *denarius.* ℞. CONCORDIA. Concordia seated l. £85

543 **Aquilia Severa,** wife of Elagabalus. AR *denarius.* ℞. CONCORDIA. Concordia stg. l. £160

544 **Julia Soaemias,** mother of Elagabalus. AR *denarius.* ℞. VENVS CAELESTIS. Venus stg. l. £65

545 **Julia Maesa,** grandmother of Elagabalus. AR *denarius.* ℞. IVNO. Juno stg. l. £45

546

550

546 **Severus Alexander,** 222-235. AR *denarius.* ℞. PAX AVG. Pax advancing l. £25

547 Æ *sestertius.* ℞. FIDES MILITVM. S . C. Fides stg. l. .. .. *F* £20

548 **Orbiana,** wife of Severus Alexander. AR *denarius.* ℞. CONCORDIA AVGG. Concordia seated l. £200

549 **Julia Mamaea,** mother of Severus Alexander. AR *denarius.* ℞. VENVS VICTRIX. Venus stg. l. £35

550 **Maximinus I,** 235-238. AR *denarius.* ℞. PAX AVGVSTI. Pax stg. l. .. £25

551 Æ *sestertius.* ℞. VICTORIA AVG. S . C. Victory advancing r... .. *F* £25

552 **Maximus Caesar,** 235-238. Æ *sestertius.* ℞. PRINCIPI IVVENTVTIS. S . C. Maximus stg. l. .. .. *F* £45

553 **Balbinus,** 238. AR *denarius.* ℞. VICTORIA AVGG. Victory stg. l. £175

554 **Pupienus,** 238. AR *denarius.* ℞. PAX PVBLICA. Pax seated l. £175

555 **Gordian III,** 238-244. Æ *denarius.* ℞. SALVS AVGVSTI. Salus stg. r. feeding serpent. £25

556 Æ *antoninianus.* ℞. ORIENS AVG. Sol stg. l. £15

557 Æ *sestertius.* ℞. AEQVITAS AVG. S . C. Aequitas stg. l. .. .. *F* £18

558

563

558 **Philip I,** 244-249. Æ *antoninianus.* ℞. ROMAE AETERNAE. Roma seated l. £16

559 Æ *sestertius.* ℞. SECVRIT. ORBIS S . C. Securitas seated l. .. .. *F* £22

560 **Otacilia Severa,** wife of Philip I. Æ *antoninianus.* ℞. PIETAS AVGVSTAE. Pietas stg. l. £22

561 **Philip II,** 247-249. Æ *antoninianus.* ℞. AETERNIT . IMPER. Sol advancing l. £22

562 **Trajan Decius,** 249-251. Æ *antoninianus.* ℞. DACIA. Dacia stg. l. .. £25

563 **Herennia Etruscilla,** wife of Trajan Decius. Æ *antoninianus.* ℞. PVDICITIA AVG. Pudicitia stg. l. £24

564 **Herennius Etruscus Caesar,** 251. Æ *antoninianus.* ℞. SPES PVBLICA. Spes advancing l. £45

565 **Hostilian Caesar,** 251. Æ *antoninianus.* ℞. PIETAS AVGVSTORVM. Sacrificial implements £65

566 **Trebonianus Gallus,** 251-253. Æ *antoninianus.* ℞. LIBERTAS AVGG. Libertas stg. l. £24

567 **Volusian,** 251-253. Æ *antoninianus.* ℞. CONCORDIA AVGG. Concordia seated l. £24

568 **Aemilian,** 252-253. Æ *antoninianus.* ℞. PACI AVG. Pax stg. l. £120

569 **Valerian I,** 253-260. Billon *antoninianus.* ℞. VICTORIA AVGG. Victory stg. l. £12

570

576

570 **Gallienus,** 253-268. Æ *antoninianus.* ℞. DIANAE CONS . AVG. Antelope £10

571 **Salonina,** wife of Gallienus. Æ *antoninianus.* ℞. PIETAS AVG. Pietas stg. l. £10

572 **Valerian II Caesar,** 253-255. Billon *antoninianus.* ℞. PIETAS AVGG. Sacrificial implements £25

573 **Saloninus Caesar,** 259. Billon *antoninianus.* ℞. SPES PVBLICA. Spes advancing l. £25

574 **Macrianus,** usurper in the East, 260-261. Billon *antoninianus.* ℞. SOL. INVICTO. Sol stg. l. £100

575 **Quietus,** usurper in the East, 260-261. Billon *antoninianus.* ℞. ROMAE AETERNAE. Roma seated l. £100

576 **Postumus,** usurper in the West, 259-268. Æ *antoninianus.* ℞. MONETA AVG. Moneta stg. l. £15

577 **Laelianus,** usurper in the West, 268. Æ *antoninianus.* ℞. VICTORIA AVG. Victory advancing r. £225

578 **Marius,** usurper in the West, 268. Æ *antoninianus.* ℞. VICTORIA AVG. Victory advancing r. £80

579 **Victorinus,** usurper in the West, 268-270. *N aureus.* ℞. LEG . XX . VAL . VICTRIX. Boar l. £10,000

580 Æ *antoninianus.* ℞. SALVS AVG. Salus stg. l. £12

581 **Claudius II Gothicus,** 268-270. Æ *antoninianus.* ℞. MARTI PACIF. Mars advancing l. £10

582 **Tetricus I,** usurper in the West, 270-273. Æ *antoninianus.* LAETITIA AVG. Laetitia stg. l. £10

583 **Tetricus II Caesar,** usurper in the West, 270-273. Æ *antoninianus.* ℞. SPES AVGG. Spes advancing l. £12

584A

584B

584C

584 **Barbarous radiates.** British and Continental copies of Æ *antoniniani,* mostly of Claudius II (A), Tetricus I (B) and Tetricus II (C) £4

585 **Quintillus,** 270. Æ *antoninianus.* ℞. FIDES MILIT. Fides stg. l. £30

586 **Aurelian,** 270-275. Æ *antoninianus.* ℞. SECVRIT . AVG. Securitas stg. l. £12

587

596

587 **Severina,** wife of Aurelian. Æ *antoninianus.* ℞. PROVIDEN . DEOR. Fides and Sol stg. £30

588 **Tacitus,** 275-276. Æ *antoninianus.* ℞. CLEMENTIA TEMP. Clementia stg. l. £22

589 **Florianus,** 276. Æ *antoninianus.* ℞. SALVS AVG. Salus stg. l. £65

590 **Probus,** 276-282. Æ *antoninianus.* ℞. ABVNDANTIA AVG. Abundantia stg. r. £12

591 **Carus,** 282-283. Æ *antoninianus.* ℞. PAX EXERCITI. Pax stg. l. £30

592 **Numerian,** 283-284. Æ *antoninianus.* ℞. ORIENS AVG. Sol advancing l. £25

593 **Carinus,** 283-285. Æ *antoninianus.* ℞. AETERNIT . AVG. Aeternitas stg. l. £22

594 **Diocletian,** 284-305, London mint reopened *c.* 297. AR *argenteus.* ℞. VIRTVS MILITVM. Tetrarchs sacrificing before camp-gate. £200

595 Æ *antoninianus.* ℞. CLEMENTIA TEMP. Diocletian and Jupiter stg. .. £14

596 Æ *follis.* ℞. GENIO POPVLI ROMANI. Genius stg. l., LON (London) *mm.* .. £35

597

600

Diocletian *continued*

597 Æ *follis*. ℞. Similar, no *mm.* (London) £30

598 — ℞. Similar, other *mms.* £20

599 **Maximianus,** 286-310. AR *argenteus*. ℞. VIRTVS MILITVM. Tetrarchs sacrificing before camp-gate £200

600 Æ *antoninianus*. ℞. SALVS AVGG. Salus stg. l. £14

601 Æ *follis*. ℞. GENIO POPVLI ROMANI. Genius stg. l., LON. *mm.* £40

602 — ℞. Similar, no *mm.* £30

603 **Carausius,** commander of the Roman Channel fleet, who took power in Britain and Northern Gaul, 287-293. *London mint* AV *aureus*. ℞. PAX AVG. Pax stg. l., no *mm.* £17,500

604

623

604 AR *denarius*. ℞. CONSER AVG. Neptune seated l. £1500

605 Æ *antoninianus*. ℞. ADVENTVS AVG. Emperor riding l. £200

606 — ℞. COHR . PRAEF. Four standards £250

607 — ℞. COMES AVG. Victory stg. l. £85

608 — ℞. CONCORD . EXERCI. Four standards £150

609 — ℞. CONCORDIA MILITVM. Clasped hands £150

610 — ℞. CONSERVAT . AVG. Sol stg. l. £200

611 — ℞. FELICIT . TEMP. Felicitas stg. l. £85

612 — ℞. FIDES MILITVM. Fides stg. l. £200

613 — ℞. FORTVNA AVG. Fortuna stg. l. £70

614 — ℞. GENIVS AVG. Genius stg. l. £200

615 — ℞. GERMANICVS MAX . V. Trophy between captives £450

616 — ℞. LAETITIA AVG. Laetitia stg. l. £70

617 — ℞. LEG . II . AVG. Capricorn l. £200

618 — ℞. LEG XX . V . V. Boar r. £220

619 — ℞. MARS VLTOR. Mars walking r. £200

620 — ℞. MONETA AVG. Moneta stg. l. £70

621 — ℞. ORIENS AVG. Sol walking r. £85

Note. Prices in this section are for VF (very fine) examples except those marked F (fine).

622 Æ *antoninianus*. ℞. PACATOR ORBIS. Bust of Sol r. £350

623 — ℞. PAX AVG. Pax stg. l. £60

624 — ℞. PIAETAS AVG. Pietas sacrificing at altar £85

625 — ℞. SALVS AVG. Salus feeding serpent £75

626 — ℞. SECVRIT . PERP. Securitas stg. l. £85

627 — ℞. VICTORIA AVG. Victory walking r. £85

628

643

628 Æ *antonianianus*. Struck in the name of Diocletian. ℞. PAX AVGGG. Pax stg. l. £75

629 Æ *antoninianus*. Struck in the name of Maximianus. ℞. PROVIDENTIA AVG. Providentia stg. l. £75

630 *Colchester or Clausentum mint.* Ꝛ *denarius*. ℞. CONCORDIA MILITVM. Clasped hands £450

631 Æ *antoninianus*. ℞. ABVNDANTIA AVG. Abundantia stg. l. £85

632 — ℞. APOLINI CON . AV. Griffin walking r. £300

633 — ℞. CONCORDIA AVGGG. Two emperors stg. £400

634 — ℞. CONSTANT . AVG. Nude male stg. r. £200

635 — ℞. EXPECTATE VENI. Britannia stg. r. £300

636 — ℞. FELICITAS AVG. Galley £150

637 — ℞. GENIO BRITANNI. Genius stg. l. £420

638 — ℞. HILARITAS AVG. Hilaritas stg. l. £75

639 — ℞. IOVI CONSERV. Jupiter stg. l. £80

640 — ℞. LEG. I. MIN. Ram stg. r. £200

641 — ℞. LIBERALITAS AVG. Carausius seated with subordinates £250

642 — ℞. PAX AVG. Pax stg. l. £70

643 — ℞. PROVID . AVG. Providentia stg. l. £75

644 — ℞. RENOVAT . ROMA. She-wolf suckling Romulus and Remus £220

645 — ℞. RESTIT . SAECVL. Carausius and Victory stg. £220

646 — ℞. ROMAE AETER. Roma seated l. £90

647 — ℞. SAECVLARES AVG. Lion walking r. £200

648 — ℞. SOLI INVICTE. Sol in quadriga £200

649 — ℞. SPES PVBLICA. Spes walking r. £75

650 — ℞. TEMP . FELICIT. Felicitas stg. l. £75

651 — ℞. VIRTVS AVG. Mars stg. r. £70

651 Æ *antoninianus*. Struck in the name of Diocletian. ℞. PAX AVGGG. Pax stg. l. £75

652 Æ *antoninianus*. Struck in the name of Maximianus. ℞. PAX AVGGG. Pax stg. l. £75

653

662

653 **Carausius, Diocletian and Maximianus.** Æ *antoninianus.* Struck by Carausius. CARAVSIVS ET FRATRES SVI. Jugate busts of three emperors l. ℞. PAX AVGGG. Pax stg. l. £1750

654 **Allectus,** chief minister and murderer of Carausius, 293-296. *London mint.* AV *aureus.* ℞. PAX AVG. Pax stg. l. £20,000

655 Æ *antoninianus.* ℞. AEQVITAS AVG. Aequitas stg. l. £70

656 — ℞. COMES AVG. Minerva stg. l. £70

657 — ℞. FORTVNA AVG. Fortuna seated l. £180

658 — ℞. HILARITAS AVG. Hilaritas stg. l. £60

659 — ℞. LAETITIA AVG. Laetitia stg. l. £80

660 — ℞. LEG . II. Lion walking l. £450

661 — ℞. ORIENS AVG. Sol stg. l. £200

662 — ℞. PAX AVG. Pax stg. l. £80

663 — ℞. PIETAS AVG. Pietas stg. l. £70

664 — ℞. PROVIDENTIA AVG. Providentia stg. l. £90

665 — ℞. SAECVLI FELICITAS. Emperor stg. r. £160

666 — ℞. SALVS AVG. Salus feeding serpent £70

667 — ℞. SPES PVPLICA. Spes holding flower £65

668 — ℞. TEMPORVM FELICI. Felicitas stg. l. £65

669 — ℞. VICTORIA AVG. Victory stg. r. £65

670 — ℞. VIRTVS AVG. Mars stg. r. £70

671 Æ *quinarius.* ℞. VIRTVS AVG. Galley £60

672 *Colchester or Clausentum mint.* Æ *antoninianus.* ℞. ABVND . AVG. Abundantia stg. l. £80

673 — ℞. ADVENTVS AVG. Emperor riding l. £240

674 — ℞. DIANAE REDVCI. Diana leading stag £200

675 — ℞. FELICITAS SAECVLI. Felicitas stg. l. £200

676 — ℞. FIDES EXERCITVS. Four standards £150

677 — ℞. IOVI CONSERVATORI. Jupiter stg. l. £200

678

681

678 — ℞. MONETA AVG. Moneta stg. l. £100

679 — ℞. PAX AVG. Pax stg. l. £80

680 — ℞. ROMAE AETERN. Roma in temple £230

681 Æ *quinarius*. ℞. LAETITIA AVG. Galley £80

682 — ℞. VIRTVS AVG. Galley. £60

683

698

683 **Constantius I,** Caesar 293-305, Augustus 305-306, campaigned in Britain and died at York. Æ *follis*. ℞. GENIO POPVLI ROMANI. Genius stg. l., no *mm*. £35

684 Æ *follis*. ℞. MEMORIA FELIX. Eagles beside altar. PLN. *mm*. £30

685 Æ *radiate*. ℞. CONCORDIA MILITVM. Constantius and Jupiter stg... .. £25

686 **Galerius,** Caesar 293-305, Augustus 305-311. Æ *follis*. ℞. GENIO IMPERATORIS. Genius stg. l. £15

687 — ℞. GENIO POPVLI ROMANI. Genius stg. l., no *mm*. £20

688 **Galeria Valeria,** wife of Galerius. Æ *follis*. ℞. VENERI VICTRICI. Venus stg. l. £85

689 **Severus II,** 306-307. Æ *follis*. ℞. FIDES MILITVM. Fides seated l. .. £75

690 Æ *follis*. ℞. GENIO POPVLI ROMANI. Genius stg. l., no *mm*. £85

691 Æ *radiate*. ℞. CONCORDIA MILITVM. Severus and Jupiter stg. £50

692 **Maximinus II,** 309-313. Æ *follis*. ℞. GENIO AVGVSTI. Genius stg. l. .. £15

693 — ℞. GENIO POP . ROM. Genius stg. l. PLN. *mm*. £25

694 **Maxentius,** 306-312, Æ *follis*. ℞. CONSERV . VRB SVAE. Roma in temple .. £25

695 **Licinius I,** 308-324. Æ *follis*. ℞. GENIO POP . ROM. Genius stg. l. PLN. *mm*. £18

696 Æ 3. ℞. SOLI INVICTO COMITI. Sol stg. l. £9

697 **Licinius II Caesar,** 317-324. Æ 3. ℞. PROVIDENTIAE CAESS. Camp gate £14

698 **Constantine I, the Great,** 307-337. Came to power in Britain, following his father's death at York. London mint closed 325. Æ *follis*. ℞. SOLI INVICTO COMITI. Sol. stg. l. PLN. *mm*. £30

699 Æ 3. ℞. BEATA TRANQVILLITAS. Altar. PLON *mm*. £15

700 Æ 3. ℞. VOT . XX in wreath £5

701

701 **Commemorative issues.** Æ 3/4, commencing A.D. 330. Bust of Roma. ℞. She-wolf suckling Romulus and Remus £8

702 Æ 3/4. Bust of Constantinopolis. ℞. Victory stg. l. £8

703 **Fausta,** wife of Constantine. Æ 3. ℞. SPES REIPVBLICAE. Fausta stg. .. £30

704 — ℞. Similar. PLON *mm*. £60

705 **Helena,** mother of Constantine. Æ 3. ℞. SECVRITAS REIPVBLICE. Helena stg. l. £25

706 — ℞. Similar. PLON *mm.* £60

707 714

707 **Theodora,** second wife of Constantius I, struck after her death. Æ 4. ℞. PIETAS ROMANA. Pietas holding child £14

708 **Crispus Caesar,** 317-326. Æ 3. ℞. CAESARVM NOSTRORVM VOT . V. Wreath £12

709 — ℞. PROVIDENTIAE CAESS. Camp gate. PLON *mm.* £15

710 **Delmatius Caesar,** 335-337. Æ 3. ℞. GLORIA EXERCITVS. Two soldiers stg. £30

711 **Hanniballianus Rex,** 335-337. Æ 4. ℞. SECVRITAS PVBLICA. Euphrates reclining £250

712 **Constantine II Caesar,** 317-337. Æ 3. ℞. BEAT . TRANQLITAS. Altar. PLON *mm.* £15

713 Æ 3/4. ℞. GLORIA EXERCITVS. Two soldiers stg. £25

714 **Constans,** 337-350. Visited Britain in 343. Æ *centenionalis.* ℞. FEL . TEMP . REPARATIO. Constans stg. on galley £15

715 723 733 741

715 **Constantius II,** 337-361. Æ *centenionalis.* ℞. FEL . TEMP . REPARATIO. Soldier spearing fallen horseman £12

716 Æ 3. ℞. PROVIDENTIAE CAESS. Camp gate. PLON *mm.* £35

717 **Magnentius,** usurper in the West, 350-353. Æ *centenionalis.* ℞. VICTORIAE DD . NN . AVG . ET CAE. Two Victories £20

718 **Decentius Caesar,** usurper in the West, 351-353. Æ *centenionalis.* ℞. VICTORIAE DD . NN . AVG . ET . CAE. Two Victories £35

719 **Constantius Gallus Caesar,** 351-354. Æ *centenionalis.* ℞. FEL . TEMP REPARATIO. Soldier spearing fallen horsemen £25

720 **Julian II,** 360-363. Æ *siliqua.* ℞. VOT . X . MVLT . XX within wreath .. £50
721 Æ 3. ℞. Similar £20
722 **Jovian,** 363-364. Æ 3. ℞. VOT . V . within wreath £50
723 **Valentinian I,** 364-375. Æ 3. ℞. SECVRITAS REIPVBLICAE. Victory advancing l. £10
724 **Valens,** 364-378. Æ *siliqua.* ℞. VRBS ROMA. Roma seated l. £40
725 Æ 3. ℞. GLORIA ROMANORVM. Valens dragging captive £10
726 **Gratian,** 367-383. Æ *siliqua.* ℞. VRBS ROMA. Roma seated l. £50
727 Æ 3. ℞. CONCORDIA AVGGG. Constantinopolis seated l. £18
728 **Valentinian II,** 375-392. Æ *siliqua.* ℞. VICTORIA AVGGG. Victory advancing l. £60
729 Æ 2. ℞. GLORIA ROMANORVM. Valentinian stg. on galley £25
730 Æ 4. ℞. SALVS REIPVBLICAE. Victory advancing l. £8
731 **Theodosius I,** 379-395. Æ 2. ℞. GLORIA ROMANORVM. Theodosius stg. on galley £25
732 Æ 4. ℞. SALVS REIPVBLICAE. Victory advancing l. £6
733 **Magnus Maximus,** usurper in the West, 383-388, proclaimed emperor by the Roman army in Britain. *AV solidus.* ℞. VICTORIA AVGG. Two emperors seated, Victory between them; AVGOB *mm.* (London) £8000
734 Æ *siliqua.* ℞. VICTORIA AVGG. Victory advancing l. AVGPS *mm.* (London) £600
735 — ℞. VIRTVS ROMANORVM. Roma seated l. £65
736 **Flavius Victor,** usurper in the West, 387-388. Æ 4. ℞. SPES ROMANORVM. Camp gate £50
737 **Eugenius,** usurper in the West, 392-394. Æ *siliqua.* ℞. VIRTVS ROMANORVM. Roma seated l. £250
738 **Arcadius,** 383-408. Æ 2. ℞. GLORIA ROMANORVM. Arcadius stg. r. .. £25
739 **Honorius,** 393-423, during whose reign the so-called "Roman withdrawal" from Britain took place. Æ *siliqua.* ℞. VIRTVS ROMANORVM. Roma seated l. £65
740 Æ 3. ℞. VIRTVS EXERCITI. Honorius stg. r. £20
741 **Constantine III,** usurper in the West, proclaimed emperor in Britain, 407-411. Æ *siliqua.* ℞. VICTORIA AVGGGG. Roma seated l. £400
742 **Valentinian III,** 425-455, during whose reign the last vestiges of Roman rule in Britain disappeared. Æ 4. ℞. VOT . PVB. Camp gate £50

Note. The prices quoted in the Roman Britain section of the catalogue are for VF (very fine) examples except those marked F (fine).

EARLY ANGLO-SAXON PERIOD, *c.* 600-*c.* 775

The withdrawal of Roman forces from Britain early in the 5th century A.D. and the gradual decline of central administration resulted in a rapid deterioration of the money supply. The arrival of Teutonic raiders and settlers hastened the decay of urban commercial life and it was probably not until late in the 6th century that renewed political, cultural and commercial links with the kingdom of the Merovingian Franks led to the appearance of small quantities of Merovingian gold *tremisses* (one-third solidus) in England. A purse containing such pieces was found in the Sutton Hoo shipburial. Native Anglo-Saxon gold *thrymsas* were minted from about the 630's, initially in the style of their continental prototypes or copied from obsolete Roman coinage and later being made in pure Anglo-Saxon style. By the middle of the 7th century the gold coinage was being increasingly debased with silver, and gold had been superseded entirely by silver by about 675.

These silver coins, contemporary with the *deniers* or *denarii* of the Merovingian Franks, are the first English pennies, though they are commonly known today as *sceattas* (a term more correctly translated as "treasure" or "wealth"). They provide important material for the student of Anglo-Saxon art.

Though the earliest sceattas are a transition from the gold thrymsa coinage, coins of new style were soon developed which were also copied by the Frisians of the Low Countries. Early coins appear to have a standard weight of 20 grains (1.29 gms) and are of good silver content, though the quality deteriorates early in the 8th century. These coins exist in a large number of varied types, and as well as the official issues there are mules and other varieties which are probably contemporary imitations. Many of the sceattas were issued during the reign of Aethelbald of Mercia, but as few bear inscriptions it is only in recent years that research has permitted their correct dating and the attribution of certain types to specific areas. Some silver sceats of groups II and III and most types of groups IV to X were issued during the period (A.D. 716-757) when Aethelbald, King of Mercia, was overlord of the southern English. In Northumbria very debased sceattas or *stycas* continued to be issued until the middle of the ninth century. Though a definitive classification has not yet been developed, the arrangement given below follows the latest work on the series: this list is not exhaustive.

The reference "*B.M.C.*" is to the type given in *British Museum Catalogue: Anglo-Saxon Coins*, and *not* the item number.

North, J. J. *English Hammered Coinage*, Vol. 1, *c.* 650-1272 (1963).
Metcalf, D. M. "A stylistic analysis of the 'porcupine' scettas". *Num. Chron.*, 7th ser., Vol. VI (1966).
Rigold, S. E. "The two primary series of sceattas", *B.N.J.*, xxx (1960).
Sutherland, C. H. V. *Anglo-Saxon Gold Coinage in the light of the Crondall Hoard* (1948).

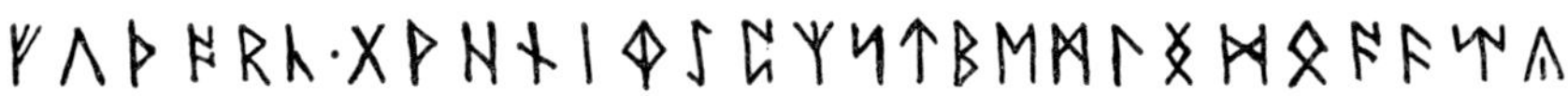

f u th o r k · z w h n i j ih p x s t b e m l ng d œ a æ ea y

Early Anglo-Saxon Runes

GOLD

A. **Anglo-Merovingian types**

751 **Thrymsa** (*c.* 1.32 gms). Name and portrait of Bishop Leudard (chaplain to Q. Bertha of Kent). ℞. Cross. *N.* 1 .. .. *Unique*

752 *Canterbury.* Bust r., moneyer's name. ℞. Cross, mint name. *N.* 2 *Extremely rare*

753 762 763

753 No mint name. Bust l. ℞. Cross. *N.* 3-5, 7 .. .. .. *Extremely rare*

754 Bust r. ℞. Cross. *N.* 6-9, 12 .. .. *Extremely rare*

755 Cross both sides. *N.* 10 .. .. *Extremely rare*

756 Bust r. ℞. Cross, runic letters. *N.* 11 .. .. *Extremely rare*

B. Roman derivatives *Fine*

757 **Solidus.** Bust r. copied from 4th cent. solidus. ℞. Various. *N.* 13, 14 *Extremely rare*

758 — Runic inscription on reverse. *N.* 15 .. .. *Extremely rare*

759 **Thrymsa.** Radiate bust r. ℞. Clasped hands. *N.* 16 .. .. *Extremely rare*

760 Bust r., hands raised to cross. ℞. Camp gate. *N.* 17 .. .. *Extremely rare*

761 Helmeted bust r. ℞. Cross, runic inscription. *N.* 18 .. .. *Extremely rare*

762 Diad. bust r. ℞. "Standard", TOV / XX in centre. *N.* 19. *M.* — .. *Extremely rare*

763 — Similar. ℞. Victory protecting "two emperors". *N.* 20 .. .. £3,000

C. "London" and derived issues

764

765

766

764 **Thrymsa.** Facing bust, no legend. ℞. Greek cross, LONDVNIV. *N.* 21 *Extremely rare*

765 Head r. or l. ℞. Plain cross, legend jumbled. *N.* 22-24 .. .. *Extremely rare*

D. "Witmen" group

766 **Thrymsa.** Bust r. with trident centre. ℞. Cross with forked limbs, moneyer's name. *N.* 25 .. .. *Extremely rare*

767 — Similar, but blundered legends both sides. *N.* 25 *var.* £3,250

768 — ℞. Cross potent. *N.* 26 .. .. £3,250

E. "York" group

769

771

772

769 **Thrymsa.** Three crosses with geometric squared design below. ℞. Small cross. *N.* 27 .. .. *Extremely rare*

F. "Regal" coinages

770 **Solidus** (4.12 gms). Diad. bust r., moneyer's name around. ℞. Cross potent on steps. *N.* 28 .. .. *Extremely rare*

771 **Thrymsa.** Diad. bust r., AVDVARLD REGES. ℞. Orb with cross, moneyer's name. *N.* 29 .. .. £3,500

772 Diad. bust l., moneyer's name around. ℞. Cross and pellets, legend of XS. *N.* 30 .. .. *Extremely rare*

773 Diad. bust r. ℞. Cross botonée, PADA in runes. *N.* 31 .. .. .. £3,250

Miscellaneous issues

774 **Thrymsa.** Crude bust r. ℞. Standing figure with arms outstretched. *N.* 33 .. .. *Extremely rare*

775 Crude bust or head r. ℞. Various. *N.* 35, 38 .. .. .. *Extremely rare*

776 Forked cross both sides, and other types. *N.* 36, 37, 39 .. .. *Extremely rare*

SILVER

I. **Transitional types struck in silver,** by thrymsa moneyers, *c.* 675-690 — *Fine*

779

780

781

777 **Sceat.** *Kentish.* As 773, diad. bust r. ℞. *Pada* in runes across field. *N.* 154 .. .. £700

778 — Obv. Similar. ℞. Cross on steps. *B.M.C.* type 2 .. .. *Extremely rare*

778A As 763. ℞. Victory over two emperors. *B.M.C.* 1 .. .. *Extremely rare*

779 — Diad. bust r., TNC to r. ℞. Cross with annulet in each angle, *Pada* in runes in legend. *B.M.C.* 3 .. .. £650

780 — "*Varimundus*" As 761, helmeted bust r. with sceptre. ℞. Cross pattée, TMVNVMVC, etc. *Rignold* VB, 4-9 .. .. £650

II. **Primary Scettas,** *c.* 690-725

783

785

786

781 Series A, *Kentish.* Radiate bust r., usually of good style, TIC to r. ℞. "Standard". *B.M.C.* 2a £100

782 Series B, *Kentish.* Diad. bust r. ℞. Bird above cross on steps. *B.M.C.* 26 £120

783 — Diad. head r. within serpent-circle or bust r. ℞. Bird above cross and two annulets, serpent-circle around. *B.M.C.* 27a £100

784 — (Bz.) Diad. head r. of poorer style. ℞. Bird and cross larger and cruder. *B.M.C.* 27b (see also 791) £150

785 Series C, *East Anglian (?) Runic.* Radiate bust r. somewhat as 781. *Epa* (etc.) in runes to r. ℞. Neat "Standard" type. *B.M.C.* 2b; *Rigold* R1 (See also 832, and for Frisian copies nos. 839 and 840) £175

786 *Early "porcupines".* Porcupine-like figure, body with annulet at one end, triangle at other. ℞. "Standard" with four pellets around central annulet. *Metcalf* D £85

787

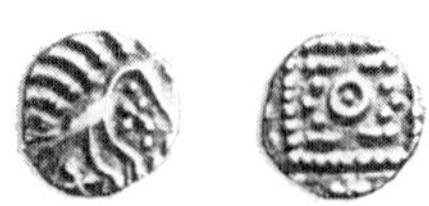
789

790

787 — "Porcupine" has insect-like body with fore-leg. ℞. "Standard" with four lines and central annulet. *Metcalf* G £90

788 — "Porcupine" with parallel lines in curve of body. ℞. "Standard" with VOIC-like symbols £90

789 — Figure developed into plumed bird. ℞. "Standard" has groups of triple pellets. *B.M.C.* type 6 .. .. £100

790 *Slightly later "porcupines" of reduced weight.* As 788 but various symbols in "standard" (some varieties are Frisian imitations—see 841-2 below) £85

III. **"Mercian" types,** *c.* 705-730. More than one mint, possibly including London; the fineness dropping from good silver to under .500.

791

792

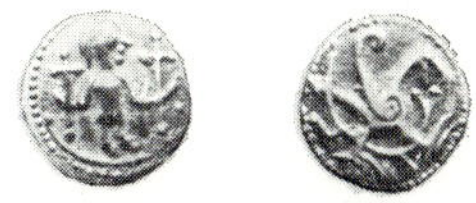

793

		Fine
791	Derivative of 784, but bird and cross larger and cruder, no serpent circles. *B.M.C.* 27b	£110
792	Two heads face-to-face, cross with trident base between. ℞. Four birds clockwise around cross. *B.M.C.* 37	£120
793	Man holding two crosses. ℞. Bird and branch. *B.M.C.* 23b	£175
794	Diad. bust r. with bird or cross. ℞. Hound and tree. *B.M.C.* 42 ..	£200
795	Diad. bust r. with chalice. ℞. Man standing with cross and bird. *B.M.C.* 20	£185
796	Diad. bust r. with cross. ℞. Wolf curled head to tail. *B.M.C.* 32a ..	£175
797	— Similar, but wolf-headed serpent.	£185
798	— Similar, but wolf-serpent within torque. *B.M.C.* 32b	£185
799	— Similar, but wolf's head r. or l. with long tongue. *B.M.C.* 33	£220
800	— Obv. Similar. ℞. Celtic cross or shield. *B.M.C.* 34	£185

IV. **Types of similar style or finess,** *of uncertain political attribution.*

800A.	Kneeling archer r., tree behind. ℞. Bird on branch r., head turned l. *B.M.C.* —	*Extremely rare*
801	As 791, but cross before head. ℞. Large and small bird. *B.M.C.* 36 ..	£150
802	Bust r., lettering around or with cable border. ℞. Bird r. in torque *B.M.C.* 38	£175
803	Bust l. within cable border. ℞. Man with two crosses. *B.M.C.* 21 ..	£200
804	Facing bust. ℞. Interlaced cruciform pattern. *B.M.C.* 52	£375

797

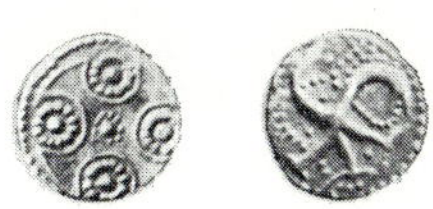

805

806

V. **South Wessex types,** *c.* 725-50. Found predominantly in excavations at Hamwic (Southampton)

805	Scutiform design (shield with bosses). ℞. Bird and branch as 794. *B.M.C.* type 39	£175
806	Jewel-head, roundels around. ℞. Bird and branch. *B.M.C.* 49	£175
807	Scutiform design. ℞. Wolf-head whorl. *B.M.C.* 48	£175

VI. South Saxon types *c.* 720-750 — *Fine*

808 Diad. bust r. cross before. ℞. "Standard". *B.M.C.* 3a — £120

809 — Similar but crude style and of very base silver. — £85

808

815

816

VII. "Dragon" types, *c.* 725-735?

810 Two standing figures, long cross between. ℞. Monster looking back to r. or l. *B.M.C.* type 41b — £175

811 One standing figure, cross either side. ℞. As last. *B.M.C.* 23a and 40 — £175

812 Four interlaced shields. ℞. As last. *B.M.C.* 43 — £175

813 Bust r., cross before. ℞. As last. *N.* 114 — *Extremely rare*

814 Wolf's head facing. ℞. As last. *N.* 122 — £350

815 Wolf and twins. ℞. Bird in vine. *B.M.C.* 7 — £200

816 Diad. bust r. + LEV. ℞. "Porcupine" l. *B.M.C.* 9 — £175

817 Facing head. ℞. Fantastic animal r. or l. *N.* 143-6 — £250

VIII. "London issue" *of around* .400 *silver content or less, c.* 740-750

818 Diad. bust r., LVNDONIA (sometimes blundered). ℞. Man holding two long crosses. *B.M C* type 12 — £400

819 — Obv. As last. ℞. "Porcupine" to l. *B.M.C.* 12/5 — £350

820 — Obv. As last. ℞. Seated figure r. holding sceptre. *B.M.C.* 13 — *Unique*

821 — Obv. As last but bust l. ℞. Scutiform design. *B.M.C.* 14 — £350

822 Diad. bust r. with cross, no legend. ℞. As 818. *B.M.C.* 15a — £200

823 — As last. ℞. Man standing with branch and cross, or two branches. *B.M.C.* 15b — £200

824 Diad. bust r. with floral scroll. ℞. As last — £200

825 — As last. ℞. Man with two crosses. *B.M.C.* 16 — £150

826 As 813 but bust 1. *B.M.C.* 17 — £175

827 Diad. bust r. with cross. ℞. Man standing with cross and bird. *B.M.C.* 18 — £200

828 Diad. bust l. with cross. ℞. As last. *B.M.C.* 19 — £200

829 Victory standing with wreath. ℞. Man with two crosses. *B.M.C.* 22 — £300

818

831

IX. "Wolf-head whorl" *types, mostly of about* .300 *silver or less, c.* 740-750

830 Man standing holding two crosses. ℞. Wolf-head whorl. *B.M.C.* 23e — £175

831 Sphinx or female centaur with outstretched wings. ℞. As above. *B.M.C.* 47 — £250

See also No. 807

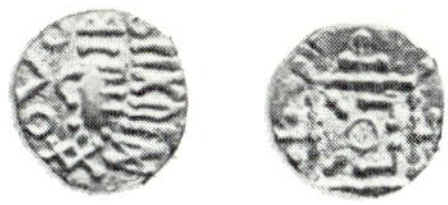

832

Fine

X. **East Anglian types,** *of about.* 500 *silver or less, c.* 735-750. Struck to a standard of 15 grs./0.97 gm. or less

832 Crude radiate bust r., *Epa, Wigraed,* or *Spi,* etc., in runes. ℞. "Standard". *Rigold* R2 (compare with 785) £135

833 — Similar. ℞. Cross with each limb ending in annulet. *Rigold* R2Z, *N.* 160 £200

833A Saltire in square. ℞. Cross ending in annulets. *B.M.C.* 51 .. .. £110

834 Bird r. looking back. ℞. "Standard" with four annulets in saltire. *B.M.C.* 46 £200

835 "Standard" both sides. *N.* 55-57 *Extremely rare*

836 Fantastic bird r. or l. ℞. Fantastic quadruped l. or r. *B.M.C.* 44 .. .. £150

836

837

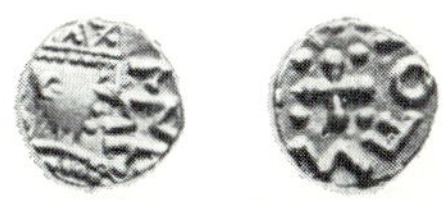

839

XI. **Late sceattas,** *on a restored silver standard, c.* 750-775. These probably include some specimen of 830 and 831 and the following types:

837 "Porcupine" ℞. *Aethili/raed* in runes in two lines. *B.M.C.* 4 .. .. £750

838 "Porcupine". ℞. Small cross, S E D E in angles. *N.* 47 *Extremely rare*

XII. **Frisian sceattas,** *c.* 700-50. A number of large sceatta hoards have been found in the Netherlands and Lower Rhine area. Some of the coins are now known to have been minted in Frisia but some also circulated in England

839 Crude radiate bust l. or r., as 832, sometimes crude runes. ℞. Plain cross with pellets or annulets in angles. *Rigold* R3. *B.M.C.* 2c £100

840 "Standard". ℞. Cross and pellets. *B.M.C.* 50 .. .. £100

841 "Porcupine" with III, XII or XIII in curve. ℞. "Standard". *Metcalf* A, B & C £100

842 "Porcupine" has a triangle attached to curve or an outline of pellets. *Metcalf* E & F £110

843

844

843 Facing "Wodan" head. ℞. Monster. *B.M.C.* 31 .. .. £135

844 — Similar ℞. Two men with staves or long cross. *B.M.C.* 30a & b .. £150

XIII. **Uncertain issues**

845

847

845 **Ecgfrith** (?possibly K. of Northumbria 670-685). Æ *sceat.* Small cross. ℞. LVXX in angles of a cross radiant *Extremely rare*

846 **Ealdfrith** (?possibly sub-king of Lindsey, c. 790). AR. *sceat.* Pellet in annulet. ℞. Fantastic animal l. with trifid tail *Extremely rare*

847 **Beonna,** King of East Anglia, *c.* 758. AR *sceat.* Pellet in annulet, Runic inscription. ℞. EFE in Roman characters around saltire cross. *Extremely rare*

KINGS OF NORTHUMBRIA

In the North, a series of silver sceats was struck with the king's name on the obverse and a fantastic animal on the reverse.

Towards the end of the eighth century the coinage degenerated to one of base silver and finally to copper or brass; from the second reign of Aethelred I the design becomes standardised with the king's name retained on the obverse but with the moneyer's name on the reverse and in the centre of both sides a cross, pellet or rosette, etc.

A parallel series of ecclesiastical coins was struck by the Archbishops of York. The coinage continued until the conquest of Northumbria by the Danes and the defeat of Osbert in 867, almost a century after introduction of the broad silver penny in Southern England.

Fine

852 **Eadberht** (737-758). AR *sceat.* . Small cross. ℞. Fantastic quadruped to l. or r. £400

Aethelwald Moll (759-765). See Archbishop Ecgberht of York

853

859

861

853 **Alcred** (765-774). AR *sceat.* As 852 .. .. £350

854 **Aethelred I,** first reign (774-779). AR *sceat.* As last £350

855 **Aelfwald I** (779-788). AR *sceat.* As last £375

856 — — . Small cross. ℞. With name of moneyer CVDBEVRT £350

857 **Aethelred I,** second reign (789-796). AR *sceat.* Similar. ℞. SCT CVD (St. Cuthbert), shrine .. .. *Extremely rare*

858 — Small cross ℞. With moneyer's name £200

The last and the rest of the *sceats*, except where otherwise stated, have on the *obv.* the king's name, and and on the *rev.* the moneyer's name: in the centre on both sides is a cross, a pellet, a rosette, etc. During the following reign the silver sceat becomes debased and later issues are only brass or copper.

859 **Eanred** (810-41). Base AR *sceat* £28

860 — Æ *sceat* £14

861 **Aethelred II,** first reign (841-844). Æ *sceat* £12

862 — ℞. Quadruped £135

Fine

863 **Redwulf** (844). Æ *sceat* £40

864 **Aethelred II,** second reign (844-849). Æ *sceat,* mainly of the moneyer EARDWVLF £18

865 **Osbert** (849-867). Æ *sceat* £55

Coins with blundered legends are worth less than those with normal readings, and to this series have been relegated those coins previously attributed to Eardwulf and Aelfwald II.

ARCHBISHOPS OF YORK

866

868

871

Fine

866 **Ecgberht** (732 *or* 734-766). AR *sceat,* with king Eadberht. As illustration, or holds cross and crozier £300

867 — — with Alchred. Cross each side .. .. *Extremely rare*

868 **Eanbald II** (796-*c.* 830). AR *sceat* £60

869 — Æ *sceat,* as last £42

870 **Wigmund** (837-854). Gold *solidus.* Facing bust. ℞. Cross in wreath .. *Unique*

871 — Æ *sceat,* various £16

872 **Wulfhere** (854-900). Æ *sceat* £80

MIDDLE ANGLO-SAXON PERIOD c. 780-973

In the kingdom of the Franks a reformed coinage of good quality *deniers* struck on broad flans had been introduced by Pepin in 755 and continued by his son Charlemagne and his descendants. A new coinage of *pennies* of similar size and weighing about 20 grains (1.3 gms.) was introduced into England, probably by Offa, the powerful king of Mercia, about 775/780; though early pennies also exist of two little known kings of Kent, Heaberht and Ecgberht, of about the same period.

The silver penny (*Lat.* "denarius", hence the *d.* of our *£. s. d.*) remained virtually the sole denomination of English coinage for almost five centuries, with the rare exception of occasional gold coins and somewhat less rare silver halfpence. The penny reached a weight of 24 grains, i.e., a "pennyweight" during the reign of Aelfred the Great. Silver pennies of this period normally bear the ruler's name, though not always his portrait, and the name of the moneyer responsible for their manufacture.

Pennies were issued by various rulers of the Heptarchy for the kingdoms of Kent, Mercia, East Anglia and Wessex (and possibly Anglian Northumbria), by the Danish settlers in the Danelaw and the Hiberno-Norse kings of York, and also by the Archbishops of Canterbury and a Bishop of London. Under Eadgar, who became the sole ruler of England, a uniform coinage was instituted throughout the country, and it was he who set the pattern for the "reformed" coinage of the later Anglo-Saxon and Norman period.

Halfpence are known from the age of Aelfred to that of Eadgar, but they are rare and were probably never made in large quantities. To provide small change pennies were sometimes cut or broken in half.

Nos. 873-1387 are all silver **pennies** except where stated.

KINGS OF KENT

Fine

873 **Heaberht** (*c.* 765). Monogram for REX. ℞. Five annulets, each containing a pellet, joined to form a cross . . . *Unique*

874 **Ecgberht** (*c.* 780). Similar. ℞. Varied . . . . *from* £1250

875 **Eadberht Praen** (796-798). As illustration. ℞. Varied £1250

875

877

876 **Cuthred** (798-807). *Canterbury*. Various types without portrait . . *from* £500

877 — As illustration £550

878

879

878 **Anonymous** (*c.* 822-823). *Canterbury*. As illustration £650

879 **Baldred** (*c.* 823-825). *Canterbury*. Head or bust r. ℞. Varied £750

880 — Cross each side £650

881 *Rochester*. Diademed bust r. ℞. Varied . . . . *Extremely rare*

ARCHBISHOPS OF CANTERBURY

882 885

No.	Description	*Fine*
882	**Jaenberht** (765-792). His name around central ornament or cross and wedges. ℞. OFFA REX in two lines	£1600
883	— His name in three lines. ℞. OFFA REX between the limbs of Celtic cross ..	£2000
884	**Aethelheard** (el. 792, cons. 793, d. 805). With Offa as overlord. First issue (792-793), with title *Pontifex*	£1500
885	— Second issue (793-796), with title *Archiepiscopus*	£1150
886	With Coenwulf as overlord. Third issue (796-805)	£1000
887	**Wulfred** (805-832). Group I (805-*c.* 810). As illustration. ℞. Crosslet (*unique*), alpha-omega .. .. *from*	£800
888	— Group II (*c.* 810). As last. ℞. DOROVERNIA C monogram	£550
889	— Group III (pre 823). Bust extends to edge of coin. ℞. As last	£600
890	— Groups IV and V (*c.* 822-823). Anonymous under Ecgberht. Moneyer's name in place of the Archbishop's. ℞. DOROBERNIA CIVITAS in three or five lines	£525
891	— Group VI (*c.* 823-825). Baldred type. Crude portrait. ℞. DRVR CITS in two lines	£550
892	— Group VII (*c.* 832). Second monogram (Ecgberht) type. Crude portrait r., PLFRED. ℞. DORIB C. Monogram as 1035	£550

887 894

No.	Description	*Fine*
893	**Ceolnoth** (833-870). Group I with name CIALNOÐ. Tonsured bust facing. ℞. Varied .. .. *from*	£500
894	— Group II. Similar but CEOLNOÐ. ℞. Types of Aethelwulf of Wessex ..	£600
895	— Group III. Diad. bust r. ℞. Moneyer's name in and between lunettes	£575

896

No.	Description	*Fine*
896	**Aethered** (870-889). Bust r. ℞. As illustration or with long cross with lozenge panel	£1500
897	— Cross pattée. ℞. ELF / STAN	*Unique*

Archbishops of Canterbury *continued*

898

Fine

898 **Plegmund** (890-914). DORO in circle. ℞. As illustration above, various moneyers . . . . *from* £375

899 — Similar, but title EPISC, and XDF in centre £600

900 — Small cross pattée. ℞. Somewhat as last £325

901 — Crosses moline and pommée on *obv.* £600

KINGS OF MERCIA

GOLD

902

903

Fine

902 **Offa** (757-796). Gold *dinar*. Copy of Arabic dinar of Caliph Al Mansur, dated 157 A.H. (A.D. 774), with OFFA REX added on *rev.* . . . . *Unique*

903 Gold *penny*. Bust r., moneyer's name. ℞. Standing figure, moneyer's name *Unique*

SILVER

904

905

904 *Canterbury*. Group I (*c.* 784-*c.* 787). Early coins without portraits, small flans. Various types . . . . *from* £850

905 — Group II (*c.* 787-*c.* 792). Various types with portrait, small flans . . *from* £1100

906 — — — Various types without portraits, small flans . . . . . . *from* £750

Offa *continued*

907 909

		Fine
907	*Canterbury*. Group III (*c*. 792-796). Various types without portrait, large flans .. .. *from*	£800
908	*East Anglia*. Copies of Group II and III, possibly struck *c*. 790. Ornate, crude, and sometimes with runic letters	£700
909	**Cynethryth** (wife of Offa). Coins as Group II of Offa. As illustration ..	£4500
910	— *O*. As *rev*. of last. ℞. EOBA on leaves of quatrefoil	£2500
911	**Eadberht** (Bishop of London, died 787/789). EADBERHT EP in three lines. ℞. Name of Offa	*Extremely rare*
	The attribution to this particular cleric is uncertain.	
912	**Coenwulf** (796-821). Group I (796-805). *Canterbury* and *London*. Without portrait. His name in three lines. ℞. Varied	£500
913	— *Canterbury*. Name around m as illus. below. ℞. Moneyer's name in two lines	*Unique*

914 915

914	— *Both mints*. "Tribrach" type as illustration	£400
915	— Group II (*c*. 805-810). *Canterbury*. With portrait. Small flans. ℞. Varied but usually cross and wedges	£500
916	— Groups III and IV (*c*. 810-820). *Canterbury*. Similar but larger flans. ℞. Varied	£500
917	— *Rochester*. Large diad. bust of coarse style. ℞. Varied. (Moneyers: Dun, Ealhstan)	£550
918	— *London*. With portrait generally of Roman style. ℞. Crosslet	£550
919	— *E. Anglia*. Crude diad. bust r. ℞. Moneyer's name LVL on leaves in arms of cross	£500
920	— — *O*. as last ℞. Various types .. .. *from*	£475

921

929

Fine

921 **Ceolwulf I** (821-823). *Canterbury*. Group I. Bust r. ℞. Varied. (Moneyers: Oba, Sigestef) £650

922 — — Group II. Crosslet. ℞. Varied £550

923 — — Group III. Tall cross with MERCIORŪ ℞. Crosslet. SIGESTEF DOROBERNIA .. .. *Unique*

924 — *Rochester*. Group I. Bust r. ℞. Varied £550

925 — — Group IIA. As last but head r. £600

926 — — Group IIB. Ecclesiastical issue by Bp. of Rochester. With mint name, DOROBREBIA, but no moneyer. .. .. *Extremely rare*

927 — *East Anglia*. Crude style and lettering with barbarous portrait. ℞. Varied £550

928 **Beornwulf** (823-825). Bust r. ℞. Moneyer's name in three lines .. £1200

929 — ℞. Cross crosslet in centre £1000

930 Crude copy of 928 but moneyer's name in two lines with crosses between *Extremely rare*

931

933

931 **Ludica** (825-827). Bust r. ℞. Moneyer's name in three lines as 928 *Extremely rare*

932 — Similar. ℞. Moneyer's name around cross crosslet in centre, as 929 *Extremely rare*

933 **Wiglaf,** first reign (827-829). Crude head r. ℞. Crosslet £1500

934

934 Second reign (830-840). Cross and pellets. ℞. Moneyer's name in and between lunettes of pellets £1500

935

No.	Description	Fine
935	**Berhtwulf** (840-852). Various types with bust .. .. .. *from*	£700
936	— Cross potent over saltire. ℞. Cross potent	£750
937	Berhtwulf with Aethelwulf of Wessex. As before. ℞. IAETHELWLF REX, cross pommée over cross pattée	*Unique*
938	**Burgred** (852-874). *B.M.C.* type A. Bust r. ℞. Moneyer's name in and between lunettes	£85
939	— — B. Similar but lunettes broken in centre of curve	£100

938 939 940 941

No.	Description	Fine
940	— — C. Similar but lunettes broken in angles	£100
941	— — D. Similar but legend divided by two lines with a crook at each end ..	£85
942	— — E. As last, but m above and below	£375
943	**Ceolwulf II** (874-*c.* 880). Bust r. ℞. Two emperors seated, Victory above	*Unique*

944

No.	Description	Fine
944	— ℞. Moneyer's name in angles of long cross with lozenge centre	£1750

KINGS OF EAST ANGLIA

946

948

Fine

Beonna (*c.* 760). See no. 847

946 **Aethelberht** (d. 794). As illustration .. .. *Only* 3 *known*

947 **Eadwald** (*c.* 798). King's name in three lines. ℞. Moneyer's name in quatrefoil or around cross. .. .. *Extremely rare*

948 **Aethelstan I** (*c.* 825-840). Bust r. or l. ℞. Crosslet or star £650

949 Bust r. ℞. Moneyer's name in three or four lines £650

950 Alpha or A. ℞. Varied £500

951 *O.* and *rev.* Cross with or without wedges or pellets in angles £500

952 — Similar, with king's name both sides £600

953 **Aethelweard** (*c.* 840-*c.* 855), A, Omega or cross and crescents. ℞. Cross with pellets or wedges £700

953

954

954 **Edmund** (855-870). Alpha or A. ℞. Cross with pellets or wedges .. £375

955 — *O.* Varied. ℞. Similar £400

For the St. Edmund coins and the Danish issues struck in East Anglia having on them the name of Aethelred I of Wessex and Alfred, see Danish East Anglia.

VIKING COINAGES

Danish East Anglia, c. 885-915

956

957

Fine

956 **Aethelstan II** (878-890), originally named Guthrum? Cross pattée. ℞. Moneyer's name in two lines £850

957 **Oswald** (unknown except from his coins). Alpha or A. ℞. Cross pattée *Extremely rare*

958 — Copy of Carolingian "temple" type. ℞. Cross and pellets *Unique fragment*

959 **Aethelred I.** As last, with name of Aethelred I of Wessex. ℞. As last, or cross-crosslet .. .. *Extremely rare*

960 **St. Edmund,** memorial coinage, Æ *penny*, type as illus. below, various legends of good style £80

961 — Similar, but barbarous or semi-barbarous legends £70

962 *Halfpenny*. Similar.. .. .. £350

961

963

963 **St. Martin of Lincoln.** As illustration £1250

964 **Alfred.** (Viking imitations, usually of very barbarous workmanship). Bust r. ℞. "LONDONIA" monogram £350

965 — Similar, but "LINCOLLA" monogram .. .. *Extremely rare*

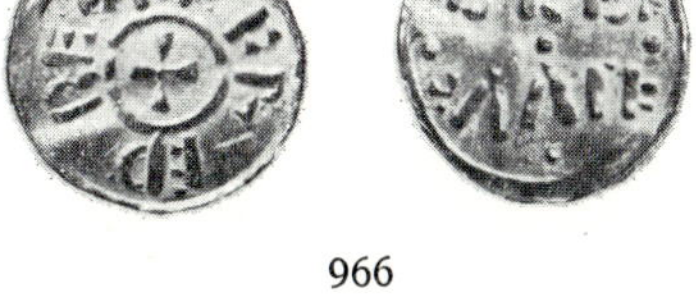

966

970

966 — Small cross, as Alfred group II (*Br.* 6), various legends, some read REX DORO *from* £200

967 — Similar. ℞. "St. Edmund," A in centre £500

968 — Two emperors seated. ℞. As 964. (Previously attributed to Halfdene) *Unique*

969 *Halfpenny*. As 964 and 965 .. .. *from* £400

970 — As 966 .. .. £350

Danish Northumbria, c. 898-915

Fine

971 **Alfred** (Imitations). ELFRED between ORSNA and FORDA. ℞. Moneyer's name in two lines £300

972 — *Halfpenny.* Similar, of very crude appearance .. .. .. *Extremely rare*

971

975

973 **Alfred/Plegmund.** *Obv.* ELFRED REX PLEGN .. .. *Extremely rare*

974 **Plegmund.** Danish copy of 900 .. .. £300

975 **Earl Sihtric.** Type as 971. SCELDFOR between GVNDI BERTVS. ℞. SITRIC COMES in two lines .. .. *Extremely rare*

Viking Coinage of York?

References are to "The Classification of Northumbrian Viking Coins in the Cuerdale hoard", by C. S. S. Lyon and B. H. I. H. Stewart, in Numismatic Chronicle, 1964, *p.* 281 *ff.*

976 **Siefred.** C . SIEFRE DIIS REX in two lines. ℞. EBRAICE CIVITAS (or contractions), small cross. *L. & S. Ia, Ie, Ii* £200

977 — Cross on steps between. ℞. As last. *L. & S. If, Ij* £275

978 — Long cross. ℞. As last. *L. & S. Ik* .. .. *Extremely rare*

979 SIEFREDVS REX, cross crosslet within legend. ℞. As last. *L. & S. Ih* .. £130

980 SIEVERT REX, cross crosslet to edge of coin. ℞. As last. *L. & S. Ic, Ig, Im* £130

981 — Cross on steps between. ℞. As last. *L. & S. Il* £240

982 — Patriarchal cross. ℞. DNS DS REX, small cross. *L. & S. Va* £150

983 — — ℞. MIRABILIA FECIT, small cross. *L. & S. VIb* £185

984 REX, at ends of cross crosslet. ℞. SIEFREDVS, small cross. *L. & S. IIIa, b* £140

985 — Long cross. ℞. As last. *L. & S. IIIc* £120

986 *Halfpenny.* Types as 977, *L. & S. Ib*; 980, *Ic*; and 983, *VIb*. .. *Extremely rare*

980

993

987 **Cnut.** CNVT REX, cross crosslet to edge of coin. ℞. EBRAICE CIVITAS, small cross. *L. & S. Io, Iq* £85

988 — — ℞. CVNNETTI, small cross. *L. & S. IIc* £90

989 — Long cross. ℞. EBRAICE CIVITAS, small cross. *L. & S. Id, In, Ir* .. £70

990 — — ℞. CVNNETTI, small cross. *L. & S. IIa, IId.* £70

991 — Patriarchal cross. ℞. EBRAICE CIVITAS, small cross. *L. & S. Ip. Is* .. £70

992 — — ℞. — KAROLUS monogram in centre. *L. & S. It* £400

993 — — ℞. CVNNETTI, small cross. *L. & S. IIb, IIe* £60

Fine

994 *Halfpenny.* Types as 987, *L. & S. Iq*; 989, *Id*; 991, *Is*; 992, *Iu*; 993, *IIb and e from* £400

995 As 992, but CVNNETTI around KAROLVS monogram. *L. & S. IIf* £400

995

998

996 **Cnut and/or Siefred.** CNVT REX, patriarchal cross. ℞. SIEFREDVS, small cross. *L. & S. IIId* £100

997 — — ℞. DNS DS REX, small cross. *L. & S. Vc.* £140

998 — — ℞. MIRABILIA FECIT. *L. & S. VId* £130

999 EBRAICE C, patriarchal cross. ℞. DNS DS REX, small cross. *L. & S. Vb* .. £110

1000 — — ℞. MIRABILIA FECIT. *L. & S. VIc* £130

1001 DNS DS REX in two lines. ℞. ALVALDVS, small cross. *L. & S. IVa* *Extremely rare*

1002 DNS DS O REX, similar. ℞. MIRABILIA FECIT. *L. & S. VIa* £250

1003 *Halfpenny.* As last. *L. & S. VIa* .. .. *Extremely rare*

1004 **"Cnut".** Name blundered around cross pattée with extended limbs. ℞. QVENTOVICI around small cross. *L. & S. VII* £300

1005 — *Halfpenny.* Similar. *L. & S. VII* £450

Possibly not Northumbrian; the reverse copied from the Carolingian coins of Quentovic, N. France.

1006 **St. Peter coinage.** Early issues. SCI PETRI MO in two lines. ℞. Cross pattée £225

1007 — Similar. ℞. "Karolus" monogram .. .. *Extremely rare*

1008 *Halfpenny.* Similar. ℞. Cross pattée £1000

1006

1009

1009 **Regnald** (blundered types). RAIENALT, head to l. or r. ℞. EARICE CT, "Karolus" monogram £1250

1010 — Open hand. ℞. Similar £1100

1011 — Hammer. ℞. Bow and arrow £1200

1012 — Similar. ℞. Sword .. .. *Extremely rare*

English Coins of the Hiberno-Norse Vikings

Early period, ***c.*** **919-925**

1013 **Sihtric** (921-927). SITRIC REX, sword. ℞. Cross or T £1500

1015

1016

Fine

1014 **St. Peter coinage.** Late issues. SCI PETRI MO, sword and hammer. ℞. EBORACEI, cross and pellets £400

1015 — Similar. ℞. Voided hammer £500

1016 — Similar. ℞. Solid hammer £850

St. Peter coins with blundered legends are rather cheaper.

Later period, 939-954 (after the battle of Brunanburh). All struck at York except the first two which were struck at Derby.

1017 **Anlaf Guthfrithsson,** 939-941. Flower type. Small cross, ANLAF REX TO D. ℞. Flower above moneyer's name £2500

1018 — Circular type. Small cross each side, ANLAF CVNVNC MOT £2500

1019 — Raven type. As illustration, CVNVNC £2000

1019

1020

1020 **Anlaf Sihtricsson,** first reign, 941-944. Triquetra type. As illus., CVNVNC. ℞. Danish standard £2000

1021 — Circular type (a). Small cross each side, CVNVNC £2000

1022 — Cross moline type, CVNVNC. ℞. Small cross .. .. .. *Extremely rare*

1023 — Two line type. Small cross. ℞. ONLAF REX. ℞. Name in two lines £1850

1024 **Regnald Guthfrithsson,** 943-944. Triquetra type. As 1020. REGNALD CVNVNC £3000

1025 — Cross moline type. As 1022, but REGNALD CVNVNC £2500

1026 **Sihtric Sihtricsson,** *c.* 942. Triquetra type. As 1020, SITRIC CVNVNC .. *Unique*

1025

1030

1027 — Circular type. Small cross each side. SITRIC CVNVNC .. .. .. *Unique*

1028 **Eric,** first reign, 948. Two line type. Small cross, ERICVS REX A; ERIC REX AL; or ERIC REX EFOR. ℞. Name in two lines £2500

1029 **Anlaf Sihtricsson,** second reign, 948-952. Circular type (b). Small cross each side. ONLAF REX £2750

1030 **Eric,** second reign, 952-954. Sword type. ERIC REX in two lines sword between. ℞. Small cross £2750

KINGS OF WESSEX

Later, KINGS OF ALL ENGLAND

All are silver pennies unless otherwise stated

BEORHTRIC, 786-802

1031

		Fine
1031	As illustration	*Extremely rare*
1032	Alpha and omega in centre. ℞. Omega in centre	*Extremely rare*

ECGBERHT, 802-839

1033	*Canterbury*. Group I. Diad. hd. r. within inner circle. ℞. Various	*from*	£1250
1034	— II. Non-portrait types. ℞. Various	*from*	£900

1035

1035	— III. Bust r. breaking inner circle. ℞. DORIB C.		£1000
1036	*London*. Cross potent. ℞. LVN / DONIA / CIVIT		*Unique*
1037	— — ℞. REDMVND MONE around TA		£1500
1038	*Rochester*, royal mint. Non-portrait types with king's name ECGBEORHT	*from*	£1200
1039	— — Portrait types, ECGBEORHT	*from*	£1400
1040	*Rochester*, bishop's mint. Bust r. ℞. SCS ANDREAS (APOSTOLVS)		£1500
1041	*Winchester*. SAXON monogram or SAXONIORVM in three lines. ℞. Cross ..		£1000

AETHELWULF, 839-858

1042

		Fine
1042	*Canterbury*. Phase I (839-*c*. 843). Head within inner circle. ℞. Various. *Br*. 3..	£325
1043	— — Larger bust breaking inner circle. ℞. A. *Br*. 1 and 2	£325
1044	— — Cross and wedges. ℞. SAXONIORVM in three lines in centre. *Br*. 10	£300
1045	— — Similar, but OCCIDENTALIVM in place of moneyer. *Br*. 11	£400
1046	— Phase II (*c*. 843-848 ?). Cross and wedges. ℞. Various, but chiefly a form of cross or a large A. *Br*. 4	£300
1047	— — New portrait, somewhat as 1043. ℞. As last. *Br*. 7	£300
1048	— — Smaller portrait. ℞. As last, with *Chi/Rho* monogram. *Br*. 7	£325
1049	— Phase III (*c*. 848/51-*c*. 855). DORIB in centre. ℞. CANT mon. *Br*. 5	£300
1050	— — CANT mon. ℞. CAN M in angles of cross. *Br*. 6	£325

1044

1051

1051	— Phase IV (*c*. 855-859). Type as Aethelberht. New neat style bust. ℞. Large voided long cross. *Br*. 8	£250
1052	*Winchester*. SAXON mon. ℞. Cross and wedges. *Br*. 9	£375

AETHELBERHT, 858-865/6

1053	As illustration below	£180
1054	*O*. Similar. ℞. Cross fleury over quatrefoil	£700

1053

1055

AETHELRED I, 865/6-871

1055	As illustration	£200
1056	Similar, but moneyer's name in four lines	£600

For another coin with the name Aethelred see 959 under Viking coinages.

ALFRED THE GREAT, 871-899

Types with portraits

Fine

1057 Bust r. ℞. As Aethelred I. *Br.* 1 .. .. £400

1058 — ℞. Long cross with lozenge centre, as 944. *Br.* 5 .. .. .. £1500

1059 — ℞. Two seated figures, as 943. *Br.* 2 .. .. *Unique*

1060 — ℞. As Archbp. Aethered; cross within large quatrefoil. *Br.* 3 .. *Unique*

1057

1062

1061 *London.* Bust r. ℞. LONDONIA monogram £500

1062 — — ℞. Similar, but with moneyer's name added £800

1063 — *Halfpenny.* Bust r. ℞. LONDONIA monogram as 1061 .. .. .. £1000

1064 *Gloucester.* ℞. ÆT GLEAPA in angles of three limbed cross .. .. .. *Unique*

Types without portraits

1065 King's name on limbs of cross, trefoils in angles. ℞. Moneyer's name in quatrefoil. *Br.* 4 .. .. *Unique*

1066

1069

1066 Cross pattée. ℞. Moneyer's name in two lines. *Br.* 6 .. .. .. £225

1067 — As last, but neater style, as Edw. the Elder £250

1068 — *Halfpenny.* As 1066 .. .. £650

1069 *Canterbury.* As last but DORO added on *obv.* *Br.* 6a £400

For other pieces bearing the name of Alfred see under the Viking coinages.

1070 *Exeter?* King's name in four lines. ℞. EXA vertically .. .. *Extremely rare*

1071 *Winchester?* Similar to last, but PIN .. .. *Extremely rare*

1072 "Offering penny". Very large and heavy. AELFRED REX SAXORVM in four lines. ℞. ELIMO in two lines ie (*Elimosina*, alms) .. .. *Extremely rare*

EDWARD THE ELDER, 899-924

1074

Fine

1073 **Rare types.** *Br.* 1. *Bath?* ℞. BA .. .. *Extremely rare*
1074 — 2. *Canterbury.* Cross moline in pommée. ℞. Moneyer's name .. £700
1075 — 3. *Chester?* Small cross. ℞. Minster £750
1076 — 4. — Small cross. ℞. Moneyer's name in single line £625
1077 — 5. — ℞. Two stars £850

1078

1082

1078 — 6. — ℞. Flower above central line, name below £850
1079 — 7. — ℞. Floral design with name across field £850
1080 — 8. — ℞. Bird holding twig .. .. *Extremely rare*
1081 — 9. — ℞. Hand of Providence £1000
1082 — 10. — ℞. City gate of Roman style .. .. *Extremely rare*
1083 — 11. — ℞. Anglo-Saxon burg £750

1084

1087

1084 **Ordinary types.** *Br.* 12. Bust l. ℞. Moneyer's name in two lines *from* £400
1085 — — As last, but in *gold* .. .. *Unique*
1086 — 12a. Similar, but bust r. of crude style £350
1087 — 13. Small cross. ℞. Similar £120
1088 *Halfpenny.* Similar to last £650

AETHELSTAN, 924-939

1089 1094

		Fine
1089	**Main issues.** Small cross. ℞. Moneyer's name in two lines	£150
1090	Diad. bust r. ℞. As last	£600
1091	— ℞. Small cross	£525
1092	Small cross both sides	£175
1093	— Similar, but mint name added	£275
1094	Crowned bust r. As illustration. ℞. Small cross	£450
1095	— Similar, but mint name added	£450

1100 1104

1096	**Local Issues.** *N.W. mints.* Star between two pellets. ℞. As 1089 ..	£550
1097	— Small cross. ℞. Floral ornaments above and below moneyer's name	£550
1098	— Rosette of pellets each side	£250
1099	— Small cross one side, rosette on the other side	£275
1100	*York.* Small cross. ℞. Tower over moneyer's name	£525
1101	— Similar, but mint name added	£750
1102	— Bust in high relief r. or l. ℞. Small cross	£475
1103	— Bust r. in high relief. ℞. Cross-crosslet	£500
1104	*Lincoln?* Helmeted bust r. ℞. As last	£525

EADMUND, 939-946

1105

1107

		Fine
1105	Small cross or rosette. ℞. Moneyer's name in two lines with crosses or rosettes between .. .. *from*	£125
1106	Crowned bust r. ℞. Small cross	£300
1107	Similar, but with mint name	£400
1108	Small cross either side, or rosette on one side	£175
1109	Cross of five pellets. ℞. Moneyer's name in two lines	£200
1110	Small cross. ℞. Flower above name	£750
1111	Helmeted bust r. ℞. Cross-crosslet	£750

1112

1112	*Halfpenny*. As 1105 .. .. *from*	£850

EADRED, 946-955

1113

1115

1113	As illustration. ℞. Moneyer's name in two lines	£100
1114	— Similar, but mint name after REX	£300
1115	Crowned bust r. As illustration	£350
1116	— ℞. Similar, with mint-name added	£400
1117	Rosette. ℞. As 1113	£125
1118	Small cross. ℞. Rosette	£135
1119	— ℞. Flower enclosing moneyer's name. *B.M.C.* II	*Extremely rare*
1120	*Halfpenny*. Similar to 1113 .. .. *from*	£650

1121

HOWEL DDA, d. 949-950 (King of Wales)?

Fine

1121 HOPÆL REX, small cross or rosette. ℞. Moneyer's name in two lines .. *Unique*

EADWIG, 955-959

1122

1122	*Br.* 1. Type as illustration	£175
1123	— — Similar, but mint name in place of crosses	£375
1124	— 2. As 1122, but moneyer's name in one line	£600
1125	— 3. Similar. ℞. Floral design	£675
1126	— 4. Similar. ℞. Rosette or small cross	£250
1127	— 5. Bust r. ℞. Small cross	*Extremely rare*

1128

1128 *Halfpenny.* Small cross. ℞. Flower above moneyer's name .. .. *Unique*

EADGAR, 959-975

It is now possible on the basis of the lettering to divide up the majority of Eadgar's coins into issues from the following regions. N.E. England, N.W. England, York, East Anglia, Midlands, S.E. England, Southern England, and S.W. England. (*Vide* "Anglo-Saxon Coins", ed. R. H. M. Dolley).

1129

1135

		Fine
1129	*Br.* 1. Small cross. ℞. Moneyer's name in two lines, crosses between, trefoils top and bottom	£75
1130	— — ℞. Similar, but rosettes top and bottom (a N.W. variety)	£75
1131	— — ℞. Similar, but annulets between	£75
1132	— — ℞. Similar, but mint name between (a late N.W. type)	£100
1133	— 2. — ℞. Floral design	£750
1134	— 4. Small cross either side	£75
1135	— — Similar, with mint name	£250
1136	— — Rosette either side	£100
1137	— — Similar, with mint name	£175
1138	— 5. Large bust to r. ℞. Small cross	£350
1139	— — Similar, with mint name	£500
1140	*Halfpenny.* (8½ grains). *Br.* 3. Small cross. ℞. Flower above name:	*Extremely rare*

See also 1141 below.

LATE ANGLO-SAXON PERIOD

In 973 Eadgar introduced a new coinage. A royal portrait now became a regular feature and the reverses normally have a cruciform pattern with the name of the mint in addition to that of the moneyer. Most fortified towns of burghal status were allowed a mint, the number of moneyers varying according to their size and importance; some royal manors also had a mint and some moneyers were allowed to certain ecclesiastical authorities. In all some seventy mints were active about the middle of the 11th century (see list of mints pp. 65-67).

The control of the currency was retained firmly in the hands of the central government, unlike the situation in France and the Empire where feudal barons and bishops controlled their own coinage. Coinage types were changed at intervals to enable the Exchequer to raise revenue from new dies and periodic demonetization of old coin types helped to maintain the currency in a good state. No halfpence were minted during this period, but pennies were often sheared into two halves.

EADGAR, 959-975 (*Continued*)

		F	*VF*
1141	**Penny.** Type 6. Small bust l. ℞. Small cross, name of moneyer and mint	£550	£1100

EDWARD THE MARTYR, 975-978

1142

1142	Type as illustration above	£700	£1400

AETHELRED II, 978-1016

1143

1144

No.	Description	F	VF
1143	First small cross type. Style of 1142. *Br.* 1; *B.M.C.* I	£325	£700
1144	First Hand type. Bust r., no sceptre. ℞. Hand of Providence. *Br.* 2; *B.M.C.* IIa	£85	£200
1145	— Similar, but bust to l. *B.M.C.* IIb	£325	£700

1146

1147

No.	Description	F	VF
1146	Second Hand type, with sceptre. *B.M.C.* IId	£75	£180
1147	Benediction type. *O.* As last. ℞. Hand giving Benediction. *B.M.C.* IIf	£500	£1200

1148

1151

No.	Description	F	VF
1148	CRVX type. *Br.* 3; *B.M.C.* IIIa	£60	£135
1149	— Lightweight issue. Small flan, sceptre into drapery	£120	£275
1150	Intermediate small cross type. Somewhat as 1143	£225	£500
1151	Long cross type. *Br.* 5; *B.M.C.* IVa	£55	£125

1152

No.	Description	F	VF
1152	Helmet type. *Br.* 4; *B.M.C.* VIII	£65	£150
1153	— — Similar, but struck in **gold**		*Unique*

		F	*VF*
1154	Last small cross type. As 1143, but different style	£55	£125
1155	— Similar, but bust to edge of coin. *B.M.C.* Id	£250	£550

1154

1156

1156 Agnus Dei type. *Br.* 6; *B.M.C.* X .. .. *Extremely rare*

CNUT, 1016-1035

Main types

1157 1158 1159 1160

		F	*VF*
1157	Quatrefoil type. *Br.* 2; *B.M.C.* VIII	£75	£175
1158	Helmet type. *Br.* 3; *B.M.C.* XIV	£65	£150
1159	Short cross type. *Br.* 4; *B.M.C.* XVI	£60	£135
1160	Jewel cross type. *Br.* 6; *B.M.C.* XX. Type as 1163	£600	£1350

Scandanavian Imitations

1161	Small cross type, as Aethelred II. *Br.* 1; *B.M.C.* 1	£250	£550
1162	Long cross type, as Aethelred II. *Br.* 1a	£250	£550

HAROLD I, 1035-1040

1163

1165

		F	VF
1163	Jewel cross type, as illustration. *Br.* 1; *B.M.C.* 1	£225	£500
1164	Long cross and trefoils type. *Br.* 2; *B.M.C.* V	£175	£400
1165	— Similar, but fleur de lis in place of trefoils. *B.M.C.* Vc	£175	£400

HARTHACNUT, 1035-1042

1167

1168

1166	**Early period, 1036.** Jewel cross type, as 1163; bust l. *Br.* 1; *B.M.C.* I	£700	£1500
1167	— Similar, but bust r. *B.M.C.* Ia	£650	£1400
1168	**Restoration, 1040-42.** Arm and sceptre type, with name Harthacnut. *Br.* 2; *B.M.C.* II	£800	£1750
1169	— Similar, but with name "Cnut"	£500	£1100

1169

1170

1170	**Danish types,** of various designs, mostly struck at Lund, Denmark (now Sweden) .. .. *from*	£135	£300

EDWARD THE CONFESSOR, 1042-1066

1171

1173

		F	*VF*
1171	PACX type, cross extends to edge of coin. *Br.* 4; *B.M.C.* IVa ..	£125	£300
1172	— Similar, but cross ends at legend. *B.M.C.* IV	£120	£275
1173	Radiate type. *Br.* 2; *B.M.C.* I	£75	£165

1174

1175

1174	Trefoil quadrilateral type. *Br.* 1; *B.M.C.* III	£75	£165
1175	Short cross type, small flans. *Br.* 3; *B.M.C.* II	£60	£145

1176

1179

1176	Expanding cross type; light issue (18 grs.). *Br.* 5; *B.M.C.* V ..	£75	£165
1177	— — heavy issue (27 grs.)	£65	£150
1178	— — Similar, but struck in **gold**		*Unique*
1179	Helmet type. *Br.* 6; *B.M.C.* VII	£65	£150
1180	— — Similar but bust l.	£275	£600

1181

1182

1181	Sovereign type. *Br.* 7; *B.M.C.* IX	£90	£200
1182	Hammer cross type. *Br.* 8; *B.M.C.* XI	£65	£140

1183

1184

		F	VF
1183	Facing bust type. *Br.* 9; *B.M.C.* XIII	£55	£120
1184	Pyramids type. *Br.* 10; *B.M.C.* XV	£75	£160

1185

1185	Large facing bust with sceptre. ℞. Similar	£950	£2000

Most York coins of this reign have an annulet in one quarter of the reverse.

HAROLD II, 1066

1186

1187

		F	VF
1186	Bust l. with sceptre. ℞. PAX across centre of *rev.* *B.M.C.* I ..	£350	£750
1187	Similar, but without sceptre. *B.M.C.* Ia	£450	£1000
1188	Bust r. with sceptre	£700	£1500

ANGLO-SAXON, NORMAN AND EARLY PLANTAGENET MINTS

In Anglo-Saxon times coins were struck at a large number of towns. The place of mintage is normally given on all coins from the last quarter of the 10th century onwards, and, generally the name of the person responsible (e.g. BRVNIC ON LVND)...Below we give a list of the mints, showing the reigns (Baronial of Stephen's reign omitted), of which coins have been found. After the town names we give one or two of the spellings as found on the coins, although often they appear in an abbreviated or extended form. On the coins the Anglo-Saxon and Norman "W" is like a P or Ƿ and the "TH" is Đ. We have abbreviated the king's names, etc.:

Alf	—	Alfred the Great	Wi	—	William I
EE	—	Edward the Elder	Wii	—	William II
A'stan	—	Aethelstan	He	—	Henry I
EM	—	Edward the Martyr	St	—	Stephen (regular issues)
Ae	—	Aethelred II	M	—	Matilda
Cn	—	Cnut	HA	—	Henry of Anjou
Hi	—	Harold I	WG	—	William of Gloucester
Ht	—	Harthacnut	T	—	"Tealby" coinage
ECfr	—	Edward the Confessor	SC	—	"short cross" coinage
Hii	—	Harold II	LC	—	"long cross" coinage

Axbridge (ACXEPO, AGEPOR) Ae, Cn, Ht.
Aylesbury (AEGEL) Ae, Cn, ECfr.

Barnstaple (BEARDA, BARDI), Edwig, Ae-Hi, ECfr, Wi, He.
Bath (BAĐAN) EE-Edmund, Edwig-ECfr, Wi, He, St.
Bedford (BEDANF, BEDEF) Edwig-T.
Bedwyn (BEDEƿIN) ECfr, Wi.
Berkeley (BEORC) ECfr
Bramber ? (BRAN) St.
Bridport (BRIPVT, BRIDI) A'stan, Ae, Cn, Ht, ECfr, Wi.
Bristol (BRICSTO) Ae-T, M, HA, LC.
Bruton (BRIVT) Ae-Cn, ECfr.
Buckingham (BVCIN) EM-Hi, ECfr.
Bury St. Edmunds (EDMVN, SEDM, SANTEA) A'stan ? ECfr, Wi, He-LC.

Cadbury (CADANB) Ae, Cn.
Caistor (CASTR) EM, Ae, Cn.
Cambridge (GRANTE) Edgar-Wii.
Canterbury (DORO, CAENT, CANTOR, CANTƿAR) Alf, A'stan, Edgar-LC.
Cardiff (CAIRDI, CARDI, CARITI) Wi, He, St, M.
Carlisle (CAR, CARDI, EDEN) Hi-LC.
Castle Gotha ? (GEOĐA, IOĐA) Ae-Ht.
Castle Rising (RISINGE) St.
Chester (LEIGECES, LEGECE, CESTRE) A'stan, Edgar-T.
Chichester (CISSAN CIV, CICES, CICST) A'stan, Edgar-St., SC.
Chippenham ? (CIPEN) St.
Christchurch, see Twynham.
Cissbury (SIĐEST) Ae, Cn.
Colchester (COLEAC, COLECES) Ae-Hi, ECfr-T.
Crewkerne (CRVCERN) Ae, Cn.
Cricklade (CROCGL, CRIC, CREC) Ae-Wii.

Derby (DEOR, DIORBI, DERBI) A'stan, Edgar-ECfr, Wi-St.
Dorchester (DORCE, DORECES) Ae-ECfr, Wi-He, WG.
Dover (DOFER) A'stan, Edgar-St.
Droitwich (PICC, PICNEH) ECfr, Hii.
Durham (DVNE, DVRE, DVRHAN) Wi, St-LC.

Exeter (EAXANC, EXEC, XECST) Alf, A'stan, Edwig-LC.

Frome ? (FRO) Cn-ECfr.

Gloucester (GLEAƿEC, GLEƿ, Gƿ) Alf, A'stan, Edgar-St, HA, T, LC.
Guildford (GILDEF) EM-Cn, Ht-Wii.

Hastings (HAESTIN) Ae-St.
Hedon, near Hull (HEDVN) St.
Hereford (HEREFOR) A'stan, Ae-St, HA, T, LC.
Hertford (HEORTF) A'stan, Edwig-Hi, ECfr, Wi, Wii.
Horncastle ? (HORN) EM, Ae.
Horndon ? (HORNIDVNE) ECfr.
Huntingdon (HVNTEN) Edwig-St.
Hythe (HIĐEN) ECfr, Wi, Wii.
Ilchester (IVELCE, GIFELCST, GIVELC) Edgar, EM-He, T, LC.
Ipswich (GIPESǷIC) Edgar-SC.
Kings Lynn (LENN, LENE) SC.
Langport (LANCPOR) A'stan, Cn, Hi, ECfr.
Launceston (LANSTF, SANCTI STEFANI) Ae, Wi, Wii, St, T.
Leicester (LIGER, LIHER, LEHRE) A'stan, Edgar-T.
Lewes (LAEǷES) A'stan, Edgar-T.
Lichfield (LIHFL) SC.
Lincoln (LINCOLNE, NICOLE) Edgar-LC.
London (LVNDENE) Alf-LC.
Louth ? (LVD) Ae.
Lydford (LYDAN) EM-Hi, ECfr.
Lympne (LIMEN) A'stan, Edgar-Cn.
Maldon (MAELDVN, MAELI) A'stan, Ae-Hi, ECfr, Wii, HA.
Malmesbury (MALD, MEALDMES) Ae-Wii.
Marlborough (MAERLEB) Wi, Wii.
Milbourne Port (MYLE) Ae, Cn.
Newark (NEPIR, NIǷOR) Edwig, Eadgar, Ae, Cn.
Newcastle (NEWEC, NIVCA) St, T, LC.
Newport (NIǷAN, NIǷEP) Edgar, ECfr.
Northampton (HAMTVN, NORHANT) Edwig, Edgar-Wi, He-LC.
Norwich (NORǷIC) A'stan-LC.
Nottingham (SNOTINC) A'stan, Ae-St.
Oxford (OXNAFOR, OXENEF) A'stan, Edmund, Edred, Edgar-St, M, T-LC.
Pembroke (PAN, PAIN) He-T.
Pershore (PERESC) ECfr.
Peterborough (MEĐE, BVR) Ae, Cn, Wi.
Petherton (PEĐR) ECfr.
Pevensey (PEFNESE, PEVEN) Wi, Wii, St.
Reading (READIN) ECfr.
Rhuddlan (RVDILI, RVLA) Wi, SC.
Rochester (ROFEC) A'stan, Edgar-He, SC.
Romney (RVME, RVMNE) Ae-Hi, ECfr-He.
Rye (RIE) St.
Salisbury (SAEREB, SALEB) Ae-ECfr, Wi-He, T.
Sandwich (SANǷIC) ECfr, Wi-St.
Shaftesbury (SCEFTESB, SCEFITI) A'stan, Ae-St.
Shrewsbury (SCROBES, SALOǷ) A'stan, Edgar-LC.
Southampton (HAMWIC, HAMTVN) A'stan, Edwig-Cn.
Southwark (SVĐGE, SVĐǷEEORC) Ae-St.
Stafford (STAFF, STAEF) A'stan, Ae-Hi, ECfr, Wi, Wii, St., T.
Stamford (STANFOR) Edgar-St.
Steyning (STAENIG) Cn-Wii.
Sudbury (SVĐBI, SVB) Ae, Cn, ECfr, Wi-St.
Swansea (SWENSEI) HA ?
Tamworth (TOMǷEARĐGE, TAMǷRĐ) A'stan, Edwig-Hi, ECfr, Wi-St.
Taunton (TANTVNE) Ae, Cn, Ht-St.
Thetford (ĐEOTFOR, TETFOR) Edgar-T.
Torksey (TORC, TVRC) EM-Cn.
Totnes (DARENT VRB, TOTANES, TOTNESE) A'stan, Edwig-Cn, Wii.
Twynham, now Christchurch (TǷIN, TVEHAM) Wi, He.
Wallingford (ǷELING, ǷALLIG) A'stan, Edgar-He, T, LC.
Wareham (ǷERHAM) A'stan, Ae, Cn, Ht-St, M, WG.
Warminster (ǷORIME) Ae-Hi, ECfr.
Warwick (ǷAERING, ǷERǷIC) A'stan, Edgar-St.
Watchet (ǷECEDPORT, ǷICEDI) Ae-ECfr, Wi-St.

Wilton (ƿILTVNE) Edgar-LC.
Winchcombe (ƿINCELE, ƿINCL) Edgar-Cn, Ht-Wi.
Winchester (ƿINTONIA, ƿINCEST) Alf-A'stan, Edwig-LC.
Worcester (ƿIHRAC, ƿIHREC) Ae-Hi, ECfr-SC.
York (EBORACI, EOFERƿIC) A'stan, Edmund, Edgar-LC.

The location of the following is uncertain.
AESTHE (*? Hastings*) Ae.
BRYGIN (which die-links with NIPAN and with *Shaftesbury*) Ae.
DERNE, DYR, (E. Anglian mint) ECfr
DEVITVN, (*?Welsh Marches* or *St. Davids*) Wi
EANBYRIG, Cn.
ORSNAFORDA, (*? Horsforth*) Alf.
WEARDBYRIG (*? Warborough*) A'stan, Edgar.

EDWARDIAN AND LATER MINTS

London, Tower: Edw. I-Geo. III.
„ *Tower Hill:* Geo. III-Eliz. II.
„ *Durham House:* Hen. VIII (posth.)-Edw. VI.
Aberystwyth: Chas. I.
„ *-Furnace:* Chas. I.
Barnstaple?: Chas. I.
Berwick-on-Tweed: Edw. I-Edw. III.
Birmingham, Heaton: Vic., Geo. V.
„ *King's Norton:* Geo. V.
„ *Soho:* Geo. III.
Bombay, India (branch mint): Geo. V.
Bristol: Edw. I, Edw. IV, Hen. VI rest., Hen. VIII-Edw. VI, Chas. I, Wm. III.
Bury St. Edmunds: Edw. I-Edw. III.
Calais: Edw. III-Hen. IV, Hen. VI.
Canterbury: Edw. I-Edw. III, Edw. IV, Hen. VII-Edw. VI.
Carlisle: Chas. I.
Chester: Edw. I, Chas. I, Wm. III.
Colchester: Chas. I.
Coventry: Edw. IV, Chas. I(?).
Durham: Edw. I-Edw. IV, Rich. III-Hen. VIII.
Exeter: Edw. I, Chas. I, Wm. III.
Kingston-upon-Hull: Edw. I.
Lincoln: Edw. I.
Llantrisant: Eliz. II (decimal coinage).
Lundy Is.?: Chas. I.
Melbourne, Australia (branch mint): Vic.-Geo. V.
Newark: Chas. I.
Newcastle-upon-Tyne: Edw. I.
Norwich: Edw. IV, Wm. III.
Ottawa, Canada (branch mint): Edw. VII-Geo. V.
Oxford: Chas. I.
Perth, Australia (branch mint): Vic.-Geo. V.
Pontefract: Chas. I.
Pretoria, South Africa (branch mint): Geo. V.
Reading: Edw. III.
Salisbury or *Sandsfoot Castle:* Chas. I.
Scarborough: Chas. I.
Shrewsbury: Chas. I.
Southwark: Hen. VIII-Edw. VI.
Sydney, Australia (branch mint): Vic.-Geo. V.
Tournai, Belgium: Hen. VIII.
Truro: Chas. I.
Weymouth: Chas. I.
Worcester (Hartlebury Cas.): Chas. I.
York: Edw. I, Edw. III-Edw. IV, Rich. III-Edw. VI, Chas. I, Wm. III.

NORMAN KINGS AND THEIR SUCCESSORS

There were no major changes in the coinage following the Norman conquest. The controls and periodic changes of type made in the previous reigns were continued. Nearly seventy mints were operating during the reign of William I; these had been reduced to about fifty-five by the middle of the 12th century and, under Henry II, first to thirty and later to eleven. By the second half of the 13th century the issue of coinage had been centralized at London and Canterbury, with the exception of two ecclesastical mints. Of the thirteen types with the name PILLEMVS, PILLELM, etc. (William), the first eight have been attributed to the Conqueror and the remaining five to his son William Rufus.

From William I to Edward II inclusive all are silver pennies unless otherwise stated

WILLIAM I, 1066-1087

1250

1251

		F	*VF*
1250	**Penny.** Profile left type. *Br.* I	£145	£300
1251	Bonnet type. *Br.* II	£120	£250

1252

1253

1252	Canopy type. *Br.* III	£175	£400
1253	Two sceptres type. *Br.* IV	£145	£325

1254

1255

1254	Two stars type. *Br.* V	£115	£250
1255	Sword type. *Br.* VI	£250	£475

1256

1257

1256	Profile right type. *Br.* VII	£375	£800
1257	PAXS type. *Br.* VIII	£60	£110

WILLIAM II, 1087-1100

1258

1259

		F	VF
1258	**Penny.** Profile type. *Br.* 1	£225	£475
1259	Cross in quatrefoil type. *Br.* 2	£225	£475

1260

1261

		F	VF
1260	Cross voided type. *Br.* 3	£225	£475
1261	Cross pattée and fleury type. *Br.* 4	£300	£650

1262

		F	VF
1262	Cross fleury and piles type. *Br.* 5	£650	£1250

HENRY I, 1100-1135

Fifteen types were minted during this reign. In 1108 provision was made for minting round halfpence again, none having been struck since the time of Eadgar, but few can have been made as only one specimen has survived. The standard of coinage manufacture was now beginning to deteriorate badly. Many genuine coins were being cut to see if they were plated counterfeits and there was a reluctance by the public to accept such damaged pieces. About 1112 an extraordinary decision was taken ordering the official mutilation of all new coins by snicking the edges, thus ensuring that cut coins had to be accepted. Pennies of types VII to XII (Nos. 1268-1273) usually have a cut in the flan that sometimes penetrated over a third of the way across the coin.

At Christmas 1124 the famous 'Assize of the Moneyers' was held at Winchester when all the moneyers in England were called to account for their activities and a number are said to have been mutilated for issuing coins of inferior quality.

1263

1263A

		F	*VF*
1263	**Penny.** *Br.* I. Annulets type	£350	£700
1263A	— II. Profile l. ℞. Cross fleury	£350	£700

1264

1265

1264	— III. PAX type	£400	£800
1265	— IV. Facing bust. ℞. Five annulets and four piles	£475	£900

1266

1267

1266	— V. — ℞. Voided cross with fleur in each angle	£600	£1200
1267	— VI. Pointing bust and stars type	£950	£2000

1268

1268	— VII. Facing bust. ℞. Quatrefoil with piles	£375	£750

1269

1270

		F	VF
1269	*Br.* VIII. Large bust l. ℞. Cross with annulet in each angle ..	£675	£1350
1270	— IX. Facing bust. ℞. Cross in quatrefoil	£525	£1000

1271

1272

1271	— X. Small facing bust in circle. ℞. Cross fleury	£325	£650
1272	— XI. Very large bust l. ℞. "Double inscription" around small cross pattée	£875	£1750

1273

1274

1273	— XII. Small bust l. ℞. Cross with annulet in each angle ..	£425	£850
1274	— XIII. Star in lozenge fleury type	£325	£650

1275

1276

1275	— XIV. Pellets in quatrefoil type	£125	£275
1276	— XV. Quadrilateral on cross fleury type	£100	£250

1277

1277 *Halfpenny*. Facing head. ℞. Cross potent with pellets in angles *Unique*

STEPHEN, 1135-1154
and the Civil War and Anarchy, 1138-53

Stephen of Blois, Count of Boulogne and a nephew of Henry I, hastily crossed the Channel on his uncle's death and secured the throne for himself, despite Henry's wishes that his daughter Matilda should succeed him. She was the widow of the German emperor Henry V, and was then married to Geoffrey, Count of Anjou. Two years later Matilda arrived in England to claim the throne, supported by her half-brother Robert of Gloucester. During the protracted civil war that ensued Matilda and, later, her son, Henry of Anjou, set up an alternative court at Bristol and held much of the west of England, striking coins at mints under their control. Many irregular coins were struck during this troublous period, some by barons in their own name. Particularly curious are the coins from the Midlands and E. Anglia which have Stephen's head defaced. In 1153, following the death of Stephen's son, Eustace, a treaty between the two factions allowed for the succession of Duke Henry and a uniform coinage was once more established throughout the kingdom.

B.M.C.—British Museum Catalogue: *Norman Kings*, 2 vols. (1916). *M.*—Mack, R. P., "Stephen and the Anarchy 1135-54", *BNJ* XXXV (1966), pp. 38-112.

STEPHEN

Regular regal issues

1278

1280

		F	VF
1278	**Penny.** Cross moline (Watford) type. Bust r., with sceptre. ℞. Cross moline with lis in angles. *B.M.C.* I; *M.* 3-42	£95	£200
1279	— Similar, but obv. reads PERERIC or PERERICM. *M.* 43-50	£600	£1250
1280	Voided cross type. Facing bust with sceptre. ℞. Voided cross pattée with mullets in angles. *Eastern mints only*. *B.M.C.* II; *M.* 53-66	£300	£600

1281

1282

1281	Cross fleury type. Bust l. with sceptre. ℞. Cross fleury with trefoils in angles. *Eastern mints only*. *B.M.C.* VI; *M.* 77-99	£700	£1350
1282	Cross pommée (Awbridge) type. Bust half-left with sceptre. ℞. voided cross pommée with lis in angles. *B.M.C.* VII; *M.* 99z-135b ..	£350	£650

For B.M.C. types III, IV & V, See 1300-1302.

Local and irregular issues of the Civil War

A. Coins struck from erased or defaced dies

1283

1288

		F	VF
1283	As 1278, with king's bust defaced with long cross. *East Anglian mints. M.* 137-147	£400	£650
1284	— Similar, but king's bust defaced with small cross. *Nottingham. M.* 149	£500	£750
1285	— Similar, but sceptre defaced with bar or cross. *Nottingham, Lincoln and Stamford. M.* 148 and 150-4	£400	£650
1286	— Similar, but king's name erased. *Nottingham. M.* 157	£500	£750
1286A.	— Other defacements.	*Extremely rare*	

B. South-Eastern variant

1287	As 1278, but king holds mace instead of sceptre. *M.* 158	*Extremely rare*	

C. Eastern variants

1288	As 1278, but roundels in centre or on limbs of cross or in angles. *M.* 159-168	£450	£750
1289	As 1278, but thick plain cross with pellet at end of limbs, lis in angles. *M.* 169-173	£450	£750
1290	— Similar, but thick plain cross superimposed on cross moline. *M.* 174	*Extremely rare*	
1290A	As 1278. ℞. Quadrilateral over voided cross. *M.* 176	*Extremely rare*	

D. Southern and S.W. variants

1291	As 1278, but with large rosette of pellets at end of obverse legend. *M.* 184-5	*Extremely rare*	
1292	— Similar, but whorled star at end of obverse legend. *M.* 187y ..	*Extremely rare*	
1293	Crowned bust r. or l. with rosette of pellets before face in place of sceptre. ℞. As 1280, but plain instead of voided cross. *M.* 181-3	*Extremely rare*	
1294	As 1278. ℞. Long cross to edge of coin, fleurs outwards in angles. *M.* 186-7	*Extremely rare*	

1295

1295	As 1278, but usually collar of annulets. ℞. Voided cross moline with annulet at centre. *M.* 207-212	£750	£1250

E. Midland variants

1296

		F	VF
1296	As 1278, but cross moline on reverse has fleured extensions into legend. *M.* 177-8	£1100	£1750
1297	As 1278 but crude work. ℞. Voided cross with lis outwards in angles. *M.* 179	*Extremely rare*	
1298	Somewhat similar obv. ℞. Voided cross with martlets in angles. *M.* 175	£1250	£2000

1298

1300

1299	As 1278. ℞. Plain cross with T-cross in each angle. *M.* 180	*Extremely rare*	
1300	Facing bust with three annulets on crown. ℞. Cross pattée, fleurs inwards in angles. *B.M.C.* III; *M.* 67-71	£1100	£2000

1301

1302

1301	Facing bust with three fleurs on crown. ℞. Lozenge fleury, annulets in angles. *B.M.C.* IV; *M.* 72-75	£1250	£2250
1302	Bust half-right with sceptre. ℞. Lozenge with pellet centre, fleurs inwards in angles. *B.M.C.* V; *M.* 76	£1250	£2250
1303	**Robert,** Earl of Leicester(?). As 1280, but reading ROBERTVS. *M.* 269	*Extremely rare*	

North-east and Scottish border variants

1304	As 1278, but star before sceptre and annulets at tips of fleurs on reverse. *M.* 188	£1000	£1800
1305	As 1278, but a voided cross extending to outer circle of reverse. *M.* 189-92	*Extremely rare*	
1306	As 1278, but crude style, with Stephen's name. *M.* 276-9 and 281-2	£700	£1200
1307	— Similar. ℞. Cross crosslet with cross-pattée and crescent in angles. *M.* 288	*Extremely rare*	

		F	VF
1308	**David I** (K. of Scotland). As 1305, but with name DAVID REX. *M.* 280	*Extremely rare*	
1309	**Henry** (Earl of Northumberland, son of K. David). As 1278. *M.* 283-5	*Extremely rare*	
1310	— Similar. ℞. Cross fleury. *M.* 286-7	£1000	£1750
1311	— As 1307, but with name NENCI : COM on obverse. *M.* 289 ..	£1250	£2000

G. "Ornamented" series. *So-called 'York Group' but probably minted in Northern France.*

1312	As 1278, with obverse inscription NSEPEFETI, STEFINEI or RODBDS. ℞. WIS Đ . GNETA, etc., with ornament(s) in legend (sometimes retrograde). *M.* 215-6 and 227	*Extremely rare*	

1313

1315

		F	VF
1313	Flag type. As 1278, but king holds lance with pennant, star to r. ℞. As 1278, mostly with four ornaments in legend. *M.* 217	£1250	£2000
1313A	— Similar, but with eight ornaments in reverse inscription. *M.* 217 ..	£1250	£2000
1314	As 1278, but STIEN and ornaments, sceptre is topped by pellet in lozenge. ℞. Cross fleury over plain cross, ornaments in place of inscription. *M.* 218..	*Extremely rare*	
1314A	King stg. facing, holding sceptre and long standard with triple-tailed pennon. ℞. Cross pattée, crescents and quatrefoils in angles, pellets around, ornaments in legend	*Unique*	
1315	**Stephen and Queen Matilda.** Two standing figures holding sceptre, as illustration. ℞. Ornaments in place of inscription. *M.* 220 ..	£2000	£3000

1316

1320

		F	VF
1316	**Eustace.** EVSTACIVS, knight stg. r. holding sword. ℞. Cross in quatrefoil, EBORACI EDTS (or EBORACI TDEFL). *M.* 221-2	*Extremely rare*	
1317	— Similar, but THOMHS FILIus VIF. *M.* 223	*Extremely rare*	
1318	— Similar, but mixed letters and ornaments in rev. legend. *M.* 224	*Extremely rare*	
1319	[EVSTA] CII . FII . IOANIS, lion passant r., collonade (or key ?) below. ℞. Cross moline with cross-headed sceptres in angles, mixed letters and ornaments in legend. *M.* 225	*Unique*	
1320	Lion rampant r., looped object below, EISTAOhIVS. ℞. Cross fleury with lis in angles, mostly, ornaments in legend. *M.* 226	£1250	£2000

F VF

1321 **Rodbert.** Knight on horse r., RODBERTVS IESTV (?). ℞. As 1314. *M.* 228 .. .. *Extremely rare*

1321 1322

1322 **Bishop Henry.** Crowned bust r., crozier and star to r., HENRICVS EPC. ℞. Somewhat as last, STEPHANVS REX. *M.* 229 .. .. *Extremely rare*

H. Uncertain issues

1323 Crowned bust r. with sceptre, -NEPΓ:. ℞. Cross pattée with annulets in angles (as Hen. I type XIII). *M.* 272 .. .. *Extremely rare*

1324 Crowned facing bust with sceptre, star to r. (as Hen. I type XIV). ℞. As last. *M.* 274 .. .. *Extremely rare*

1325 Other types .. .. *Extremely rare*

ANGEVINS

1326 1331

1326 **Matilda,** Dowager Empress, Countess of Anjou (in England 1139-1148). As 1278, but cruder style, MATILDI IMP. etc. *M.* 230-240 .. £2000 £3000

1326A Obv. similar. ℞. Cross pattée over cross fleury (Cardiff hoard) .. *Extremely rare*

1326B Similar, but triple pellets or plumes at end of cross .. .. .. *Extremely rare*

1327 **Duke Henry,** son of Matilda and Geoffrey of Anjou, Duke of Normandy from 1150 (in England 1147-1149-50 and 1153-54). As 1278 but HENRICVS, etc. *M.* 241-5 .. .. £1750 £3000

1327A As 1295 but HENRIC. *M.* 246 .. .. *Extremely rare*

1327B As 1326B, but HENNENNVS R, etc... .. .. *Extremely rare*

1328 Obverse as 1278. ℞. Cross crosslet in quatrefoil. *M.* 254 .. *Extremely rare*

1329 Crowned bust r. with sceptre. ℞. Cross fleury over quadrilateral fleury. *M.* 248-253 .. .. £1750 £3000

1330 Crowned facing bust, star each side. ℞. Cross botonnée over a quadilateral pommée. *M.* 255-258 .. .. £1750 £3000

1331 Obverse as 1330. ℞. Voided cross botonnée over a quadrilateral pommée. *M.* 259-261 .. .. £1750 £3000

1332 **William,** Earl of Gloucester (succeded his father, Earl Robert, in 1147). Type as Henry of Anjou, no. 1329. *M.* 262 .. .. *Unique*

1333 Type as Henry of Anjou, no. 1330. *M.* 263 .. .. *Unique*

1334 Type as Henry of Anjou, no. 1331. *M.* 264-268 .. .. .. £1850 £3500

1335 **Brian Fitzcount,** Lord of Wallingford (?). Type as Henry of Anjou, no. 1330. *M.* 270.. .. .. *Unique*

1336 **Patrick,** Earl of Salisbury (?). Helmeted bust r. holding sword, star behind. ℞. As Henry of Anjou, no. 1329. *M.* 271 .. .. *Extremely rare*

HENRY II, 1154-1189

Cross-and-crosslets ("Tealby") Coinage, 1158-80

Coins of Stephen's last type continued to be minted until 1158. Then a new coinage bearing Henry's name replaced the currency of the previous reign which contained a high proportion of irregular and sub-standard pennies. The new Cross and Crosslets issue is more commonly referred to as the "Tealby" coinage, over 5000 of these pennies having been discovered at Tealby, Lincolnshire in 1807. Thirty mints were employed in this recoinage, but once the re-minting had been completed not more than a dozen mints were kept open. The issue remained virtually unchanged for twenty-two years apart from minor variations in the king's portrait. The coins tend to be poorly struck.

A

B

C

Penny

			Fair	*F*
1337	Class A.	No hair	£22	£60
1338	— B.	Similar but mantle varies	£26	£70
1339	— C.	Decorated collar, curl of hair	£22	£60

D

E

F

1340	— D.	Decoration continues along shoulder	£24	£65
1341	— E.	Similar bust, but shoulder not decorated	£25	£70
1342	— F.	Hair in long ringlet to r. of bust	£25	£70

Mints and classes of the Cross-and-Crosslets coinage

Approximate dates for the various classes are as follows:
A 1158-61, B and C 1161-65, D 1165-68, E 1168-70 and F 1170-80.

Bedford	A–––––	Ilchester	ABCD–F	Pembroke ..	A–––––
Bristol	ABCDEF	Ipswich	–BCDEF	Salisbury	A–––––
Bury St. Edmunds	ABCDEF	Launcester ..	A–––––	Shrewsbury ..	A–––––
Canterbury ..	ABCDEF	Leicester	A–––––	Stafford	A–C–––
Carlisle	A–CDEF	Lewes	––––?F	Thetford	A–CD–F
Chester	A––D––	Lincoln	ABCDEF	Wallingford ..	A–––––
Colchester ..	A–C–E–	London	ABCDEF	Wilton	A–––––
Durham	ABC–––	Newcastle ..	A–CDEF	Winchester ..	A–CD?–
Exeter	ABCD––	Northampton ..	A–C?––	York	A–CD––
Gloucester ..	A–––––	Norwich	ABCD–F		
Hereford	A–C–––	Oxford	A—DE–		

"Short cross" coinage of Henry II (1180-1189)

In 1180 a coinage of new type, known as the Short Cross coinage, replaced the Tealby issue. The new coinage is remarkable in that it covers not only the latter part of the reign of Henry II, but also the reigns of his sons Richard and John and his grandson Henry III, and the entire issue bears the name "hENRICVS". There are no English coins with names of Richard or John. The Short Cross coins can be divided chronologically into various classes: eleven mints were operating under Henry II and tables of mints, moneyers and classes are given for each reign.

1a 1b 1c

		F	*VF*
1343	Class 1a. Narrow face, square E, sometimes square C, round M ..	£150	£325
1344	— 1b. Curls usually 2 to l., 5 to r., round ϵ and C, square M, stop before REX	£35	£85
1345	— 1c. First evidence of degradation, more curls to r. than to l., no stop in *obv.* legend..	£35	£75

Mints, moneyers, and classes for Henry II

		F
London: Aimer (1b, c), Alain (1b,c), Alain V (1b), Alward (1b), Davi (1b, c), Filip Aimer (1a, b), Gilebert (1c), Godard (1b), Henri (1a, b), Henri Pi (1a, b), Iefrei or Gefrei (1a, b, c), Oohan (1a, b), Osber (1b), Pieres (1a, b, c), Pieres M (1a, b), Randul (1a, b), Raul (1b, c), Reinald (1b), Ricard (1c), Stivene (1c), Willelm (1a, b, c)	*from*	£35
Carlisle: Alain (1a, b, c)	*from*	£80
Exeter: Asketil (1a, b), Iordan (1a, b), Osber (1a, b), Raul (1b), Ricard (1b, c), Roger (1b)	*from*	£60
Lincoln: Edmund (1b, c), Girard (1b), Hugo (1b), Lefwine (1b, c), Rodbert (1b), Walter (1b), Will . D.F. (1b), Willelm (1b, c)	*from*	£50
Northampton: Filipe (1a, b), Gefrei (1b), Hugo (1a, b), Raul (1a, b), Simund (1b), Walter (1a, b, c), Willelm (1a, b)	*from*	£65
Norwich: Reinald (1b, c), Willelm (1b) .. .. (Current research may indicate that these coins are of the Northampton mint).	*from*	£65
Oxford: Asketil (1b), Iefri (1b), Owein (1b), Ricard (1b), Rodbert (1b), Robert F . B . (1b), Sagar (1b)	*from*	£65
Wilton: Osber (1a, b), Rodbert (1a, b)	*from*	£60
Winchester: Adam (1b, c), Clement (1a, b), Gocelm (1a, b, c), Henri (1a), Osbern (1a, b), Reinir (1b), Ricard (1b), Rodbert (1a, b)	*from*	£48
Worcester: Edric (1b), Godwine (1b), Osber (1b, c), Oslac (1b)	*from*	£60
York: Alain (1b), Everard (1a, b, c), Gerard (1b), Hugo (1b, c), Hunfrei (1b), Isac (1a, b), Turkil (1a, b, c), Willem (1b)	*from*	£40

RICHARD I, 1189-1199

Pennies of Short Cross type continued to be issued throughout the reign, all bearing the name HENRICVS. The coins of class 4, which have very crude portraits, continued to be issued in the early years of the next reign. The only coins bearing Richard's name are from his territories of Aquitaine and Poitou in western France.

2 3a 3b 4a 4b

	"Short-cross" coinage (reading HENRICVS)	*F*	*VF*
1346	Class 2a. Round face; 5 pearls in crown; mass of small curls at both sides of head	£70	£150
1347	— 3a. Long thin face; 7 or more pearls in crown; 3 or 4 curls at either side of head; beard of small curls, large pellet eyes	£60	£135
1347A	— 3b. Similar, but annulet eyes	£55	£110
1348	— 4a. Similar, but beard of pellets	£35	£80
1348A	— 4b. Very crude bust, hair represented by only one or two crescents each side	£35	£80
1348B	— 4a*. As 4a, but colon stops on reverse	£40	£90

Mints, moneyers, and classes for Richard I

		F
London: Aimer (2-4b), Alain (4a), Davi (2), Fulke (3-4b), Goldwine (4a), Henri (4a-4b), Pieres (2), Raul (2), Ricard (2-4b), Stivene (2-4b), Wilhelm (2-4b).	*from*	£35
Canterbury: Goldwine (2-4b), Hernaud (4b), Io(h)an (4b), Meinir (2-4b), Reinald (2-4a), Reinaud (4b), Roberd (2-4b), Samuel (4b), Ulard (3-4b) ..	*from*	£35
Carlisle: Alain (3-4b)	*from*	£100
Durham: Adam (4a), Alain (4a-b)	*from*	£100
Exeter: Ricard (3)	*from*	£80
Lichfield: Ioan (2)	*Extremely rare*	
Lincoln: Edmund (2), Lefwine (2) Willem (2, 4a), ...	*from*	£45
Northampton: Geferi (4a), Roberd (3), Waltir (3)	*from*	£60
Norwich: Randal (4a-b), Willelm (4a-b)	*from*	£60
Shrewsbury: Ive (4b), Reinald (4a), Willem (4a)	*from*	£110
Winchester: Gocelm (2-3), Osbern (3-4), Pires (3), Willelm (2-4)	*from*	£55
Worcester: Osber (2)	*Extremely rare*	
York: Davi (4b ?), Everard (2-4b), Hue (3-4b), Nicole (4b), Turkil (2-4b) ..	*from*	£40

JOHN, 1199-1216

"Short cross" coinage *continued.* All with name hENRICVS

The Short Cross coins of class 4 will have continued during the early years of John's reign, but in 1205 a re-coinage was initiated and new Short Cross coins of better style replaced the older issues. Coins of classes 5a and 5b were issued in the recoinage in which sixteen mints were employed. Only ten of these mints were still working by the end of class 5. The only coins to bear John's name are the pennies, halfpence and farthings issued for Ireland.

4c 5a 5b 5c 6a1 6a2

		F	VF
1349	Class 4c. Somewhat as 4b, but letter S is reversed	£45	£100
1350	— 5a. New coinage of neat style and execution; realistic face; 5 pearls to crown; letter S is reversed; *mm* cross pommée	£45	£95
1350A	— — with ornamented letters	£55	£120
1350B	— 5a/5b or 5b/5a mules	£40	£85
1351	— 5b. Similar, but S normal and *mm* reverts to cross pattée	£20	£45
1352	— 5c. Similar, but letter X composed of 4 strokes in the form of a St. Andrew's cross	£20	£45
1353	— 6a1. Coarser style; letter X composed of 2 strokes in the form of a St. Andrew's cross	£20	£45
1353A	— 6a2. Similar, but letter X has arms at right angles and with rounded ends	£20	£45

Mints, moneyers and classes for John

		F
London: Abel (5c-6a), Adam (5b-c), Alexander (5a ?), Andreu (5b), Arnaud (5b), Beneit (5b-c), Fulke (4c-5b), Henri (4c-5b), Ilger (5b-6a), Iohan (5a-b), Rauf (5c-6a), Rener (5b-c), Ricard (4c-5b), Ricard B (5b-c), Ricard T (5b), Walter (5c-6a), Willelm (4c-5b), Willelm B (5b-c), Willelm L (5b-c), Willelm T (5b-c)	*from*	£20
Bury St. Edmunds: Fulke (5b-c)	*from*	£25
Canterbury Andreu (5b), Arnaud (5a-c), Coldwine (4c-5c), (H)erraud (5a), Hue (4c-5c), Io(h)an (4c-5c), Iohan B (5b-c), Iohan M (5b-c), Rauf (Vc ?), Roberd (4c-5c), Samuel (4c-5c), Simon (5a-c), Simun (4c-5b), Walter (5b) ..	*from*	£20
Carlisle: Tomas (5b)	*from*	£90
Chichester: Pieres (5b), Rauf (5a-b), Simon (5a-b), Willelm (5b)	*from*	£40
Durham: Pieres (4c-6a)	*from*	£90
Exeter: Gilebert (5a-b), Iohan (5a-b), Ricard (5a-b)	*from*	£40
Ipswich: Alisandre (5a-c), Iohan (5b-c)	*from*	£35
Kings Lynn: Iohan (5b), Nicole (5b), Willelm (5b)	*from*	£120
Lincoln: Alain (5a), Andreu (5a-c), Hue (5b-c), Iohan (5a), Rauf (5a-b), Ricard (5a), Tomas (5b)	*from*	£35
Northampton: Adam (5b-c), Randul (4c), Roberd (5b), Roberd T (5b) ..	*from*	£40

		F
Norwich: Gifrei (5b-c), Iohan (5a-c), Reinald (5a), Reinaud (5a-b)	*from*	£40
Oxford: Ailwine (5b), Henri (5b), Miles (5b)	*from*	£40
Rhuddlan: An irregular issue probably struck during this reign. Halli, Tomas, Simond	*from*	£70
Rochester: Alisandre (5b), Hunfrei (5b)	*from*	£65
Winchester: Adam (5a-c), Andreu (5b-c), Bartelme (5b-c), Henri (5a), Iohan (5a-c), Lukas (5b), Miles (5a-c), Rauf (5b-c), Ricard (5b)	*from*	£25
York: Davi (4c-5b), Iohan (5a-b), Nicole (4c-5c), Renaud (5b), Tomas (5b)	*from*	£28

HENRY III, 1216-1272

"Short cross" coinage *continued* (1216-47)

The Short Cross coinage continued for a further thirty years during which time the style of portraiture and workmanship deteriorated. By the 1220's minting had been concentrated at London and Canterbury, one exception being the mint of the Abbot of Bury St. Edmunds.

6b 6c 7 early 7 middle 7 late

"Short-cross" coinage, 1216-1247	F	VF
1354 Class 6b. Very tall lettering; early coins have a head similar to 6a, but later issues have a long thin face	£16	£38
1355 — 6c. Pointed face	£16	£38
1355A — — Ornamental lettering	£55	£120
1356 — 7. No stops between words in rev. legend; no neck	£11	£25

8a 8b1 8b2 8b3

	F	VF
1357 — 8a. New style; *mm* cross pattée; letter X curule shaped	£35	£110
1357A — 8b1. Similar; *mm* cross pommée	£35	£110
1357B — 8b2. Cruder version; wedge shaped letter X	£35	£110
1357C — 8b3. Very crude version; letter X is cross pommée	£35	£110

Mints, moneyers, and classes for Henry III "short-cross" coinage

		F
London: Abel (6b-7), Adam (7), (H)elis (7), Giffrei (7), Ilger (6b-7), Ledulf (7), Nicole (7-8), Rau(l)f (6b-7), Ricard (7), Terri (7), Walter (6b-6c)	*from*	£11
Bury St. Edmunds: Io(h)an (7-8), Norman (7), Rauf (6b-7), Simund (7), Willelm (7)	*from*	£18
Canterbury: Henri (6b-7), Hiun (6b-c), Iun (7), Io(h)an (6b-8), Ioan Chic (7), Ioan F. R. (7), Nicole (7-8), Norman (7), Osmund (7), Roberd (6b-7), Robert Vi (7), Roger (6b-7), Roger of R (7), Salemun (7), Samuel (6b-7), Simon (7), Simun (6b-7), Tomas (7), Walter (6b-7), Willem (7-8), Willem Ta (7)	*from*	£11
Durham: Pieres (7)	*from*	£65
Winchester: Henri (6c), Iohan (6c)	*from*	£20
York: Iohan (6c), Peres (6c), Tomas (6c), Willelm (6c)	*from*	£18

"Long Cross" coinage (1247-72)

By the middle of Henry's reign the coinage in circulation was in a poor state, being worn and clipped. In 1247 a fresh coinage was ordered, the new pennies having the reverse cross extended to the edge of the coin to help safeguard the coins against clipping. The earliest of these coins have no mint or moneyers' names. A number of provincial mints were opened for producing sufficient of the Long Cross coins, but these were closed again in 1250, only the royal mints of London and Canterbury and the ecclesiastical mints of Durham and Bury St. Edmunds remaining open.

In 1257, following the introduction of new gold coinages by the Italian cities of Brindisi (1232), Florence (1252) and Genoa (1253), Henry III issued a gold coinage in England. This was a Gold "Penny" valued at 20 silver pence and twice the weight of the silver penny. The coinage was not a success, being undervalued, and coinage ceased after a few years—few have survived.

Without sceptre *F* *VF*

Ia

Ib

		F	*VF*
1358	Class Ia. hENRICVS : REX. ℞. ANGLIE TERCI	£70	£150
1359	Ib. hENRICVS REX. ANG. ℞. LIE TERCI LON (*London*), CAN (*Canterbury*) or AED (*Bury St. Edmunds*) .. .. *from*	£40	£85
1360	— I/II mule	£45	£95
1361	— II. hENRICVS REX TERCI'. ℞. Moneyer and mint	£30	£65

II

IIIa

IIIb

IIIc

1362	— IIIa. hENRICVS REX · III, thin face as class II	£11	£25
1363	— IIIb. Smaller, rounder face	£11	£25
1364	— IIIc. Face with pointed chin, neck indicated by two lines, usually REX : III	£11	£25

With sceptre

IVa

IVb

Va

Vb

Vc

		F	VF
1365	Class IVa. Similar to last, but with sceptre	£55	£120
1366	— IVb. Similar, but new crown with half-fleurs and large central fleur	£65	£135
1367	— Va. With class IV bust, round eyes, from now on legend begins at 10 o'clock	£14	£32
1368	— Vb. Narrower face, wedge-tailed R, round eyes	£11	£25
1369	— Vc. As last, but almond-shaped eyes	£11	£25

Vd Ve Vf Vg Vh

		F	VF
1370	— Vd. Portrait of quite different style; new crown with true-shaped fleur	£40	£85
1371	— Ve. Similar, with jewelled or beaded crown	*Extremely*	*rare*
1372	— Vf. New style larger face, double-banded crown	£20	£45
1373	— Vg. Single band to crown, low central fleur, curule chair shaped X	£18	£40
1374	— Vh. Crude copy of Vg, with pellets in lieu of fleur	£25	£55
1375	— Vi. Similar to last, but triple line of pellets for beard	*Extremely*	*rare*

Vi

1376

1376 **Gold penny** of 20d. As illustration .. .. *Extremely rare*

Mints, Moneyers, and classes for Henry III "Long-Cross" coinage — F

	F
London: Davi or David (IIIc.-Vf), Henri (IIIa-Vd, f, g), Ion, Ioh, Iohs, or Iohan (Vc-g), Nicole (Ib/II mule, II-Vc), Renaud (Vg-i), Ricard (IIIc-Vg), Robert (Vg), Thomas (Vg), Walter (Vc-g), Willem (Vc-g and gold penny) .. .. *from*	£11
Bristol: Elis (IIIa, b, c), Henri (IIIb), Iacob (IIIa, b, c), Roger (IIIa, b, c), Walter (IIIb, c) .. *from*	£24
Bury St. Edmunds: Ion or Iohs (II-Va, Vg, h, i), Randulf (Va-f), Renaud (Vg), Stephane (Vg) .. *from*	£18
Canterbury: Alein (Vg, h), Ambroci (Vg), Gilbert (II-Vd/c mule, Vf, g), Ion, Ioh, Iohs, or Iohanes (IIIe-Vd, f, g), Nicole or Nichole (Ib/II mule, II-Vh), Ricard (Vg, h), Robert (Vc-h), Walter (Vc-h), Willem or Willeme (Ib/II mule, II-Vd, f, g). *from*	£11
Carlisle: Adam (IIIa, b), Ion (IIIa, b), Robert (IIIa, b), Willem IIIa, b) .. *from*	£70
Durham: Philip (IIIb), Ricard (V, b, c), Roger (Vg), Willem (Vg) .. .. *from*	£80
Exeter: Ion (II-IIIc), Philip (II-IIIc), Robert (II-IIIc), Walter (II-IIIb) .. *from*	£40

		F
Gloucester: Ion (II-IIIc), Lucas (II-IIIc), Ricard (II-IIIc), Roger (II-IIIc)	*from*	£22
Hereford: Henri (IIIa, b), Ricard (IIIa, b, c), Roger (IIIa, b, c), Walter (IIIa, b, c)	*from*	£35
Ilchester: Huge (IIIa, b, c), Ierveis (IIIa, b, c), Randulf (IIIa, b, c), Stephe (IIIa, b, c)	*from*	£50
Lincoln: Ion (II-IIIc), Ricard (II-IIIc), Walter (II-IIIc), Willem (II-IIIc)	*from*	£25
Newcastle: Adam (IIIa, b), Henri (IIIa, b, c), Ion (IIIa, b, c), Roger (IIIa, b, c)	*from*	£22
Northampton: Lucas (II-IIIb), Philip (II-IIIc), Tomas (II-IIIc), Willem (II-IIIc)	*from*	£28
Norwich: Huge (II-IIIc), Iacob (II-IIIc), Ion (II-IIIc), Willem (II-IIIc) ..	*from*	£35
Oxford: Adam (II-IIIc), Gefrei (II-IIIc), Henri (II-IIIc), Willem (II-IIIc)	*from*	£40
Shrewsbury: Lorens (IIIa, b, c), Nicole (IIIa, b, c), Peris (IIIa, b, c), Ricard (IIIa, b, c)	*from*	£50
Wallingford: Alisandre (IIIa, b), Clement (IIIa, b), Ricard (IIIa, b), Robert (IIIa, b)	*from*	£42
Wilton: Huge (IIIb, c), Ion (IIIa, b, c), Willem (IIIa, b, c)	*from*	£42
Winchester: Huge (II-IIIc), Iordan (II-IIIc), Nicole (II-IIIc), Willem (II-IIIc)	*from*	£24
York: Alain (II-IIIb), Ieremie (II-IIIb), Ion (II-IIIc), Rener (II-IIIc), Tomas (IIIb, c)	*from*	£28

EDWARD I, 1272-1307

"Long Cross" coinage *continued* (1272-79). With name hENRICVS

The earliest group of Edward's Long Cross coins are of very crude style and only known of Durham and Bury St. Edmunds. Then, for the last class of the type, pennies of much improved style were issued at London, Durham and Bury, but in 1279 the Long Cross coinage was abandoned and a completely new coinage substituted.

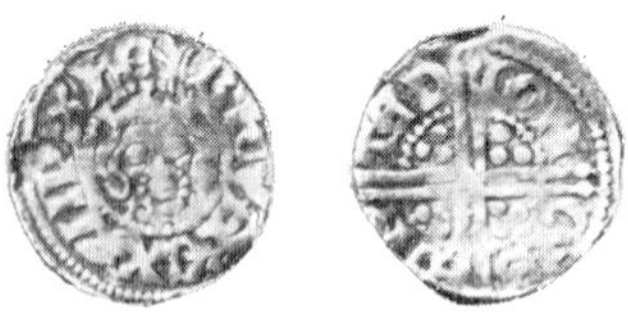

VI

VII

		F	VF
1377	Class VI. Crude face with new realistic curls, ϵ and N ligate ..	£16	£45
1378	— VII. Similar, but of improved style, usually with Lombardic U.	£85	£200

Mints, moneyers, and classes for Edward I "Long Cross" coinage

London: Phelip (VII), Renaud (VII)	*from*	£85
Bury St. Edmunds: Ioce (VII), Ion or Ioh (VI, VII)	*from*	£16
Durham: Roberd (VI), Robert (VII)	*from*	£100

New Coinage (from 1279).

A major recoinage was embarked upon in 1279 which introduced new denominations. In addition to the penny, halfpence and farthings were also minted and, for the first time, a four penny piece called a "Groat" (from the French *Gros*).

As mint administration was now very much centralized, the practice of including the moneyer's name in the coinage was abandoned (except for a few years at Bury St. Edmunds). Several provincial mints assisted with the recoinage during 1279-81, then minting was again restricted to London, Canterbury, Durham and Bury.

The provincial mints were again employed for a subsidiary re-coinage in 1299-1302 in order to remint light-weight coins and the many illegal *esterlings* (foreign copies of the English pennies or *Sterlings*, mainly from the Low Countries, are usually poorer quality than the English coins).

1379

		F	VF
1379	**Groat.** (=4d.; wt. 89grs.). Type as illustration but several minor varieties	£1000	£2500

Most extant specimens show traces of having been mounted on the obverse and gilded on the reverse; unmounted coins are worth more.

1a

1b

1c

		F	*VF*
1380	**Penny.** *London.* Class 1a. Crown with plain band, ЄDW RЄX; Lombardic N	£50	£120
1381	— 1b. — ЄD RЄX; no drapery on bust, Roman N	£175	£425
1382	— 1c. — ЄDW RЄX; Roman N, normal or reversed; small lettering ..	£16	£35
1383	— 1d. — ЄDW R;—; large lettering and face	£14	£30
1384	— — — Annulet below bust (for the Abbot of Reading)	£135	£325

1d

2a

2b

1385	— 2a. Crown with band shaped to ornaments; large face and short neck similar to 1d; usually broken left petal to central fleur of crown ..	£18	£40
1386	— 2b. — tall bust; long neck; N reversed	£14	£30

3a 3b 3c

			F	VF
1387	— 3a.	Crescent-shaped contraction marks; pearls in crown, drapery is foreshortened circle	£20	£45
1388	— 3b.	— — drapery is segment of a circle	£12	£26
1389	— 3c.	— normal crown; drapery in one piece, hollowed in centre	£10	£22

3e 3f 3g

1390	— 3d.	— — drapery in two pieces, broad face	£12	£26
1391	— 3e.	— long narrow face (mostly Northern mints)	£14	£30
1392	— 3f.	— broad face, large nose, rougher work, late S first used	£20	£45
1393	— 3g.	— small neat bust, narrow face	£9	£20

4a 4b 4c 4d 4e

			F	VF
1394	— 4a.	Comma-shaped contration mark, late S always used, C and Є open	£12	£26
1395	— 4b.	Similar, but face and hair shorter	£9	£20
1396	— 4c.	Larger face with more copious hair; unbarred A first used	£9	£20
1397	— 4d.	Pellet at beginning of *obv.* and/or *rev.* inscription	£12	£26
1398	— 4c.	Three pellets on breast; pellet in *rev.* legend	£14	£30

5a 5b

1399	— 5a.	Well spread coins, pellet on breast, A normally unbarred	£30	£65
1400	— 5b.	Coins more spread, tall lettering, long narrow face, pellet on breast	£30	£65

6a 6b 7a

		F	VF
1401	— 6a. Smaller coins, initial cross almost plain, crown with wide fleurs	£40	£85
1402	— 6b. Initial cross well pattée; lettering of good style; closed ϵ (from now on)	£35	£75
1403	— 7a. Rose on breast; almond-shaped eyes; double barred N ..	£32	£70

7b 8a 8b 9a 9b

		F	VF
1404	— 7b. — — longer hair, new crown	£40	£85
1405	— 8a. Smaller crown; top-tilted S; longer neck	£24	£50
1406	— 8b. Not unlike 9a, but top-tilted S	£24	£50
1407	— 9a. Narrow face, flatter crown, star on breast	£16	£35
1408	— 9b. Small coins; Roman N, normal, un-barred, or usually of pot-hook form; often star or pellet on breast	£8	£17

10a 10b 10d 10f

		F	VF
1409	— 10a. Bi-foliate crown (from now on), long narrow face, narrow-waisted lettering, ϵDWARD R	£16	£35
1410	— 10b. — — — ϵDWAR R	£16	£35
1411	— 10c. — — — ϵDWA R	£9	£20
1412	— 10d. Broader face and larger crown, more ornate lettering ..	£6	£15
1413	— 10e. Square face with short neck; thin intitial cross	£6	£15
1414	— 10f. Thicker and more dumpy initial cross	£10	£22

The prices for the above types are for London. We can sometimes supply coins of the following mints; types struck in brackets.

Berwick type 1 Type II Type III Type IV

			F	*VF*
1415	*Berwick-on-Tweed.* (Blunt types I-IV)	*from*	£18	£40
1416	*Bristol.* (2; 3b; c, d; 3f, g; 9b)	*from*	£16	£34
1417	*Bury St. Edmunds.* Robert de Hadelie (3c, d, g; 4a, b c)	*from*	£45	£95
1418	— Villa Sci Edmundi (4e; 5b; 6b; 7a; 8a-10f)	*from*	£18	£40
1419	*Canterbury.* (2; 3b-g; 4; 5; 7a; 9; 10)	*from*	£9	£20
1420	*Chester.* (3g; 9b)	*from*	£35	£75
1421	*Durham.* King's Receiver (9b; 10a, b, e, f)	*from*	£35	£75
1422	— Bishop de Insula (2; 3b, c, e, g; 4a)	*from*	£18	£40
1423	— Bishop Bec (4b, c, d; 5b; 6b; 7a; 8b; 9; 10b-f) mostly with *mm.* cross moline	*from*	£18	£40
1424	— — (4b) cross moline in one angle of *rev.*		£120	£250
1425	*Exeter.* (9b)		£35	£75
1426	*Kingston-upon-Hull.* (9b)		£55	£125
1427	*Lincoln.* (3c, d, f, g)	*from*	£16	£34
1428	*Newcastle-on-Tyne.* (3e; 9b; 10)	*from*	£18	£40
1429	*York.* Royal mint (2; 3b, c, d, f; 9b)	*from*	£12	£26
1430	— Archbishop's mint (3e, g; 9b). ℞. Quatrefoil in centre	*from*	£18	£40

1431

1436

1431	**Halfpenny,** *London.* Class IIIb. Drapery is segment of circle		£30	£70
1432	— IIIc. Normal drapery		£28	£65
1433	— IIIg. Similar, larger letters, wider crown		£45	£100
1434	— IVe. Usually three pellets on breast, one on *rev.*		£45	£100
1435	— VII. Double barred N		£42	£95
1436	— IX. Pot-hook N, usually no star on breast		£30	£70
1437	— X. EDWAR R ANGL DNS hYB		£30	£70

The above prices are for London; halfpence of the mints given below were also struck.

1438	*Berwick-on-Tweed.* (Blunt types II and III)	*from*	£75	£200
1439	*Bristol.* (IIIc; IIIg)		£65	£175
1440	*Lincoln.* (IIIc)		£55	£135
1441	*Newcastle.* (IIIe). With single pellet in each angle of *rev.*		£90	£225
1442	*York.* (IIIb IIIc)		£85	£200

1443

1445

		F	VF
1443	**Farthing,** *London.* Class I. Heavy weight (6.85 grains), EDWARDVS REX. ℞. LONDONIENSIS	£60	£130
1444	— II. Similar, but reversed N's	£55	£120
1445	— IIIc. As class I, but different bust	£50	£110
1446	— IIIg. Lighter weight (5.5 grs.), E R ANGLIE	£55	£120
1447	— VII. Similar	£60	£130
1448	— VIII. E R ANGL DN	£55	£120
1449	— IX. pot-hook N	£55	£120
1450	— X. EDWARDVS REX A or AN	£45	£110

The above prices are for London; farthings of the mints given below were also struck.

1452

		F	VF
1451	*Berwick-on-Tweed.* (Blunt type III)	£150	£325
1452	*Bristol.* (II; III as illustration) .. .. *from*	£100	£225
1453	*Lincoln.* (III) .. .. *from*	£135	£300
1454	*York.* (II; III) .. .. *from*	£125	£275

For further information on the pennies of Edward I and II see the articles by K. A. Jacob in "Notes on English Silver Coins, 1066-1648," *and for the mint of Berwick on Tweed, see the article by C. E. Blunt, in the Num. Chron.,* 1931.

EDWARD II, 1307-27

The coinage of this reign differs only in minor details from that of Edward I. No groats were issued in the years *c.* 1282-1351.

11a

12

13

14

15a

15b

15c

		F	VF
1455	**Penny,** *London.* Class 11a. Broken spear-head or pearl on l. side of crown; long narrow face, straight-sided N	£12	£26
1456	— 11b. — Є with angular back (till 15b), N with well-marked serifs	£12	£26
1457	— 11c. — — A of special form	£22	£50
1458	— 12. Central fleur of crown formed of three wedges	£30	£65
1459	— 13. Central fleur of crown as Greek double axe	£18	£40
1460	— 14. Crown with tall central fleur; large smiling face with leering eyes	£14	£30
1461	— 15a. Small flat crown with both spear-heads usually bent to l.; face of 14	£18	£40
1462	— 15b. — very similar, but smaller face	£18	£40
1463	— 15c.— large face, large Є	£20	£45

The prices of the above types are for London. We can sometimes supply coins of the following mints; types struck in brackets.

Type 5

Type 6

Type 7

			F	VF
1464	*Berwick-on-Tweed.* (Blunt types V, VI and VII)	*from*	£27	£60
1465	*Bury St. Edmunds.* (11; 12; 13; 15)	*from*	£18	£40
1466	*Canterbury.* (11; 12; 13; 14; 15)	*from*	£18	£40
1467	*Durham.* King's Receiver (11a; 14); *mm.* plain cross	*from*	£25	£55
1468	— Bishop Bek. (11a), *mm.* cross moline		£18	£40
1469	— Bishop Kellawe (11; 12; 13), crozier on *rev.*	*from*	£24	£50
1470	— Bishop Beaumont (13; 14; 15), *mm.* lion with lis	*from*	£24	£50
1471	— Sede Vacante (15c); *mm.* plain cross		£55	£135
1472	**Halfpenny** of *London.* ЄDWARDVS REX A(NG)		£55	£135
1473	— — *Berwick-on-Tweed.* (Blunt type V)		£80	£200
1474	**Farthing** of *London.* ЄDWARDVS REX (AN)G		£75	£175
1475	— *Berwick-on-Tweed.* (Blunt type V)		*Extremely rare*	

EDWARD III, 1327-77

During Edward's early years small quantities of silver coin were minted following the standard of the previous two reigns, but in 1335 halfpence and farthings were produced which were well below the .925 Sterling silver standard. In 1344 an impressive gold coinage was introduced comprising the Florin or Double Leopard valued at six shillings, and its half and quarter, the Leopard and the Helm. The design of the Florin was based on the contemporary gold of Philip de Valois of France. The first gold coinage was not successful and it was replaced later the same year by a heavier coinage, the Noble valued at 6s. 8d, i.e., 80 pence, half a mark or one third of a pound, together with its fractions. The Noble was lowered in weight in two stages over the next few years, being stabilized at 120 grains. With the signing of the Treaty of Bretigni in 1360 Edward's title to the Kingdom of France was omitted from the coinage, but it was resumed again in 1369.

In 1344 the silver coinage had been re-established at the old sterling standard, but the penny was reduced in weight to just over 20 grains and in 1351 to 18 grains. Groats were minted again in 1351 and were issued regularly henceforth until the reign of Elizabeth.

Subsequent to the treaty with France which gave England a cross-channel trading base at Calais, a mint was opened there in 1363 for minting gold and silver coins of English type. In addition to coins of the regular English mints the Abbot of Reading also minted silver pence and a halfpence with a scallop shell badge while coins from Berwick display one or two boars' heads.

Mintmarks

6 1 2 3 74 4 5 7a

1334-51	Cross pattée (6)	1356	Crown (74)
1351-2	Cross 1 (1)	1356-61	Cross 3 (4)
1351-7	Crozier on cross end (76a, *Durham*)	1361-9	Cross potent (5)
1352-3	Cross 1 broken (2)	1369-77	Cross pattée (6)
1354-5	Cross 2 (3)		Plain cross (7a)
			Cross potent and four pellets

The figures in brackets refer to the plate of mintmarks on page 309.

GOLD

Third coinage, 1344-51

First period, 1344

1476

1477

1478

1476 **Florin** or **Double Leopard.** (=6s.; wt. 108 grs.). King enthroned beneath canopy; fleured field. ℞. Cross in quatrefoil, etc... .. *Extremely rare*

1477 **Half-florin** or **Leopard.** Leopard sejant with banner l. ℞. Somewhat as last .. .. *Extremely rare*

1478 **Quarter-florin** or **Helm.** Helmet on fleured field. ℞. Floriate cross *Extremely rare*

Second period, 1344-6

		F	VF
1479	**Noble** (=6s. 8d., wt. $138\frac{6}{13}$ grs.). King stg. facing in ship with sword and shield. ℞. L in centre of royal cross in tressure	*Extremely rare*	
1480	**Quarter-noble.** Shield in tressure. ℞. As last	£550	£1100

Third period, 1346-51

		F	VF
1481	**Noble** (wt. $128\frac{4}{7}$ grs.). As 1479, but є in centre; large letters	£600	£1400
1482	**Half-noble.** Similar	*Extremely rare*	
1483	**Quarter-noble.** As 1480, but є in centre	£200	£400

Fourth coinage, 1351-77

Reference: L. A. Lawrence, *The Coinage of Edward III from* 1351.

Pre-treaty period, 1351-61. With French title.

1488

1498

		F	VF
1484	**Noble** (wt. 120 grs.), series B (1351). Open є and c, Roman M; *mm.* cross 1 (1)	£450	£850
1485	— — *rev.* of series A (1351). Round lettering, Lombardic M and N; closed inverted є in centre	£525	£950
1486	C (1351-2). Closed є and c, Lombardic M; *mm.* cross 1 (1)	£375	£750
1487	D (1352-3). *O.* of series C. ℞. *Mm.* cross 1 broken (2)	£600	£1100
1488	E (1354-5). Broken letters, V often has a nick in r. limb; *mm.* cross 2 (3)	£375	£750
1489	F (1356). *Mm.* crown (74)	£500	£900
1490	G (1356-61). *Mm.* cross 3 (4). Many varieties	£350	£700
1491	**Half-noble,** B. As noble with *rev.* of series A, but closed є in centre not inverted	£300	£600
1492	C. *O.* as noble. *Rev.* as last	£325	£650
1493	E. As noble	£625	£1100
1494	G. As noble. Many varieties	£275	£525
1495	**Quarter-noble,** B. Pellet below shield. ℞. Closed є in centre	£150	£300
1496	C *O.* of series B. *Rev.* details as noble	£175	£350
1497	E. *O.* as last. *Rev.* details as noble, pellet in centre	£200	£400
1498	G. *Mm.* cross 3 (4). Many varieties	£125	£250

Transitional treaty period, 1361. Aquitaine title added and FRANC omitted on the noble and, rarely, the half-noble; irregular sized letters; *mm.* cross potent (5).

		F	*VF*
1499	**Noble.** ℞. Pellets or annulets at corners of central panel	£450	£850
1500	**Half-noble.** Similar	£275	£550
1501	**Quarter-noble.** Similar. Many varieties	£150	£300

1499

1503

Treaty period, 1361-9. Omits FRANC, new letters, usually curule-shaped X; *mm.* cross potent (5).

1502	**Noble.** *London.* Saltire before ЄDWARD	£350	£700
1503	— Annulet before ЄDWARD	£350	£700
1504	*Calais.* C in centre of *rev.*, flag at stern of ship	£425	£850
1505	— — without flag	£400	£800

1506

1508

1506	**Half-noble.** *London.* Saltire before ЄDWARD	£250	£500
1507	— Annulet before ЄDWARD	£250	£500
1508	*Calais.* C in centre of *rev.*, flag at stern of ship	£400	£800
1509	— — without flag	£400	£800
1510	**Quarter-noble.** *London.* As 1498. ℞. Lis in centre	£125	£275
1511	— — annulet before ЄDWARD	£125	£275
1512	*Calais.* ℞. Annulet in centre	£150	£300
1513	— — cross in circle over shield	£165	£325
1514	— ℞. Quatrefoil in centre; cross over shield	£185	£375
1515	— — crescent over shield	£275	£550

Post-treaty period, 1369-77. French title resumed.

No.	Description	*F*	*VF*
1516	**Noble.** *London.* Annulet before ED. ℞. Treaty period die	£375	£750
1517	— — — crescent on forecastle	£400	£800
1518	— — post-treaty letters. ℞. E and pellet in centre	£350	£700
1519	— — — ℞. E and saltire in centre	£425	£850
1520	*Calais.* Flag at stern. ℞. E in centre	£375	£750

1521

No.	Description	*F*	*VF*
1521	— — *Rev.* as 1518, with E and pellet in centre	£335	£650
1522	— As 1520, but without flag. ℞. C in centre	£350	£700
1523	**Half-noble.** *London.* *O.* Treaty die. *Rev.* as 1518	*Extremely rare*	
1524	*Calais.* Without AQT, flag at stern. ℞. E in centre	£450	£900
1525	— — ℞. Treaty die with C in centre	£475	£950

SILVER

First coinage, 1327-35 (.925 fineness)

1526 1530 1535

No.	Description	*F*	*VF*
1526	**Penny.** *London.* As Edw. II; class XVd with Lombardic n's	£160	£350
1527	*Bury St. Edmunds.* Similar	*Extremely rare*	
1528	*Canterbury; mm.* cross pattée with pellet centre	£140	£300
1529	— — three extra pellets in one quarter	£140	£300
1530	*Durham.* ℞. Small crown in centre	£350	£750
1531	*York.* As 1526, but quatrefoil in centre of *rev.*	£90	£200
1532	— — — pellet in each quarter of *mm.*	£90	£200
1533	— — — three extra pellets in one quarter	£90	£200
1534	— — — Roman N on *obv*	£90	£200
1535	*Berwick* (1333-42, Blunt type VIII). Bear's head in one quarter of *rev.*	£225	£500
1536	**Halfpenny.** *London.* EDWARDVS REX AII(G)*, neat work, flat crown	£100	£225
1537	*Berwick* (Bl. VIII). Bear's head in one or two qtrs.	£90	£200
1538	**Farthing.** *London.* EDWARDVS REX A*, flat crown	£175	£375
1539	*Berwick* (Bl. VIII). As 1537	£160	£350

1537 1540

Second coinage, 1335-43 (.833 fineness)

		F	VF
1540	**Halfpenny.** *London.* EDWARDVS REX A(NG)*, rough work, tall crown	£30	£70
1541	*Reading.* Escallop in one quarter	£175	£375
1542	**Farthing.** *London.* As halfpenny	£125	£250

Third or florin coinage, 1344-51. Bust with bushy hair.

1543 1555

1543	**Penny.** *London.* Class 1, EDW, Lombardic n's	£20	£45
1544	— 2, EDWA, n's, but sometimes N's on *rev.*	£17	£36
1545	— 3, EDW, N's, sometimes reversed or n's on *rev.*	£14	£30
1546	— 4, EDW, no stops, reversed N's, but on *rev.* sometimes n's, N's or double-barred N's	£15	£32

*There are also five unusual varieties of *obv.*

1547	*Canterbury.* EDWA, n's	£45	£95
1548	— EDW, reversed N's	£40	£85
1549	*Durham,* Sede Vacante (1345). A, EDW R. ℞. No marks	£40	£85
1550	— — B, similar, EDWAR R	£55	£120
1551	— Bp. Hatfield. C, similar, but pellet in centre of *rev.*	£55	£120
1552	— — — Crozier on *rev.*	£55	£120
1553	— — — — with pellet in centre of *rev.*	£55	£120
1554	— — D, EDWARDVS REX AIn, crozier on *rev.*	£90	£185
1555	*Reading.* *O.* as 1546. ℞. Escallop in one quarter	£185	£450
1556	*York.* *O.* as 1546. ℞. Quartrefoil in centre	£22	£50
1557	**Halfpenny.** *London.* EDWARDVS REX(An)	£20	£45
1558	— — pellet either side of crown	£25	£55
1559	— — saltire either side of crown and in one quarter of *rev.*	£22	£50
1560	*Reading.* *O.* similar. ℞. Escallop in one quarter	£185	£450
1561	*Continental imitation.* Mostly reading EDWARDIENSIS	£18	£45
1562	**Farthing.** *London.* EDWARDVS REX	£110	£235

Fourth coinage, 1351-77

Reference: L. A. Lawrence, *The Coinage of Edward III from* 1351.

Pre-treaty period, 1351-61. With French title.

1567

1570

		F	VF
1563	**Groat** (=4d., 72 grs.). *London*, series B (1351). Roman M, open C and Є; *mm.* cross 1	£110	£250
1564	— — — crown in each quarter		*Unique*
1565	— C (1351-2). Lombardic m, closed C and Є, R with wedge-shaped tail; *mm.* cross 1	£24	£70
1566	— D (1352-3). R with normal tail; *mm.* cross 1 or cross 1 broken (2)	£30	£85
1567	— E (1354-5). Broken letters, V often with nick in r. limb; *mm.* cross 2 (3)	£22	£65
1568	— — — lis on breast	£24	£70
1569	— F (1356). *Mm.* crown (74)	£30	£85
1570	— G (1356-61). Usually with annulet in one qtr. and sometimes under bust, *mm.* cross 3 (4). Many varieties	£24	£70
1571	*York*, series D. As London	£40	£100
1572	— E. As London	£32	£90

1573

1574

		F	VF
1573	**Halfgroat.** *London*, series B. As groat	£70	£150
1574	— C. As groat	£20	£50
1575	— D. As groat	£22	£55
1576	— E. As groat	£20	£50
1577	— F. As groat	£25	£60
1578	— G. As groat	£22	£55
1579	— — — annulet below bust	£25	£60

		F	VF
1580	*York*, series D. As groat	£25	£60
1581	— E. As groat	£20	£50
1582	— — — lis on breast	£35	£85

1584 1587 1591

		F	VF
1583	**Penny.** *London.* Series A (1351). Round letters, Lombardic m and n, annulet in each quarter; *mm.* cross pattée	£30	£60
1584	— C. Details as groat, but annulet in each quarter	£12	£30
1585	— D. Details as groat, but annulet in each quarter	£12	£30
1586	— E. Sometimes annulet in each quarter	£12	£30
1587	— F. Details as groat	£15	£35
1588	— G. Details as groat	£12	£30
1589	— — — annulet below bust	£15	£35
1590	— — — saltire in one quarter	£25	£50
1591	*Durham*, Bp. Hatfield. Series A. As 1583, but extra pellet in each quarter, VIL LA crozier DVRREM	£90	£200
1592	— C. Details as groat. ℞. Crozier, CIVITAS DVNELMIE	£25	£50
1593	— D — — —	£25	£50
1594	— E — — —	£18	£40
1595	— F — ℞. Crozier, CIVITAS DVREME	£22	£45
1596	— G — — —	£12	£30
1597	— — — — — annulet below bust	£15	£35
1598	— — — — — saltire in one quarter	£15	£35
1599	— — — — — annulet on each shoulder	£14	£32
1600	— — — — — trefoil of pellets on breast	£20	£42
1601	— — — ℞. Crozier, CIVITAS DVRELMIE	£26	£55
1602	*York*, Royal Mint. Series D	£22	£45
1603	— — E	£14	£30
1604	— Archb. Thorsby. Series D. ℞. Quatrefoil in centre	£20	£42
1605	— — G —	£14	£30
1606	— — — — annulet or saltire on breast	£15	£35
1607	**Halfpenny.** *London.* Series E. EDWARDVS REX An	£75	£175
1608	— G, but with *obv.* of F (*mm.* crown). Annulet in one quarter ..	*Extremely rare*	
1609	**Farthing.** *London.* Series E. EDWARDVS REX	*Extremely rare*	

Transitional treaty period, 1361. French title omitted, irregular sized letters; *mm.* cross potent (5).

		F	*VF*
1610	**Groat.** *London.* Annulet each side of crown	£110	£240
1611	**Halfgroat.** Similar, but only seven arches to tressure	£90	£200

1611

1612

1612	**Penny,** *London.* Omits REX, annulet in two upper qtrs. of *mm.* ..	£50	£110
1613	*York,* Archb. Thoresby. Similar, but quatrefoil enclosing pellet in centre of *rev.*	£50	£110
1614	*Durham,* Bp. Hatfield. Similar. ℞. Crozier, CIVITAS DORELME ..	£50	£110
1615	**Halfpenny.** Two pellets over *mm.*, EDWARDVS REX An	£75	£150

Treaty period, 1361-9. French title omitted, new letters, usually "Treaty" X; *mm.* cross potent (5).

1616	**Groat,** *London.* Many varieties	£35	£90
1617	— Annulet before EDWARD	£38	£95
1618	— Annulet on breast	£65	£150
1619	*Calais.* As last	£75	£185

1621

1635

1620	**Halfgroat,** *London.* As groat	£22	£50
1621	— — Annulet before EDWARDVS	£17	£40
1622	— — Annulet on breast	£45	£110
1623	*Calais.* As last	£42	£100
1624	**Penny,** *London.* EDWARD AnGL R, etc.	£17	£38
1625	— — — pellet before EDWARD	£22	£50
1626	*Calais.* ℞. VILLA CALESIE	£55	£135
1627	*Durham.* ℞. CIVITAS DVNELMIS	£28	£60
1628	— ℞. Crozier, CIVITAS DVREME	£17	£38
1629	*York,* Archb. Thoresby. Quatrefoil in centre of *rev.*, EDWARDVS DEI G REX An	£32	£75
1630	— — — EDWARDVS REX ANGLI	£16	£40
1631	— — — — quatrefoil before ED and on breast	£15	£38
1632	— — — — annulet before ED	£22	£50
1633	— — — EDWARD AnGL R DnS HYB	£30	£70

		F	VF
1634	**Halfpenny.** EDWARDVS REX An, pellet stops	£22	£50
1635	— Pellet before ED, annulet stops	£26	£60
1636	**Farthing.** EDWARDVS REX, pellet stops	£90	£200

Post-treaty period, 1369-77. French title resumed, X like St. Andrew's cross; *mm.* 5, 6, 7a.

1637 1638

1637	**Groat.** Various readings, *mm.* cross pattée	£60	£180
1638	— — row of pellets across breast (chain mail)	£180	£550
1639	— row of annulets below bust (chain mail); *mm.* cross potent with four pellets	£160	£485
1640	**Halfgroat.** Various readings	£60	£150
1641	— row of pellets one side of breast (chain mail)	£235	£600
1642	**Penny,** *London.* No marks on breast	£32	£75
1643	— Pellet or annulet on breast	£40	£100
1644	— Cross or quatrefoil on breast	£38	£90
1645	*Durham,* Bp. Hatfield. *Mm.* 7a, CIVITAS DVNOLM, crozier	£25	£65
1646	— — — — annulet on breast	£28	£70
1647	— — — — lis on breast	£32	£75
1648	*York,* Archb. Thoresby or Neville. ℞. Quatrefoil in centre ..	£22	£55
1649	— — — lis on breast	£40	£85
1650	— — — annulet on breast	£25	£55
1651	— — — cross on breast	£25	£55
1652	**Farthing.** EDWARD REX ANGL, large head without neck	£200	£400

RICHARD II, 1377-99

There was no significant change in the coinage during this reign. Noteworthy is the first appearance of symbols on the ship's rudder on some of the gold coins. The earlier silver coins have a portrait like that on the coins of Edward III, but the king's head and the style of lettering were altered on the later issues.

Reference: *Silver coinages of Richard II, Henry IV and V.* (B.N.J. 1959-60 and 1963).

Mintmark: cross pattée (6) 

GOLD

1655

1657

			F	*VF*
1653	**Noble,** *London.* With altered *obv.* and/or *rev.* die of Edw. III	*from*	£750	£1650
1654	— Lettering as Edw. III, lis over sail		£625	£1350
1655	— Straight-sided letters, annulet over sail		£550	£1200
1656	— Late issue, fish-tail lettering; no marks, or trefoil by shield ..		£600	£1300
1657	— — — lion or lis on rudder		£800	£1750
1658	— — small dumpy lettering; escallop or crescent on rudder and/or trefoil over sail or by shield	*from*	£700	£1500

1658

1662

1659	*Calais.* Flag at stern, otherwise as 1653	*from*	£650	£1400
1660	— — as 1655, but quatrefoil over sail		£600	£1300
1661	— — as 1656; no marks		£625	£1350
1662	— — — lion on rudder		£700	£1500
1663	— — as 1658		£600	£1300

1664

1672/3

		F	VF
1664	**Half-noble,** *London.* As 1653	£650	£1450
1665	— as 1655	£550	£1250
1666	— as 1656; lion on rudder	£600	£1350
1667	— as 1658; crescent on rudder	£650	£1450
1668	*Calais.* Flag at stern, otherwise as 1653	£600	£1350
1669	— — as 1655; quatrefoil over sail	£600	£1350
1670	— — as 1656; lion on rudder	£550	£1250
1671	— — as 1658, but one var. has saltire behind rudder	£650	£1450
1672	**Quarter-noble,** *London.* R in centre of *rev.*	£275	£550
1673	— Lis or pellet in centre of *rev.*	£250	£500
1674	— — *obv.* die of Edw. III altered	£300	£600
1675	— — escallop over shield	£325	£650
1676	— — trefoil of annulets over shield	£285	£575
1677	— — quatrefoil, cross or slipped trefoil over shield .. .. *from*	£250	£500

SILVER

		F	VF
1678	**Groat.** I. Style of Edw. III, F (*i.e. et*) before FRANC, etc.	£250	£600
1679	II. New lettering, retrograde Z before FRANC, etc.	£200	£500
1680	III. Bust with bushy hair, "fishtail" serifs to letters	£250	£600
1681	IV. New style bust and crown, crescent on breast	£850	£2000

1682

		F	VF
1682	**Halfgroat.** II. New lettering	£175	£400
1683	III. As 1680	£185	£425
1684	— — with *rev.* die of Edw. III	£375	£850
1685	IV. As 1681, but no crescent	£550	£1200

No.	Description	F	VF
1686	**Penny,** *London.* I. Lettering as 1678, RICARDVS REX ANGLIE	£175	£450
1687	— — lis on breast	£200	£500
1688	— II. As 1679, Z FRANC	£175	£450
1689	— III. As 1680, RICARD REX ANGLIE	£200	£500

1689

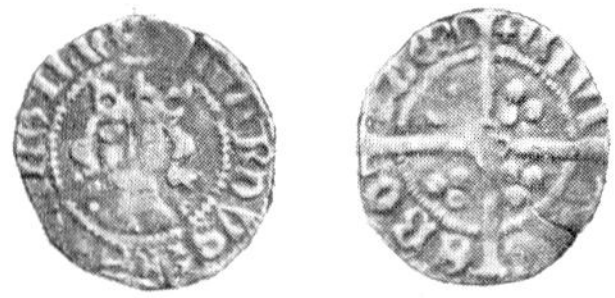
1692

No.	Description	F	VF
1690	*York.* I. Early style, usually with cross or lis on breast, quatrefoil in centre of *rev.* *Fair* £20	£60	
1691	— II. New bust and letters, no marks on breast *Fair* £22	£65	
1692	— Local dies. Pellet above each shoulder, cross on breast, REX ANGLIE *Fair* £20	£50	
1693	— — — REX DNS EB *Fair* £22	£60	
1694	— — — REX ANG FRANC *Fair* £22	£60	
1695	— III. As 1680, REX ANGL Z FRANC *Fair* £20	£55	
1696	— IV. Very bushy hair, new letters, no crescent. R. R in centre of quatrefoil	£225	£475
1697	*Durham.* Cross or lis on breast, DVNOLM	£200	£450

1699

1704

No.	Description	F	VF
1698	**Halfpenny.** Early style. LONDON, saltire or annulet on breast	£50	£110
1699	Intermediate style. LONDON, no marks on breast	£30	£65
1700	Late style. Similar, but fishtail letters	£45	£95
1701	**Farthing.** Small bust and letters	£150	£300
1702	— — rose after REX	£175	£350
1703	Large head, no bust	£200	£400
1704	Rose in each angle of *rev.* instead of pellets	£350	£700

HENRY IV, 1399-1413

In 1412 the standard weights of the coinage were reduced, the noble by 12 grains and the penny by 3 grains, partly because there was a scarcity of bullion and partly to provide revenue for the king, as Parliament had not renewed the royal subsidies. As in France, the royal arms were altered, three fleur-de-lis taking the place of the four or more lis previously displayed.

Mintmark: cross pattée (6)

Heavy coinage, 1399-1412 GOLD

1707

1708

		F	VF
1705	**Noble** (120 grs.), *London.* Old arms with four lis in French qtrs.; crescent or annulet on rudder	*Extremely rare*	
1706	— New arms with three lis; crescent, pellet or no marks on rudder	*Extremely rare*	
1707	*Calais.* Flag at stern, old arms; crown on or to l. of rudder	*Extremely rare*	
1708	— — new arms; crown or star on rudder	*Extremely rare*	
1709	**Half-noble,** *London.* Old arms	*Extremely rare*	
1710	— new arms	*Extremely rare*	
1711	*Calais.* New arms	*Extremely rare*	
1712	**Quarter-noble,** *London.* Crescent over old arms	£500	£1000
1713	— — — new arms	£450	£900
1714	*Calais.* New arms. ℞ *Mm.* crown	£625	£1250

1710

1715

Light coinage, 1412-13

		F	VF
1715	**Noble** (108 grs.). Trefoil, or trefoil and annulet, on side of ship. ℞. Trefoil in one qtr.	£1500	£3000
1716	**Half-noble.** Similar, but always with annulet	*Extremely rare*	
1717	**Quarter-noble.** Trefoils, or trefoils and annulets beside shield, lis above. ℞. Lis in centre	£400	£800

SILVER

Heavy coinage, 1399-1412

1718

1722

1723

		F	*VF*
1718	**Halfgroat** (36 grs.). Star on breast	£700	£1750
1719	**Penny,** *London.* Similar, early bust with long neck	£500	£1000
1720	— later bust with shorter neck, no star	£500	£1000
1721	*York.* Early bust with long neck	£425	£800
1722	— later bust with broad face, round chin	£425	£800
1723	**Halfpenny.** Early small bust	£275	£550
1724	Later large bust, with rounded shoulders annulets by neck	£275	£550
1725	**Farthing.** Face without neck	£400	£800

Light coinage, 1412-13

1728

1731

1737

1726	**Groat** (60 grs.). I. Pellet to l., annulet to r. of crown; altered die of Richard II	£1250	£3000
1727	New dies; II. Annulet to l., pellet to r. of crown, 8 or 10 arches to tressure	£1000	£2500
1728	— III. Similar but 9 arches to tressure	£1000	£2500
1729	**Halfgroat.** Pellet to l., annulet to r. of crown	£725	£1750
1730	Annulet to l., pellet to r. of crown	£700	£1750
1731	**Penny,** *London.* Annulet and pellet by crown; trefoil on breast and before CIVI	£475	£950
1732	— — annulet or slipped trefoil before LON	£475	£950
1733	— Pellet and annulet by crown		*Unique*
1734	*York.* Annulet on breast. ℞. Quatrefoil in centre	£425	£850
1735	*Durham.* Trefoil on breast, DVnOLM	£575	£1150
1736	**Halfpenny.** Struck from heavy dies	£300	£600
1737	New dies; annulet either side of crown or none	£300	£600
1738	**Farthing.** Face, no bust; slipped trefoil after REX	£475	£950

HENRY V, 1413-22

There was no change of importance in the coinage of this reign. There was, however, a considerable development in the use of privy marks which distinguished various issues, except for the last issue of the reign when most marks were removed. The Calais mint, which had closed in 1411, did not re-open until early in the next reign.

Mintmarks

Cross pattée (4, but with pellet centre). Pierced cross (18).

GOLD

1744 1755

		F	*VF*
1739	**Noble.** A. Quatrefoil over sail and in second qtr. of *rev.* Short broad letters, no other marks	*Extremely rare*	
1740	— B. Ordinary letters; similar, or with annulet on rudder	£750	£1250
1741	— C. Mullet by sword arm, annulet on rudder	£700	£1150
1742	— — — broken annulet on side of ship	£500	£900
1743	— D. Mullet and annulet by sword arm, trefoil by shield, broken annulet on ship	£550	£950
1744	— E. Mullet, or mullet and annulet by sword arm, trefoil by shield, pellet by sword point and in one qtr., annulet on side of ship	£575	£1000
1745	— — Similar, but trefoil on ship instead of by shield	£625	£1100
1746	— F. Similar, but no pellet at sword point, trefoil in one qtr.	£625	£1100
1747	— G. No marks; annulet stops, except for mullet after first word	£850	£1500
1748	**Half-noble.** B. As noble; Hen. IV *rev.* die	*Extremely rare*	
1749	— C. Broken annulet on ship, quatrefoil below sail	£500	£900
1750	— — Mullet over shield, broken annulet on *rev.*	£450	£800
1751	— F. Similar, but no annulet on ship, usually trefoil by shield	£525	£950
1752	— F/E. As last, but pellet in 1st and annulet in 2nd qtr.	£600	£1100
1753	— G. As noble, but quatrefoil over sail, mullet sometimes omitted after first word of *rev.*	£650	£1350
1754	**Quarter-noble.** A. Lis over shield and in centre of *rev.* Short broad letters; quatrefoil and annulet beside shield, stars at corners of centre on *rev.*	£250	£450
1755	— C. Ordinary letters; quatrefoil to l., quat. and mullet to r. of shield	£165	£325
1756	— — — annulet to l., mullet to r. of shield	£150	£300

		F	VF
1757	**Quarter-noble.** F. Ordinary letters; trefoil to l., mullet to r. of shield	£200	£400
1758	— G — no marks, except mullet after first word	£200	£400

SILVER

1759

1762

		F	VF
1759	**Groat.** A. Short broad letters; 'emaciated' bust	£400	£850
1760	— — muled with Hen. IV *obv.* or *rev.*	£450	£950
1761	— — muled with later *rev.* of Hen. V	£400	£850
1762	B. Ordinary letters; 'scowling' bust	£250	£500
1763	— — muled with Hen. IV or later Hen. V	£275	£600
1764	C. Normal bust	£65	£130
1765	— — mullet on r. shoulder	£45	£90
1766	— — mullet in centre of breast	£125	£275
1767	G. Normal bust; no marks	£100	£200
1768	**Halfgroat.** A. As groat, but sometimes with annulet and pellet by crown	£250	£500
1769	B. Ordinary letters; no marks	£120	£250
1770	— — muled with Hen. IV or class C	£160	£325
1771	C. Tall neck, broken annulet to l. of crown	£65	£135
1772	— — — mullet on r. shoulder	£60	£120

1773

1774

		F	VF
1773	— — — mullet in centre of breast	£100	£200
1774	F. Annulet and trefoil by crown, mullet on breast	£85	£175
1775	G. New neat bust: no marks	£75	£160

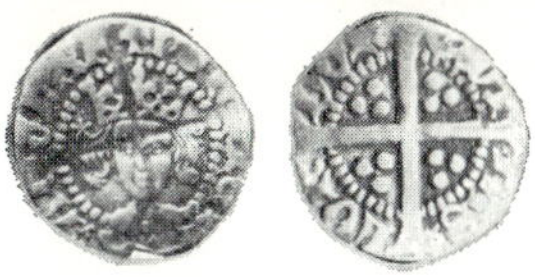

1778

1791

		F	*VF*
1776	**Penny.** *London.* A. Letters, bust and marks as 1768	£55	£130
1777	— B. Altered A *obv.*, with mullet and broken annulet added by crown. ℞. Ordinary letters	£70	£175
1778	— C. Tall neck, mullet and broken annulet by crown	£25	£60
1779	— D. Similar, but whole annulet	£30	£85
1780	— F. Mullet and trefoil by crown	£35	£90
1781	— G. New neat bust, no marks, DI GRA	£30	£85
1782	*Durham.* C. As 1778 but quatrefoil at end of legend	£40	£100
1783	— D. As 1779	£35	£90
1784	— G. Similar, but new bust. ℞. Annulet in one qtr.	£45	£120
1785	*York.* C. As 1778, but quatrefoil in centre of *rev.*	£25	£65
1786	— D. Similar, but whole annulet by crown	£25	£65
1787	— E. As last, but pellet above mullet	£50	£120
1788	— F. Mullet and trefoil by crown	£35	£85
1789	— — Trefoil over mullet to l., annulet to r. of crown	£28	£70
1790	— G. Mullet and trefoil by crown (London dies)	£28	£70
1791	— — Mullet and lis by crown, annulet in one qtr. (usually local dies)	£28	£70

1795

1798

1792	**Halfpenny.** A. Emaciated bust, annulets by crown	£32	£80
1793	— altered dies of Hen. IV	£38	£100
1794	C. Ordinary bust, broken annulets by crown	£20	£45
1795	D. Annulets, sometimes broken, by hair	£20	£45
1796	F. Annulet and trefoil by crown	£22	£50
1797	G. New bust; no marks	£24	£55
1798	**Farthing.** G. Small face with neck	£80	£200

HENRY VI, 1422-61

The supply of gold began to dwindle early in the reign, which accounts for the rarity of gold after 1426. The Calais mint was re-opened in 1424 and for some years a large amount of coin was struck there. It soon stopped minting gold; the mint was finally closed in 1440. A royal mint at York was opened for a short time in 1423/4.

Marks used to denote various issues become more prominent in this reign and can be used to date coins to within a year or so.

Reference: *Heavy Coinage of Henry VI*, by C. A. Whitton (B.N.J. 1938-41).

Mintmarks

7a 105 18 — 8 9 15

1422-60	Plain cross (7a, intermittently)	1427-34	Cross patonce (8)
	Lis (105, on gold)		Cross fleurée (9)
1422-27	Pierced cross (18)	1434-35	Voided cross (15)
1422-34	Cross pommée	1435-60	Cross fleury (9)
		1460	Lis (105, on *rev.* of some groats)

For Restoration marks see p. 121.

GOLD

Annulet issue, 1422-7

1799

		F	*VF*
1799	**Noble.** *London.* Annulet by sword arm, and in one spandril on *rev.*; trefoil stops on *obv.* with lis after hENRIC, annulets on *rev.*, with mullet after IhC	£475	£850
1800	— Similar, but *obv.* from Henry V die	£750	£1400
1801	— As 1799, but Flemish imitative coinage	£375	£700
1802	*Calais.* As 1799, but flag at stern and C in centre of *rev.*	£675	£1250
1803	— — with h in centre of *rev.*	£575	£1100
1804	*York.* As London, but with lis over stern	£675	£1250
1805	**Half-noble.** *London.* As 1799	£300	£625
1806	— Similar, but *obv.* from Henry V die	£400	£800
1807	*Calais.* As noble, with C in centre of *rev.*	£700	£1300
1808	— — with h in centre of *rev.*	£425	£900
1809	*York.* As noble	£450	£950

		F	VF
1810	**Quarter-noble.** *London.* Lis over shield; *mm.* large lis	£150	£300
1811	— — — trefoil below shield	£250	£500
1812	— — — pellet below shield	*Extremely rare*	
1813	*Calais.* Three lis over shield; *mm.* large lis	£250	£500
1814	— Similar but three lis around shield	£325	£600
1815	— As 1810, but much smaller *mm.*	£225	£450
1816	*York.* Two lis over shield	£325	£600

1814

1819

Rosette-mascle issue, 1427-30

		F	VF
1817	**Noble.** *London.* Lis by sword arm and in *rev.* field; stops, rosettes, or rosettes and mascles	£600	£1300
1818	*Calais.* Similar, with flag at stern	£675	£1500
1819	**Half-noble.** *London.* Lis in *rev.* field; stops, rosettes and mascles	£500	£1050
1820	*Calais.* Similar, flag at stern; stops, rosettes	£625	£1350
1821	**Quarter-noble.** *London.* As 1810; stops, as noble	£250	£525
1822	— without lis over shield	£225	£500
1823	*Calais.* Lis over shield, rosettes r. and l., and rosette stops	£350	£550

Pinecone-mascle issue, 1430-4

		F	VF
1824	**Noble.** *London.* Stops, pinecones and mascles	£625	£1350
1825	**Half-noble.** *London.* *O.* Rosette-mascle die. ℞. As last	*Extremely rare*	
1826	**Quarter-noble.** As 1810, but pinecone and mascle stops		*Unique*

Leaf-mascle issue, 1434-5

		F	VF
1827	**Noble.** Leaf in waves; stops, saltires with two mascles and one leaf	£1000	£2400
1828	**Half-noble.** (Fishpool Hoard)		*Unique*
1829	**Quarter-noble.** As 1810; stops, saltire and mascle; leaf on inner circle of *rev.*	£1350	£2750

Leaf-trefoil issue, 1435-8

		F	VF
1830	**Noble.** Stops, leaves and trefoils	*Extremely rare*	
1831	**Quarter-noble.** Similar		*Unique*

Trefoil issue, 1438-43

		F	VF
1832	**Noble.** Trefoil below shield and in *rev.* legend	£1000	£2400

Leaf-pellet issue, 1445-54

		F	VF
1833	**Noble.** Annulet, lis and leaf below shield	£1000	£2400

Cross-pellet issue, 1454-60

		F	VF
1834	**Noble.** Mascle at end of obv. legend		*Unique*

SILVER

Annulet issue, 1422-7

1835 1840

		F	VF
1835	**Groat.** *London.* Annulet in two quarters of *rev.*	£28	£65
1836	*Calais.* Annulets at neck. ℞. Similar	£20	£45
1837	— — no annulets on *rev.*	£26	£60
1838	*York.* Lis either side of neck. ℞. As 1835	£500	£900
1839	**Halfgroat.** *London.* As groat	£22	£48
1840	*Calais.* As 1836	£20	£42
1841	— — no annulets on *rev.*	£25	£55
1842	— — only one annulet on *rev.*	£28	£65
1843	*York.* As groat	£500	£950
1844	**Penny.** *London.* Annulets in two qtrs.	£20	£45
1845	*Calais.* Annulets at neck. ℞. As above	£18	£40
1846	— — only one annulet on *rev.*	£19	£42
1847	*York.* As London, but lis at neck	£500	£900
1848	**Halfpenny.** *London.* As penny	£22	£45
1849	*Calais.* Similar, but annulets at neck	£20	£42
1850	*York.* Similar, but lis at neck	£350	£650
1851	**Farthing.** *London.* As penny, but *mm.* cross pommée	£130	£275
1852	*Calais.* Similar, but annulets at neck	£250	£500

1843 1849 1852

Annulet-trefoil sub-issue

1853	**Groat.** *London.* As 1835, but trefoil of pellets to l. of crown (*North*)	£55	£130
1854	*Calais.* Similar, but annulets by neck also	£50	£120
1855	**Halfgroat.** *Calais.* Similar	£55	£130
1856	**Penny.** *Calais.* Similar	£55	£130
1857	— — only one annulet on *rev.*	£55	£130

Rosette-mascle issue, 1427-30. All with rosettes (early) or rosettes and mascles somewhere in the legends.

		F	*VF*
1858	**Groat.** *London*	£28	£65
1859	*Calais*	£22	£50
1860	— mascle in two spandrils (as illus. 1863)	£50	£125

1861 1863 1872

		F	*VF*
1861	**Halfgroat.** *London*	£28	£65
1862	*Calais*	£20	£42
1863	— mascle in two spandrils, as illustrated	£50	£125
1864	**Penny,** *London*	£24	£50
1865	*Calais*	£18	£40
1866	*York.* Archb. Kemp. Crosses by hair, no rosette	£18	£40
1867	— — Saltires by hair, no rosette	£18	£40
1868	— — Mullets by crown	£18	£40
1869	*Durham,* Bp. Langley. Large star to l. of crown, no rosette, DVnOLMI	£65	£150
1870	**Halfpenny,** *London*	£22	£45
1871	*Calais*	£18	£40
1872	**Farthing,** *London*	£110	£225
1873	*Calais. Mm.* cross pommée	£120	£250

1879 1884

Pinecone-mascle issue, 1430-4. All with pinecones and mascles in legends

		F	*VF*
1874	**Groat,** *London*	£40	£90
1875	*Calais*	£28	£65
1876	**Halfgroat,** *London*	£25	£60
1877	*Calais*	£24	£55
1878	**Penny,** *London*	£35	£80
1879	*Calais*	£24	£55
1880	*York,* Archb. Kemp. Mullet by crown, quatrefoil in centre of *rev.*	£20	£42
1881	— — rosette on breast, no quatrefoil	£18	£40
1882	— — mullet on breast, no quatrefoil	£40	£85
1883	*Durham,* Bp. Langley. DVnOLMI	£75	£175
1884	**Halfpenny,** *London*	£20	£45
1885	*Calais*	£20	£45

Pinecone-mascle issue, *continued.*

		F	VF
1886	**Farthing,** *London*	£100	£225
1887	*Calais. Mm.* cross pommée	£150	£325

Leaf-mascle issue, 1434-5. Usually with a mascle in the legend and a leaf somewhere in the design.

		F	VF
1888	**Groat,** *London.* Leaf below bust	£50	£125
1889	— — *rev.* of last or next coinage	£45	£110
1890	*Calais.* Leaf below bust, and usually below MЄVM	£35	£90
1891	**Halfgroat,** *London.* No leaf, pellet under TAS and DON	£32	£80
1892	*Calais.* Leaf below bust, and sometimes on *rev.*	£35	£90
1893	**Penny,** *London.* Leaf on breast, no stops on *rev.*	£24	£55
1894	*Calais.* Leaf on breast and below SIЄ	£20	£45
1895	**Halfpenny,** *London.* Leaf on breast and on *rev*	£20	£45
1896	*Calais.* Leaf on breast and below SIЄ	£45	£100

1892 1897 1912

Leaf-trefoil issue, 1435-8. Mostly with leaves and trefoil of pellets in the legends.

		F	VF
1897	**Groat,** *London.* Leaf on breast	£42	£100
1898	— without leaf on breast	£35	£85
1899	*Calais.* Leaf on breast	£60	£150
1900	**Halfgroat,** *London.* Leaf on breast; *mm.* plain cross	£24	£55
1901	— *O. mm.* cross fleury; leaf on breast	£24	£55
1902	— — without leaf on breast	£24	£55
1903	**Penny,** *London.* Leaf on breast	£20	£45
1903A	*Calais.* Similar		*Unique*
1904	*Durham,* Bp. Neville. Leaf on breast. ℞. Rings in centre, no stops, DVnOLM	£60	£150
1905	**Halfpenny,** *London.* Leaf on breast	£22	£50
1906	— without leaf on breast	£24	£55
1907	**Farthing,** *London.* Leaf on breast; stops, trefoil and saltire on *obv.*	£100	£250

Trefoil issue, 1438-43. Trefoil of pellets either side of neck and in legend, leaf on breast.

		F	VF
1908	**Groat,** *London.* Sometimes a leaf before LON	£38	£90
1909	— Fleurs in spandrils, sometimes extra pellet in two qtrs.	£42	£100
1910	— Trefoils in place of fleurs at shoulders, none by neck, sometimes extra pellets	£35	£85
1911	*Calais*	£100	£250
1912	**Halfpenny,** *London*	£45	£100

Trefoil-pellet issue, 1443-5

		F	*VF*
1913	**Groat.** Trefoils by neck, pellets by crown, small leaf on breast; sometimes extra pellet in two qtrs.	£45	£100

Leaf-pellet issue, 1445-54. Leaf on breast, pellet each side of crown, except where stated.

		F	*VF*
1914	**Groat.** AnGL; extra pellet in two qtrs.	£40	£90
1915	Similar, but AnGLI	£30	£70
1916	— — trefoil in *obv.* legend	£40	£90
1917	Leaf on neck, fleur on breast, often extra pellet in two qtrs.	£35	£80
1918	As last, but two extra pellets by hair	£65	£140
1919	**Halfgroat.** As 1914	£24	£55
1920	Similar, but *mm.* plain cross; sometimes no leaf on breast and no stops on *rev.*	£24	£55
1921	**Penny,** *London.* Usually extra pellets in two qtrs.	£24	£55
1922	— — pellets by crown omitted	£24	£55
1923	— — trefoil in legend	£30	£70
1924	*York,* Archb. Booth. ℞. Quatrefoil and pellet in centre	£24	£55
1925	— — two extra pellets by hair (local dies)	£18	£40
1926	*Durham,* Bp. Neville. Trefoil in *obv.* legend. B. Two rings in centre of cross	£85	£200
1927	— — Similar, but without trefoil	£85	£200
1928	**Halfpenny.** Usually extra pellet in two qtrs.	£30	£65
1929	— *mm.* plain cross	£30	£65
1930	**Farthing.** As last	£120	£250

1914 1927 1935

Unmarked issue, 1453-54

		F	*VF*
1931	**Groat.** No marks on *obv.*; two extra pellets on *rev.*	£120	£250
1932	— four extra pellets on *rev.*	£130	£275
1933	**Halfgroat.** As 1931	£130	£275

Cross-pellet issue, 1454-60

		F	*VF*
1934	**Groat.** Saltire either side of neck, pellets by crown, leaf and fleur on breast, extra pellets on *rev.*	£60	£150
1935	Saltire on neck, no leaf, pellets by crown, usually mullets in legend; extra pellets on *rev.*	£40	£100
1936	— Similar, but mascles in place of mullets on *obv.*	£40	£100
1937	— — pellets by hair instead of by crown	£55	£130
1938	**Halfgroat.** Saltire on neck, pellets by crown and on *rev.*, mullets in legend	£90	£200

Cross-pellet issue, *continued.*

		F	*VF*
1939	**Penny,** *London.* Saltire on neck, pellets by crown and on *rev.*, mascle(s), or mullet and mascle in legend	£75	£175
1940	*York,* Archb. Wm. Booth. Saltires by neck, usually leaf on breast, pellets by crown. ℞. Cross in quatrefoil in centre. Illustrated below	£40	£90
1941	*Durham,* Bp. Laurence Booth. Saltire and B at neck, pellets by crown. ℞. Rings in centre	£85	£200
1942	**Halfpenny.** Saltires by neck, usually two extra pellets on *rev.* ..	£50	£110
1943	Similar, but saltire on neck, sometimes mullet after hENRIC	£100	£225
1944	**Farthing.** Saltire on neck, pellets by crown and on *rev.*	£120	£250

1940

1945

Lis-pellet issue, 1456-60.

1945	**Groat.** Lis on neck; pellets by crown. ℞. Extra pellets	£120	£250

EDWARD IV, First Reign, 1461-70

In order to increase the supply of bullion to the mint the weight of the penny was reduced to 12 grains in 1464, and the current value of the noble was raised to 8s. 4d. Later, in 1465, a new gold coin was issued, the Ryal or "Rose Noble," weighing 120 grains and having a value of 10s. However, as 6s. 8d. had become the standard professional fee the old noble was missed, and a new coin was issued to take its place, the Angel of 80 grains.

Royal mints were opened at Canterbury and York to help with the re-coinage, and other mints were set up at Bristol, Coventry and Norwich, though they were not open for long.

Reference: C. E. Blunt and C. A. Whitton, *The Coinage of Edward IV and Henry VI (Restored)*, B.N.J. 1945-7.

Mintmarks

105 9 7a 33 99 28 74 11

1461-4	Lis (105)	1467-70	Lis (105, *York*)	
	Cross fleury (9)	1467-8	Crown (74)	often combined
	Plain cross (7a)		Sun (28)	
1464-5	Rose (33 and 34)	1468-9	Crown (74)	sometimes combined
1464-7	Pall (99, *Canterbury*)		Rose (33)	
1465-6	Sun (28)	1469-70	Long cross fitchée (11)	often combined
1466-7	Crown (74)		Sun (28)	

GOLD

Heavy coinage, 1461-64

		F	*VF*
1946	**Noble** (=6s. 8d., wt. 108 grs.). Normal type, but *obv.* legend commences at top left, lis below shield; *mm.* -/lis	£4000	£8000
1947	— Quatrefoil below sword arm; *mm.* rose/lis	*Extremely rare*	
1948	— ℞. Roses in two spandrils; *mm.* rose	*Extremely rare*	
1949	**Quarter noble**		*Unique*

1946

1950

Light coinage, 1464-70.

1950	**Ryal** or rose-noble (=10s., wt. 120 grs.), *London*. Type as next illus. Large fleurs in spandrils; *mm.* 33-74	£375	£650
1951	— — Small trefoils in spandrils; *mm.* 74-11	£350	£625
1952	— Flemish imitative coinage (mostly 16th cent.)	£225	£450

Light coinage, *continued.*

		F	VF
1953	*Bristol.* B in waves, large fleurs; *mm.* 28, 74	£450	£900
1954	— — small fleurs in spandrils; *mm.* 74, 28	£450	£900
1955	*Coventry.* C in waves; *mm.* sun	£1000	£2000
1956	*Norwich.* N in waves; *mm.* sun, rose?	£1250	£2500
1957	*York.* E in waves, large fleurs in spandrils, *mm.* 28, 105	£475	£950
1958	— — small fleurs, *mm.* 105, 28	£475	£950
1959	**Half-ryal,** *London.* As 1950	£225	£475
1960	*Bristol.* B in waves; *mm.* 28-28/74	£625	£1300
1961	*Coventry.* C in waves; *mm.* sun	£850	£1800
1962	*Norwich.* N in waves; *mm.* rose	£750	£1600

1963

		F	VF
1963	*York.* E in waves; *mm.* 28, 105, 33/105	£300	£625
1964	**Quarter-ryal.** Shield in tressure of eight arcs, rose above. R. Somewhat as half ryal; *mm.* 28/33		*Unique?*
1965	Shield in quatrefoil, E above, rose on l., sun on r.; *mm.* 33/28-74/33	£175	£375
1966	— — sun on l., rose on r.; *mm.* 74-11	£200	£425

1967

1967 **Angel** (=6s. 8d., wt. 80 grs.). St. Michael spearing dragon. R. Ship, rays of sun at masthead, large rose and sun beside mast; *mm.* -/34 *Extremely rare*

1968 — — small rose and sun at mast; *mm.* -/74 *Extremely rare*

First Reign

SILVER

1972 1985

Heavy coinage, 1461-64

		F	*VF*
1969	**Groat** (60 grs.). Group I, lis on neck, pellets by crown; *mm.* 9, 7a, 105, 9/105	£75	£150
1970	— Lis on breast, no pellets; *mm.* plain cross, 7a/105	£75	£150
1971	— — with pellets at crown; *mm.* plain cross	£75	£150
1972	II, quatrefoils by neck, crescent on breast; *mm.* rose	£75	£150
1973	III, similar, but trefoil on breast; *mm.* rose	£75	£150
1974	— — — eye in *rev.* inner legend, *mm.* rose	£75	£150
1975	— Similar, but no quatrefoils by bust	£85	£175
1976	— — Similar, but no trefoil on breast	£85	£175
1977	IV, annulets by neck, eye after TAS; *mm.* rose	£80	£165
1978	**Halfgroat.** I, lis on breast, pellets by crown and extra pellets in two qtrs.; *mm.* 9, 7a	£140	£300
1979	II, quatrefoils at neck, crescent on breast; *mm.* rose	£160	£350
1980	III, similar, but trefoil on breast, eye on *rev.; mm.* rose	£160	£350
1981	— Similar, but no mark on breast	£150	£325
1982	IV, annulets by neck, sometimes eye on *rev.; mm.* rose	£140	£300
1983	**Penny** (15 grs.), *London.* I, marks as 1978, but mascle after REX; *mm.* plain cross	£150	£325
1984	— II, quatrefoils by neck; *mm.* rose	£140	£300
1985	— III, similar, but eye after TAS; *mm.* rose	£130	£275
1986	— IV, annulets by neck; *mm.* rose	£140	£300
1987	*York*, Archb. Booth. Quatrefoils by bust, voided quatrefoil in centre of *rev.; mm.* rose	£120	£250
1988	*Durham.* O. of Hen. VI. ℞. DVnOLIn	£160	£350

Some of the Durham pennies from local dies may belong to the heavy coinage period, but if so they are indistinguishable from the light coins.

1989	**Halfpenny.** I, as 1983, but no mascle	£120	£250
1990	II, quatrefoils by bust; *mm.* rose	£80	£175
1991	— saltires by bust; *mm.* rose	£120	£250
1992	III, no marks by bust; *mm.* rose	£90	£200
1993	IV, annulets by bust; *mm.* rose	£90	£200
1994	**Farthing.** I, as 1989		2 *known*

Light coinage, 1464-70. There is a great variety of groats and we give only a selection. Some have pellets in one quarter of the reverse, or trefoils over the crown; early coins have fleurs on the cusps of the tressure, then trefoils or no marks on the cusps, while the late coins have only trefoils.

No.	Description	*F*	*VF*
1995	**Groat** (48 grs.), *London.* Annulets at neck, eye after TAS; *mm.* 33 (struck from heavy dies, IV)	£65	£160
1996	— — — Similar, but new dies, eye after TAS or DOn	£60	£145
1997	— Quatrefoils at neck, eye; *mm.* 33 (heavy dies, III)	£65	£160
1998	— — — Similar, but new dies	£55	£135
1999	— No marks at neck, eye; *mm.* 33	£75	£185

2000

2002

No.	Description	*F*	*VF*
2000	— Quatrefoils at neck, no eye; *mm.* 33, 74, 28, 74/28, 74/33, 11/28 ..	£24	£55
2001	— — — rose or quatrefoil on breast; *mm.* 33, 74/28	£28	£65
2002	— No marks at neck; *mm.* 28, 74, 11/28, 11	£28	£65
2003	— Trefoils at neck; *mm.* 11/33, 11/28, 11	£28	£65
2004	*Bristol.* B on breast, quatrefoils at neck; *mm.* 28/33, 28, 28/74, 74, 74/28	£30	£70
2005	— — trefoils at neck; *mm.* 28	£40	£85
2006	— — no marks at neck; *mm.* 28	£42	£90
2007	— Without B, quatrefoils at neck; *mm.* 28	£35	£80

Bristol is variously rendered as BRESTOLL, BRISTOLL, BRESTOW, BRISTOW.

No.	Description	*F*	*VF*
2008	*Coventry.* C on breast, quatrefoils at neck, COVETRE; *mm.* 28/33, 28 ..	£50	£120
2009	— — Local dies, similar; *mm.* rose	£60	£150
2010	— — — as last, but no C or quatrefoils	£70	£175
2011	*Norwich.* n on breast, quatrefoils at neck, nORWIC or nORVIC, *mm.* 28/33, 28	£48	£110
2012	*York.* € on breast, quatrefoils at neck, €BORACI; *mm.* 28, 105/74, 105, 105/28	£35	£80
2013	— Similar, but without € on breast, *mm.* 105	£42	£90
2014	— € on breast, trefoils at neck; *mm.* 105/28, 105	£28	£65
2015	**Halfgroat,** *London.* Annulets by neck (heavy dies); *mm.* 33 ..	£85	£185
2016	— Quatrefoils by neck; *mm.* 33/-, 28/-, 74, 74/28	£24	£55
2017	— Saltires by neck; *mm.* 74, 74/28	£28	£65
2018	— Trefoils by neck; *mm.* 74, 74/28, 11/28	£24	£55
2019	— No marks by neck; *mm.* 11/28	£50	£120

Light coinage, silver, *continued.*

		F	VF
2020	**Halfgroat,** *Bristol.* Saltires or crosses by neck; *mm.* 33/28, 28, 74, 74/-	£50	£120
2021	— Quatrefoils by neck; *mm.* 28/-, 74, 74/-	£50	£120
2022	— Trefoils by neck; *mm.* 74	£60	£150
2023	— No marks by neck; *mm.* 74/28	£60	£150
2024	*Canterbury,* Archb. Bourchier (1464-7). Knot below bust; quatrefoils by neck; *mm.* 99/-, 99, 99/33, 99/28	£24	£50
2025	— — — quatrefoils omitted	£24	£50
2026	— — — saltires by neck; *mm.* 99/-, 99/28	£25	£55

2027 2030

		F	VF
2027	— — — wedges by hair and/or neck; *mm.* 99, 99/33, 99/28	£26	£60
2028	— — As 2024 or 2025, but no knot	£30	£70
2029	— Royal mint (1467-69). Quatrefoils by neck; *mm.* 74, 74/-	£22	£48
2030	— — Saltires by neck; *mm.* 74/-, 74	£25	£55
2031	— — Trefoils by neck; *mm.* 74, 74/-, 74/28, 33	£25	£55
2032	— No marks by neck; *mm.* 28	£55	£135
2033	*Coventry.* Crosses by neck; *mm.* sun		*Unique*
2034	*Norwich.* Saltires by neck; *mm.* sun	*Extremely rare*	
2035	*York.* Quatrefoils by neck; *mm.* sun, lis, lis/-	£40	£90
2036	— Saltires by neck; *mm.* lis	£40	£90
2037	— Trefoils by neck; *mm.* lis, lis/-	£40	£90
2038	— є on breast, quatrefoils by neck; *mm.* lis/-	£38	£85
2039	**Penny** (12 grs.), *London.* Annulets by neck (heavy dies); *mm.* 33	£70	£160
2040	— Quatrefoils by neck; *mm.* 28, 74	£22	£50
2041	— Trefoil and quatrefoil by neck; *mm.* 74	£30	£65
2042	— Saltires by neck; *mm.* 74	£30	£65
2043	— Trefoils by neck; *mm.* 74, 11	£22	£50
2044	— No marks by neck; *mm.* 11	*Extremely rare*	
2045	*Bristol.* Crosses, quatrefoils or saltires by neck, BRISTOW; *mm.* crown	£60	£150
2046	— Quatrefoils by neck; BRI(trefoil)STOLL	£75	£185
2047	— Trefoil to r. of neck BRISTOLL		*Unique?*
2048	*Canterbury,* Archb. Bourchier. Quatrefoils or saltires by neck, knot on breast; *mm.* pall	£35	£80
2049	— — Similar, but no marks by neck	£55	£125
2050	— — As 2048, but no knot	£40	£90
2051	— — Crosses by neck, no knot	£40	£90
2052	— Royal mint. Quatrefoils by neck; *mm.* crown	£90	£200

Light coinage silver, *continued.*

		F	*VF*
2053	**Penny,** *Durham*, King's Receiver (1462-4). Local dies, mostly with rose in centre of *rev.; mm.* 7a, 33	£22	£50
2054	— Bp. Lawrence Booth (1465-70). B and D by neck, B on *rev.; mm.* 33	£24	£55
2055	— — Quatrefoil and B by neck; *mm.* 28	£26	£60
2056	— — B and quatrefoil by neck; *mm.* 74	*Extremely rare*	
2057	— — D and quatrefoil by neck; *mm.* 74	£28	£65
2058	— — Quatrefoils by neck; *mm.* crown	£34	£80
2059	— — Trefolis by neck; *mm.* crown	£34	£80
2060	— — Lis by neck; *mm.* crown	£34	£80
2061	*York*, Sede Vacante (1464-5). Quatrefoils at neck, no quatrefoil in centre of *rev.; mm.* 28, 33	£55	£125
2062	— Archb. Neville (1465-70). Local dies, G and key by neck, quatrefoil on *rev.; mm.* 33, 7a	£55	£125

2063

2068

		F	*VF*
2063	— — London-made dies, similar; *mm.* 28, 105, 11	£20	£42
2064	— — Similar, but no marks by neck; *mm.* large lis	*Extremely rare*	
2065	— — — Quatrefoils by neck; *mm.* large lis	£22	£45
2066	— — — Trefoils by neck; *mm.* large lis	£32	£65
2067	**Halfpenny,** *London.* Saltires by neck; *mm.* 34, 28, 74	£25	£55
2068	— Trefoils by neck; *mm.* 28, 74, 11	£22	£45
2069	— No marks by neck; *mm.* 11		*Unique?*
2070	*Bristol.* Crosses by neck; *mm.* 74	£90	£200
2071	— Trefoils by neck; *mm.* 74	£80	£175
2072	*Canterbury*, Archb. Bourchier. No marks; *mm.* pall	£100	£225
2073	— Royal mint. Saltires by neck; *mm.* crown	£65	£140
2074	— — Trefoils by neck; *mm.* crown	£60	£125
2075	*York*, Royal mint. Saltires by neck; *mm.* lis/-	£65	£140
2076	— — Trefoils by neck; *mm.* lis/-	£60	£125
2077	**Farthing.** EDWARD DI GRA REX		*Unique*

HENRY VI RESTORED, Oct. 1470-Apr. 1471

The coinage of this short restoration follows closely that of the previous reign. Only angel gold was issued, the ryal being discontinued. Many of the coins have the king's name reading hENRICV—a distinguishing feature.

Mintmarks

6 13 44 33 10 12

Cross pattée (6)
Restoration cross (13)
Trefoil (44 and 45)
Rose (33, Bristol)
Lis (105)
Short cross fitchée (12)

GOLD

2079

		F	*VF*
2078	**Angel,** *London,* As illus. but no B; *mm.* -/6, 13, -/105, none	£600	£1250
2079	*Bristol.* B in waves; *mm.* -/13, none	£850	£1750
2080	**Half-angel,** *London.* As 2078; *mm.* -/6, -/13, -/105	£800	£1600
2081	*Bristol.* B in waves; *mm.* -/13		*Unique*

SILVER

2082

2084

		F	*VF*
2082	**Groat,** *London.* Usual type; *mm.* 6, 6/13, 6/105, 13, 13/6, 13/105, 13/12..	£90	£200
2083	*Bristol.* B on breast; *mm.* 13, 13/33, 13/44, 44, 44/13, 44/33, 44/12 ..	£135	£300
2084	*York.* € on breast; *mm.* lis, lis/sun	£100	£225
2085	**Halfgroat,** *London.* As 2082; *mm.* 13, 13/-	£160	£350
2086	*York.* € on breast; *mm.* lis		*Extremely rare*
2087	**Penny,** *London.* Usual type; *mm.* 6, 13, 12	£175	£400
2087A	*Bristol.* Similar; *mm.* 12		*Unique?*
2088	*York.* G and key by neck; *mm.* lis	£150	£325
2089	**Halfpenny,** *London.* As 2087; *mm.* 12	£175	£400
2090	*Bristol.* Similar; *mm.* cross		*Unique?*

EDWARD IV, Second Reign, 1471-83

The Angel and its half were the only gold denominations issued during this reign. The main types and weight standards remained the same as those of Edward's first reign light coinage. The use of the "initial mark" as a mintmark to denote the date of issue was now firmly established.

Mintmarks

33 12 55 44 55 28 56 17

37 6 18 19 20 31 11 38

1471-83 Rose (33, *York & Durham*)
1471 Short cross fitchée (12)
1471-2 Annulet (large, 55)
Trefoil (44)
Rose (33, *Bristol*)
1471-3 Pansy (30, *Durham*)
1472-3 Annulet (small, 55)
Sun (28, *Bristol*)
1473-7 Pellet in annulet (56)
Cross and four pellets (17)
Cross in circle (37)

1473-7 Cross pattée (6)
Pierced cross 1 (18)
1477-80 Pierced cross and pellet (19)
Pierced cross 2 (18)
Pierced cross, central pellet (20)
Rose (33, *Canterbury*)
1480-3 Heraldic cinquefoil (31)
Long cross fitchée (11, *Canterbury*)
Halved sun and rose (38) ?

GOLD

2092

2093

2094

			F	*VF*
2091	**Angel,** *London.* Type as illus.; *mm.* 12, 55, 56, 17, 18, 19, 31	..	£225	£475
2092	*Bristol.* B in waves; *mm.* 55	..	£650	£1400
2093	**Half-angel.** As illus.; *mm.* 55, cross in circle, 19, 20/19, 31	..	£200	£425
2094	King's name and title on *rev.; mm.* 12/-	..	£375	£800
2095	King's name and title both sides; *mm.* 55/-	..	£300	£650

SILVER

2101 2106

		F	VF
2096	**Groat,** *London.* Trefoils on cusps, no marks by bust; *mm.* 12-37	£28	£65
2097	— — roses by bust; *mm.* 56	£50	£120
2098	— Fleurs on cusps, no marks by bust; *mm.* 18-20	£28	£65
2099	— — pellets by bust; *mm.* 18 (2)	£60	£140
2100	— — rose on breast; *mm.* 31	£28	£65
2101	*Bristol.* B on breast; *mm.* 33, 33/55, 28/55, 55, 55/-, 28	£35	£85
2102	*York.* ϵ on breast; *mm.* lis	£42	£100
2103	**Halfgroat,** *London.* As 2096; *mm.* 12-31	£26	£60
2104	*Bristol.* B on breast; *mm.* 33/12	*Extremely rare*	
2105	*Canterbury* (Royal mint). As 2103; *mm.* 31, 11	£22	£50
2106	— C on breast; *mm.* rose	£22	£50
2107	— — ℞. C in centre; *mm.* rose	£22	£50
2108	— — ℞. Rose in centre; *mm.* rose	£24	£55
2109	*York.* ϵ on breast; *mm.* lis	£65	£150
2110	**Penny,** *London.* No marks by bust; *mm.* 12-31	£28	£65
2111	*Bristol.* Similar; *mm.* rose		*Unique?*
2112	*Canterbury* (Royal). Similar; *mm.* 33, 11	£65	£140
2113	— C on breast; *mm.* 33	£80	£175

2115 2116 2123

		F	VF
2114	*Durham,* Bp. Booth (1471-6). No marks by neck; *mm.* 12, 44	£24	£55
2115	— — D in centre of *rev.;* B and trefoil by neck; *mm.* 44, 33, 56	£25	£60
2116	— — — two lis at neck; *mm.* 33	£25	£55
2117	— — — crosses over crown, and on breast; *mm.* 33	£22	£50
2118	— — — crosses over crown, V under CIVI; *mm.* 33, 30	£22	£50
2119	— — — B to l. of crown, V on breast and under CIVI	£22	£50
2120	— — — As last but crosses at shoulders	£22	£50
2121	— Sede Vacante (1476). ℞. D in centre; *mm.* 33	£60	£140
2122	— Bp. Dudley (1476-83). V to r. of neck; as last	£24	£55
2123	— — D and V by neck; as last, but *mm.* 31	£22	£50

Nos. 2117-2123 are from locally-made dies.

Second reign, silver, *continued.*

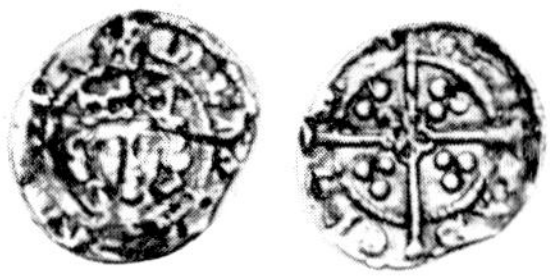

2125

2134

No.		F	VF
2124	*York*, Archb. Neville (1471-2). Quatrefoils by neck. ℞. Quatrefoil; *mm.* 12 (over lis)	*Extremely rare*	
2125	— — Similar, but G and key by neck; *mm.* 12	£14	£30
2126	— Neville suspended (1472-5). As last, but no quatrefoil in centre of *rev.*	£16	£34
2127	— — No marks by neck, quatrefoil on *rev.; mm.* 55, cross in circle, 33	£15	£32
2128	— — Similar but E and rose by neck; *mm.* 33	£15	£32
2129	— Archb. Neville restored (1475-6). As last, but G and rose ..	£18	£38
2130	— — Similar, but G and key by bust	£15	£32
2131	— Sede Vacante (1476). As 2127, but rose on breast; *mm.* 33 ..	£18	£38
2132	— Archb. Lawrence Booth (1476-80). B and key by bust, quatrefoil on *rev.; mm.* 33, 31..	£14	£30
2133	— Sede Vacante (1480). Similar, but no quatrefoil on *rev.; mm.* 33 ..	£16	£34
2134	— Archb. Rotherham (1480-83). T and slanting key by neck, quatrefoil on *rev.; mm.* 33	£14	£30
2135	— — — Similar, but star on breast	*Extremely rare*	
2136	— — — Star on breast and to r. of crown	£75	£150
2137	**Halfpenny,** *London.* No marks by neck; *mm.* 12-31	£16	£38
2138	— Pellets at neck; *mm.* 18	£18	£40
2139	*Canterbury* (Royal). C on breast and in centre of *rev.; mm.* rose ..	£65	£135
2140	— C on breast only; *mm.* rose	£55	£115
2141	— Without C either side; *mm.* 11 (?)	£65	£135
2142	*Durham*, Bp. Booth. No marks by neck. ℞. DERAM, D in centre; *mm.* rose	£85	£175
2143	— — — Similar, but V to l. of neck	£85	£175

EDWARD IV or V

Mintmark: Halved sun and rose. 

The consensus of opinion now favours the last year of Edward IV for the introduction of the halved-sun-&-rose mintmark. Even if that is the case the first pieces struck under the new young king may have been from these Edw. IV dies. The coins are very rare.

GOLD

		F	*VF*
2144	**Angel.** As 2091	£650	£1500
2145	**Half-angel.** As 2093	*Extremely rare*	

2145

2146

SILVER

2146	**Groat.** As 2098	£325	£750
2147	**Penny.** As 2110	£400	£800
2148	**Halfpenny.** As 2137	£275	£550

EDWARD V, 1483

On the death of Edward IV, 9th April, 1483, the 12-year-old Prince Edward was placed under the guardianship of his uncle, Richard, Duke of Gloucester but within eleven weeks Richard usurped the throne and Edward and his younger brother were confined to the Tower and were later murdered there. Very few coins of this reign have survived. The boar's head was a personal badge of Richard, Edward's "Protector".

Mintmarks: Boar's head on *obv.*, halved sun and rose on *rev.*  

GOLD

		F	*VF*
2149	**Angel.** As 2091	*Extremely rare*	
2150	**Half-angel.** Similar	*Unique*	

SILVER

2151

		F	VF
2151	**Groat.** As 2098	£1500	£3250
2152	**Halfgroat.** As 2103	*Unknown?*	
2153	**Penny.** As 2110	*Unknown?*	

RICHARD III, 1483-5

Richard's brief and violent reign was brought to an end on the field of Bosworth. His coinage follows the pattern of the previous reigns. The smaller denominations of the London mint are all rare.

Mintmarks

38 62 63 105 33

Halved sun and rose, 3 styles (38, 39 and another with the sun more solid, see *North*).
Boar's head, narrow (62) wide (63).
Lis (105, *Durham*).
Rose only (33).

GOLD

		F	VF
2154	**Angel.** Reading EDWARD but with R (over E) and rose by mast; *mm.* sun and rose	*Unique*	
2155	— Similar, but boar's head *mm.* on *obv.*	*Extremely rare*	

2156

2158

		F	VF
2156	Reading RICARD or RICAD. ℞. R and rose by mast; *mm.* various combinations	£700	£1500
2157	— Similar, but R by mast over E (?)	£750	£1600
2158	**Half-angel.** ℞. R and rose by mast; *mm.* boar's head	*Extremely rare*	

SILVER

2159

2160

		F	VF
2159	**Groat,** *London.* *Mm.* various combinations	£200	£400
2160	— Pellet below bust—	£200	£400
2161	*York.* *Mm.* sun and rose (*obv.*)	£400	£850
2162	**Halfgroat.** *Mm.* sun and rose or on *obv.* only	£600	£1250
2163	Pellet below bust; *mm.* sun and rose	£650	£1350
2164	— *mm.* boar's head (*obv.*)	£700	£1500
2165	**Penny,** *London.* *Mm.* boar's head (*obv.*)		*Unique*

The only known specimen was stolen from our premises Feb. 1962.

2168

2169

2166	*York*, Archb. Rotherham. ℞. Quatrefoil in centre; *mm.* sun and rose	£300	£550
2167	— — T and upright key at neck; *mm.* rose	£200	£375
2168	— — — *mm.* boar's head	£200	£375
2169	*Durham*, Bp. Sherwood. S on breast. ℞. D in centre; *mm.* lis	£165	£325
2170	**Halfpenny,** *London.* *Mm.* sun and rose	£325	£600
2171	— *Mm.* boar's head		*Extremely rare*

HENRY VII, 1485-1509

For the first four years of his reign Henry's coins differ only in name and mintmark from those of his predecessors, but in 1489 radical changes were made in the coinage. Though the pound sterling had been a denomination of account for centuries a pound coin had never been minted. Now a magnificent gold pound was issued which, from the design of the king enthroned in majesty, was called a 'Sovereign'. The reverse had the royal arms set in the centre of a Tudor rose. A few years later the angel was restyled and St. Michael, who is depicted about to thrust Satan into the Pit with a cross-topped lance, is no longer a feathered figure but is clad in armour of Renaissance style. A gold ryal of ten shillings was also minted again for a brief period.

The other major innovation was the introduction of the Shilling in the opening years of the 16th century. It is remarkable for the very fine profile portrait of the King which replaces the representational image of a monarch that had served on the coinage for the past couple of centuries. This new portrait was also used on groats and halfgroats but not on the smaller denominations.

Mintmarks

39 41 40 42 33 11 7a 123

105 76b 31 78 30 91 43 57

85 94 118 21 33 53

1485-87	Halved sun and rose (39)
	Lis upon sun and rose (41)
	Lis upon half rose (40)
	Lis-rose dimidiated (42)
	Rose (33, *York*)
1487	Lis (105)
	Cross fitchy (11)
1487-88	Rose (33)
	Plain cross (7a, *Durham*)
1488-89	No marks
1489-93	Cinquefoil (31)
	Crozier (76b, *Durham*)
1492	Cross fitchy (11, gold only)
1493-95	Escallop (78)
	Dragon (118, gold only)
	Lis (105, *Canterbury* and *York*)
	Tun (123, *Canterbury*)
1495-98	Pansy (30)
	Tun (123, *Canterbury*)
	Lis (105, *York*)
1498-99	Crowned leopard's head (91)
	Lis issuant from rose (43)
	Tun (123, *Canterbury*)
1499-1502	Anchor (57)
1502-4	Greyhound's head (85)
	Lis (105, profile issue only)
	Martlet (94, *York*)
1504-5	Cross-crosslet (21)
1504-9	Martlet (94, *York* and *Canterbury*)
	Rose (33, *York* and *Canterbury*)
1505-9	Pheon (53)

The coins are placed in groups, as in Brooke, *English Coins*, to correspond to the classification of the groats.

GOLD

F *VF*

2172 **Sovereign** (20s; wt. 240 grs). Group I. Large figure of king sitting on throne with low back. ℞. Large Tudor rose bearing small shield; *mm.* 11. .. .. *Extremely rare*

2173 II. *O.* Somewhat similar but no lis as background. ℞. Large shield crowned on large Tudor rose; *mm.* 31 .. .. *Unique*

2174

		F	VF
2174	III. King on high-backed very ornamental throne, with greyhound and dragon on side pillars. ℞. Shield on Tudor rose; *mm.* 118 ..	£8000	£16500
2175	IV. Similar but throne with high canopy breaking legend and broad seat, *mm.* 105/118	£7500	£15000
2176	— Similar but narrow throne with a portcullis below the king's feet (like Henry VIII); *mm.* 105/21, 105/53	£7750	£15500
2177	**Double-sovereign** and **Treble-sovereign** from sovereign dies. These *piedforts* were probably intended as presentation pieces ..		*Unique*

2178

2178 **Ryal** (10s.). As illustration: *mm.* 11 .. .. *Extremely rare*

2181 2183

Gold

		F	VF
2179	**Angel** (6s. 8d). I. Angel of old type with one foot on dragon. ℞. PER CRVCEM, etc., *mm.* 39, 41, 40, 33	£300	£650
2180	— — Name altered from RICARD and h on *rev.* altered from є	£425	£925
2181	II. As 2179, but *mm.* none, 31/-, 31/78	£250	£550
2182	— — ℞. IhC AVTЄ TRANSIЄNS etc.; *mm.* none	£350	£750
2183	III. New dies, angel with both feet on dragon; *mm.* 78, 30, 43, 57, 85 (large straight lettering)	£275	£550
2184	— — ℞. IhC AVT TRANSIЄNS, etc.; *mm.* 78	£325	£700
2185	IV. Small square lettering; *mm.* 85	£275	£600
2186	— Tall thin lettering; *mm.* 21	£275	£550
2187	V. Large crook-shaped abbreviation after hЄNRIC; *mm.* 21, 21 and 53, 53	£275	£550
2188	**Half-angel or angelet.** I. *Mm.* 39 (old dies altered), 41	£300	£575
2189	III. Angel with both feet on dragon: *mm.* 30, 57/30, 57/85	£185	£400
2190	IV. Small square lettering; *mm.* 33	£200	£425
2191	— Tall thin lettering; *mm.* 33/21	£200	£425
2192	V. As angel; *mm.* pheon	£185	£400

SILVER

Facing bust issues. Including "Sovereign" type pennies.

2194

2195

2193	**Groat.** I. Open crown; *mm.* 39, 40, 40/41, 41, 42	£55	£130
2194	— — crosses by neck, 33, 11, 105	£100	£250
2195	II. Crown with two unjewelled arches; *mm.* none, 31	£35	£85
2196	— — similar but crosses by neck; *mm.* none, -/105	£40	£100
2197	— — ℞. Portcullis over long cross; *mm.* -/lis	*Extremely rare*	

2198

2199

2201

2198	IIIa. Crown with two jewelled arches; *mm.* 31, 78, 30	£36	£90
2199	IIIb. Crown with one plain and one jewelled arch; *mm.* 30, 91, 43, 43/57, 57/85, 85	£32	£75
2200	IVa. Similar, but plainer lettering; *mm.* 85, 21/85, 21	£40	£100
2201	IVb. Single-arched crown, 85, 85/33, 21	£36	£90

		F	VF
2202	**Halfgroat,** *London.* I. Open crown, tressure unbroken; *mm.* 41	£100	£250
2203	— IIIa. Double-arched crown; *mm.* 78	£35	£80
2204	— — — ℞. Lozenge panel in centre; *mm.* lis	£35	£80
2205	— — — Similar, but also with lis on breast	£35	£80
2206	— IIIb. Unarched crown with tressure broken. ℞. Lozenge panel in centre; *mm.* lis	£24	£60

2211

2214

		F	VF
2207	*Canterbury*, Archb. Morton. I. Open crown, crosses by neck. ℞. m in centre; *mm.* tun	£40	£95
2208	— — II. Similar, but double-arched crown; *no mm.*	£22	£50
2209	— King and Archb. jointly. As last but without m; (a) early lettering, trefoil stops; *mm.* lis, tun and lis/lis	£18	£40
2210	— — (b) ornate lettering, rosette stops; *mm.* tun and lis/-, tun/lis, tun	£18	£40
2211	— — (c) — saltire or no stops; *mm.* 123, 123 & 30/123	£16	£38
2212	*York*, Royal Mint. (a) Double-arched crown, lis on breast (rarely omitted). ℞. Lozenge panel in centre; *mm.* lis	£25	£55
2213	— — (b) Similar, but unarched crown, tressure broken	£18	£40
2214	— Archb. Savage. (a) Double-arched crown, keys at neck, no tressure; ornate lettering; *mm.* martlet	£18	£40
2215	— — (b) Similar, but fleured tressure, small square lettering	£18	£40
2216	— — (c) As last, but tall thin lettering	£18	£40
2217	— Sede Vacante (1507/8). As last but no keys	£25	£55

2221

2226

		F	VF
2218	**Penny.** Old type. *London; mm.* 41	£80	£200
2219	— — — — crosses by bust, *mm.* uncertain	*Extremely rare*	
2220	— *Canterbury*, Archb. Morton. Open crown, *mm.* tun. ℞. m in centre	£100	£250
2221	— — King and Archb. jointly, arched crown; *mm.* tun	£45	£100
2222	— *Durham*, Bp. Sherwood. S on breast. ℞. D in centre; *mm.* 7a	£75	£175
2223	— *York*, Archb. Rotherham. With or without cross on breast, *mm.* 41; T and cross at neck. ℞. h in centre	£40	£90
2224	— — — — T and trefoil at neck. ℞. Quatrefoil in centre and two extra pellets	£35	£80

Facing bust issues.

		F	VF
2225	**Penny.** "Sovereign" type. *London.* Early lettering, trefoil stops, no pillars to throne; no *mm.*	£45	£110
2226	— — — single pillar; no *mm.* or 31	£20	£50
2227	— — Ornate letters, rosette stops, single pillar; *mm.* lis	£25	£60
2228	— — — saltire stops, two pillars; *mm.* none, 30	£20	£50
2229	— — Similar, but small square lettering; no *mm.*	£20	£50
2230	— — Similar, but lettering as profile groats; *mm.* 21, 53	£25	£60
2231	— *Durham*, Bp. Sherwood. Crozier to r. of king, throne with one pillar. ℞. D and S beside shield	£28	£70
2232	— — Throne with two pillars, no crozier. ℞. As last	£28	£70
2233	— — Bp. Fox. Throne with one pillar. ℞. Mitre above shield, RD or DR at sides	£25	£60
2234	— — Similar, but two pillars	£28	£70

2231

2233

2235

		F	VF
2235	*York*, Archb. Rotherham. Keys below shield; early lettering, trefoil stops, no pillars to throne	£20	£50
2236	— — — single pillar	£20	£50
2237	— — — ornate lettering, rosette or no stops, single pillar	£20	£50
2238	— — — — — — two pillars	£20	£50

2245

2248

		F	VF
2239	**Halfpenny,** *London.* I. Open crown; *mm.* 41, 42	£45	£100
2240	— — — trefoils at neck; no *mm.*	£45	£100
2241	— — — crosses at neck; *mm.* 33, 11	£30	£70
2242	— II. Arched crown; *mm.* cinquefoil, none?	£20	£45
2243	— — — saltires at neck; no *mm.*	£18	£40
2244	— III. Crown with lower arch, ornate lettering; no *mm.*	£20	£45
2245	— V. Much smaller portrait; *mm.* pheon	£26	£60
2246	*Canterbury*, Archb. Morton. I. Open crown. ℞. m in centre ..	£80	£175
2247	— — II. Similar, but arched crown, saltires by bust; *mm.* profile eye (82)?	£100	£225
2248	— King and Archb. III. Arched crown; *mm.* none, 105	£50	£110
2249	*York*, Archb. Savage. Arched crown, key below bust	£50	£110
2250	**Farthing,** HENRIC DI GRA REX (A)	£150	£300

Profile issue

2253

		F	*VF*
2251	**Testoon** (1s.). Type as groat. hENRIC(VS); *mm.* lis	£4000	£8500
2252	— hENRIC VII; *mm.* lis	£4500	£10000
2253	— hENRIC SEPTIM; *mm* lis	£6000	£12500

2254

2258

2254	**Groat,** *Tentative issue* (contemporary with full-face groats). Double band to crown, hENRIC VII; *mm.* none, 105/-, -/105: 105/85, 105, 85, 21	£150	£350
2255	— — — tressure on *obv.; mm.* 21	£1750	£4000
2256	— — hENRIC (VS); *mm.* 105, -/105, 105/85	£300	£650
2257	— — hENRIC SEPTIM; *mm.* -/105	£2000	£5000
2258	*Regular issue.* Triple band to crown; *mm.* 21, 21 and 53/21, 21/21 and 53, 53	£50	£150
2259	**Halfgroat,** *London.* As last; *mm.* 105, 53/105, 53	£45	£100
2260	— — no numeral after king's name, no *mm.*	£150	£350
2261	*Canterbury*, King and Archb. As London, but *mm.* 94, 33	£35	£80
2262	*York*, Archb. Bainbridge. As London, but two keys below shield; *mm.* 94, 33	£35	£80
2263	— — XB beside shield; *mm.* 33/94	£150	£350

HENRY VIII, 1509-1547

Henry VIII is held in ill-regard by numismatists as being the author of the debasement of England's gold and silver coinage; but there were also other important numismatic innovations during his reign. For the first sixteen years of the reign the coinage closely followed the pattern of the previous issues, even to the extent of retaining the portrait of Henry VII on the larger silver coins.

In 1526, in an effort to prevent the drain of gold to continental Europe, the value of English gold was cried up by 10%, the sovereign to 22s. 0d. and the angel to 7s. 4d., and a new coin valued at 4s. 6d.—the Crown of the Rose—was introduced as a competitor to the French *écu au soliel*. The new crown was not a success and within a few months it was replaced by the Crown of the Double Rose valued at 5 shillings but made of gold of only 22 carat fineness, the first time gold had been minted below the standard 23¾ carat. At the same time the sovereign was again revalued to 22s. 6d. and the angel at 7s. 6d., with a new coin, the George Noble, valued at 6s. 8d. (one-third pound).

The royal cyphers on some of the gold crowns and half-crowns combine the initial of Henry with those of his queens: Katherine of Aragon, Anne Boleyn and Jane Seymour. The architect of this coinage reform was the Chancellor, Cardinal Thomas Wolsey, but besides his other changes he had minted at York a groat bearing his initials and cardinal's hat in addition to the other denominations normally authorized for the ecclesiastical mints.

In view of Henry's final break with Rome in 1534, followed by the Act Supremacy of 1535, it was hardly surprising that the Church's coining privileges in England were finally terminated and the mints of Durham and York (ecclesiastical) were closed.

In 1544, to help finance the king's inordinate extravagances, it was decided to extend the process of debasement. Initially all the 'fine' gold coins were reduced in quality to 23 carat then the following year gold was issued of 22 carat and later of 20 carat fineness. Concurrently the silver coins were reduced from the sterling standard fineness of 11 oz. 2 dwt. (i.e. .925 silver) to 9 oz. (.750), and later to 6 oz. (.500) and eventually 4 oz. (.333) fineness. Henry's nickname of 'Old Coppernose' was earned, not through his own personal characteristics, but by his last poor 'silver' coins which soon displayed their two-thirds copper content once they became slightly worn.

Mintmarks

53 69 70 108 33 94 73 11

105 22 23 30 78 15 24 110

1509-26	Pheon (53)		Lis (105, *Canterbury, Durham*)
	Castle (69)	1509-14	Martlet (94, *York*)
	Castle with H (70, gold)	1509-23	Radiant star (22, *Durham*)
	Portcullis crowned (108)	1514-26	Star (23, *York*)
	Rose (33, *Canterbury*)		Pansy (30, *York*)
	Martlet (94, *Canterbury*)		Escallop (78, *York*)
	Pomegranate (73, but broader, *Cant.*)		Voided cross (15, *York*)
	Cross fitchée (11, *Cant.*)	1523-6	Spur rowel (24, *Durham*)

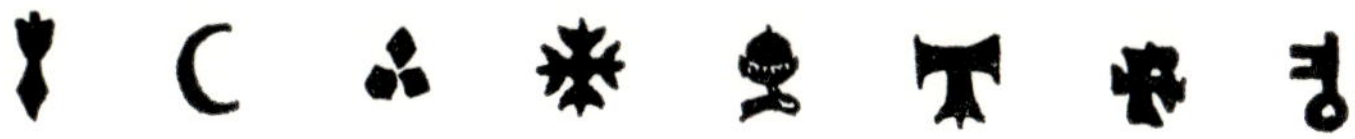

52 72a 44 8 65a 114 121 90

36 106 56 S ϵ 116

1526-44	Rose (33)	1526-32	Cross patonce (8, *Cant.*)
	Lis (105)		T (114, *Canterbury*)
	Sunburst (110)		Uncertain mark (121, *Canterbury*)
	Arrow (52)	1529-44	Radiant star (22, *Durham*)
	Pheon (53)	1530-44	Key (90, *York*)
	Lis (106)	1533-44	Catherine wheel (36, *Canterbury*)
	Star (23, *Durham*)	1544-47	Lis (105 and 106)
1526-9	Crescent (72a, *Durham*)		Pellet in annulet (56)
	Trefoil (44 variety, *Durham*)		S
	Flower of eight petals and circle centre (*Durham*)		ϵ or E
1526-30	Cross (7a, sometimes slightly voided, *York*)	1546-7	WS monogram (116, *Bristol*)
	Acorn (65a, *York*)		

GOLD

First coinage, 1509-26

2264

		F	*VF*
2264	**Sovereign** (20s.). As last sov. of Hen. VII; *mm.* 108	£4000	£8500
2265	**Angel** (6s. 8d.). As Hen. VII, but hϵnRIC ? VIII DI GRA RϵX, etc.; *mm.* 53, 69, 70, 108	£250	£600
2266	**Half-angel.** Similar; *mm.* 69, 70, 108	£215	£450

Second coinage, 1526-44

2267	**Sovereign** (22s. 6d.). As 2264, but *mm.* 110, 105, 105/52	£3500	£8000
2268	**Angel** (7s. 6d.). As 2265, but hϵnRIC VIII D G R etc.; *mm.* 110, 105	£400	£850
2269	**Half-angel.** Similar; *mm.* 105	£600	£1200

Second coinage gold.

2270

2272

		F	VF
2270	**George-noble** (6s. 8d.). As illustration; *mm.* rose	£4000	£9000
2271	**Half-George-noble.** Similar		*Unique*
2272	**Crown of the rose** (4s. 6d.). As illustration; *mm.* rose		*Extremely rare*

2279

2285

		F	VF
2273	**Crown of the double-rose** (5s.). Double-rose crowned, hK (Henry and Katherine of Aragon) both crowned in field. ℞. Shield crowned; *mm.* rose	£210	£475
2274	— hK both sides; *mm.* rose/lis, lis, arrow	£220	£500
2275	— hK / hA or hA / hK; *mm.* arrow	£325	£725
2276	— hR / hK or hI / hR; *mm.* arrow		*Both unique*
2277	— hA (Anne Boleyn); *mm.* arrow	£350	£700
2278	— hA / hR; *mm.* arrow		*Extremely rare*
2279	— hI (Jane Seymour); *mm.* arrow	£275	£600
2280	— hK / hI; *mm.* arrow	£350	£775
2281	— hR / hI; *mm.* arrow	£410	£800
2282	— hR (Rex); *mm.* arrow	£220	£500
2283	— — but with HIBERIE REX; *mm.* pheon	£450	£1100
2284	**Halfcrown.** Similar but king's name on *rev.*, no initials; *mm.* rose	£200	£400
2285	— hK uncrowned on *obv.*; *mm.* rose	£185	£375
2286	— hK uncrowned both sides; *mm.* rose/lis, lis, arrow	£190	£385
2287	— hI uncrowned both sides; *mm.* arrow	£220	£425
2288	— hR uncrowned both sides; HIB REX; *mm.* pheon	£350	£800

Third coinage, 1544-7

2291

		F	*VF*
2289	**Sovereign,** I (20s., wt. 200 grs., 23 ct.). As illustration but king with larger face and larger design; *mm.* lis	£4500	£10000
2290	II (20s., wt. 200 or 192 grs., 23, 22 or 20 ct.). *London.* As illustration; *mm.* lis, pellet in annulet/lis	£1850	£4200
2291	— *Southwark.* Similar; *mm.* s, є/s	£1750	£4000
2292	— — Similar but є below shield; *mm.* s/є	£2000	£4250
2293	— *Bristol.* As London but *mm.* ws/-	£2000	£4250
2294	**Half-sovereign** (wt. 96 grs.), *London.* As illus.; *mm.* lis, pellet in annulet	£250	£575
2295	— Similar, but with annulet on inner circle (*rev.*)	£275	£600
2296	*Southwark. Mm.* s	£275	£600
2297	— є below shield; *mm.* s, є	£250	£550
2298	*Bristol.* Lombardic lettering; *mm.* ws/ ws/-	£400	£900

2303

2304

2299	**Angel.** Annulet by angel's head and on ship, hENRIC' 8; *mm.* lis ..	£185	£450
2300	— Similar, but annulet one side only or none	£200	£475
2301	**Half-angel.** Annulet on ship; *mm.* lis	£165	£425
2302	— No annulet in ship	£200	£475
2303	— Three annulets on ship; *mm.* lis	£225	£500
2304	**Quarter-angel.** *Mm.* lis	£185	£375

No.	Description	F	VF
2305	**Crown,** *London.* As 2283, but hENRIC' 8; Lombardic lettering; *mm.* 56	£160	£335
2306	— without RVTILANS; *mm.* 56	£175	£350
2307	— — — with annulet on inner circle	£200	£400
2308	*Southwark.* As 2305; *mm.* S, E, E/S, S/E	£200	£400
2309	*Bristol.* hENRIC VIII. R. DEI GRA, etc.; *mm.* WS, -/WS	£150	£335
2310	— Similar but hENRIC(VS) 8	£150	£325
2311	**Halfcrown,** *London.* As 2288 but hENRIC' 8; *mm.* 56	£125	£250
2312	— — with annulet on inner circle	£135	£260
2313	*Southwark.* As 2311; *mm.* S	£160	£325
2314	— *O.* hENRIC 8 ROSA SINE SPIN. R. DEI GRA, etc.; *mm.* E	£175	£350
2315	*Bristol.* *O.* RVTILANS, etc. R. hENRIC 8; *mm.* WS/-	£170	£325

For other gold coins in Henry's name, see page 142.

SILVER

First coinage, 1509-26

2316 2327

No.	Description	F	VF
2316	**Groat.** Portrait of Hen. VII. *London; mm.* 5, 69, 108	£50	£135
2317	— *Tournai; mm.* crowned T. R. CIVITAS TORNACEN	£175	£500
2318	**Halfgroat.** Portrait of Hen. VII. *London; mm.* 108	£48	£120
2319	— *Canterbury*, Archb. Warham. POSVI *rev.; mm.* rose	£90	£200
2320	— — — WA above shield; *mm.* martlet	£45	£110
2321	— — — WA beside shield; *mm.* cross fitchée	£55	£140
2322	— — CIVITAS CANTOR *rev.*, similar; *mm.* 73, 105, 11/105	£45	£110
2323	— *York*, POSVI *rev.*, Archb. Bainbridge (1508-14). Keys below shield; *mm.* martlet	£45	£110
2324	— — — XB beside shield; *mm.* martlet	£60	£150
2325	— — — Archb. Wolsey (1514-30). Keys and cardinal's hat below shield; *mm.* 94, 22	£85	£200
2326	— — CIVITAS EBORACI *rev.* Similar; *mm.* 22, 23, 30, 78, voided cross	£32	£80
2327	— — As last with TW beside shield; *mm.* voided cross	£35	£90

2332

2335

2336

		F	VF
2328	**Penny,** "Sovereign" type, *London; mm.* 69, 108	£24	£55
2329	— *Canterbury.* WA above shield; *mm.* martlet	£85	£175
2330	— — — WA beside shield; *mm.* 73	£40	£90
2331	— *Durham*, Bp. Ruthall (1509-23). TD above shield; *mm.* lis	£24	£55
2332	— — — TD beside shield; *mm.* lis, radiant star	£32	£75
2333	— — Bp. Wolsey (1523-9). DW beside shield, cardinal's hat below; spur rowel	£70	£175
2334	**Halfpenny.** Facing bust, hENRIC DI GRA REX (AGL). *London; mm.* 69, 108	£40	£90
2335	— *Canterbury.* WA beside bust; *mm.* 73	£50	£120
2336	**Farthing.** *O. Mm.* portcullis, hENRIC DI GRA REX, a portcullis as type. ℞. CIVITAS LONDON, rose in centre of long cross	*Extremely rare*	

Second coinage, 1526-44

2337a

2337c

2337	**Groat.** His own young portrait. *London;* bust l., with short hair; Roman letters, except Lombardic h, *mm.* rose	£80	£220
2337A	— — Bust 2, hair just touches collar; mostly Lombardic letters, *mm.* rose	£55	£120
2337B	— — Bust 3, similar, but hair over collar; *mm.* rose	£28	£75
2337C	— — — Similar, all Lombardic letters; *mm.* 105-53 (sometimes muled)	£30	£80
2338	— — with Irish title HIB; *mm.* 53, 53/105, 105/53, 105 (b.s.)	£325	£800
2339	— *York*, Archb. Wolsey. TW beside shield, cardinal's hat below; *mm.* voided cross, acorn, sometimes muled	£60	£160
2340	— — — omits TW; *mm.* voided cross	£250	£600

Second Coinage Silver.

2343 2348 2354

		F	VF
2341	**Halfgroat.** Similar. *London; mm.* rose to arrow	£45	£100
2342	— — with Irish title HIB; *mm.* pheon	£450	£1200
2343	— *Canterbury*, Archb. Warham (—1532). ℞. CIVITAS CAnTOR, WA beside shield; *mm.* 121, 121/33, 8, 8/T, T	£25	£60
2344	— — — nothing by shield; *mm.* 121, 121/-	£45	£100
2345	— — Archb. Cranmer (1533—). TC beside shield; *mm.* 36, 36/- ..	£30	£75
2346	— *York*, Archb. Wolsey (—1530). ℞. CIVITAS ЄBORACI, TW beside shield, hat below; *mm.* voided cross	£30	£75
2347	— — Sede Vacante (1530/1). No marks; *mm.* key	£38	£80
2348	— — Archb. Lee (1531-44). EL or LE beside shield; *mm.* key ..	£32	£70
2349	**Penny,** "Sovereign" type, h . D . G . ROSA SInЄ SPInA, *London; mm.* rose to arrow	£22	£50
2350	— *Canterbury.* WA beside shield; *mm.* 121, 8, T	£60	£135
2351	— — TC beside shield; *mm.* 36	£50	£120
2352	— *Durham*, Bp. Wolsey (—1529). TW beside shield, hat below; *mm.* 23, 72a, 44	£30	£70
2353	— — Sede Vacante (1529-30). No marks; *mm. obv.* only, 23/-, 22/-	£32	£75
2354	— — Bp. Tunstall (1530—). CD beside shield; *mm* 23, 23/-, 22/- ..	£26	£60
2355	— *York.* EL beside shield; *mm.* key	£65	£150
2356	**Halfpenny.** Facing bust, h D G ROSA SIЄ SPIA. *London; mm.* rose to sunburst	£25	£55
2357	— *Canterbury.* WA beside bust; *mm.* 8 ?, T	£22	£50
2358	— — TC beside bust; *mm.* 36	£50	£110

2359

		F	VF
2359	— *York.* TW beside bust; *mm.* cross voided	£60	£140
2360	— — Sede Vacante. Key below bust; *mm.* cross voided	£55	£120
2361	— — EL or LE beside bust; *mm.* key	£48	£100
2362	**Farthing.** *O.* RVTILANS ROSA, portcullis; *mm.* lis ? ℞. HD . . . . ., long cross with pellet in each angle	*Extremely rare*	
2363	— — *mm.* arrow. ℞. hЄ. . D G . . AC, rose on long cross	*Extremely rare*	

Third coinage, 1544-7.

2365

		Fair	Fine
2364	**Testoon.** *Tower.* hᴇɴʀɪᴄ'. ᴠɪɪɪ, etc. ℞. Crowned rose between h and ʀ. ᴘᴏsᴠɪ, etc.; *mm.* lis, two lis, and pellet in annulet	£115	£325
2365	— hᴇɴʀɪᴄ' 8; *mm.* lis, pellet in annulet	£100	£300
2366	— — annulet on inner circle of *rev.; mm.* pellet in annulet ..	£125	£350
2367	*Southwark.* As 2365. ℞. ᴄɪᴠɪᴛᴀs ʟᴏɴᴅᴏɴ; *mm.* s, ᴇ ..	£115	£325
2368	*Bristol.* *Mm.* -/ws monogram	£140	£400

Bust 1

Bust 2

Bust 3

		F	VF
2369	**Groat.** *Tower.* As 2365, busts 1, 2, 3; *mm.* lis	£30	£130
2370	— — annulet on inner circle	£40	£160
2371	*Southwark.* As 2367, busts 1, 2, 3, 4; no *mm.* or lis; s or s and ᴇ in forks	£35	£140
2372	*Bristol.* *Mm.* -/ws monogram	£37	£150
2373	*Canterbury.* Busts 1 var., 2; no *mm.*, 105/-	£37	£150
2374	*York.* Busts 1 var., 2, 3, no *mm.*..	£37	£150
2375	**Halfgroat.** *Tower.* As 2365, bust 1; *mm.* lis, none	£55	£140
2376	*Southwark.* As 2367, bust 1; no *mm.;* s or ᴇ in forks	£45	£120
2377	*Bristol.* *Mm.* -/ws monogram	£36	£100
2378	*Canterbury.* Bust 1; no *mm.*	£24	£80
2379	*York.* Bust 1; no *mm.*	£32	£90
2380	**Penny.** *Tower.* Facing bust; no *mm.* or lis	£32	£70
2381	*Southwark.* Facing bust; *mm.* s, ᴇ	£42	£90
2382	*Bristol.* Facing bust; no *mm.*	£36	£80
2383	*Canterbury.* Facing bust; no *mm.*	£38	£90
2384	*York.* Facing bust; no *mm.*	£36	£85
2385	**Halfpenny.** *Tower.* Facing bust; no *mm.* or lis	£42	£90
2386	*Bristol.* Facing bust; no *mm.*	£70	£150
2387	*Canterbury.* Facing bust; no *mm.*	£45	£100
2388	*York.* Facing bust; no *mm.*	£45	£100

HENRY VIII POSTHUMOUS COINAGE, 1547-51

Coins struck during the reign of Edward VI but bearing the name of Henry VIII and, except in the case of the half-sovereigns, his figure or bust. Most of these coins have Roman lettering.

Mintmarks

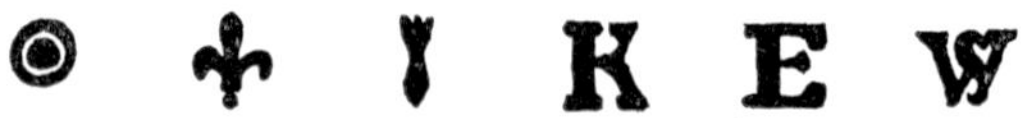

56 105 52 K E 116

66 115 33 122 t 94

1547	Annulet and pellet (56)	1549	TC monogram (115, *Bristol*)
1547-8	Lis (105)		Lis (105, *Canterbury*)
1547-9	Arrow (52)		Rose (33, *Canterbury*)
	K		Grapple (122)
	Roman E (*Southwark*)	1549/50	t (*Canterbury*)
	WS monogram (116, *Bristol*)	1550/51	Martlet (94)
1548-9	Bow (66, *Durham House*)		

GOLD

		F	*VF*
2389	**Sovereign,** *London.* As no. 2290, but Roman lettering; *mm.* lis ..	£1850	£4500
2390	— *Bristol.* Similar but *mm.* WS	£2000	£5000

2391 2395

2391	**Half-sovereign.** As no. 2294, but with youthful portrait. *London; mm.* 52, 105, 122, 94	£250	£575
2392	— — — K below shield; *mm.* -/K, none	£275	£600
2393	— — — grapple below shield; *mm.* grapple, none	£300	£625
2394	— *Southwark.* *Mm.* E, and usually E below shield	£250	£575
2395	**Crown.** As no. 2305. *London, mm.* 52, -/K, 122, 94	£250	£575
2396	— Similar but king's name on *rev.* without numeral; *mm.* arrow/- ..	£325	£675
2397	— *Southwark.* Similar; *mm.* E	*Extremely rare*	
2398	— — King's name on *obv.; mm.* E/-	*Extremely rare*	
2399	**Halfcrown.** As no. 2311. *London; mm.* 52, K/-, 122/-, 94	£225	£450
2400	— *Southwark.* *Mm.* E, E/-, -/E	£225	£450

SILVER

		Fair	*Fine*
2401	**Testoon.** *Tower.* As 2365 with sleeve stops one side; no *mm.* or 56	£110	£300
2402	*Southwark.* As 2367; *mm.* S/E	£140	£425

Some of the Bristol testoons, groats and halfgroats with WS monogram were struck after the death of Henry VIII but cannot be distinguished from those struck during his reign.

Bust 4

Bust 5

Bust 6

		F	*VF*
2403	**Groat.** *Tower.* Busts 4, 5, 6 (and, rarely, 2). ℞. POSVI, etc.; *mm.* 105, 52, -/52, K/-, -/K, K,-/122, -/94, 94, 94/105, -/105, 105/94, none	£32	£120
2404	*Southwark.* Busts 4, 5, 6. ℞. CIVITAS LONDON; no *mm.* lis, -/E; S and Є or roses in forks	£34	£130
2405	*Durham House.* Bust 6. ℞. REDDE CVIQUE QVOD SVVM EST; *mm.* bow	£110	£350
2406	*Bristol. Mm.* WS on *rev.*	£45	£165
2407	— — *Mm.* TC on *rev.*	£70	£250
2408	*Canterbury.* Busts 5, 6; no *mm.* or rose	£30	£110
2409	*York.* Busts, 4, 5, 6; no *mm.* or lis	£32	£120
2410	**Halfgroat.** Bust 1. *Tower.* POSVI, etc.; *mm.* 52, -/52, 52/K, -/K, 52/122, -/122, 105/94	£22	£60
2411	— *Southwark.* CIVITAS LONDON; *mm.* 52, E, -/E, none	£20	£55
2412	— *Durham House.* ℞. REDD, etc.; *mm.* bow	£135	£300
2413	—*Bristol. Mm.* WS on *rev.*	£25	£65
2414	— — *mm.* TC on *rev.*	£38	£100
2415	— *Canterbury.* No *mm.* or t	£20	£55
2416	— *York.* No *mm.* (also bust 6)	£22	£60

2422

2418

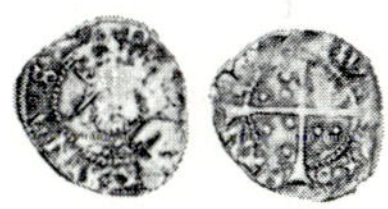
2427

2417	**Penny.** *Tower.* CIVITAS LONDON. Facing bust; *mm.* 52/-, -/52, -/K, 122/-, -/122, none	£18	£50
2418	— — three-quarter bust; no *mm.*	£18	£50
2419	*Southwark.* As 2417; *mm.* E	£55	£120
2420	*Durham House.* As groat but shorter legend	£135	£300
2421	*Bristol.* Facing bust; no *mm.*	£22	£60
2422	*Canterbury.* Similar	£18	£50
2423	— three-quarters facing bust; no *mm.*	£18	£50
2424	*York.* Facing bust; no *mm.*	£18	£50
2425	— three-quarters facing bust; no *mm.*	£22	£60
2426	**Halfpenny.** *Tower.* 52 ?, none	£42	£85
2427	*Canterbury.* No *mm.*	£24	£55
2428	*York.* No *mm.*	£42	£85

EDWARD VI, 1547-53

Coinage in his own name.

While base coins continued to be issued bearing the name of Henry VIII, plans were made early in Edward's reign to reform the coinage. As a first step, in 1549, the standard of the gold was raised to 22 carat and "silver" was increased to 50% silver content. Baser shillings were issued in 1550, but finally, in 1551, it was decided to resume the coinage of some "fine" gold and a new silver coinage was ordered of 11 oz. 1 dwt. fineness, i.e. almost up to the ancient standard. At the same time four new denominations were added to the coinage—the silver crown, halfcrown, sixpence and threepence. Pennies continued to be struck in base silver.

The first dates on English coinage appear in Roman numerals during this reign; MDXLVIII = 1548; MDXLVIX = 1549; MDL = 1550; MDLI = 1551.

Mintmarks

66 52 35 115 E 53 122

44 t T 111 Y 126 94

92 105 y 97 123 78 26

1548-9	Bow (66, *Durham House*)	1549-50	**6** (126, gold only)
1549	Arrow (52)	1550	Martlet (94)
	Rose (35)	1550-1	Lion (92)
	TC monogram (115, *Bristol*)		Lis (105)
	Roman E (*Southwark*)		Rose (33)
	Pheon (53)	1552	Y (117)
	Grapple (122)		Ostrich's head (97, gold only)
	Trefoil (44 variety)		
	t or T (*Canterbury*)	1551-3	Tun (123)
1549-50	Swan (111)		Escallop (78)
	Roman Y	1552-3	Pierced mullet (26, *York*)

GOLD

First period, Apr. 1547-Jan. 1549.

2429 2431

		F	*VF*
2429	**Half-sovereign.** As 2391, but reading EDWARD 6. *Tower; mm.* arrow	£375	£750
2430	— *Southwark* (Usually with E or Є below shield); *mm.* E	£325	£650

F *VF*

2431 **Crown.** RVTILANS, etc, crowned rose between E R both crowned. ℞. EDWARD 6 etc., crowned shield between ER both crowned; *mm.* arrow .. *Unique*

2432 **Halfcrown.** Similar, but initials not crowned.. .. .. .. *Extremely rare*

Second period, Jan. 1549-Apr. 1550.

2433

2433 **Sovereign.** As illustration; *mm.* arrow, Y £1750 £4000

2435 2438

2434 **Half-sovereign.** Uncrowned bust. *London.* TIMOR etc., MDXLIX on *obv.; mm.* arrow.. .. .. *Extremely rare*

2435 — — SCVTVM, etc. as illustration; *mm.* arrow, **6,** Y £700 £1650

2436 — *Durham House.* Similar with MDXLVIII at end of *obv.* legend; *mm.* bow .. .. *Extremely rare*

2437 — — LVCERNA, etc. on *obv.; mm.* bow .. .. *Extremely rare*

2438 Crowned bust. *London.* EDWARD VI etc. ℞. SCVTVM, etc.; *mm.* 52, 122, 111, Y, 94 .. .. £600 £1500

2439 — *Durham House.* Half-length bust; *mm.* bow .. .. .. *Unique*

2440 — — King's name on *obv.* and *rev.; mm.* bow .. .. .. *Extremely rare*

2441 2444

2441 **Crown.** Uncrowned bust as 2435; *mm.* arrow, **6,** Y £675 £1600

2442 Crowned bust, as 2438; *mm.* 52, 122, 111, Y £650 £1500

Second period gold.

		F	*VF*
2443	**Halfcrown.** Uncrowned bust; *mm.* arrow, Y	£450	£1000
2444	Crowned bust as illus. above; *mm.* 52, 52/111, 122, Y	£400	£900
2445	Similar, but king's name on *rev.; mm.* 52, 122	£450	£1000

Third period, 1550-3.

		F	*VF*
2446	**"Fine" sovereign** (=30s.). King on throne; *mm.* 97, 123	*Extremely rare*	
2447	**Double sovereign.** From the same dies	*Extremely rare*	

2448

2451

		F	*VF*
2448	**Angel** (=10s.). As illustration; *mm.* 97, 123	£5000	£10000
2449	**Half-angel.** Similar, *mm.* 97	*Unique*	
2450	**Sovereign.** (=20s.). Half-length figure of king r., crowned and holding sword and orb. ℞. Crowned shield with supporters; *mm.* y, tun	£1100	£2500
2451	**Half-sovereign.** As illustration above; *mm.* y, tun	£900	£2000
2452	**Crown.** Similar, but for *rev.* legend; *mm.* y, tun	£800	£1750
2453	**Halfcrown.** Similar	£800	£1750

SILVER

First period, Apr. 1547-Jan. 1549.

2459

2460

		F	*VF*
2454	**Shilling.** *Durham House.* Crowned bust r. ℞. TIMOR, etc MDXLVIII, crowned garnished shield, ER at sides; *mm.* bow	£700	£1850
2455	**Groat.** Similar. *Tower.* ℞. Shield over cross, POSVI, etc.; *mm.* arrow	£325	£850
2456	— *Southwark.* ℞. CIVITAS LONDON; *mm.* E or none	£350	£900
2457	**Halfgroat.** *Tower.* As groat	£300	£700
2458	*Southwark.* As groat; *mm.* arrow, E	£250	£600
2459	*Canterbury.* Similar. No *mm.*	£250	£600
2460	**Penny.** *Tower.* As halfgroat, but E.D.G. etc. ℞. CIVITAS LONDON; *mm.* arrow	£225	£550
2461	— *Southwark.* As last, but *mm.* E	£225	£550
2462	*Bristol.* Similar, but no *mm.*	£225	£550

		F	VF
2463	**Halfpenny.** *Tower.* *O.* As 2460, *mm.* E (?). ℞. Cross and pellets	*Extremely rare*	
2464	— *Bristol.* Similar, but no *mm.*	£275	£600

Second period, Jan. 1549-Apr. 1550

2471

		fair	*fine*
2465	**Shilling.** As illus. *London.* MDXLIX or MDL; *mm.* 52-94 ..	£25	£75
2466	— — Similar, but legends transposed, MDXLIX; *mm.* 52, 35, Y or none	£30	£90
2467	— *Bristol.* MDXLIX; *mm.* TC	£200	£600
2468	— *Canterbury.* MDXLIX; *mm.* T or t	£50	£150
2469	— *Durham House.* ℞. TIMOR etc. MDXLIX; *mm.* bow ..	£140	£450
2470	— — Similar, but legends transposed	£160	£500
2471	— — No date. ℞. INIMICOS etc.	£80	£250
2472	— — Similar, but legends transposed	£100	£300

Third period, 1550-3
Base issue

2473

2475

2477

2473	**Shilling.** As 2465, MDL, MDLI; *mm.* lis, lion, rose	£45	£150

For coins of Edward VI countermarked, see p. 154.

2474	**Penny.** *London.* *O.* Rose. ℞. Shield; *mm.* escallop ..	£38	£100
2475	— — *York.* *Mm.* mullet, as illustration	£26	£60
2476	**Halfpenny.** As penny, but single rose..	£80	£250
2477	**Farthing.** *O.* Portcullis. ℞. Cross and pellets	*Extremely rare*	

Fine silver issue

2478

		F	VF
2478	**Crown.** King on horseback with date below horse. ℞. Shield on cross; *mm.* y, 1551; tun, 1551-3	£350	£850

2479

		F	VF
2479	**Halfcrown.** Walking horse with plume; *mm.* y, 1551	£275	£650
2480	Galloping horse without plume; *mm.* tun, 1551-2	£325	£750
2481	Large walking horse without plume; *mm.* tun, 1553	£450	£1100
2482	**Shilling.** Facing bust, rose l., value XII r. *mm.* y, tun	£35	£110

2482

2483

2486

		F	VF
2483	**Sixpence.** *London.* As illustration	£42	£120
2484	*York.* As last, but CIVITAS EBORACI; *mm.* mullet	£175	£450
2485	**Threepence.** *London.* As sixpence, but III; *mm.* tun	£120	£350
2486	*York.* As 2484, but III by bust	£200	£500
2487	**Penny.** "Sovere ·;n" type; *mm.* tun	*Extremely rare*	

MARY, 1553-4

All Mary's gold coin was struck in 23 carat 3½ grain gold, the "crown" gold denominations being temporarily discontinued. The mintmarks appear at the end of the first word of the legends.

Mintmarks

Pomegranate (73)  Half-rose (or half-rose and castle) 

GOLD

2488

		F	*VF*
2488	**"Fine" Sovereign** (=30s.). Queen enthroned. ℞. Shield on rose, MDLIII, MDLIIII and undated	£2250	£5500
2489	**Ryal** (=15s.). Queen in ship, MDLIII	*Extremely rare*	
2490	**Angel** (=10s.). Usual type; *mm.* pomegranate, half-rose	£500	£1100
2491	**Half-angel.** Similar; *mm.* pomegranate	*Extremely rare*	

2489

2492

SILVER

2492	**Groat.** Crowned bust l. ℞. VERITAS, etc.	£45	£160
2493	**Halfgroat.** Similar	£300	£750
2494	**Penny.** Similar, but M . D . G . ROSA, etc.	£300	£750
2495	— As last. ℞. CIVITAS LONDON	£250	£650

PHILIP AND MARY, 1554-58

The groats and smaller silver coins of this period have Mary's portrait only, but the shillings and sixpences show the bust of the queen's husband, Philip of Spain.

Mintmarks

Lis (105)  Half-rose and H (or castle.) 

GOLD

2496

		F	*VF*
2496	**Angel.** As illustration; *mm.* lis	£1500	£3500
2497	**Half-angel.** Similar	*Extremely rare*	

SILVER

2505

2510

		F	*VF*
2498	**Shilling.** Busts face-to-face, full titles, undated	£140	£400
2499	— — — also without mark of value	£250	£650
2500	— — 1554	£120	£350
2501	— English titles only, 1554, 1555	£130	£400
2502	— — without mark of value, 1554, 1555	£300	£800
2503	— — date below bust, 1554, 1555	*fair* £175	
2504	— — As last, but without ANG., 1555	£200	
2505	**Sixpence.** Similar. Full titles, 1554	£135	£450
2506	— English titles only, 1555, 1557	£125	£400
2507	— — date below bust, 1554, 1557	*fair* £150	
2508	**Groat.** Crowned bust of Mary l. ℞. POSIMVS etc.; *mm.* lis	£55	£175
2509	**Halfgroat.** Similar, but POSVIM	£350	£850
2510	**Penny.** Similar to 2495, but P . Z . M . etc.; *mm.* lis	£300	£750
2511	**Base penny.** Similar to 2474, but P . Z . M . etc.; *mm.* halved rose and H (or castle)	£48	£125

Note. Similar pence of the York mint were made for currency in Ireland (see *Coins and Tokens of Ireland*, no. 4502).

ELIZABETH I, 1558-1603

Elizabeth's coinage is particularly interesting on account of the large number of different denominations issued. "Crown" gold coins were again issued as well as the "fine" gold denominations. In 1559 the base shillings of Edward VI second and third coinages were called in and countermarked for re-circulation at reduced values. The normal silver coinage was initially struck at .916 fineness as in the previous reign but between 1560 and 1577 and after 1582 the old sterling standard of .925 was restored. Between 1578 and 1582 the standard was slightly reduced and the weights were reduced by 1/32nd in 1601. Gold was similarly reduced slightly in quality 1578-1582, and there was a slight weight reduction in 1601.

To help alleviate the shortage of small change, and avoid the expense of minting an impossibly small silver farthing, a threefarthing piece was introduced which would provide change if a penny was tendered for a farthing purchase. The sixpence, threepence, threehalfpence and threefarthings were marked with a rose behind the queen's head to distinguish them from the shilling, groat, halfgroat and penny.

Coins of exceedingly fine workmanship were produced in a screw press introduced by Eloye Mestrelle, a French moneyer, in 1561. With parts of the machinery powered by a horse drawn mill, the coins produced came to be known as "mill money". The Company of Moneyers eyed this foreign gadgetry with extreme suspicion as a threat to their employment. Mestrelle's dismissal was engineered in 1572 and six years later he was hanged for counterfeiting.

Mintmarks

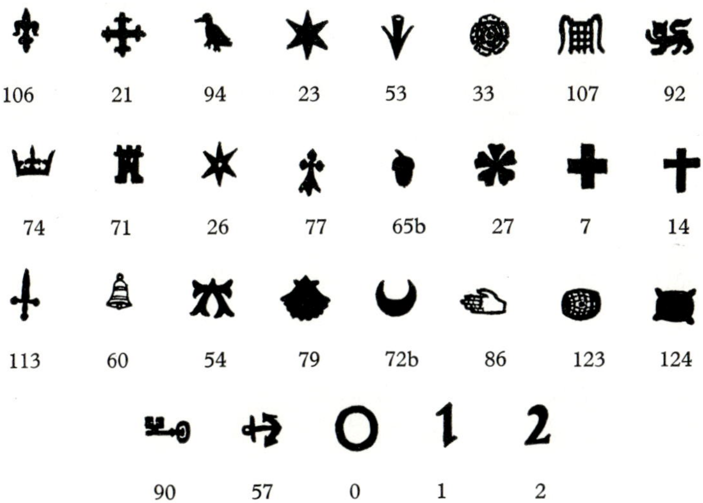

1558-60	Lis (106)	1578-79	Greek cross (7)
1560-61	Cross crosslet (21)	1580-81	Latin cross (14)
	Martlet (94)	1582	Sword (113)
1560-66	Star (23, milled)	1582-83	Bell (60)
1561-65	Pheon (53)	1582-84	A (54)
1565	Rose (33)	1584-86	Escallop (79)
1566	Portcullis (107)	1587-89	Crescent (72b)
1566-67	Lion (92)	1590-92	Hand (86)
1567-70	Coronet (74)	1592-95	Tun (123)
	Lis (105, milled)	1594-96	Woolpack (124)
1569-71	Castle (71)	1595-98	Key (90)
1570	Pierced mullet (26, milled)	1597-1600	Anchor (57)
1572-73	Ermine (77)	1600	**0**
1573-74	Acorn (65b)	1601	**1**
1573-77	Eglantine (27)	1602	**2**

GOLD

Hammered Coinage

First to Third issues, 1559-1578. ("Fine" gold of ·979, "Crown" gold of ·916 fineness. Sovereigns of 240 grs. wt.). Mintmarks: lis to eglantine.

2512

		F	*VF*
2512	**"Fine" Sovereign** of 30 sh. Queen enthroned, tressure broken by throne. ℞. Arms on rose; *mm.* lis, cross-crosslet	£2300	£6000
2513	**Angel.** St. Michael. ℞. Ship. Wire line inner circles; *mm.* lis, 21	£400	£825
2514	— — Similar, but beaded inner circles; ship to r.; *mm.* 106, 21, 74, 77-27	£325	£675
2515	— — — Similar, but ship to l.; *mm.* 77-27	£350	£725
2516	**Half Angel.** As 2513, wire line inner circles; *mm.* lis	*Extremely rare*	
2517	— As 2514, beaded inner circles; *mm.* 106, 21, 74, 77-27	£225	£500
2518	**Quarter Angel.** Similar; *mm.* 106, 74, 77-27	£200	£450

2513

2519

2519	**Half Pound** of 10 sh. Young crowned bust l. ℞. Arms. Wire line inner circles; *mm.* lis	£500	£1200
2520	— Similar, but beaded inner circles; *mm.* 21, 33-71	£375	£950
2521	**Crown.** As 2519; *mm.* lis	*Extremely rare*	
2522	— As 2520; *mm.* 21, 33-71	£325	£750
2523	**Half Crown.** As 2519; *mm.* lis	*Extremely rare*	
2524	— As 2520; *mm.* 21, 33-71	£375	£825

Fourth Issue, 1578-82 ("Fine" gold only of ·976). Mintmarks: Greek cross, Latin cross and sword.

		F	VF
2525	**Angel.** As 2514; *mm.* 14, 113	£375	£775
2526	**Half Angel.** As 2517; *mm.* 7, 113	£225	£475
2527	— Similar, but without E and rose above ship; *mm.* 14	£425	£900
2528	**Quarter Angel.** As last; *mm.* 14, 113	£185	£400

Fifth Issue, 1583-1600 ("Fine" gold of ·979, "crown" gold of ·916; Pound of 174·5 grs. wt.). Mintmarks: bell to **O**

2529

		F	VF
2529	**Sovereign** (30 sh.). As 2512, but tressure not broken by back of throne; *mm.* 54-124	£2000	£5000
2530	**Ryal** (15 sh.). Queen in ship; *mm.* 54-86	£2400	£6500
2531	**Angel.** As 2514; *mm.* 60-123, 90-**O**	£300	£650
2532	**Half Angel.** As 2517; *mm.* 60-57	£200	£475
2533	**Quarter Angel.** As 2518; *mm.* 60-57	£200	£450
2534	**Pound** (20 sh.). Old bust l., with elaborate dress and profusion of hair; *mm.* 123-**O**	£1200	£3000
2535	**Half Pound.** Similar; *mm.* 132-**O**	£450	£1150
2536	**Crown.** Similar; *mm.* 123-90, **O**	£350	£750
2537	**Half Crown.** Similar; *mm.* 123-57	£325	£775

2534

2541

Sixth Issue, 1601-1603 ("Fine" gold of ·979, "crown" gold of ·916; Pound of 172 grs. wt.). Mintmarks: **1** and **2**

		F	*VF*
2538	**Angel.** As 2514; *mm.* **1, 2**	£400	£825
2539	**Pound.** As 2534; *mm.* **1, 2**	£1300	£3250
2540	**Half Pound.** As 2535; *mm.* **1, 2**	£900	£2100
2541	**Crown.** As 2536; *mm.* **1, 2**	£550	£1200
2542	**Half Crown.** As 2537; *mm.* **1, 2**	£350	£800

Milled Coinage, 1561-1570.

2543	**Half Pound.** Crowned bust l.; *mm.* star, lis	£875	£2000
2544	**Crown.** Similar; *mm.* star, lis	£1100	£2500
2545	**Half Crown.** Similar; *mm.* star, lis	£1850	£3750

SILVER

Hammered Coinage

Countermarked Edward VI base shillings (1559)

2546

2547

2546 **Fourpence-halfpenny.** Edward VI 2nd period shillings countermarked on obverse with a portcullis; *mm.* 66, 52, t, 111 and y .. *Extremely rare*

2547 **Twopence-farthing.** Edward VI 3rd period shillings countermarked on obverse with a seated greyhound; *mm.* 92, 105 and 33 .. *Extremely rare*

First Issue, 1559-60 (·916 fine, shillings of 96 grs.).

2548

2548	**Shilling.** Without rose or date, ELIZABET(H), wire-line inner circles; *mm.* lis	£150	£450
2549	— Wire-line and beaded circles; *mm.* lis	£100	£300

2551

		F	VF
2550	**Groat.** Without rose or date, wire-line inner circles; *mm.* lis ..	£110	£275
2551	— Wire-line and beaded circles; *mm.* lis	£50	£120
2552	**Halfgroat.** Without rose or date, wire-line inner circles; *mm.* lis ..	£100	£250
2553	**Penny.** Without rose or date, wire-line inner circles; *mm.* lis ..	£90	£225
2554	Similar, but dated 1558		*Unique*

Second Issue, 1560-61 (·925 fineness, shilling of 96 grs.).

2555	**Shilling.** Without rose or date, beaded circles, ET instead of Z; *mm.* cross crosslet, martlet	£40	£120
2556	**Groat.** As last, *mm.* cross crosslet, martlet	£40	£120
2557	**Halfgroat.** As last, *mm.* cross crosslet, martlet	£38	£90
2558	**Penny.** As last, *mm.* cross crosslet, martlet	£16	£40

Third Issue, 1561-77 (Same fineness and weight as last).

2561

2567

2571

2559	**Sixpence.** With rose and date 1561, large flan (27 *mm.*), large bust with hair swept back; *mm.* pheon..	£80	£200
2560	— large flan, small regular bust; *mm.* pheon	£26	£65
2561	— 1561-77, regular flan (25 mm.); *mm.* pheon to eglantine	£18	£50
2562	Without rose, 1561; *mm.* pheon	*Extremely rare*	
2563	Without date; *mm.* lion, crown, ermine	*Extremely rare*	
2564	**Threepence.** With rose and date 1561, large flan (21 mm.); *mm.* pheon	£32	£75
2565	— 1561-77, regular flan (19 mm.); *mm.* pheon to eglantine	£18	£50
2566	Without rose, 1568; *mm.* coronet	*Extremely rare*	
2567	**Halfgroat.** Without rose or date; *mm.* portcullis to castle	£40	£90
2568	**Threehalfpence.** With rose and date 1561, large flan (12 mm.); *mm.* pheon	£45	£100
2569	— 1561-2, 1564-70, 1572-77, regular flan (11 mm.); *mm.* pheon to eglantine	£28	£65
2570	**Penny.** Without rose or date; *mm.* 33-71, 27	£14	£36
2571	**Threefarthings.** With rose and date 1561-2, 1568, 1572-7; *mm.* 53, 74, 77-27 .. .. *fair* £35	£100	£250

Fourth Issue, 1578-82 (·921 fineness, shilling of 95·6 grs.).

				F	VF
2572	**Sixpence.** As 2561, 1578-82; *mm.* 7-113			£24	£65
2573	**Threepence.** As 2565, 1578-82; *mm.* 7-113			£25	£70
2574	**Threehalfpence.** As 2569, 1578-79, 1581-82; *mm.* 7-113			£25	£70
2575	**Penny.** As 2570; *mm.* 7-113			£18	£40
2576	**Threefarthings.** As 2571, 1578-9, 1581-82; *mm.* 7-113	*fair*	£35	£100	£250

2573

2577

2581

Fifth Issue, 1582-1600 (·925 fineness, shilling of 96 grs.).

		F	VF
2577	**Shilling.** Without rose and date, ELIZAB; *mm.* bell to **O**	£32	£85
2578	**Sixpence.** With rose and date 1582-1600; *mm.* bell to **O**	£24	£65
2579	**Halfgroat.** Without rose and date, E, D, G, ROSA etc., two pellets behind bust. ℞. CIVITAS LONDON; *mm.* bell to **O**	£14	£36
2580	**Penny.** As last, but no marks behind bust; *mm.* bell to **O**	£14	£36
2581	**Halfpenny.** Portcullis. ℞. Cross and pellets; *mm.* none, A to **O**	£35	£90

Sixth Issue, 1601-02 (·925 fineness, shilling of 93 grs.).

		F	VF
2582	**Crown.** As illustration; *mm.* 1, 2	£475	£1500

2583

		F	VF
2583	**Halfcrown.** Similar, *mm.* 1, 2	£325	£900
2584	**Shilling.** As 2577, *mm.* 1, 2	£35	£100
2585	**Sixpence.** With rose and date 1601-2; *mm.* 1, 2	£30	£85
2586	**Halfgroat.** As 2579, *mm.* 1, 2	£16	£40
2587	**Penny.** As 2580, *mm.* 1, 2	£16	£40
2588	**Halfpenny.** As 2581, *mm.* 1, 2	£40	£100

Milled coinage.

2592

		F	VF
2589	**Shilling.** Without rose or date; *mm.* star. Plain dress, large size ..	£160	£425
2590	— decorated dress, large size (over 31 mm.)	£100	£300
2591	— — intermediate size (30-31 mm.)	£85	£250
2592	— — small size (under 30 mm.)	£90	£275
2593	**Sixpence.** Small bust, large rose, 1561; *mm.* star	£24	£75

2594

2601

		F	VF
2594	Tall narrow bust with plain dress, large rose, 1561-2, *mm.* star *from*	£24	£75
2595	— similar, but decorated dress, 1562	£22	£65
2596	Large broad bust, elaborately decorated dress, small rose, 1562; *mm.* star	£22	£65
2597	— — cross pattée on *rev.*, 1562-4; *mm.* star	£30	£100
2598	— similar, but with low ruff, pellet border, 1563-64, 1566	£32	£110
2599	Small bust, 1567-8; *mm.* lis	£30	£100
2600	Large crude bust breaking legend; 1570, *mm.* lis; 1571, *mm.* castle ..	£90	£225
2601	**Groat.** As illustration	£125	£350
2602	**Threepence.** With rose, small bust with plain dress, 1561 ..	£65	£175
2603	Tall narrow bust with large rose, 1562	£55	£150
2604	Short bust with small rose, 1562	£60	£160
2605	Cross pattée on *rev.*, 1563-4	£120	£325
2606	**Halfgroat.** As groat	£135	£400
2607	**Threefarthings.** E . D . G . ROSA, etc., with rose. ℞. CIVITAS LONDON, shield with 1563 above	*Extremely rare*	

Portcullis money.

Trade coins of 8, 4, 2 and 1 Testerns were coined at the Tower Mint in 1600/1 for the first voyage of the incorporated 'Company of Merchants of London Trading into the East Indies'. The coins bear the royal arms on the obverse and a portcullis on the reverse and have the *mm.* **O.** They were struck to the weights of the equivalent Spanish silver 8, 4, 2 and 1 reales.

JAMES I, 1603-25

With the accession of James VI of Scotland to the English throne, the royal titles and coat of arms are altered on the coinage; on the latter the Scottish rampant lion and the Irish harp now appear in the second and third quarters. In 1604 the weight of the gold pound was reduced and the new coin became known as the "Unite". Fine gold coins of 23½ carat and crown gold of 22 carat were both issued, and a gold four-shilling piece was struck 1604-1619. In 1612 all the gold coins had their values raised by 10%; but in 1619 the Unite was replaced by a new, lighter 20s. piece—the "Laurel", and a lighter rose-ryal, spur-ryal and angel Wece minted.

In 1613 the King granted Lord Harrington a licence to coin farthings of copper as a result of repeated public demands for a low value coinage; this was later taken over by the Duke of Lennox. Towards the end of the reign coins made from silver sent to the mint from the Welsh mines had the Prince of Wales's plumes inserted over the royal arms.

Mintmarks

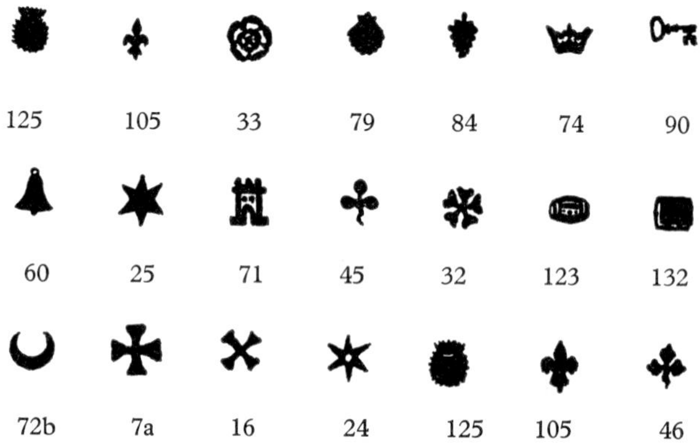

First coinage
1603-4 Thistle (125)
1604-5 Lis (105)
Second coinage
1605-6 Rose (33)
1606-7 Escallop (79)
1607 Grapes (84)
1607-9 Coronet (74)
1609-10 Key (90)
1610-1 Bell (60)
1611-2 Mullet (25)
1612-3 Tower (71)
1613 Trefoil (45)
1613-5 Cinquefoil (32)
1615-6 Tun (123)
1616-7 Closed book (132)
1617-8 Crescent (72b, gold)
1618-9 Plain cross (7a)
1619 Saltire cross (16)
Third coinage
1619-20 Spur rowel (24)
1620-1 Rose (33)
1621-3 Thistle (125)
1623-4 Lis (105)
1624 Trefoil (46)

GOLD

First coinage, 1603-4 (Obverse legend reads D'. G'. ANG : SCO : etc.).

2608

2612

2608	**Sovereign** (=20s.). King crowned r., half-length, first bust with plain armour. ℞. EXVRGAT, etc.; *mm.* thistle..	£850	£2000
2609	— second bust with decorated armour; *mm.* 125, 105	£900	£2250
2610	**Half-sovereign.** Crowned bust r. ℞. EXVRGAT, etc.; *mm.* thistle..	*Extremely rare*	
2611	**Crown.** Similar. ℞. TVEATVR, etc.; *mm.* 125, 105/125	*Extremely rare*	
2612	**Halfcrown.** Similar; *mm.* thistle, lis	£550	£1100

N.B. The Quarter-Angel of this coinage is considered to be a pattern, having the reverse of the half-crown.

Second coinage, 1604-19 (Obverse legend reads D' G' MAG : BRIT : etc.).

2613

2614

2613	**Rose-ryal** (=30s, 33s. from 1612). King enthroned. ℞. Shield on rose; *mm.* 33-90, 25-132	£1100	£2750
2614	**Spur ryal** (=15s, 16s. 6d. from 1612). King in ship; *mm.* 33, 79, 74, 25-32, 132	£2250	£6000
2615	**Angel** (=10s., 11s. from 1612). Old type; *mm.* 33-74, 60-16 ..	£400	£1000
2616	— pierced for use as touch-piece	£225	£450
2617	**Half-angel** (=5s., 5s. 6d. from 1612). Similar; *mm.* 71-132, 7a, 16	*Extremely rare*	

Second coinage gold.

2620

2627

		F	*VF*
2618	**Unite** (=20s, 22s. from 1612). Half-length second bust r. ℞. FACIAM etc.; *mm.* lis or rose	£350	£725
2619	— fourth bust; *mm.* rose to cinquefoil	£300	£625
2620	— fifth bust; *mm.* cinquefoil to saltire	£275	£575
2621	**Double-crown.** Third bust r. ℞. HENRICVS, etc.; *mm.* lis or rose	£225	£525
2622	Fourth bust; *mm.* rose to bell	£225	£525
2623	Fifth bust; *mm.* mullet to saltire	£250	£550
2624	**Britain crown.** First bust r.; *mm.* lis to coronet	£150	£300
2625	Third bust; *mm.* key to cinquefoil	£150	£300
2626	Fifth bust; *mm.* cinquefoil to saltire	£135	£275
2627	**Thistle crown** (=4s.). As illus.; *mm.* lis to cross	£135	£275
2628	— IR only on one side	£150	£300
2629	**Halfcrown.** I' D' G' ROSA SINE SPINA. First bust; *mm.* lis to coronet	£120	£215
2630	Third bust; *mm.* key to trefoil	£125	£225
2631	Fifth bust; *mm.* cinquefoil to cross	£115	£200

Third coinage, 1619-25

2632	**Rose-ryal.** (=30s.; 196½ grs.) King enthroned. ℞. XXX above shield; lis, lion and rose emblems around; *mm.* 24-105	£1500	£4250
2633	Similar but plain back to throne; *mm.* 46	£1600	£4500

2634

2635

2634	**Spur-ryal.** (=15s.) As illus.; *mm.* 24-125, 46	£1750	£3750
2635	**Angel** (=10s.) of new type; *mm.* 24-46	£700	£1500
2636	— pierced for use as touch-piece	£275	£600

		F	VF
2637	**Laurel** (=20s.; 140½ grs.). First (large) laur. bust l.; *mm.* 24 ..	£350	£750
2638	Second to fourth busts; *mm.* 24-46	£300	£650
2639	Fifth, small rather crude bust; *mm.* trefoil	*Extremely rare*	

2640

2642

2640	**Half-laurel.** First bust; *mm.* spur rowel	£275	£575
2641	Fourth bust; *mm.* 24-46	£235	£500
2642	**Quarter-laurel.** Second or fourth bust; *mm.* 24-46	£125	£275

For busts on the laurels, see North.

SILVER

First coinage, 1603-4

2643	**Crown.** King on horseback. ℞. EXVRGAT, etc., shield; *mm.* thistle, lis	£450	£1250
2644	**Halfcrown.** Similar	£250	£700
2645	**Shilling.** First bust, square-cut beard. ℞. EXVRGAT, etc.; *mm.* thistle	£32	£100
2646	— Second bust, pointed beard; *mm.* thistle, lis	£28	£85

2647

2648

2647	**Sixpence.** First bust; 1603, *mm.* thistle	£22	£65
2648	Second bust; 1603-4; *mm.* thistle, lis	£20	£60
2649	**Halfgroat.** As illustration but II; *mm.* thistle, lis	£20	£45
2650	**Penny.** Similar, but I behind head; *mm.* thistle, lis	£18	£40

2650

2651

2651	**Halfpenny.** As illustration; *mm.* thistle, lis	£17	£38

Second coinage, 1604-19

		F	*VF*
2652	**Crown.** King on horseback. ℞. QVAE DEVS, etc.; *mm.* 105-84 ..	£350	£900
2653	**Halfcrown.** Similar; *mm.* 105, 79, 123	£275	£750
2654	**Shilling.** Third bust, beard cut square and stands out (*cf.* illus. 2657); *mm.* lis, rose..	£26	£85
2655	— Fourth bust, armour plainer (*cf.* 2658); *mm.* 33-74	£22	£75
2656	— Fifth bust, similar, but hair longer; *mm.* 74-7a	£24	£80

2657

2658

2657	**Sixpence.** Third bust; 1604-5; *mm.* lis, rose	£20	£55
2658	— Fourth bust; 1605-15; *mm.* rose to tun	£17	£50
2658A	— Fifth bust, 1618; *mm.* plain cross		*Unique*

2660

2663

2659	**Halfgroat.** As illus. but larger crown on *obv.; mm.* lis to coronet ..	£10	£22
2660	— Similar, but smaller crown on *obv.; mm.* coronet to cross	£15	£32
2661	**Penny.** As halfgroat but no crowns; *mm.* lis to cross and none ..	£10	£22
2662	— As before but TVEATVR legend both sides; *mm.* mullet	*Extremely rare*	
2663	**Halfpenny.** As illus.; *mm.* lis to mullet, cinquefoil	£16	£35

Third coinage, 1619-25

2664	**Crown.** As 2652, but mostly with bird-headed harp, colon stops on *obv.*, no stops on *rev.; mm.* 33-46..	£275	£750
2665	— — plume over shield; *mm.* 125-46	£300	£800

2666

2667

2666	**Halfcrown.** As 2664; all have bird-headed harp	£120	£300
2667	— — plume over shield; *mm.* 125-46	£130	£350

		F	VF
2668	**Shilling.** Sixth (large) bust, hair longer and very curly; *mm.* 24-46	£22	£75
2669	— — plume over shield; *mm.* 125-46	£42	£125

2670

2672

2670	**Sixpence.** Sixth bust; 1621-4; *mm.* 33-46	£20	£55
2671	**Halfgroat.** As 2660 but no stops on *rev.; mm.* 24-46 and none ..	£9	£20
2672	**Penny.** As illus.; *mm.* 24, 105, 46 and none	£10	£22
2673	**Halfpenny.** As 2663, but no *mm.*	£15	£32

COPPER

For mintmarks, see our *British Copper Coins and Their Values*, or *English Copper Tin and Bronze Coins in the British Museum, 1558-1958.*

2674

2676

2679

2674	**Farthing.** "Harington", small size 1a, letter or other mark below crown (originally tinned surface) .. .. *from*	£25	£65
2675	— — 1b, central jewel on circlet with *mm.* below crown or unmodified	£30	£70
2676	— normal size 2, *mm.* on *rev.*	£15	£35
2677	"Lennox" 3a; *mm. rev.* only	£8	£25
2678	— 3b; *mm.* both sides	£5·50	£16
2679	— — 3c; *mm. obv.* only	£5·50	£16
2680	— — 3d; larger crown	£5·50	£16
2681	— 4; oval type, legend starts at bottom l.	£22	£45

CHARLES I, 1625-1649

Numismatically, this reign is one of the most interesting of all the English monarchs. Some outstanding machine-made coins were produced by Nicholas Briot, a French die-sinker, but they could not be struck at sufficient speed to supplant hand-hammering methods. In 1637 a branch mint was set up at Aberystwyth to coin silver extracted from the Welsh mines. After the king's final breach with Parliament the parliamentary government continued to issue coins at London with Charles's name and portrait until the king's trial and execution. The coinage of copper farthings continued to be manufactured privately under licences held first by the Duchess of Richmond, then by Lord Maltravers and later by various other persons. The licence was finally revoked by Parliament in 1644.

During the Civil War coins were struck at a number of towns to supply coinage for those areas of the country under Royalist control. Many of these coins have an abbreviated form of the "Declaration" made at Wellington, Shropshire, Sept., 1642, in which Charles promised to uphold the Protestant Religion, the Laws of England and the Liberty of Parliament. Amongst the more spectacular pieces are the gold triple unites and the silver pounds and half-pounds struck at Shrewsbury and Oxford, and the emergency coins, made from odd-shaped pieces of silver plate during the sieges of Newark, Scarborough, Carlisle and Pontefract.

Mintmarks

105 10 96 71 57 88 101 35

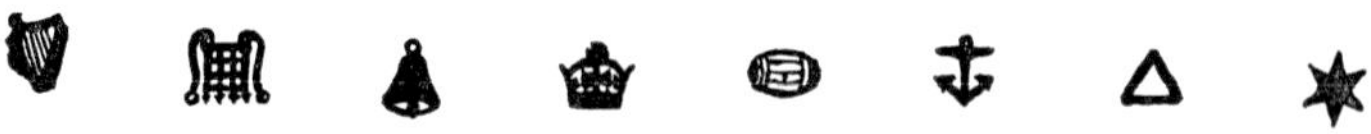

87 107 60 75 123 57 119a 23

119b 98 112 81 120 109

Tower Mint under Charles I
1625 Lis (105)
1625-6 Cross Calvary (10)
1626-7 Negro's head (96)
1627-8 Castle (71)
1628-9 Anchor (57)
1629-30 Heart (88)
1630-1 Plume (101)
1631-2 Rose (35)
1632-3 Harp (87)
1633-4 Portcullis (107)
1634-5 Bell (60)
1635-6 Crown (75)
1636-8 Tun (123)
1638-9 Anchor (57)
1639-40 Triangle (119a)
1640-1 Star (23)
1641-3 Triangle in circle (119b)

Tower Mint under Parliament
1643-4 P in brackets (98)
1644-5 R in brackets (112)
1645 Eye (81)
1645-6 Sun (120)
1646-8 Sceptre (109)

59 B 58 *var* 58

Briot's Mint
1631-2 Flower and B (59)
1632 B
1638-9 Anchor and B (58)
Anchor and mullet

Footnote. On mint mark no. 58 the 'B' below the anchor should be shown as

61 104 35 92 103 6 65b 71

89 91 *var.* 131 84 94 *var.* 64 93 34

102 67 127 128 129 25 83 100

71 130 A B 75

Provincial Mints

1638-42	Book (61, *Aberystwyth*)
1642	Plume (104, *Shrewsbury*)
	Pellets or pellet (*Shrewsbury*)
1642-3	Rose (35, *Truro*)
1642-4	Lion (92, *York*)
1642-6	Plume (103, *Oxford*)
	Pellet or pellets (*Oxford*)
	Lis (105, *Oxford*)
1643	Cross pattée (6, *Bristol*)
	Acorn (65b, *Bristol*)
	Castle (71, *Weymouth*)
	Helmet (89, *Weymouth* and ? *Salisbury*)
1643-4	Leopard's head (91 *var.* ? *Weymouth*)
	Two lions (131, *Weymouth*)
	Lis (105, *Wey.* or *Sal.*)
	Bunch of grapes (84, *Weymouth* or *Salisbury*)
	Bird (*Wey.* or *Sal.*)
1643-4	Boar's head (*Wey.* or *Sal.*)
	Lion rampant (93)
	Rosette (34, *Wey.* or *Sal.*)
1643-5	Plume (102, *Bristol*)
	Br. (67, *Bristol*)
	Pellets (*Bristol*)
	Rose (35, *Exeter*)
	Rosette (34, *Oxford*)
1643-6	Floriated cross (127, *Oxford*)
1644	Cross pattée (6, *Oxford*)
	Lozenge (128, *Oxford*)
	Billet (129, *Oxford*)
	Mullet (25, *Oxford*)
1644-6	Gerb (83, *Chester*)
	Pear (100, *Worcester*)
	Lis (105, *uncertain mint*)
	Castle (71, *Exeter*)
	Plume (130, see p. 182)
	A (Ditto)
1646	B (Ditto)
1648-9	Crown (75, *Aberystwyth-Furnace*)

GOLD

Tower mint, under the King, 1625-42.

2687

2682	**Angel.** As for James I last issue, without mark of value; *mm.* lis and cross calvary	£650	£1400
2683	— — pierced for use as touch-piece	£300	£600

Tower Gold

		F	*VF*
2684	— x in field to r.; *mm.* 96-88	£550	£1150
2685	— — — pierced for use as touch-piece	£300	£600
2686	— x in field to l.; *mm.* 96, 88, 35-119a, 119b	£500	£1100
2687	— — — pierced for use as touch-piece	£250	£500

2688

2697

2688	**Unite** (=20s.). First bust with ruff and collar of order, high double-crown. ℞. Square-topped shield; *mm.* 105, 10	£300	£625
2689	— Similar, but flat single-arched crown	£300	£650
2690	Second bust with ruff and armour nearly concealed with scarf; *mm.* 10-101	£275	£625
2691	— — *mm.* anchor below bust	*Extremely rare*	
2692	Third bust, more armour visible. ℞. Oval shield with CR at sides; *mm.* 101, 35	£300	£650
2693	Fourth bust, small lace collar, Garter ribbon on breast. ℞. Oval shield with crowned CR at sides; *mm.* 87-23	£325	£675
2694	Sixth (Briot's) bust, large lace collar. ℞. Similar; *mm.* 57-119b	£350	£725
2695	— — with Briot's *rev.; mm.* 57	*Extremely rare*	
2696	**Double-crown.** First bust. ℞. Square-topped shield; *mm.* 105, 10	£210	£475
2697	Second bust. ℞. Similar; *mm.* 10-101	£190	£425
2698	Third bust. ℞. Oval shield with CR at sides; *mm.* 101, 35	£275	£575
2699	Fourth bust. ℞. Oval shield with crowned CR at sides; *mm.* 87-57	£225	£500
2700	Fifth bust as Aberystwyth silver. ℞. Similar; *mm.* 57, 119a	£300	£625
2701	Sixth bust. ℞. Normal; *mm.* 57-119b	£275	£575
2702	— ℞. Briot's square-topped shield; *mm.* 57	*Extremely rare*	
2703	**Crown.** First bust. ℞. Square-topped shield; *mm.* 105, 10	£135	£250
2704	Second bust. ℞. Similar; *mm.* 10-101	£125	£225
2705	— — ℞. As next; 101, 35	£150	£275
2706	Third bust. ℞. Oval shield with CR at sides; *mm.* 101	*Extremely rare*	
2707	Fourth bust. ℞. Oval shield with crowned CR at sides; *mm.* 87-119b	£135	£250
2708	Fifth (Aberystwyth) bust. ℞. Similar; *mm.* 57	£185	£350
2709	Sixth (Briot's) bust. ℞. Similar; *mm.* 57		*Unique*

Gold

2703

2714

Tower mint, under Parliament, 1643-8. All Charles I types.

		F	*VF*
2710	**Unite.** Fourth bust, as 2693; *mm.* (P)	£450	£950
2711	Sixth bust, as 2964; *mm.* (P), (R)	£525	£1100
2712	Seventh bust, cruder style; *mm.* 81-109	£550	£1200
2713	**Double-crown.** Fourth bust, as 2699; *mm.* eye	*Extremely rare*	
2714	Fifth bust, as 2700; *mm.* sun, sceptre	£425	£900
2715	Sixth bust, as 2701; *mm.* (P)	£525	£1150
2716	Seventh bust, as 2712; *mm.* sun		*Unique*
2717	**Crown.** Fourth bust, as 2707; *mm.* (P) to sceptre	£375	£800

Nicholas Briot's coinage, 1631-2.

2718 **Angel.** Type as Tower but smaller and neater; *mm.* -/B .. .. *Extremely rare*

2719

2719	**Unite.** As illustration. ℞. FLORENT etc.	£900	£2250
2720	**Double-crown.** Similar but X. ℞. CVLTORES, etc.	£750	£1750
2721	**Crown.** Similar; *mm.* B	*Extremely rare*	

Provincial issues, 1638-49.

Unknown mint (Chester ?)

2722 **Unite.** As Tower. Sixth bust but CR not crowned; *mm.* plume *Extremely rare*

Shrewsbury mint, 1642

2723 **Triple unite,** 1642. Half-length figure l. holding sword and olive-branch; *mm.* : ℞. EXVRGAT, etc., around RELIG PROT, etc., in two wavy lines, III and three plumes above, date below .. .. .. *Unique ?*

Oxford mint, 1642-6

2724

No.	Description	F	VF
2724	**Triple unite.** As last, but *mm.* plume, tall narrow bust, 1642 ..	£2750	£6500
2725	Similar, but "Declaration" on continuous scroll, 1642-3	£3000	£7000
2726	As last, but larger bust, with scarf behind shoulder, 1643	£3250	£7500
2727	Similar, but without scarf, 1643	£2500	£6500
2728	Similar, but OXON below 1643, rosette stops	*Extremely rare*	
2729	Smaller size, 1644 / OXON	£3000	£7000
2730	— 1644 / OX	£3250	£7500
2731	**Unite.** Tall thin bust. ℞. "Declaration" in two wavy lines, 1642 ..	£650	£1400
2732	— ℞. "Declaration" in three lines on continuous scroll, 1642-3 ..	£650	£1400
2733	Larger bust. ℞. Similar, 1643	£750	£1600
2734	Shorter bust. ℞. Similar, 1643, 1645; *mm.* plume	£550	£1250

2735

No.	Description	F	VF
2735	— — 1644 / OX; *mm.* plume	£650	£1400
2736	Tall bust to edge of coin. ℞. Similar, 1643	£800	£1700
2737	As 2734. ℞. "Declaration" in three straight lines, 1644 / OX ..	*Extremely rare*	
2738	Longer, narrower bust. ℞. Similar	£725	£1550
2739	— ℞. Single plume above "Declaration", 1645-6 / OX	£800	£1700
2740	**Half-unite.** "Declaration" in three straight lines, 1642	*Extremely rare*	
2741	"Declaration" on scroll; *mm.* plume; 1642-3	£925	£1900
2742	Bust to bottom of coin, 1643	£750	£1550
2743	— 1644 / OX	*Extremely rare*	

Bristol mint, 1645

2744 **Unite.** Somewhat as 2734; *mm.* Br; 1645 .. .. *Extremely rare*

2745 **Half-unite.** Similar .. .. *Unique?*

Truro mint, 1642-3

2746 **Unite.** *Mm.* rose. ℞. FLORENT, etc., crowned oval shield between C R .. .. *Unique*

2747 — ℞. CVLTORES, etc., similar but no C R .. .. *Extremely rare*

Weymouth mint, 1643-4

2748 **Unite.** No *mm.* ℞. FLORENT, etc., double annulet stops, crowned oval shield, lion's paws on either side of garniture .. .. .. *Extremely rare*

Salisbury (or Sandsfoot Castle) mint, 1644

2749 **Unite.** As last, but *mm.* lis .. .. *Unique?*

Colchester besieged, 1648

2750 **Ten shillings.** Gateway of castle between CR; below OBS COL 16 $\frac{S}{X}$ 48 *Extremely rare*

Pontefract besieged, 1648-9. After the death of Charles I, in the name of Charles II.

2751 **Unite.** DVM : SPIRO : SPERO around CR crowned. ℞. CAROLVS : SECVNDVS : 1648, castle, OBS on l., PC above. *Octagonal* .. .. *Extremely rare*

2752 CAROL : II, etc., around HANC : DEVS, etc. ℞. POST : MORTEM, etc., around castle. *Octagonal* .. .. *Extremely rare*

SILVER

Tower mint, under the King, 1625-42.

2759

		F	VF
2753	**Crown.** King on horseback with raised sword. 1a. Horse caparisoned with plume on head and crupper. ℞. Square-topped shield over long cross fourchée; *mm.* 105, 10	£300	£850
2754	— 1b. Similar, but plume over shield, no cross; *mm.* 105, 10, 71 ..	£750	£1750
2755	— 2a. Smaller horse, plume on hd. only, cross on housings, king holds sword on shoulder. ℞. Oval garnished shield over cross fourchée, CR above; *mm.* harp	£275	£700
2756	— 2b^1. — — plume divides CR, no cross; *mm.* 101, 35	£320	£800
2757	— 2b^2. — — — with cross; *mm.* harp	£400	£1000

Tower Silver

		F	VF
2758	— 3a. Horse with caparisons. ℞. Oval shield without CR; *mm.* 60-23	£300	£750
2759	— 3b. — — plume over shield; *mm.* 107, 75, 123	£320	£800
2760	"Briot" horse with ground-line; *mm.* 119b	£600	£1500

2762

2761	**Halfcrown.** As 2753. $1a^1$. Rose on housings, ground-line; *mm.* lis ..	£80	£200
2762	— $1a^2$. Similar, but no rose or ground-line; *mm.* lis	£90	£225
2763	— $1a^3$. As last but clumsier horse and shield not over cross; *mm.* 10-71	£75	£185
2764	— $1a^4$. — — with ground-line; *mm.* lis	£450	£1000
2765	— 1b. — — plume over shield; *mm.* lis to anchor	£350	£750
2766	— 2/1b. As 2755 but rose on housings. ℞. As last; *mm.* heart, plume	£425	£1000
2767	— 2a. As 2755. ℞. Flattened oval garnished shield without cross, CR above; *mm.* plume, rose	£40	£110
2768	— 2b. Similar, but plume between the CR	£150	£325
2769	— 2c. As 2a, but differently garnished oval shield with CR at sides; *mm.* harp, portcullis	£38	£90
2770	— 2d. Similar, but with plume over shield; *mm.* harp	£275	£625

2771

2775

2771	— $3a^1$. No caparisons on horse, upright sword, scarf flies out from waist. ℞. Round garnished shield, no CR; *mm.* 57, 60-123.. ..	£20	£75
2772	— 3b. — — plume over shield; *mm.* 107-123	£130	£325
2773	— $3a^2$. — cloak flies from king's shoulder; *mm.* 123-23	£20	£75
2774	— — — — rough ground beneath horse; *mm.* 119a, 23	£20	£75
2775	— 4. Foreshortened horse, mane before chest, tail between legs; *mm.* 23, 119b	£18	£70

Tower Silver

2776

		F	*VF*
2776	**Shilling.** 1. Bust in ruff. ℞. Square-topped shield over cross fourchée; *mm.* lis, cross Calvary (Normal weight $92\frac{3}{4}$ grs.)	£25	£75
2777	— — — light weight ($81\frac{33}{47}$ grs.); *mm.* 10	£85	£185
2778	— $1b^1$. As 2776, but plume over shield, no cross; *mm.* 105, 10 ..	£100	£250
2779	— 1a. Bust in ruff and armour concealed by scarf. ℞. As 2776; 10-71	£35	£90
2780	— — — — light weight; *mm.* cross Calvary	£90	£225
2781	— $1b^2$. As 2779, but plume over shield, no cross; *mm.* 10-101 ..	£38	£100
2782	— $1b^3$. — — — cross; *mm.* negro's head	£350	£750
2783	— 2a. More armour visible. ℞. Oval shield, CR above; *mm.* plume, rose	£22	£70
2784	— 2b. — — plume over shield; *mm.* 101, 35	£100	£250
2785	— 3^1. Bust with lace collar. ℞. Flattish oval shield, CR at sides; *mm.* harp, portcullis	£20	£62
2786	— 3^2. — — plume over shield; *mm.* harp	£225	£450
2787	— 3a. — no inner circles, rounder shield without CR; *mm.* 60-123 ..	£18	£60
2788	— 3b. — — plume over shield; *mm.* 60-123	£55	£125

2787

2791

2793

2789	— 4^1. Large Aberystwyth bust, small XII. ℞. Square-topped shield over cross fleury; *mm.* tun..	£20	£65
2790	— 4^1. var. Similar, but rounder shoulders, large XII; *mm.* 57, 119a..	£15	£50
2791	— 4^2. Smaller Aberystwyth bust with small double-arched crown, small XII; *mm.* tun	£16	£55
2792	— 4^3. — single-arches, large XII; *mm.* 123, 57, 119a	£15	£50
2793	— 4^4. Older (Briot's style) bust, very pointed beard; *mm.* 57-119b	£14	£45

Tower Silver

2797

2799

		F	VF
2794	**Sixpence.** 1. As 2776, but dated 1625-6; *mm.* 105, 10	£28	£80
2795	— 1a^{1}. As 2779, but dated 1625-9; *mm.* 10-88	£32	£95
2796	— 1a^{2}. — no cross, 1629-30; *mm.* 88, 101	£38	£110
2797	— 2a. As 2783, no date; *mm.* plume, rose	£25	£80
2798	— 2b.— plume dividing CR; *mm.* plume and rose	£22	£65
2799	— 3. As 2785; *mm.* harp, portcullis	£20	£60
2800	— 3a. — no inner circles; *mm.* 60-123	£15	£45
2801	— 4^{1}. As first Aberystwyth sixpence, large VI. ℞. Square-topped shield over cross; *mm.* tun	£18	£55
2802	— 4^{1}. var. — similar, but small VI; *mm.* tun and anchor	£24	£75
2803	— 4^{2}. Second Aberystwyth bust, double-arched crown; *mm.* 57, 119a	£13	£40
2804	— 4^{2}. var. — single-arched crown; *mm.* 119a	£26	£80
2805	— 4^{3}. Older (Briot's style) bust; *mm.* 119a-119b	£12	£35

2806

2808

2818

		F	VF
2806	**Halfgroat.** 1. Crowned rose type; *mm.* 105-96	£9	£25
2807	— 1a. — without inner circles; *mm.* 96-101	£9	£25
2808	— 2a. King's bust in ruff and mantle. ℞. Oval shield; *mm.* plume, rose	£9	£25
2809	— 2b. Similar, but with plume over shield	£22	£55
2810	— 3^{1}. Bust with lace collar. ℞. Oval shield between CR; no inner circles; *mm.* harp, crown, portcullis	£9	£25
2811	— 3^{2}. — — inner circles; *mm.* harp, portcullis	£9	£25
2812	— 3^{3}. — — inner circle on *rev.; mm.* similar	£10	£30
2813	— 3^{4}. — — inner circle on *obv.; mm.* similar	£9	£25
2814	— 3^{5}. — — no CR, i.cs.; *mm.* portcullis	£9	£25
2815	— 3^{6}. — — — i.c. on *obv.; mm.* portcullis	£9	£25
2816	— 3a^{1}. — ℞. Rounder shield, different garniture, no i.cs.; *mm.* 60-119b	£9	£25
2817	— 3a^{2}. — — i.c. on *obv.; mm.* triangle	£9	£25
2818	— 3a^{3}. — — i.cs. both sides; *mm.* 119a-119b	£9	£25
2819	— 3a^{4}. Aberystwyth bust, no i.cs.; *mm.* anchor	£9	£25
2820	— 3a^{5}. — i.c. on *rev.; mm.* anchor	£9	£25
2821	— 3a^{6}. Very small bust, no i.cs.; *mm.* anchor	£9	£25

Tower Silver

2822 2829 2837

		F	VF
2822	**Penny.** 1. Rose each side; i.cs.; *mm.* negro's head, lis/:, one or two pellets	£8	£25
2823	— 1a. — no i.cs.; *mm.* lis, one or two pellets, anchor	£8	£25
2824	— 1b. — i.c. on *rev.; mm.* negro's head/two pellets	£10	£30
2825	— 2. Bust in ruff and mantle. ℞. Oval shield; i.cs.; *mm.* plume	£10	£30
2826	— 2^1. — — no i.cs.; *mm.* plume	£12	£35
2827	— $2a^1$. More armour visible; no i.cs.; *mm.* plume, rose	£9	£25
2828	— $2a^2$. — i.c. on *obv.; mm.* plume, rose	£12	£35
2829	— $2a^3$. — i.c.s. both sides; *mm.* plume, rose	£10	£30
2830	— $2a^4$. — i c. on *rev.; mm.* rose/plume	£20	£55
2831	— 3^1. Bust in lace collar. ℞. CR at sides of shield; no i.cs.; *mm.* harp, one or two pellets	£9	£25
2832	— 3^2. — similar but no CR; *mm.* as last and 107	£10	£30
2833	— 3^3. — — i.c. on *obv.; mm.* harp	£10	£30
2834	— 3^4. — — i.c. on *rev.; mm.* harp	£10	£30
2835	— $3a^1$. — similar, but shield almost round and with scroll garniture; no i.cs.; *mm.* bell, triangle, one or two pellets	£8	£22
2836	— $3a^3$. Aberystwyth bust; *mm.* one or two pellets or none	£8	£22
2837	**Halfpenny.** Rose each side; no legend or *mm.*	£18	£48

Tower mint, under Parliament, 1642-8. All Charles I type.

		F	VF
2838	**Crown.** 4. Foreshortened horse; *mm.* (P) to sun	£285	£725
2839	— 5. Tall spirited horse; *mm.* sun	£325	£850
2840	**Halfcrown.** $3a^3$. As 2773, but coarse work; *mm.* (P) to sun	£17	£65
2841	— 4. Foreshortened horse; *mm.* (P)	*Extremely rare*	
2842	— 5. Tall horse; *mm.* sun, sceptre	£30	£100
2843	**Shilling.** 4^4. Briot style bust but coarse work; *mm.* (P) to sun	£14	£45

2844 2845

		F	VF
2844	— 4^5. Long narrow coarse bust; *mm.* sun, sceptre	£20	£65
2845	— 4^6. Short broad older bust; *mm.* sceptre	£24	£80

Tower Silver

		F	VF
2846	**Sixpence.** 4^3. Briot style bust; *mm.* (P) to sun	£28	£80
2847	— 4^4. Late Aberystwyth bust; *mm.* (R) to sceptre	£20	£60
2848	— 4^5. Squat bust of crude style; *mm.* eye and sun	£70	£200
2849	**Halfgroat.** $3a^3$. As 2818; *mm.* (P) to sceptre	£16	£50
2850	— $3a^7$. Older, shorter bust, pointed beard; *mm.* eye to sceptre ..	£16	£50
2851	**Penny.** $3a^2$. Older bust; *mm.* pellets	£15	£45

Nicholas Briot's coinage, 1631-9.

First milled issue, 1631-2.

		F	VF
2852	**Crown.** King on horseback. ℞. Crowned shield between C R crowned; *mm.* flower and B / B	£400	£900
2853	**Halfcrown.** Similar	£250	£550
2854	**Shilling.** Briot's early bust with falling lace collar. ℞. Square-topped shield over long cross fourchée; *mm.* as before..	£140	£300
2855	**Sixpence.** Similar, but VI behind bust	£70	£150

2855

2856

		F	VF
2856	**Halfgroat.** Briot's bust, B below, II behind. ℞. IVSTITIA, etc., square-topped shield over long cross fourchée	£40	£90
2857	**Penny.** Similar, but I behind bust	£35	£80

Second milled issue, 1638-9.

2858

		F	VF
2858	**Halfcrown.** As 2853, but *mm.* anchor and B	£175	£450
2859	**Shilling.** Briot's late bust, the falling lace collar is plain with broad lace border, no scarf. ℞. As 2854 but cross only to inner circle; *mm.* anchor and B	£65	£150
2860	**Sixpence.** Similar, but VI; *mm.* 57, anchor and mullet	£40	£100

Briot's hammered issue, 1638-9

		F	*VF*
2861	**Halfcrown.** King on Briot's style horse with ground line. ℞. Square-topped garnished shield; *mm* anchor, triangle over anchor	£450	£1000
2862	**Shilling.** As 2859; *mm.* anchor, triangle over anchor. ℞. Square-topped shield over short cross fleury	£350	£800

Provincial and Civil War issues, 1638-49

York mint, 1643-4. *Mm.* lion.

2863	**Halfcrown.** 1. Ground-line below horse. ℞. Square-topped shield between CR	£200	£550
2864	— 2. — ℞. Oval shield as Tower 3a	£225	£650
2865	— 3. No ground-line. ℞. Shield somewhat flattened	£185	£525
2866	— 4. As last, but EBOR below horse with head held low. Base metal, often very base	£160	£475
2867	— 5. Tall horse, mane in front of chest, EBOR below. ℞. Crowned square-topped shield between CR, flowers in legend	£150	£450
2868	— 6. As last, but shield is oval, garnished	£135	£425

2869

2869	— 7. Similar, but horse's tail shows between legs. ℞. Shield as last, but with lion's skin garniture, no CR or flowers	£120	£400
2870	**Shilling.** 1. Bust as Tower 3^1. ℞. EBOR above square-topped shield over cross fleury	£80	£250
2871	— 2. Similar, but bust in plain armour, mantle; coarse work	£100	£300
2872	— 3. — ℞. EBOR below oval shield	£100	£300
2873	— 4. — Similar, but crowned oval shield	£80	£250
2874	— 5. — As last, but lion's skin garniture	£80	£250

2876

2877

2875	**Sixpence.** Crowned oval shield	£135	£300
2876	— — C R at sides	£100	£225
2877	**Threepence.** As type 1 shilling, but III behind bust	£65	£135

Aberystwyth mint, 1638/9-42. *Mm.* book.
Plume 1=with coronet and band. Plume 2=with coronet only.

		F	VF
2878	**Halfcrown.** King on horseback, small plume 2 behind. ℞. Oval garnished shield with large plume above	£300	£750
2879	— plume 1 behind King, ground below horse	£350	£850
2880	As 2878, but more spirited horse, no ground, FRAN ET HIB	£400	£950
2881	**Shilling.** Bust with large square lace collar, plume 2 before, small XII. ℞. As before. No inner circles	£135	£300
2882	— inner circle on *rev.*	£150	£350
2883	As 2881, but large plume 1, large XII, inner circles	£135	£300
2884	As last, but small head, rounded lace collar	£150	£350
2885	Briot's bust as Tower 4[4], small square lace collar, plume 2, inner circles	£175	£400

2886

		F	VF
2886	**Sixpence.** As 2881, but small VI; no inner circles	£140	£325
2887	As 2884, but plume 2, inner circle *obv.*	£175	£385
2888	Similar, but with inner circles both sides	£140	£325
2889	— — later *rev.* with smaller square-shaped plume	£135	£300
2890	Bust as the first Oxford sixpence; with crown cutting inner circle	£175	£385
2891	**Groat.** Large bust, lace collar, no armour on shoulder Crown breaks inner circle. ℞. Shield, plume 1 or 2	£38	£80
2892	— Similar, armour on shoulder, shorter collar. ℞. Similar	£42	£90
2893	— Smaller, neater bust not breaking circle. ℞. Similar	£38	£80

2892

2894

2895-9

		F	VF
2894	**Threepence.** Small bust, reads M . B . FR . ET . H. ℞. Shield, plume 1 or 2 above	£28	£60
2895	— Similar, but HI. ℞. Shield, plume 2 above	£30	£65
2896	— M : B : FR : ET . HI : ℞. Similar	£30	£65
2897	— M . B . F . ET . HIB. ℞. Similar	£35	£75
2898	— M : B : F : ET : HIB : ℞. Similar	£35	£75
2899	— MAG : B : F : ET . H : ℞. Similar	£32	£70

	Aberystwyth, *continued*	*F*	*VF*
2900	**Halfgroat.** Bust as 2881. ℞. Large plume. No i.cs.	£75	£200
2901	Bust with round lace collar; inner circles	£75	£200
2902	Briot's bust, square lace collar; inner circles	£75	£200

2905

2907

2903	**Penny.** As 2900; CARO; no inner circles	£50	£135
2904	As 2901; CARO; inner circles	£50	£135
2905	As 2903; CAROLVS; inner circles	£45	£120
2906	Similar, but Briot's bust; inner circles	£60	£150
2907	**Halfpenny.** No legend. *O.* Rose. ℞. Plume	£100	£250

Aberystwyth-Furnace mint, 1648-9. *Mm.* crown.

2908	**Halfcrown.** King on horseback. ℞. As 2878	£600	£1500
2909	**Shilling.** Aberystwyth type, but *mm.* crown	*Extremely rare*	
2910	**Sixpence.** Similar	*Extremely rare*	

2911

2913

2911	**Groat.** Similar	£135	£275
2912	**Threepence.** Similar	£175	£350
2913	**Halfgroat.** Similar. ℞. Large plume	£185	£375
2914	**Penny.** Similar	£600	£1250

Uncertain mint

2915

		fair	*fine*
2915	**Halfcrown.** As illustration, dated 1645	£600	£1500
2916	— — undated	*Extremely rare*	

Shrewsbury mint, 1642. *Mm.* plume without band.

		F	VF
2917	**Pound.** King on horseback, plume behind, Aberystwyth style. R. Declaration between two straight lines, XX and three Shrewsbury plumes above, 1642 below	£650	£1500
2918	Similar, but Shrewsbury horse walking over pile of arms	£600	£1350
2919	As last, but cannon amongst arms and only single plume and XX above Declaration	£750	£1750
2920	**Half-pound.** As 2917, but X	£375	£950
2921	Similar, but only two plumes on *rev.*	£450	£1150
2922	Shrewsbury horseman with ground-line	£375	£950
2923	— with cannon and arms below horse	£325	£850
2924	— no cannon in arms, no plume on *obv.*	£325	£850

2926

2925	**Crown.** Aberystwyth horseman		*Unique*
2926	Shrewsbury horseman with ground-line	£300	£750
2927	**Halfcrown.** *O.* From Aberystwyth die; *mm.* book. R. Single plume above Declaration, 1642	£250	£625
2928	Aberystwyth horseman, fat plume behind. R. Three plumes above Declaration	£165	£400
2929	Shrewsbury horseman. R. As 2927, single plume	£185	£475
2930	— R. 2: plume: 6. above Declaration	£300	£750
2931	— with ground-line. R. Similar	£275	£650
2932	— — R. As 2927, single plume	£175	£450
2933	— — R Three thin plumes above Declaration	£110	£300
2934	— — — no plume behind king	£125	£325
2935	**Shilling.** *O.* From Aberystwyth die; *mm.* book. R. Declaration type	£135	£300
2936	*O.* From Shrewsbury die. R. Similar	£150	£350

Oxford mint, 1642/3-6. *Mm.* usually plume with band, except on the smaller denominations when it is lis or pellets. There were so many dies used at this mint that we can only give a selection of the more identifiable varieties.

		F	VF
2937	**Pound.** Large horseman over arms, no exergual line, fine workmanship. R. Three Shrewsbury plumes and XX above Declaration, 1642 below	£1000	£2500

2937

2938	— Similar, but three Oxford plumes, 1643	£1000	£2500
2939	Shrewsbury horseman trampling on arms, exergual line. ℞. As last, 1642	£800	£2000
2940	— — cannon amongst arms, 1642-3	£750	£1850
2941	— as last but exergue is chequered, 1642	£900	£2250
2942	Briot's horseman, 1643	£1350	£3000
2943	*O*. As 2937. ℞. Declaration in cartouche, single large plume above, 1644 OX below	£1500	£3500
2944	**Half-pound.** As next. ℞. Shrewsbury die, 1642	£375	£850
2945	Oxford dies both sides, 1642-3	£350	£800
2946	**Crown.** *O*. Shrewsbury die with ground-line. ℞. As last but v	£375	£850
2947	Oxford horseman with grass below, 1643	£500	£1250
2948	By Rawlins. King riding over a view of the city. ℞. Floral scrolls above and below Declaration, 1644 / OXON below (Beware forgeries!)	*Extremely rare*	

Note. An extremely fine specimen sold at auction in June 1974 for £20,000.

2949	**Halfcrown.** *O*. From Shrewsbury die, 1642	£150	£450
2950	℞. From Shrewsbury die, 1642	£120	£350
2951	Both Oxford dies, but Shrewsbury type horse, ground-line, 1642 ..	£80	£225
2952	— — without ground-line, 1642..	£100	£300
2953	Oxford type horse, ground-line, 1643	£85	£265

2954

2954	— without ground-line, 1643	£80	£250

Oxford Silver *continued*

No.	Description	*F*	*VF*
2955	**Halfcrown.** Briot's horse, grass below, 1643	£90	£275
2956	— — large central plume, 1643, 1644 / ox	£100	£325
2957	— lumpy ground, 1643, 1643 / ox	£90	£250
2958	— — large central plume, 1643-4 / ox	£90	£275
2959	— plain ground, 1644-5 / ox	£90	£275
2960	— — large central plume, 1644 / ox	£90	£275
2961	— — — Similar, but large date in script	£120	£400
2962	— — — two small plumes at date, 1644 / ox	£250	£600
2963	Large horse (as Briot's, but clumsier), plain ground, 1644-5 / ox	£100	£350
2964	— lumpy ground, 1644-5 / ox	£100	£350
2965	— — large central plume, 1644 / ox	£100	£350
2966	— pebbly ground, 1645-6 / ox	£100	£350
2967	— — pellets or annulets by plumes and at date, 1645-6 / ox	£100	£350
2968	— grass below, 1645-6 / ox	£110	£380
2969	— — rosettes by plumes and at date, 1645 / ox	£125	£450
2970	**Shilling.** *O.* From Shrewsbury die. ℞. Declaration type, 1642	£85	£225
2971	Both Oxford dies. Small bust, 1642-3	£65	£175
2972	Similar, but coarser work, 1643	£65	£175
2973	Large bust of fine work, 1643	£65	£175
2974	— 1644-6 / ox	£75	£200
2975	Bust with bent crown, 1643	£75	£200
2976	— 1644 / ox	£75	£200
2977	Rawlins' dies. Fine bust with R on truncation, 1644	£90	£265
2978	— — 1644 / ox	£100	£300
2979	Small size, 1646, annulets or pellets at date	£110	£325

2980

No.	Description	*F*	*VF*
2980	**Sixpence.** *O.* Aberystwyth die. ℞. With three Oxford plumes, 1642-3	£135	£300
2981	— ℞. With three Shrewsbury plumes, 1643	£135	£300
2982	— ℞. With Shrewsbury plume and two lis, 1644 / ox	£150	£350

2985

2991

No.	Description	*F*	*VF*
2983	**Groat.** *O.* Aberystwyth die. ℞. As 2985	£50	£125
2984	As last but three plumes above Declaration	£100	£235

Oxford Silver *continued*

		F	VF
2985	**Groat.** As illustration, with lion's head on shoulder	£60	£175
2986	Large bust reaching to top of coin. ℞. As last	£60	£175
2987	Large bust to bottom of coin, lion's head on shoulder, legend starts at bottom l. ℞. As last	£70	£200
2988	Rawlins' die; similar, but no i.c., and with R on shoulder. ℞. As last	£70	£200
2989	*O.* As 2985. ℞. Large single plume and scroll above Declaration, 1645	£70	£200
2990	*O.* As 2987. ℞. As last	£70	£200
2991	*O.* As 2988. ℞. Large single plume above Declaration, which is in cartouche, 1645-6	£100	£265
2992	**Threepence.** *O.* Aberystwyth die. ℞. Declaration type, 1644 / ox	£50	£130
2993	Rawlins' die, R below shoulder. ℞. Aberystwyth die with oval shield; *mm.* book	£50	£130
2994	— ℞. Declaration type, three lis above, 1644 below	£50	£130
2995	— Similar, without the R, 1646 (over 1644)	£50	£130
2996	**Halfgroat.** ℞. Aberystwyth type with large plume	£60	£150
2997	— ℞. Declaration type, 1644 / ox	£85	£180

2995

2999

		F	VF
2998	**Penny.** *O.* Aberystwyth die; *mm.* book. ℞. Type, small plume	£75	£175
2999	— — ℞. Type, large plume	£75	£175
3000	— Rawlins' die with R. ℞. Type, small plume	£75	£175
3001	— Wider bust similar to the halfgroat. ℞. Similar	£90	£250
3002	— — ℞. Declaration type, 1644	£200	£550

Bristol mint, 1643-5. *Mm.* usually plume or Br., except on small denominations.

		F	VF
3003	**Halfcrown.** *O.* Oxford die. ℞. Declaration, three Bristol plumes above, 1643 below	£95	£335
3004	— — Br. *mm.* on *rev.*, 1643	£90	£325
3005	King wears unusual flat crown, *obv. mm.* acorn? between four pellets. ℞. As 3003, 1643	£110	£350
3006	— Br. *mm.* on *rev.*, 1643-4	£110	£350
3007	Shrewsbury plume behind king. ℞. As last	£80	£250
3008	— Br. below date, 1644	£85	£300

Bristol Silver *continued*

3009

3024

		F	VF
3009	**Halfcrown.** Br. below horse and below date, 1644-5	£125	£375
3010	Br. also *mm.* on *rev.*, 1644-5	£100	£300
3011	**Shilling.** *O.* Oxford die. ℞. Declaration, 1643	£85	£250
3012	— — Similar, but Br. as *rev. mm.*, 1643-4	£85	£250
3013	Crude bust. ℞. As 3011, 1643	£85	£250
3014	— — Similar, but Br. as *rev. mm.*, 1644	£85	£250
3015	Bust of good style, plumelet before. ℞. As last, 1644-5	£85	£250
3016	— — Similar, but Br. below date instead of as *mm.*, 1644	£90	£275
3017	Bust with round collar, *mm.* Br. on its side. ℞. As last, 1644-5 ..	£90	£275
3018	Bust with square collar. ℞. Br. as *mm.*, 1645	£85	£250
3019	**Sixpence.** Coarse bust, nothing before. ℞. Declaration, 1643 ..	£140	£500
3020	— Plumelet before face, 1644	£125	£400
3021	**Groat.** Bust l. ℞. Declaration, 1644	£80	£250
3022	— Plumelet before face, 1644	£110	£350
3023	— Br. below date, 1644	£100	£300
3024	**Threepence.** *O.* Aberystwyth die, *mm.* book. ℞. Declaration, 1644	£100	£350
3025	Bristol die, plume before face, no *mm.*, 1644	£90	£300
3026	**Halfgroat.** Br. in place of date below Declaration	£100	£350
3027	**Penny.** Similar bust, I behind. ℞. Large plume with bands ..	£200	£550

Late issues connected with Thomas Bushell, 1645-6

(Previously given as Lundy Island and/or Appledore and Barnstaple/Bideford, it seems likely that coins marked A, 1645 one probably of Aberystwyth, 1645/6 and coins marked B or with plumes, 1646 are from an unidentified mint.

		F	VF
3028	**Halfcrown.** A below horse and date and as *rev. mm.*, 1645	£700	£2000
3029	Similar but *rev.* from altered Bristol die (i.e. the A is over Br.) ..	£525	£1500
3030	As 3028 but without A below date 1645	£475	£1450
3031	A below horse and as *rev. mm.* Scroll above Declaration, B below 1646	*Extremely rare*	
3032	Plumelet below horse. ℞. *Mm.* Shrewsbury plume; scroll above Declaration, 1646	£400	£1100
3033	— Similar, but plumelet below date	£450	£1250
3034	**Shilling.** Crowned bust l., *mm.* plume. ℞. Declaration type; *mm.* A and A below 1645	£400	£850
3035	— Similar, but plumelet before face	£400	£850
3036	— — ℞. Scroll above Declaration, 1646, *mm.* plumelet ..	£175	£400
3037	Large Shrewsbury plume before face. ℞. As last but *mm.* pellet ..	£200	£450

Late West Country Silver *continued*

3039

3044

		F	VF
3038	**Sixpence.** *O.* Plumelet before face; *mm.* ⊳; 1645	£250	£600
3039	*O.* Large Shrewsbury plume before face; *mm.* B. ℞. Scroll above Declaration, 1646	£120	£275
3040	**Groat.** As 3038	*Extremely rare*	
3041	Somewhat similar, but *obv. mm.* plumelet; 1646	£100	£225
3042	**Threepence.** Somewhat as last but only single plumelet above Declaration, no line below, 1645	£95	£250
3043	— Scroll in place of line above, 1646 below	£85	£200
3044	**Halfgroat.** Bust l., II behind. ℞. Large plume with bands dividing 1646	£200	£450

The penny listed under Bristol may belong to this series.

Truro mint, 1642-3. *Mm.* rose.

		F	VF
3045	**Half-pound.** King on horseback, face turned frontwards. ℞. CHRISTO, etc., round garnished shield. Struck from crown dies on thick flan	*Extremely rare*	
3046	**Crown.** Similar type	£200	£500
3047	— Shield garnished with twelve even scrolls	£225	£600
3048	King's face in profile, well-shaped flan, finer workmanship	£250	£650

3049

		F	VF
3049	**Halfcrown.** King on spirited horse galloping over arms. ℞. Oval garnished shield, 1642 in cartouche below	£1000	£3250
3050	Similar, but no arms. ℞. Oblong shield, CR at sides	£800	£2600
3051	Galloping horse, king holds sword. ℞. Similar	£750	£2400
3052	— ℞. Similar, but CR above	£700	£2000
3053	Trotting horse. ℞. Similar, but CR at sides	£300	£750

Truro Silver *continued*

		F	*VF*
3054	**Halfcrown.** Walking horse, king's hd. in profile. ℞. Similar	£275	£725
3055	— ℞. Similar, but CR above	£325	£850
3056	**Shilling.** Small bust of good style. ℞. Oblong shield	£450	£1200
3057	— ℞. Round shield with eight even scrolls	£575	£1400
3058	— ℞. Oval shield with CR at sides	£250	£700
3059	Normal bust with lank hair. ℞. As last	£150	£450
3060	— ℞. As 3057	£475	£1300
3061	— ℞. Round shield with six scrolls	£150	£450

Truro or Exeter mint *Mm.* rose.

3064

3067-69

3062	**Halfcrown.** King on horseback, sash tied in bow. ℞. Oblong shield with CR at sides	£125	£320
3063	— ℞. Round shield with eight even scrolls	£75	£210
3064	— ℞. Round shield with six scrolls	£85	£225
3065	King's sash flies out behind. ℞. As 3063	£120	£300
3066	— ℞. Oblong shield, curved sides, little garniture	*Extremely rare*	
3067	Briot's horse with groundline. ℞. As 3063	£120	£300
3068	— ℞. As 3066		*Unique*
3069	— ℞. As 3064	£120	£300

Exeter mint, 1643-6. *Mm.* rose except where stated.

3070	**Crown.** As 3046, but 1644 divided by *rev. mm.*	£140	£400
3071	Similar, but 1644 to l. of *mm.*	£125	£350
3072	Similar, but 1645 and *rev. mm.* EX	£140	£400
3073	King's sash in two loose ends; *mm.* castle/rose, 1645	£125	£350
3074	— *mm.* castle/EX, 1645	£175	£450
3075	— *mm.* castle, 1645	£125	£350
3076	**Halfcrown.** As 3049, but 1644 in legend	*Extremely rare*	
3077	Similar, but *mm.* castle, 1645		*Unique*
3078	Short portly figure, leaning backwards on ill-proportioned horse, 1644, 16 rose 44	£185	£500
3079	Briot's horse and groundline; 1644	£130	£375

Exeter Silver *continued*

3080

		F	VF
3080	**Halfcrown.** Horse with twisted tail; 1644-5	£125	£375
3081	— ℞. *Mm.* castle, 1645	£180	£500
3082	— ℞. *Mm.* EX, 1645	£180	£500
3083	— ℞. Declaration type; *mm.* EX, 1644-5	£800	£2250
3084	— — — EX also below 1644	£600	£1750
3085	**Shilling.** As 3061. 1644, 16 rose 44, 1645	£100	£265
3086	— ℞. Declaration type, 1645	£350	£1250
3087	**Sixpence.** As 3085. 1644, 16 rose 44	£85	£275
3088	**Groat.** Somewhat similar but 1644 at beginning of *obv.* legend ..	£60	£160

3089

3091

		F	VF
3089	**Threepence.** As illustration, 1644	£50	£150
3090	**Halfgroat.** Similar, but II. ℞. Oval shield, 1644	£80	£240
3091	— ℞. Large rose, 1644	£100	£300
3092	**Penny.** As last but I behind head	£135	£400

Weymouth mint, 1643-4

3096

Weymouth Silver *continued*

		F	*VF*
3093	**Halfcrown.** King on horseback l., W below; *mm.* two lions. ℞. Declaration type 1644	£325	£825
3094	— ℞. Square-topped shield; *mm.* helmet castle	£250	£650
3095	— ℞. Oval shield; *mm.* helmet	£260	£700
3096	Similar but grass indicated; *mm.* castle. ℞. Square-topped shield; helmet or none. (Illustrated at foot of previous page)...	£250	£650
3097	— ℞. Oval draped shield lis or lions in legend	£275	£750
3098	— ℞. Oval shield CR at sides roses in legend	£300	£800
3099	— ℞. FLORENT etc., oval garnished shield with lion's paws each side	£375	£1000
3100	Tall king, no W or *mm.* ℞. Oval shield, lis, roses, lions or stars in legend	£250	£650
3101	— ℞. Square-topped shield; *mm.* helmet	£300	£800
3102	— ℞. FLORENT, etc., oval shield	£375	£1000
3103	Briot type horse, sword slopes foreward, ground-line. ℞. Oval Shield, roses in legend	£250	£675
3104	— Similar, but CR at sides	£300	£800
3105	Dumpy, portly king, crude horse. ℞. As 3100	£250	£675

3106

3106	Thin king and horse. ℞. Oval shield, stars in legend	£225	£650

Weymouth or Sandsfoot Castle (or Salisbury) mint

3111

3117

3107	**Shilling.** Bust of king l., faithfully rendered. ℞. Square-topped shield; *mm.* castle	£350	£1000
3108	— ℞. CR above shield; *mm.* helmet and lion	£350	£1000
3109	— ℞. Oval shield; *mm.* lion, pear	£325	£900

		F	*VF*
3110	**Shilling.** Bust a somewhat crude copy of last; *mm.* bird, lis. ℞. Square-topped shield with lion's paws above and at sides; *mm.* boar's head, helmet	£350	£1000
3111	— — CR above; *mm.* scroll	£350	£1000
3112	— ℞. Oval shield, lis in legend; *mm.* lis	£300	£850
3113	— ℞. Round shield; *mm.* various	£325	£900
3114	Bust r.; *mm.* pear. ℞. Oval shield, rose and lis in legend		*Unique*
3115	**Sixpence.** As 3110; *mm.* castle, castle/boar's hd.	£500	£1250
3116	**Groat.** As 3112; *mm.* lis/helmet, rose/helmet	£375	£850
3117	**Threepence.** Similar; *mm.* lis *obv.*	£250	£650
3118	**Halfgroat.** Similar; *mm.* lis (*O.*) various (℞.)	£275	£675

Sandsfoot Castle (or Salisbury) mint, 1644

		F	*VF*
3119	**Halfcrown.** King on horseback l. SA below; *mm.* lis. ℞. Oval shield; *mm.* helmet	*Extremely rare*	
3120	— ℞. FLORENT, etc., oval shield, no *mm.*	*Extremely rare*	
3121	— SA erased or replaced by large pellet or cannon ball; *mm.* lis in legend, helmet	£1200	£2750
3122	Tall horse and king, nothing below; *mm.* lis. ℞. Large round shield with crude garniture; *mm.* helmet	£525	£1250
3123	— ℞. Small uncrowned square-topped shield with lion's paw above and at sides; *mm.* helmet	£575	£1400
3124	— ℞. Small oval shield; *mm.* various	£525	£1250
3125	— ℞. As 3120	£600	£1500
3126	Cruder work with little or no mane before horse. ℞. Round shield	£525	£1250
3127	Grass beneath horse. ℞. Similar; *mm.* lis or rose	£525	£1250
3128	Ground below horse. ℞. As 3120	£575	£1400

Worcester mint, 1646

3129

		F	*VF*
3129	**Halfcrown.** *O. Mm.* pear. ℞. HC (Hartlebury Castle) in garniture below shield; *mm.* three pears	£750	£1650

Chester mint, 1644

3130

		F	VF
3130	**Halfcrown.** As illus. ℞. Oval shield; *mm.* three gerbs	£425	£1000
3131	As last. ℞. Crowned oval shield; *mm.* prostrate gerb, -/cinquefoil, and -/ ∴	£450	£1100
3132	— ℞. Crowned square-topped shield with CR at sides both crowned; *mm.* cinquefoil, rose in *rev.* legend	£525	£1350
3133	As 3130, but without plume or CHST. ℞. Declaration type, 1644; *mm.* plume, ∴	£475	£1200
3134	**Threepence.** ℞. Square-topped shield; *mm.* prostrate gerb ..	£275	£600

Coventry (or Corfe Castle) mint? *Mm.* two interlocked C's

3135	**Halfcrown.** King on horseback l. ℞. Oval shield	*Extremely rare*	

Carlisle besieged, 1644-5

3136	**Three shillings.** Large crown above C . R / . III . S. ℞. OBS . CARL / · 1645	*Extremely rare*	
3137	Similar but : OBS : / · : CARL : · / · 1645 ·	£1400	£3000

3138

3138	**Shilling.** As illustration	£900	£2000
3139	℞. Legend and date in two lines	£1000	£2250

Newark besieged, several times 1645-6, surrendered May 1646

3140

		F	VF
3140	**Halfcrown.** Large crown between CR; below, XXX. ℞. OBS / NEWARK / 1645 or 1646	£250	£550
3141	**Shilling.** Similar but curious flat shaped crown, NEWARKE, 1645 ..	£225	£500
3142	Similar but high arched crown, 1645	£150	£375
3143	— NEWARK, 1645 or 1646	£140	£350
3144	**Ninepence.** As halfcrown but IX, 1645 or 1646	£150	£375
3145	— NEWARKE, 1645	£140	£350
3146	**Sixpence.** As halfcrown but VI, 1646	£185	£475

Pontefract besieged, June 1648-March, 1648-9

		F	VF
3147	**Two shillings** (lozenge shaped). DVM : SPIRO : SPERO around CR crowned. ℞. Castle surrounded by OBS, PC, sword and 1648 ..	*Extremely rare*	
3148	**Shilling** (lozenge shaped, octagonal or round). Similar	£375	£850
3149	— Similar but XII to r. dividing PC	£325	£750

After the death of Charles I (30 Jan. 1648/9), in the name of Charles II

3149

3150

		F	VF
3150	**Shilling** (octagonal). *O.* As last. ℞. CAROLVS : SECVNDVS : 1648, castle gateway with flag dividing PC, OBS on l., cannon protrudes on r.	£275	£650
3151	CAROL : II : etc., around HANC : DEVS : etc. ℞. POST MORTEM, etc., gateway etc. as last	£275	£650

Scarborough besieged, July 1644-July 1645

3165

3168

Type I. Castle with gateway to left, value punched below

3152	**Five shillings and eightpence.**	*Extremely rare*
3153	**Crown.** Similar but SC also punched	*Extremely rare*
3154	**Three shillings and fourpence.** As 3152	*Extremely rare*
3155	**Three shillings.** Similar	*Extremely rare*
3156	**Two shillings and tenpence.** Similar	£4000
3157	**Halfcrown.** Similar	£3250
3158	**Two shillings and fourpence.** Similar	*Extremely rare*
3159	**Two shillings and twopence.** Similar	*Extremely rare*
3160	**Two shillings.** Similar	*Extremely rare*
3161	**One shilling and ninepence.** Similar	*Extremely rare*
3162	**One shilling and sixpence.** Similar	*Extremely rare*
3163	**One shilling and fourpence.** Similar	*Extremely rare*
3164	**One shilling and threepence.** Similar	*Extremely rare*
3165	**Shilling.** As illustration	*Extremely rare*
3166	**Sixpence.** Similar	*Extremely rare*
3167	**Groat.** Similar	*Extremely rare*

Type II. Castle with two turrets, value punched below

3168	**Two shillings.** Two castles	*Extremely rare*
3170	**One shilling and sixpence.** Single castle	*Extremely rare*
3171	**One shilling and fourpence.** Similar	£3000
3172	**One shilling and threepence.** Similar	*Extremely rare*
3173	**One shilling and twopence.** Similar	*Extremely rare*
3174	**One shilling and one penny.** Similar	*Extremely rare*
3175	**Shilling.** Similar	£3500
3176	**Elevenpence.** Similar	*Extremely rare*
3177	**Tenpence.** Similar	*Extremely rare*
3178	**Ninepence.** Similar	*Extremely rare*
3179	**Sevenpence.** Similar	*Extremely rare*
3180	**Sixpence.** Similar	*Extremely rare*

COPPER

For mintmarks see *English Copper, Tin & Bronze Coins in the British Museum, 1558-1958*, by C. Wilson Peck.

3186

3191

3194

		F	*VF*
3181	**Royal farthing.** "Richmond" round, colon stops, 1a. CARO over IACO; *mm.* on *obv*...	£7·50	£22
3182	— — 1b. CARA; *mm.* on *obv.*	£75	£150
3183	— — 1c. CARO; *mm.* on *obv.*	£4	£12
3184	— apostrophe stops. 1d. Eagle-headed harp	£6·50	£20
3185	— 1e. Beaded harp	£5·50	£16
3186	— 1f. Scroll-fronted harp, 5 jewels on circlet	£12	£35
3187	— 1g. — — 7 jewels on circlet	£5	£15
3188	Transitional issue, double-arched crowns	£13	£40
3189	"Maltravers" round, 3a; *mm.* on *obv.* only	£10	£32
3190	— 3b. *Mm.* both sides	£4	£12
3191	— 3c. Different *mm.* either side	£6	£17·50
3192	"Richmond" oval. 4a. CARO over IACO; *mm.* both sides	£22	£45
3193	— — — *mm.* on *obv.*	£22	£45
3194	— 4b. CARO, colon stops; *mm.* on *obv.*	£16	£35
3195	— — — — *mm.* on *rev.*	£16	£35
3196	— — — — *mm.* both sides	£16	£35
3197	— 4c. apostrophe stops; *mm.* rose on *obv.*	£18	£40
3198	— — — — *mm.* rose both sides	£22	£45
3199	— — — — *mm.* rose (*obv.*); scroll (*rev.*)	£18	£40
3200	"Maltravers" oval. 5. CAROLVS; *mm.* lis both sides	£22	£45

3101

3207

3201	**Rose farthing.** 1a. Double-arched crowns; double rose; sceptres within inner circle, BRIT	£8	£25
3202	— 1b. — — sceptres just break circle, BRIT	£7·50	£22
3203	— 1c. — — sceptres almost to outer circle, BRIT	£4·50	£14
3204	— 1d. — — — BRI	£4·50	£14
3205	Transitional mules of types 1d/2, with double and single arched crowns	£5·50	£16
3206	— 2. Single-arched crowns; single rose	£3	£9
3207	— 3. Sceptres below crown	£8	£25

COMMONWEALTH, 1649-1660

The coins struck during the Commonwealth have inscriptions in English instead of Latin which was considered to savour too much of Papacy. St. George's cross and the Irish harp take the place of the royal arms. The silver halfpenny was issued for the last time.

Coins with *mm.* anchor, were struck during the Protectorship of Richard Cromwell.

Mintmarks

1649-57 Sun  1658-60 Anchor 

GOLD

3208 3213

			F	*VF*
3208	**Unite.** As illustration; *mm.* sun, 1649-57		£500	£1150
3209	— *mm.* anchor, 1658, 1660		£1100	£2750
3210	**Double-crown.** As illus., but X; *mm.* sun, 1649-55, 57		£450	£1000
3211	— *mm.* anchor, 1660		£1200	£2500
3212	**Crown.** As illus., but V; *mm.* sun, 1649-55, 57		£300	£600
3213	— *mm.* anchor, 1658-1660		£950	£2000

SILVER

3214	**Crown.** Same type; *mm.* sun, 1649, 51-4, 56		£275	£650
3215	**Halfcrown.** Similar; *mm.* sun, 1649, 1651-6		£120	£250
3216	— *mm.* anchor, 1658, 1660	*Fair* £150	£325	
3217	**Shilling.** Similar; *mm.* sun, 1649, 1651-7		£55	£125
3218	— *mm.* anchor, 1658-60	*Fair* £120	£275	
3219	**Sixpence.** Similar; *mm.* sun, 1649, 1651-7		£60	£150
3220	— *mm.* anchor, 1658-60	*Fair* £85	£200	

3221 3223

3221	**Halfgroat.** As illustration		£16	£35
3222	**Penny.** Similar, but I above shields		£17	£38
3223	**Halfpenny.** As illustration		£18	£40

Oliver Cromwell. All said to be only patterns, but some circulated, especially the 1656 halfcrown and the shillings. Half broads exist, but are not contemporary.

GOLD

3224 **Fifty shillings.** Head l. ℞. Shield, 1656. Inscribed edge .. *Extremely rare*

3225

			VF	*EF*
3225	**Broad** (=20s.). Similar, but grained edge	.. ..	£2750	£6500

SILVER

3227

			F	*VF*
3226	**Crown.** Bust l. ℞. Shield, 1658. Inscribed edge	.. ..	£650	£1500
3227	**Halfcrown.** Similar, 1656, 1658	.. ..	£350	£700
3228	**Shilling.** Similar, but grained edge, 1658	.. ..	£275	£600
3229	**Sixpence.** Similar	.. ..	*Extremely rare*	

COPPER

3230

3230	**Farthing.** Dr. bust l. ℞. CHARITIE AND CHANGE, shield	.. ..	£950	£1500

There are also other reverses.

SEVENTEENTH CENTURY TOKENS

As there was no authorized copper coinage under the Commonwealth, towns and traders took it into their own hands to issue small change. Between 1648 and 1672 there was an enormous and very varied issue of these tokens. They were mostly farthings and halfpennies, but there were also some pennies. No collection is representative unless it contains at least a few. Many collectors specialize in those of their own town or county.

	F
Price of commoner pennies	£20·00
— — — round halfpennies	£5·00
— — — octagonal halfpennies	£10 00
— — — heart-shaped halfpennies	£40·00
— — — square or lozenge-shaped halfpennies	£35·00
— — — round farthings	£4·00

For further details of seventeenth century tokens see "Trade Tokens issued in the Seventeenth Century" by G. C. Williamson.

CHARLES II, 1660-85

For the first two years after the Restoration the same denominations, apart from the silver crown, were struck as were issued during the Commonwealth. In 1662 the hand hammering of coins was abandoned in favour of manufacture by the Roettiers improved mill and screw presses. As a prevention against clipping the larger coins were made with the edge inscribed DECVS ET TVTAMEN and the regnal year and the medium sized coins were given a grained edge.

The new gold coins were current for 100s., 20s. and 10s., and they came to be called "guineas" as the gold from which some of them were made was imported from Guinea by the Africa Company (whose badge was the Elephant and Castle). It was not until some years later that the guinea increased in value to 21s. and more. The Africa Co. badge is also found on some silver, and so is the plume symbol indicating silver from the Welsh mines. The four smallest silver denominations, though known today as "Maundy Money," were actually issued for general circulation: at this period the silver penny was probably the only coin distributed at the royal Maundy ceremonies. The smaller "machine" made coins were perhaps minted later than 1662.

A good regal copper coinage was issued for the first time in 1672, but later in the reign farthings were struck in tin (with a copper plug) in order to help the Cornish tin industry.

For the emergency issues struck in the name of Charles II in 1648/9, see the siege pieces of Pontefract listed under Charles I, nos. 3150-51.

Mintmark: Crown.

GOLD

Hammered coinage, 1660-62.

First issue. Without mark of value.

3302

3305

			F	*VF*
3301	**Unite.** (=20s.)	Type as illustration	£850	£1800
3302	**Double-crown.**	As illustration	£900	£1900
3303	**Crown.**	Similar	£900	£1900

Second issue. With mark of value.

			F	*VF*
3304	**Unite.**	Type as illustration	£650	£1350
3305	**Double-crown.**	As illustration	£575	£1250
3306	**Crown.**	Similar	£575	£1250

SILVER

First issue. Without inner circles or mark of value.

			F	*VF*
3307	**Halfcrown.**	Crowned bust, as 3309	£500	£1500
3308	**Shilling.**	Similar	£175	£450
3309	**Sixpence.**	Similar	£150	£400

		F	VF
3310	**Twopence.** Similar	£16	£40
3311	**Penny.** Similar	£18	£45
3312	As last, but without mintmark	£18	£45

3308

3313

3322

Second issue. Without inner circles, but with mark of value.

		F	VF
3313	**Halfcrown.** Crowned bust	£500	£1500
3314	**Shilling.** Similar	£300	£750
3315	**Sixpence.** Similar	£450	£1150
3316	**Twopence.** Similar, but *mm.* on *obv.* only	£14	£35
3317	Similar, but *mm.* both sides (machine made)	£12	£30
3318	Bust to edge of coin, legend starts at bottom l. (machine made)	£12	£30
3319	**Penny.** As 3317	£14	£35
3320	As 3318	£12	£30

3310

3317

3326

Third issue. With inner circles and mark of value.

		F	VF
3321	**Halfcrown.** Crowned bust	£75	£275
3322	**Shilling.** Similar	£45	£135
3323	**Sixpence.** Similar	£65	£175
3324	**Fourpence.** Similar	£14	£28
3325	**Threepence.** Similar	£14	£28
3326	**Twopence.** Similar	£12	£24
3327	**Penny.** Similar	£15	£30

GOLD

Milled Coinage

3328

3335

3328 Five guineas. First bust, pointed truncation

	F £	*VF* £		*F* £	*VF* £		*F* £	*VF* £
1668 ..	1000·00	2100·00	1672 ..	975·00	2100·00	1676 ..	1200·00	2500·00
1669 ..	1100·00	2200·00	1673 ..	975·00	2100·00	1677 ..	1000·00	2150·00
1670 ..	885·00	1850·00	1674 ..	1125·00	2300·00	1678 ..	925·00	1950·00
1671 ..	1150·00	2400·00	1675 ..	1025·00	2150·00			

3329 — with elephant below bust

1668 ..	850·00	1800·00	1675 ..	1425·00	3000·00
1669 ..	1425·00	3000·00	1677/5	*Extremely rare*	

3330 — with elephant and castle below

1675 ..	*Extremely rare*		1677 ..	1200·00	2500·00
1676 ..	1125·00	2200·00	1678 ..	1300·00	2650·00

3331 Second bust, rounded truncation

1678 ..	1300·00	2650·00	1681 ..	925·00	1950·00	1684 ..	825·00	1700·00
1679 ..	925·00	1950·00	1682 ..	900·00	1950·00			
1680 ..	1025·00	2150·00	1683 ..	975·00	2050·00			

3332 — with elephant and castle below

1680 ..	*Extremely rare*		1682 ..	1100·00	2200·00	1684 ..	885·00	1850·00
1681 ..	1300·00	2650·00	1683 ..	1300·00	2650·00			

3333 Two guineas. First bust, pointed truncation

1664 ..	625·00	1400·00	1669 ..	*Extremely rare*	
1665 ..	*Extremely rare*		1671 ..	750·00	1600·00

3334 — with elephant below, 1664 .. .. 425·00 900·00

3335 Second bust, rounded truncation

1675 ..	600·00	1400·00	1679 ..	525·00	1150·00	1683 ..	450·00	950·00
1676 ..	550·00	1200·00	1680 ..	750·00	1700·00	1684 ..	575·00	1300·00
1677 ..	450·00	1000·00	1681 ..	500·00	1050·00			
1678 ..	425·00	950·00	1682 ..	500·00	1050·00			

3336 — with elephant and castle below

1676 ..	450·00	1100·00	1678 ..	550·00	1200·00	1683 ..	800·00	2000·00
1677 ..	*Extremely rare*		1682 ..	550·00	1200·00	1684 ..	750·00	1650·00

3337 — with elephant only below, 1678 *Extremely rare*

N.B. Overstruck dates are listed only if commoner than the normal date or if no normal date is known.

Note. Values for coins in EF (extremely fine) condition can be three or more times the value of VF (very fine) specimens.

Milled gold

3343

3345

		F	VF
3338	**Guinea.** First bust, 1663	900·00	2100·00
3339	— with elephant below, 1663	700·00	1600·00
3340	Second bust, 1664	600·00	1450·00
3341	— with elephant below, 1664	*Extremely rare*	

3342 Third bust, normal portrait

	F £	*VF* £		*F* £	*VF* £		*F* £	*VF* £
1664 ..	400·00	850·00	1668 ..	350·00	775·00	1672 ..	450·00	1000·00
1665 ..	400·00	850·00	1669 ..	450·00	1000·00	1673 ..	700·00	1500·00
1666 ..	400 00	850·00	1670 ..	400·00	850·00			
1667 ..	400·00	850·00	1671 ..	400·00	850·00			

3343 — with elephant below

1664 ..	450·00	1000·00	1665 ..	450·00	1000·00	1668	*Extremely rare*	

3344 Fourth bust, rounded truncation

1672 ..	325·00	675·00	1677 ..	250·00	525·00	1682 ..	350·00	725·00
1673 ..	325·00	725·00	1678 ..	275·00	575·00	1683 ..	250·00	525·00
1674 ..	500·00	1100·00	1679 ..	225·00	500·00	1684 ..	375·00	800·00
1675 ..	400·00	850·00	1680 ..	250·00	550·00			
1676 ..	275·00	575·00	1681 ..	350·00	725·00			

3345 — with elephant and castle below

1674 ..	*Extremely rare*		1678 ..	550·00	1325·00	1682 ..	450·00	1050·00
1675 ..	500·00	1100·00	1679 ..	500·00	1100·00	1683 ..	650·00	1650·00
1676 ..	275·00	650·00	1680 ..	650·00	1650·00	1684 ..	450·00	1050·00
1677 ..	275·00	650·00	1681 ..	425·00	1000·00			

3346 — with elephant below

1677 ..	*Extremely rare*		1678 ..	*Extremely rare*	

3347 **Half-guinea.** First bust, pointed truncation

1669 ..	325·00	775·00	1671 ..	525·00	1300·00
1670 ..	225·00	575·00	1672 ..	525·00	1300·00

3348 Second bust, rounded truncation

1672 ..	275·00	675·00	1677 ..	275·00	675·00	1682 ..	500·00	1125·00
1673 ..	685·00	1600·00	1678 ..	325·00	725·00	1683 ..	275·00	650·00
1674 ..	685·00	1600 00	1679 ..	225·00	525·00	1684 ..	225·00	400·00
1675 ..	*Extremely rare*		1680 ..	685·00	1600·00			
1676 ..	250·00	625·00	1681 ..	685·00	1600·00			

3349 — with elephant and castle below

1676 ..	*Extremely rare*		1680 ..	*Extremely rare*		1684 ..	325·00	675·00
1677 ..	630·00	1600·00	1682 ..	685·00	1700·00			
1678/7	525·00	1300·00	1683 ..	*Extremely rare*				

SILVER

Milled coinage

3350

		F	VF
3350	**Crown.** First bust, rose below, edge undated, 1662	38·00	125·00
3351	— — edge dated, 1662	48·00	160·00
3352	— no rose, edge dated, 1662	58·00	195·00
3353	— — edge not dated, 1662	42·00	165·00
3354	— — new reverse, shields altered, 1663, regnal year on edge in Roman figures ANNO REGNI XV	42·00	150·00

3355

3355 Second bust, regnal year on edge in Roman figures

	F £	VF £		F £	VF £		F £	VF £
1664 ..	47·50	150·00	1665 ..	160·00	700·00	1666 ..	70·00	225·00

		F	VF
3356	— — elephant below bust, 1666	155·00	500·00

3357 — regnal year on edge in words (e.g. 1667 = DECIMO NONO)

1667 ..	57 50	170·00	1669 ..	90·00	225·00	1671 ..	55·00	160·00
1668 ..	52·00	160·00	1670 ..	57·50	170·00			

3358 Third bust

1671 ..	38·00	115·00	1675/3	185·00	550·00	1679 ..	38·00	115·00
1672 ..	38·00	115·00	1676 ..	35·00	110·00	1680 ..	75·00	225·00
1673 ..	38·00	115·00	1677 ..	48·00	175·00			
1674 ..	*Extremely rare*		1678/7	80·00	350·00			

3359 Fourth bust

1679 ..	48·00	125·00	1681 ..	52·00	135·00	1683 ..	75·00	190·00
1680 ..	52·00	135·00	1682/1	80·00	135·00	1684 ..	75·00	190·00

3360 — elephant and castle below bust, 1681 .. .. *Extremely rare*

Milled Silver

3367

3369

3370

			F	VF
3361	**Halfcrown.** First bust, regnal year on edge in Roman figures, 1663	.. ..	38·00	125·00
3362	Second bust, 1664	.. ..	60·00	175·00
3363	Third bust, 1666	.. ..	470·00	1050·00
3364	— elephant below bust, 1666	.. ..	365·00	735·00

3365 — regnal date on edge in words

	F £	VF £		F £	VF £		F £	VF £
1667/4	*Extremely rare*		1669/4	65·00	235·00			
1668/4	55·00	125·00	1670 ..	32·00	125·00			

3366 — Third bust variety

1671 ..	30·00	115·00	1672 ..	35·00	125·00

3367 Fourth bust

1672 ..	90·00	210·00	1677 ..	32·00	105·00	1682 ..	48·00	170·00
1673 ..	32·00	105·00	1678 ..	75·00	365·00	1683 ..	38·00	115·00
1674 ..	55·00	160·00	1679 ..	30·00	95·00	1684/3	105·00	265·00
1675 ..	38·00	125·00	1680 ..	85·00	165·00			
1676 ..	28·00	100·00	1681 ..	42·00	120·00			

3368 — plume below bust

1673 .. *Extremely rare* 1683 .. *Extremely rare*

3369 — plume below bust and in centre of *rev.*, 1673 .. .. .. *Extremely rare*

3370 — elephant and castle below bust, 1681 .. .. *Extremely rare*

3371

3376

3380

3371	**Shilling.** First bust, 1663	.. ..	35·00	140·00

3372 First bust variety

1663 .. 35·00 130·00 1668 .. 140·00 325·00 1669/6 *Extremely rare*

3373	— elephant below bust, 1666	.. ..	140·00	500·00
3374	Guinea head, elephant below bust, 1666	.. ..	230·00	725·00

3375 Shilling. Second bust

	F £	VF £		F £	VF £		F £	VF £
1666 ..	*Extremely rare*		1673 ..	58·00	180·00	1679 ..	40·00	150·00
1668 ..	38·00	150·00	1674 ..	58·00	180·00	1680	*Extremely rare*	
1669 ..	*Extremely rare*		1675 ..	90·00	255·00	1681 ..	75·00	215·00
1670 ..	60·00	200·00	1676 ..	40·00	160·00	1682/1	*Extremely rare*	
1671 ..	80·00	225·00	1677 ..	40·00	160·00	1683	*Extremely rare*	
1672 ..	42·00	160·00	1678 ..	52·00	185·00			

3376 — plume below bust and in centre of *rev.*

1671 ..	100·00	400·00	1675 ..	115·00	400·00	1679 ..	115·00	400·00
1673 ..	110·00	425·00	1676 ..	100·00	375·00	1680 ..	200·00	625·00
1674 ..	100·00	400·00						

3377 — plume *rev.* only, 1674 .. .. 150·00 440·00

3378 — plume *obv.* only

1677 ..	175·00	550·00	1679 ..	125·00	360·00

3379 — elephant and castle below bust, 1681 .. .. *Extremely rare*

3380 Third (large) bust

1674 ..	80·00	185·00	1675 ..	60·00	140·00

3381 Fourth (large) bust, older features

1683 ..	62·00	220·00	1684 ..	52·00	200·00

3382 Sixpence

1674 ..	25·00	65·00	1678/7	30·00	75·00	1682/1	33·00	75·00
1675 ..	25·00	65·00	1679 ..	30·00	75·00	1683 ..	25·00	65·00
1676 ..	27·00	75·00	1680 ..	33·00	90·00	1684 ..	27·00	62·00
1677 ..	25·00	65·00	1681 ..	25·00	65·00			

3384 3386 3388 3390

3383 Fourpence. Undated. Crowned bust l. to edge of coin, value behind. ℞. Shield .. .. 6·00 13·00

3384 Dated. *O.* As illustration. ℞. Four c's

1670 ..	4·00	9·50	1675 ..	3·75	9·00	1680 ..	3·25	8·00
1671	4·00	9·50	1676	3·75	9·00	1681 ..	3·25	8·00
1672/1	3·75	9·00	1677 ..	3·50	8·50	1682 ..	3·50	8·50
1673 ..	3·75	9·00	1678 ..	3·50	8·50	1683 ..	3·25	8·00
1674 ..	3·75	9·00	1679 ..	3·25	8·00	1684/3	3·25	8·00

3385 Threepence. Undated. As 3383 .. .. 7·50 17·00

3386 Dated. As illustration

1670 ..	5·50	9·00	1675 ..	5·50	9·00	1680 ..	4·75	8·50
1671 ..	5·00	8·50	1676 ..	5·00	8·50	1681 ..	4·75	8·50
1672/1	5·00	8·50	1677 ..	5·00	8·50	1682 ..	4·75	8·50
1673 ..	5·00	8·50	1678 ..	5·00	8·50	1683 ..	4·75	8·50
1674 ..	5·00	8·50	1679 ..	4·25	7·50	1684 ..	4·75	8·50

Note. Values for coins in EF (extremely fine) condition can be three or more times the value of VF (very fine) specimens.

Milled Silver

	F £	VF £
3387 **Twopence.** Undated. As 3383	6·00	11·00

3388 Dated. As illustration

	F £	VF £		F £	VF £		F £	VF £
1668 ..	3·75	7·50	1675 ..	3·50	7·00	1680 ..	3·50	7·00
1670 ..	3·50	7·00	1676 ..	3 50	7·00	1681 ..	3 50	7·00
1671 ..	3·50	7·00	1677 ..	3·75	7·50	1682 ..	3·50	7·00
1672/1	3·50	7·00	1678 ..	3·50	7·00	1683 ..	3·50	7·00
1673 ..	3·75	7·50	1679 ..	3·50	7·00	1684 ..	4·00	7·50
1674 ..	3·50	7·00						

	F	VF
3389 **Penny.** Undated. As 3383	8·50	16·00

3390 Dated. As illustration

	F	VF		F	VF		F	VF
1670 ..	7·50	16·00	1675 ..	7·50	16·00	1680 ..	7·50	16·00
1671 ..	7·50	16·00	1676 ..	8·00	17·00	1681 ..	8·50	18·00
1672/1	7·50	16·00	1677 ..	7·50	16·00	1682 ..	8·00	17·00
1673 ..	7·50	16·00	1678 ..	7·50	16·00	1683 ..	7·50	16·00
1674 ..	7·50	16·00	1679 ..	13·00	25·00	1684 ..	8 00	17·00

	F	VF
3391 **Maundy Set.** Undated. The four coins	55·00	110·00

3392 Dated. The four coins. Uniform dates

	F	VF		F	VF		F	VF
1670 ..	40·00	80·00	1675 ..	38·00	75·00	1680 ..	38·00	75·00
1671 ..	38·00	75·00	1676 ..	38·00	70·00	1681 ..	42·00	85·00
1672 ..	40·00	80·00	1677 ..	38·00	75·00	1682 ..	40·00	80·00
1673 ..	38·00	75·00	1678 ..	42·00	85·00	1683 ..	38·00	75·00
1674 ..	38·00	75·00	1679 ..	40·00	80·00	1684 ..	40·00	80·00

	F	VF
3392a Mixed dates	21·00	40·00

COPPER and TIN

3393

3394

3393 Copper **halfpenny.**

	F	VF		F	VF		F	VF
1672 ..	18·00	60·00	1673 ..	16·00	55·00	1675 ..	18·00	60·00

3394 Copper **farthing.** As illustration

	F	VF		F	VF		F	VF
1672 ..	12·00	25·00	1674 ..	15·00	40·00	1679 ..	18·00	50·00
1673 ..	12·00	25·00	1675 ..	16·00	45·00			

3395 Tin **farthing.** Somewhat similar, but with inscribed edge and copper plug

	fair	*F*	*VF*
1684	21·00	65·00	160·00
1685			*Extremely rare*

N.B. Overstruck dates are listed only if commoner than the normal date or if no normal date is known.

JAMES II, 1685-88

Tin halfpence and farthings provided the only base metal coinage during this short reign. All genuine tin coins of this period have a copper plug.

GOLD

			F	VF
3396	**Five guineas.** Bust l., sceptres misplaced, 1686		1350·00	3250·00

3397 — with sceptres normal

	F £	*VF* £		*F* £	*VF* £		*F* £	*VF* £
1687 ..	1250·00	3000·00	1688 ..	1200·00	2750·00			

3398 — elephant and castle below bust

1687 ..	1350·00	3500·00	1688 ..	1450·00	3500·00

3399 **Two guineas.** Similar

1687 ..	850·00	2500·00	1688/7	900·00	2600·00

3403

3404

3400 **Guinea.** First bust

1685 ..	325·00	750·00	1686 ..	425·00	1025·00

3401 — elephant and castle below

1685 ..	375·00	925·00	1686 ..	*Extremely rare*	

3402 Second bust

1686 ..	275·00	650·00	1687 ..	275·00	650·00	1688 ..	275·00	650·00

3403 Elephant and castle below

1686 ..	475·00	1075·00	1687 ..	325·00	700·00	1688 ..	325·00	700·00

3404 **Half-guinea**

1686 ..	250·00	700·00	1687 ..	450·00	1050·00	1688 ..	275·00	750·00

3405 Elephant and castle below, 1686 .. .. 600·00 1500·00

SILVER

3406 **Crown.** First bust, 1686 .. .. 95·00 275·00

3407 Second bust

1687 ..	85·00	260·00	1688 ..	85·00	265·00

3408

1st bust 2nd bust

3408 Halfcrown. First bust

	F	VF		F	VF		F	VF
	£	£		£	£		£	£
1685 ..	45·00	185·00	1686 ..	45·00	185·00	1687 ..	45·00	185·00

3409 Second bust

1687 ..	60·00	200·00	1688 ..	55·00	190·00

3410 Shilling

1685 ..	40·00	200·00	1687/6	40·00	200·00
1686 ..	40·00	200 00	1688 ..	45·00	210·00

3411 Plume in centre of *rev.*, 1685 .. .. *Extremely rare*

3412 Sixpence. Early type shields

1686 ..	35·00	90·00	1687 ..	35·00	95·00

3413 Late type shields

1687 ..	32·00	85·00	1688 ..	35·00	95·00

3414 3415 3416 3417

3414 Fourpence. *O.* As illus. ℞. IIII crowned

1686 ..	6·00	14·00	1687/6	6·00	13·00	1688 ..	6·00	14·00

3415 Threepence. As illustration

1685 ..	6·00	13·00	1687 ..	6·00	13·00
1686 ..	6·00	13·00	1688 ..	6·00	13·00

3416 Twopence. As illustration

1686 ..	6·00	13·00	1687 ..	6·00	13·00	1688 ..	6·50	13·50

3417 Penny. As illustration

1685 ..	11·00	23·00	1687 ..	11·00	23 00
1686 ..	11·00	23·00	1688 ..	11·00	23·00

3418 Maundy Set. As last four. Uniform dates

1686 ..	45·00	95·00	1687 ..	45·00	95·00	1688 ..	45·00	95·00

TIN

3419

	fair	*F*	*VF*
3419 Halfpenny			
1685	22·00	58·00	155·00
1686	27·00	68·00	180·00
1687	22·00	58·00	155·00
3420 Farthing. Cuirassed bust			
1684	*Extremely rare*		
1685	22·00	55·00	155·00
1686	27·00	68·00	180·00
1687	*Extremely rare*		
3421 Draped bust, 1687	38·00	95·00	210·00

WILLIAM AND MARY, 1688-94

Due to the poor state of the silver coinage, much of it worn hammered coin, the guinea, which was valued at 21s. 6d. at the beginning of the reign, circulated for as much as 30s. by 1694. The tin halfpennies and farthings were replaced by copper coins in 1694. The rampant lion of Orange is now placed as an inescutcheon on the centre of the royal arms.

GOLD

3422 Five guineas. Conjoined heads r.

	F £	*VF* £		*F* £	*VF* £		*F* £	*VF* £
1691 ..	1250·00	2750·00	1693 ..	1200·00	2750·00			
1692 ..	1200·00	2750·00	1694 ..	1350·00	3250·00			

3423 — elephant and castle below

1691 ..	1450·00	3300·00	1693 ..	1700·00	4000·00
1692 ..	1850·00	3500·00	1694 ..	1600·00	3750·00

3424 Two guineas. Conjoined heads r.

1693 ..	950·00	1650·00	1694 ..	750·00	1650·00

3425 — elephant and castle below

1691 ..	*Extremely rare*		1693 ..	875·00	2000·00	1694 ..	875·00	2000·00

3427

3426 Guinea. Conjoined heads r.

1689 ..	350·00	750·00	1691 ..	450·00	900·00	1693 ..	425·00	875·00
1690 ..	400·00	825·00	1692 ..	425·00	875·00	1694 ..	375·00	800·00

3427 — elephant and castle below

1689 ..	350·00	750·00	1691 ..	425·00	875·00	1693 ..	*Extremely rare*	
1690 ..	600·00	1200·00	1692 ..	475·00	950·00	1694 ..	475·00	975·00

3428 — elephant only below

1692 ..	400·00	950·00	1693 ..	*Extremely rare*	

3429

3430

3429 Half-guinea. First heads, 1639 .. .. 325·00 750·00

3430 Second head, normal portraits

1690 ..	375·00	800·00	1692 ..	350·00	800·00	1694 ..	275·00	600·00
1691 ..	400·00	875·00	1693 ..	*Extremely rare*				

3431 — — elephant and castle below

1691 ..	325·00	675·00	1692 ..	300·00	650·00

3432 — — elephant only below, 1692 .. *Extremely rare*

SILVER

3433 Crown. Conjoined busts, as 3436 below

	F	*VF*		*F*	*VF*		*F*	*VF*
	£	£		£	£		£	£
1691 ..	250·00	600·00	1692 ..	250·00	600·00			

3434

3435

3434 Halfcrown. First busts and first shields, 1689 .. .. .. 25·00 70·00

3435 — and second shield

1689 ..	40·00	130·00	1690 ..	45·00	130·00

3436 Second busts. ℞. As illustration below

1691 ..	45·00	140·00	1692 ..	45·00	150·00	1693 ..	40·00	130·00

3436

3438

3437 Shilling. Similar

1692 ..	42·00	115·00	1693 ..	40·00	110·00

3438 Sixpence. Similar

1693 ..	35·00	90·00	1694 ..	50·00	120·00

3439 Fourpence. First busts, no tie to wreath

1689 ..	7·00	16·00	1691 ..	8·50	19·00
1690 ..	7·00	16·00	1694 ..	8·00	17·00

3440 Second busts, tie to wreath

1691 ..	9·00	20·00	1693 ..	10·00	21·00
1692 ..	8·00	18·00	1694 ..	10·00	21·00

3441 Threepence. First busts, no tie

1689 ..	7·00	14·00	1690 ..	7·00	14·00	1691 ..	12·00	28·00

3442 Second busts, tie to wreath

1691 ..	7·50	19·00	1693 ..	6·50	17·00
1692 ..	7·50	19·00	1694 ..	6·50	16·00

3443 Twopence

	F	VF		F	VF		F	VF
	£	£		£	£		£	£
1689 ..	6·50	13·00	1692 ..	6·50	13·00	1694 ..	8·00	15·00
1691 ..	6·50	14·00	1693 ..	6·50	13·00			

3444 Penny. Legend continuous over heads, 1689 .. .. .. 60·00 125·00

3445 — Legend broken by heads

1690 ..	15·00	26·00	1692 ..	15·00	26·00	1694 ..	14·00	25·00
1691 ..	14·00	25·00	1693 ..	14·00	25·00			

3446

3446 Maundy Set. As last pieces. Uniform dates

1689 ..	140·00	270·00	1692 ..	50·00	95·00	1694 ..	50·00	95·00
1691 ..	50·00	95·00	1693 ..	60·00	105·00			

TIN AND COPPER

3447 Tin **Halfpenny.** Small draped busts, 1689 .. .. *Extremely rare*

3448 Large cuirassed busts; date only on edge

	fair	*F*	*VF*
1690	22·00	58·00	160·00

3449 — — date in exergue and on edge

1691	22·00	58·00	160·00
1692	22·00	58·00	160·00

3450 Tin **Farthing.** Small draped busts

1689 .. *Extremely rare* 1689/90 *Extremely rare*

3451 Large cuirassed busts

1689/90		*Extremely rare*	
1690	22·00	58·00	160·00
1691	22·00	58·00	160·00
1692	22·00	70·00	170·00

3453

3452 Copper **Halfpenny,** 1694 .. .. 12·00 35·00

3453 Copper **Farthing,** 1694 .. .. 15·00 45·00

N.B. Overstruck dates are listed only if commoner than the normal date or if no normal date is known.

Note. Values for coins in EF (extremely fine) condition can be three or more times the value of VF (very fine specimens.

WILLIAM III, 1694-1702

In 1696 a great recoinage was undertaken to replace the hammered silver that made up most of the coinage in circulation, much of it being clipped and badly worn. Branch mints were set up at Bristol, Chester, Exeter, Norwich and York to help with the recoinage. For a short time before they were finally demonetized unclipped hammered coins were allowed to circulate freely providing they were officially pierced in the centre. Silver coins with roses between the coats of arms were made from silver obtained from the West of England mines.

GOLD

3454

3457

3454 Five guineas. First bust

	F £	VF £		F £	VF £		F £	VF £
1699 ..	1200·00	2650·00	1700 ..	1250·00	2750·00			

3455 — elephant and castle below, 1699 .. ..1400·00 3000·00
3456 Second bust ("fine work"), 1701 .. ..1150·00 2500·00
3457 **Two guineas** ("fine work"), 1701 .. .. 800·00 2000·00

3458

3460

3458 Guinea. First bust
1695 .. 250·00 600·00 1696 .. 400·00 800·00 1697 .. 385·00 750·00

3459 — elephant and castle below
1695 .. 400·00 800·00 1696 .. *Extremely rare*

3460 Second bust, human-headed harp
1697 .. 350·00 675·00 1699 .. 385·00 850·00 1701 .. 250·00 550·00
1698 .. 250·00 550·00 1700 .. 250·00 550·00

3461 — elephant and castle below
1697 .. 750·00 1600·00 1699 .. *Extremely rare*
1698 .. 385·00 800·00 1700 .. 800·00 1700·00

3462 — R. Large lettering and large date, 1698 .. .. 250·00 550·00
3463 — R. Scrolled harp, 1701 .. .. 255·00 500·00
3464 — — elephant and castle, 1701 .. .. *Extremely rare*
3465 Third bust ("fine work"), 1701 .. .. 525·00 1100·00
3466 **Half-guinea.** R. With early harp, 1695 .. .. 175·00 425·00

3467 **Half-guinea.** Elephant and Castle. ℞. With early harp.

	F £	VF £		F £	VF £		F £	VF £
1695 ..	500·00	1150·00	1696 ..	200·00	475·00			

3468 ℞. With late harp

	F £	VF £		F £	VF £		F £	VF £
1697 ..	330·00	700·00	1699 ..	*Extremely rare*		1701 ..	175·00	375·00
1698 ..	185·00	425·00	1700 ..	185·00	425·00			

3469 — elephant and castle, 1698 .. .. 400·00 1000·00

SILVER

3470 **Crown.** First bust, first harp

1695 .. 30·00 120·00 1696 .. 30·00 120·00

3471 Second bust (hair across breast), 1696 .. .. *Unique*

3472 Third bust, first harp, 1696 .. .. 32·00 125·00

3473 — second harp, 1697 .. .. 260·00 650·00

3474 Third bust variety, third harp, 1700 .. .. 48·00 140·00

3490

3475 **Halfcrown.** Small shields, 1696 .. .. 20·00 75·00

3476 — B (*Bristol*) below bust, 1696 .. .. 30·00 95·00

3477 — C (*Chseter*) below bust, 1696 .. .. 50·00 140·00

3478 — E (*Exeter*) below bust, 1696 .. .. 80·00 250·00

3479 — N (*Norwich*) below bust, 1696 .. .. 44·00 115·00

3480 — y (*York*) below bust, 1696 .. .. 34·00 135·00

3481 Large shield, early harp, 1696 .. .. 20·00 75·00

3482 — — B (*Bristol*) below bust, 1696 .. .. 34·00 95·00

3483 — — C (*Chester*) below bust, 1696 .. .. 40·00 105·00

3484 — — E (*Exeter*) below bust, 1696 .. .. 50·00 130·00

3485 — — N (*Norwich*) below bust, 1696 .. .. 85·00 225·00

3486 — — y (*York*) below bust, 1696 .. .. 34·00 95·00

3487 Large shields, ordinary harp

1696 .. 75·00 225·00 1697 .. 20·00 75·00

3488 — — B (*Bristol*) below bust, 1697 .. .. 20·00 75·00

3489 — — C (*Chester*) below bust

1696 .. 85·00 225·00 1697 .. 30·00 85·00

3490 — — E (*Exeter*) below bust

1696 .. 85·00 225·00 1697 .. 34·00 90·00

3491 — — N (*Norwich*) below bust

1696 .. 125·00 265·00 1697 .. 34·00 90·00

3492 — — y (*York*) below bust, 1697 .. .. 32·00 90·00

3493 Second bust (hair across breast), 1696 .. .. *Unique*

3494	**Half-crown.** Modified large shields							
	F	*VF*		*F*	*VF*		*F*	*VF*
	£	£		£	£		£	£
1698 ..	22·00	60·00	1700 ..	24·00	65·00			
1699 ..	27·00	95·00	1701 ..	24·00	75·00			

3495 Elephant and castle below bust, 1701 .. .. .. *fair* £135 525·00

3496 Plumes in angles on *rev.*, 1701 .. .. 45·00 120·00

1st bust

2nd bust

3rd bust

3507

3rd bust var.

4th bust

5th bust

3497	**Shilling.** First bust							
1695 ..	22·00	60·00	1696 ..	17·00	35·00	1697 ..	17·00	35·00
3498	— B (*Bristol*) below bust							
1696 ..	19·00	55·00	1697 ..	24·00	60·00			
3499	— C (*Chester*) below bust							
1696 ..	24·00	70·00	1697 ..	24·00	70·00			
3500	— E (*Exeter*) below bust							
1696 ..	22·00	60·00	1697 ..	22·00	60·00			
3501	— N (*Norwich*) below bust							
1696 ..	22·00	60·00	1697 ..	20·00	52·00			
3502	— y (*York*) below bust							
1696 ..	24·00	65·00	1697 ..	24·00	65·00			
3503	— Y (*York*) below bust							
1696 ..	26·00	60·00	1697 ..	26·00	90·00			

3504 Second bust (hair across breast), 1696 .. .. *Unique*

3505 Third bust, 1697 .. .. 18·00 35·00

3506 — B (*Bristol*) below bust, 1697 .. .. 32·00 85·00

3507	— C (*Chester*) below bust				
1696 ..	85·00	210·00	1697 ..	27·00	80·00

3508 — E (*Exeter*) below bust, 1697 .. .. 32·00 80·00

3509 — N (*Norwich*) below bust, 1697 .. .. 30·00 75·00

3510	— y (*York*) below bust				
1696 ..	*Extremely rare*		1697 ..	30·00	75·00
3511	Third bust variety				
1697 ..	22·00	40·00	1698 ..	28·00	55·00

3512 — B (*Bristol*) below bust, 1697 .. .. 30·00 75·00

No.	Description	Year	F £	VF £	Year	F £	VF £	Year	F £	VF £
3513	Third bust variety C (*Chester*) below bust, 1697							..	45·00	140·00
3514	— ℞. Plumes in angles, 1698							..	45·00	140·00
3515	Fourth bust ("flaming hair")	1698 ..	50·00	140·00	1699 ..	50·00	140·00			
3516	Fifth bust (hair high)	1699 ..	35·00	100·00	1700 ..	25·00	65·00	1701 ..	28·00	85·00
3517	— ℞. Plumes in angles	1699 ..	50·00	140·00	1701 ..	50·00	140·00			
3518	— ℞. Roses in angles, 1699							..	75·00	170·00
3519	— plume below bust, 1700							..	575·00	—

3520

3542

No.	Description	Year	F £	VF £	Year	F £	VF £	Year	F £	VF £
3520	**Sixpence.** First bust, early harp	1695 ..	20·00	60·00	1696 ..	12·00	25·00			
3521	— — B below bust, 1696							..	14·00	25·00
3522	— — C below bust, 1696							..	15·00	30·00
3523	— — E below bust, 1696							..	18·00	35·00
3524	— — N below bust, 1696							..	16·00	30·00
3525	— — y below bust, 1696							..	15·00	28·00
3526	— — Y below bust, 1696							..	30·00	60·00
3527	— later harp, large crowns, 1696							..	27·00	70·00
3528	— — — B below bust	1696 ..	35·00	75·00	1697 ..	25·00	45·00			
3529	— — — C below bust, 1697							..	30·00	75·00
3530	— — — E below bust, 1697							..	25·00	40·00
3531	— — small crowns	1696 ..	25·00	65·00	1697 ..	12·00	32·00			
3532	— — — B below bust	1696 ..	18·00	45·00	1697 ..	12·00	30·00			
3533	— — — C below bust	1696 ..	25·00	75·00	1697 ..	12·00	32·00			
3534	— — — E below bust, 1697							..	12·00	35·00
3535	— — — N below bust	1696 ..	30·00	70·00	1697 ..	15·00	45·00			
3536	— — — y below bust, 1697							..	18·00	35·00
3537	Second bust	1696 ..	*Extremely rare*		1697 ..	45·00	150·00			
3538	Third bust, large crowns	1697 ..	10·00	22·00	1699 ..	35·00	90·00	1701 ..	13 00	27·00
		1698 ..	12·00	26·00	1700 ..	9·00	25·00			
3539	— — B below bust, 1697							..	18·00	45·00
3540	— — C below bust, 1697							..	34·00	75·00
3541	— — E below bust, 1697							..	40·00	80·00

		F £	VF £
3542	**Sixpence.** Third bust small crowns, 1697	18·00	35·00
3543	— — C below bust, 1697	40·00	80·00
3544	— — E below bust, 1697	24·00	60·00
3545	— — Y below bust, 1697	29·00	53·00

3546 — R. Plumes in angles

Date	F £	VF £	Date	F £	VF £
1698 ..	23·00	50·00	1699 ..	20·00	45·00

		F £	VF £
3547	— R. Roses in angles, 1699	35·00	90·00
3548	— plume below bust, 1700	*Extremely rare*	

3549 3550 3551 3552

3549 Fourpence. R. 4 crowned

Date	F	VF	Date	F	VF	Date	F	VF
1697 ..	*Unique*		1699 ..	11·50	21·00	1701 ..	12·00	22·00
1698 ..	12·00	20·00	1700 ..	11·00	19·00	1702 ..	11·00	19·00

3550 Threepence. R. 3 crowned

Date	F	VF	Date	F	VF
1698 ..	11·00	19·00	1700 ..	11·00	19·00
1699 ..	12·00	20·00	1701 ..	11·00	19·00

3551 Twopence. R. 2 crowned

Date	F	VF	Date	F	VF
1698 ..	11·00	19·00	1700 ..	10·00	19·00
1699 ..	10·00	18·50	1701 ..	9·50	18·00

3552 Penny. R. 1 crowned

Date	F	VF	Date	F	VF
1698 ..	11·00	19·00	1700 ..	12·00	20·00
1699 ..	12·00	20·00	1701 ..	11·00	19·00

3553 Maundy set. As last four. Uniform dates

Date	F	VF	Date	F	VF
1698 ..	55·00	110·00	1700 ..	65·00	120·00
1699 ..	65·00	120·00	1701 ..	55·00	110·00

COPPER

3554 Halfpenny. First issue. Britannia with r. hand raised

Date	F	VF	Date	F	VF
1695 ..	8·00	35·00	1697 ..	7·00	30·00
1696 ..	7·00	30·00	1698 ..	9·00	45·00

3555 Second issue. R. Date in legend

Date	F	VF	Date	F	VF
1698 ..	6·00	35·00	1699 ..	7·00	30·00

3556 Third issue. R. Britannia with r. hand on knee

Date	F	VF	Date	F	VF	Date	F	VF
1699 ..	7·00	30·00	1700 ..	7·00	30·00	1701 ..	7·50	32·50

3557 3558

3557 Farthing. First issue

Date	F	VF	Date	F	VF	Date	F	VF
1695 ..	10·00	40·00	1697 ..	9·00	35·00	1699 ..	9·00	35·00
1696 ..	9·00	35·00	1698 ..	60·00	175·00	1700 ..	9·00	35·00

3558 Second issue. R. Date at end of legend

Date	F	VF	Date	F	VF
1698 ..	18·00	80·00	1699 ..	12·00	45·00

ANNE 1702-14

The Act of Union of 1707, which effected the unification of the ancient kingdoms of England and Scotland into a single realm, resulted in a change in the royal arms—on the after-Union coinage the English leopards and Scottish lion are emblazoned per pale on the top and bottom shields. After the Union the rose in the centre of the reverse of the gold coins is replaced by the Garter star.

Following a successful Anglo-Dutch expedition against Spain, bullion seized in Vigo Bay was sent to be minted into coin, and the coins made from this metal had the word VIGO placed below the queen's bust.

GOLD

Before Union with Scotland

3560 Five guineas

	F	*VF*		*F*	*VF*		*F*	*VF*
	£	£		£	£		£	£
1705	1500·00	3100·00	1706	1200·00	2600·00			

3561 VIGO below bust, 1703 .. .. *Extremely rare*

3562 Guinea

1702	300·00	675·00	1706	400·00	900·00
1705	400·00	900·00	1707	475·00	1050·00

3563 VIGO below bust, 1703 .. .. 2000·00 4650·00

3564 Half-guinea

1702	375·00	825·00	1705	375·00	825·00

3565 VIGO below bust, 1703 .. .. 1875·00 4150·00

3562

3574

After Union with Scotland. The shields on the reverse are changed.

3566 Five guineas. Ordinary bust, 1706 .. .. 1200·00 2350·00

3567 — broader shields, 1709 .. .. 1300·00 2600·00

3568 Last (coarse) bust

1711	1100·00	2150·00	1713	1300·00	2600·00	1714	1200·00	2350·00

3569 Two guineas

1709	650·00	1500·00	1713	650·00	1500·00
1711	550·00	1300·00	1714	725·00	1650·00

3570 Guinea. First bust

1707	325·00	750·00	1708	*Extremely rare*	

3571 — elephant and castle below, 1707 .. .. 750·00 1650·00

3572 Second bust

1707	*Extremely rare*		1708	250·00	575·00	1709	285·00	625·00

3573 — elephant and castle below

1708	650·00	1500·00	1709	500·00	1150·00

3574 Third bust

1710	225·00	525·00	1712	250·00	575·00	1714	185·00	425·00
1711	225·00	525·00	1713	185·00	450·00			

3575 Half-guinea

1707	215·00	475·00	1710	150·00	350·00	1713	165·00	375·00
1708	275·00	625·00	1711	165·00	365·00	1714	165·00	375·00
1709	200·00	425·00	1712	215·00	475·00			

SILVER

Before Union with Scotland

3576

		F £	*VF* £
3576	**Crown.** VIGO below bust, 1703	130·00	550·00
3577	R. Plumes in angles, 1705	135·00	450·00
3578	R. Roses and plumes in angles		
	1706 .. *F* 80·00 *VF* 302·00 — 1707 .. *F* 70·00 *VF* 275·00		
3579	**Halfcrown.** No marks below bust or on *rev.* (i.e. plain), 1703 ..	250·00	700·00
3580	VIGO below bust, 1703	40·00	125·00
3581	R. Plumes in angles		
	1704 .. 65·00 145·00 — 1705 .. 55·00 110·00		
3582	R. Roses and plumes in angles		
	1706 .. 40·00 110·00 — 1707 .. 30·00 100·00		

3583 3589

		F £	*VF* £
3583	**Shilling.** First bust, 1702	30·00	80·00
3584	— R. Plumes in angles, 1702	38·00	135·00
3585	— VIGO below bust, 1702	33·00	125·00
3586	Second bust, VIGO below, 1703	28·00	100·00
3587	— plain		
	1704 .. *Extremely rare* — 1705 .. 50·00 130·00		
3588	— R. Plumes in angles		
	1704 .. 50·00 120·00 — 1705 .. 35·00 95·00		
3589	— R. Roses and plumes in angles		
	1705 .. 30·00 95·00 — 1707 .. 35·00 105·00		

3592

		F	VF
3590	**Sixpence.** VIGO below bust, 1703	12·00	40·00
3591	Plain, 1705	38·00	100·00
3592	℞. Early shields, plumes in angles, 1705	22·00	60·00
3593	℞. Late shields, plumes in angles, 1705	30·00	80·00

3594 ℞. Roses and plumes in angles

	F £	VF £		F £	VF £		F £	VF £
1705	22·00	60·00	1707	22·00	60·00			

3595 Fourpence. ℞. Crowned 4

1703	7·00	13·00	1706	6·00	12·00	1710	6·00	12·00
1704	6·00	12·00	1708	6·00	12·00	1713	6·00	12·00
1705	7·00	13·00	1709	6·00	12·00			

3596 Threepence. ℞. Crowned 3

1703	7·50	13·00	1706	6·00	12·00	1709	6·00	12·00
1704	6·50	11·50	1707	6·00	12·00	1710	6·00	12·00
1705	6·50	11·50	1708	6·00	12·00	1713	6·00	12·00

3597 Twopence. ℞. Crowned 2

1703	6·50	13·50	1706	6·50	13·50	1709	7·00	13·50
1704	6·00	12·50	1707	6·50	13·50	1710	6·00	12·50
1705	6·00	12·50	1708	6·00	12·50	1713	6·00	12·50

3598 Penny. ℞. Crowned 1

1703	11·00	21·00	1708	11·00	21·00	1713	11·00	21·00
1705	10·00	19·00	1709	10·00	19·00			
1706	10·00	19·00	1710	14·00	30·00			

3599

3599 Maundy set. As last four. Uniform dates

1703	48·00	85·00	1708	48·00	85·00	1713	48·00	85·00
1705	48·00	85·00	1709	48·00	85·00			
1706	45·00	75·00	1710	55·00	100·00			

Note. Values for coins in EF (extremely fine) condition can be three or more times the value of VF (very fine) specimens.

After Union with Scotland

The shields on reverse are changed. The Edinburgh coins have been included here as they are now coins of Great Britain.

3600 Crown. Second bust, E (Edinburgh) below

	F	*VF*		*F*	*VF*		*F*	*VF*
	£	£		£	£		£	£
1707 ..	40·00	140·00	1708 ..	45·00	145·00			

3601 — plain

1707 ..	45·00	160·00	1708 ..	45·00	160·00

3602 ℞. Plumes in angles, 1708 .. .. 70·00 220·00

3603 Third bust. ℞. Roses and plumes, 1713 .. .. 75·00 210·00

3604

3604 Halfcrown. Plain

1707 ..	25·00	85·00	1709	25·00	85·00
1708 ..	25·00	85·00	1713 ..	30·00	95·00

3605 Halfcrown. E below bust

1707 ..	24·00	75·00	1708 ..	25·00	80·00	1709 ..	45·00	175·00

3606 ℞. Plumes in angles, 1708 .. .. 35·00 100·00

3607 ℞. Roses and plumes in angles

1710 ..	30·00	95·00	1713 ..	30·00	95·00
1712 ..	25·00	85·00	1714 ..	25·00	85·00

3609

3608 Shilling. Second bust, E below

1707 ..	20·00	65·00	1708 ..	30·00	95·00

3609 — E* below

1707 ..	35·00	95·00	1708 ..	30·00	60·00

3610 Third bust, plain

1707 ..	14·00	50·00	1709 ..	14·00	55·00
1708 ..	14·00	50·00	1711 ..	35·00	90·00

3611 — ℞. Plumes in angles

1707 ..	25·00	80·00	1708 ..	20·00	70·00

3612 — E below

1707 ..	15·00	50·00	1708 ..	30·00	70·00

			F £	VF £
3613	**Shilling.** Second bust. ℞. Roses and plumes, 1708		60·00	300·00

3614 Third bust. ℞. Roses and plumes

	F £	VF £		F £	VF £		F £	VF £
1708 ..	35·00	65·00	1710 ..	20·00	50·00			

3615 "Edinburgh" bust, E* below

1707 ..	*Extremely rare*		1708 ..	25·00	75·00	1709 ..	35·00	90·00

3616 — E below, 1709 .. .. *Extremely rare*

3617 Fourth bust. ℞. Roses and plumes

1710 ..	22·00	60·00	1713/2	20·00	55·00
1712 ..	18·00	50·00	1714 ..	18·00	50·00

3618 — plain, 1711 .. .. 13·00 50·00

3623

3620

3619 **Sixpence.** Normal bust. ℞. Plain

1707 ..	10·00	22·00	1708 ..	11·00	25·00	1711 ..	9·00	20·00

3620 — E below bust

1707 ..	12·00	25·00	1708 ..	13·00	30·00

3621 — E* below bust, 1708 .. .. 14·00 35·00

3622 "Edinburgh" bust, E* below, 1708 .. .. 16·00 40·00

3623 Normal bust. ℞. Plumes in angles

1707 ..	15·00	30·00	1708 ..	16·00	35·00

3624 ℞. Roses and plumes in angles, 1710 .. .. 20·00 65·00

COPPER

3625

	F	VF	EF
3625 **Farthing,** 1714	75·00	160·00	325·00

N.B. Overstruck dates are listed only if commoner than normal date or if no normal date is known.

GEORGE I, 1714-27

The coins of the first of the Hanoverian kings have the arms of the Duchy of Brunswick and Luneberg on one of the four shields, the object in the centre of the shield being the crown of Charlemagne. The king's German titles also appear, in abbreviated form, and name him "Duke of Brunswick and Luneberg, Arch-treasurer of the Holy Roman Empire, and Elector", and on the guinea of 1714, "Prince Elector". A quarter-guinea was struck for the first time in 1718, but it was an inconvenient size and the issue was discontinued.

Silver coined from bullion supplied to the mint by the South Sea Company in 1723 shows the company's initials S.S.C.; similarly Welsh Copper Company bullion has the letters W.C.C. below the king's bust and plumes and an interlinked CC on the reverse. Roses and plumes together on the reverse indicate silver supplied by the Company for Smelting Pit Coale and Sea Coale.

GOLD

3626 Five guineas

	F £	*VF* £		*F* £	*VF* £		*F* £	*VF* £
1716 ..	1850·00	4250·00	1720 ..	2000·00	4750·00			
1717 ..	2200·00	5250·00	1726 ..	1850·00	4250·00			

3627 Two guineas

1717 ..	750·00	1550·00	1720 ..	775·00	1650·00	1726 ..	625·00	1350·00

3627

3628

3628 Guinea. First head. R. Legend ends ET PR . EL (Prince Electror),
1714 .. .. 500·00 1350·00

3629 Second head, tie with two ends, 1715 .. .. 275·00 525·00

3630 Third head, no hair below truncation

1715 ..	175·00	450·00	1716 ..	275·00	575·00

3631 Fourth head, tie with loop and one end

1716 ..	175·00	450·00	1719 ..	175·00	450·00	1722 ..	175·00	450·00
1717 ..	200·00	500·00	1720 ..	175·00	450·00	1723 ..	275·00	575·00
1718 ..	*Extremely rare*		1721 ..	225·00	550·00			

3632 — elephant and castle below

1721 .. *Extremely rare* 1722 .. *Extremely rare*

3633 Fifth (older) head, tie with two ends

1723 ..	250·00	550·00	1725 ..	250·00	550·00	1727 ..	350·00	800·00
1724 ..	250·00	550·00	1726 ..	200·00	475·00			

3634 — elephant and castle below, 1726 .. .. 800·00 1800·00

3633

3638

3635 **Half-guinea.** First head

	F	*VF*		*F*	*VF*		*F*	*VF*
	£	£		£	£		£	£
1715 ..	225·00	550·00	1719 ..	135·00	350·00	1722 ..	175·00	425·00
1717 ..	175·00	425·00	1720 ..	300·00	775·00	1723 ..	*Extremely rare*	
1718 ..	125·00	325·00	1721 ..	*Extremely rare*		1724 ..	250·00	600·00

3636 — elephant and castle below, 1721 .. .. *Extremely rare*

3637 Second (older) bust

1725 ..	135·00	350·00	1726 ..	150·00	400·00	1727 ..	150·00	425·00

3638 **Quarter-guinea,** 1718 .. .. 50·00 110·00

SILVER

3639 **Crown.** R. Roses and plumes in angles

1716 ..	185·00	325·00	1720/18	200·00	400·00
1718/6	200·00	350·00	1726 ..	225·00	550·00

3640 R. SSC (South Sea Company) in angles, 1723 .. .. .. 200·00 500·00

3641 **Halfcrown.** Plain (proof only), 1715 *EF* £2000

3642 R. Roses and plumes in angles

1715 ..	70·00	200·00	1717 ..	70·00	200·00	1720/17	70·00	200·00

3643 R. SSC in angles, 1723 .. .. 80·00 190·00

3644 R. Small roses and plumes, 1726 .. .. 600·00 1000·00

3647

3650

3645 **Shilling.** First bust. R. Roses and plumes

1715 ..	30·00	80·00	1718 ..	27·00	75·00	1721/0	30·00	85·00
1716 ..	45·00	140·00	1719 ..	40·00	125·00	1722 ..	30·00	80·00
1717 ..	30·00	80·00	1720 ..	30·00	80·00	1723 ..	30·00	80·00

3646 — plain (i.e. no marks either side)

1720 ..	18·00	70·00	1721 ..	75·00	175·00

3647 R. SSC in angles, 1723 .. .. 15·00 50·00

3648 Second bust, bow to tie. R. Similar, 1723 .. .. .. 20·00 60·00

3649 R. Roses and plumes

1723 ..	25·00	60·00	1725 ..	25·00	60·00	1727 ..	100·00	250·00
1724 ..	25·00	60·00	1726 ..	100·00	250·00			

3650 — W.C.C. (Welsh Copper Company) below

1723 ..	110·00	325·00	1725 ..	110·00	325·00
1724 ..	110·00	325·00	1726 ..	110·00	325·00

3651 **Sixpence.** R. Roses and plumes in angles

1717 ..	25·00	75·00	1720 ..	25·00	75·00

3652 R. SSC in angles, 1723 .. .. 15·00 27·00

3653 R. Small roses and plumes, 1726 .. .. 27·00 60·00

3654 3655 3656 3657

3654 Fourpence

	F	VF		F	VF		F	VF
	£	£		£	£		£	£
1717 ..	8·50	16·00	1723 ..	8·50	16·00			
1721 ..	8·50	16·00	1727 ..	9·50	17·00			

3655 Threepence

1717 ..	9·00	17·00	1723 ..	9·50	18·00
1721 ..	9 50	18·00	1727 ..	9·50	18·00

3656 Twopence

1717 ..	6·00	9·50	1723 ..	6·50	10·00	1727 ..	6·50	10·00
1721 ..	5·50	9·00	1726 ..	5·50	9·00			

3657 Penny

1716 ..	4·00	6·50	1723 ..	4·50	7·00	1726 ..	6·00	9·50
1718 ..	4·00	6·50	1725 ..	4·00	6·50	1727 ..	6·00	9·50
1720 ..	4·00	6·50						

3658 Maundy set. As last four. Uniform dates

1723 ..	30·00	60·00	1727 ..	30·00	60·00

COPPER

3661 3662

3659 Halfpenny. "Dump" issue

1717 ..	7·50	35·00	1718 ..	7·00	32·50

3660 Second issue

1719 ..	4·50	25·00	1721 ..	4·50	25·00	1723 ..	5·00	27·50
1720 ..	4·50	25·00	1722 ..	5·00	27·50	1724 ..	4·50	25·00

3661 Farthing. "Dump" issue, 1717 .. .. 35·00 90·00

3662 Second issue

1719 ..	5·00	27·50	1721 ..	5·50	30·00	1723 ..	6·00	32·50
1720 ..	5·00	27·50	1722 ..	6·00	32·50	1724 ..	6·00	32·50

GEORGE II, 1727-60

Silver was only coined spasmodically by the Mint during this reign and no copper was struck after 1754. Gold coins made from bullion supplied by the East India Company bear the company's initials; and some of the treasure seized by Admiral Anson during his circumnavigation of the globe, 1740-44, and by other privateers, was made into coin which had the word LIMA below the king's bust to celebrate the expedition's successful harassment of the Spanish colonies in the New World. Hammered gold was finally demonetized in 1733.

GOLD

3664

3663 Five guineas. Young head

	F £	VF £		F £	VF £		F £	VF £
1729 ..	950·00	2400·00	1735 ..	1250·00	2750·00	1741 ..	850·00	2000·00
1731 ..	1350·00	2850·00	1738 ..	1000·00	2500·00			

3664 — E.I.C. (East India Company) below, 1729 .. .. 900·00 2100·00

3665 Old head, LIMA below, 1746 .. ..1100·00 2650·00

3666 — plain

1748 ..	850·00	2150·00	1753 ..	850·00	2150·00

3667* Two guineas. Young head

1734/3	1200·00	3000·00	1738 ..	325·00	650·00
1735 ..	450·00	950·00	1739 ..	350·00	750·00

3668 Intermediate head

1739 ..	300·00	550·00	1740 ..	325·00	625·00

3669* Old head

1748 ..	350·00	750·00	1753 ..	675·00	1850·00

* N.B. Beware recent forgeries.

3670

3674

3670 Guinea. First young head, small lettering, 1727 .. .. .. 600·00 1650·00

3671 — larger lettering, smaller shield

1727 ..	500·00	1150·00	1728 ..	550·00	1225·00

N.B. Overstruck dates are listed only if commoner than normal date or if no normal date is known.

3672 Guinea. Second (narrower) young head

	F £	VF £		F £	VF £		F £	VF £
1729 ..	*? proof or pattern only*		1731 ..	210·00	450·00			
1730 ..	350·00	825·00	1732 ..	275·00	600·00			

3673 — E.I.C. below

1729 ..	600·00	1350·00	1731 ..	350·00	850·00	1732 ..	325·00	700·00

3674 — larger lettering on *obv.*

1732 ..	*Extremely rare*		1735 ..	225·00	500·00	1737 ..	300·00	650·00
1733 ..	200·00	450·00	1736 ..	275·00	600·00	1738 ..	250·00	550·00
1734 ..	210·00	475·00						

3675 — — E.I.C. below, 1732 .. .. 450·00 900·00

3676 Intermediate head

1739 ..	210·00	450·00	1741/39	*Extremely rare*	
1740 ..	250·00	550·00	1743 ..	*Extremely rare*	

3677 — E.I.C. below, 1739 .. .. 400·00 850·00

3678 — larger lettering on *obv.*

1745 ..	350·00	850·00	1746 ..	225·00	500·00

3679 — LIMA below, 1745 .. .. 600·00 1425·00

3680 Old head

1747 ..	250·00	550·00	1751 ..	225·00	500·00	1756 ..	200·00	450·00
1748 ..	225·00	500·00	1752 ..	225·00	500·00	1758 ..	190·00	425·00
1749 ..	225·00	500·00	1753 ..	225·00	500·00	1759 ..	175·00	400·00
1750 ..	250·00	550·00	1755 ..	275·00	600·00	1760 ..	185·00	425·00

3681

3679

3685

3681 Half-guinea. Young head

1728 ..	250·00	575·00	1732 ..	250·00	575·00	1736 ..	225·00	550·00
1729 ..	225·00	550·00	1733 ..	*? exists*		1737 ..	*Extremely rare*	
1730 ..	*Extremely rare*		1734 ..	200·00	500·00	1738 ..	175·00	450·00
1731 ..	325·00	750·00	1735 ..	*? exists*		1739 ..	175·00	450·00

3682 — E.I.C. below

1729 ..	400·00	925·00	1731 ..	*Extremely rare*		1739 ..	*Extremely rare*	
1730 ..	550·00	1250·00	1732 ..	*Extremely rare*				

3683 Intermediate head

1740 ..	275·00	700·00	1745 ..	275·00	700·00
1743 ..	*? Unique*		1746 ..	175·00	450·00

3684 — LIMA below, 1745 .. .. 625·00 1550·00

3685 Old head

1747 ..	275·00	650·00	1751 ..	225·00	500·00	1756 ..	140·00	300·00
1748 ..	200·00	450·00	1752 ..	225·00	500·00	1758 ..	150·00	325·00
1749 ..	*Extremely rare*		1753 ..	150·00	325·00	1759 ..	125·00	275·00
1750 ..	165·00	375·00	1755 ..	150·00	325·00	1760 ..	125·00	275·00

Note. Values for coins in EF (extremely fine) condition can be three or more times the value of VF (very fine) specimens.

SILVER

3686 **Crown.** Young bust. R. Roses and plumes in angles

	F £	VF £		F £	VF £		F £	VF £
1732 ..	150·00	315·00	1735 ..	160·00	335·00			
1734 ..	160·00	335·00	1736 ..	155·00	325·00			

3687 R. Roses in angles

1739 ..	140·00	300·00	1741 ..	140·00	300·00

3688 Old head. R. Roses in angles, 1743 .. .. 140·00 310·00

3689 — LIMA below, 1746 .. .. 150·00 325·00

3690 Plain (i.e. no marks either side)

1750 ..	175·00	350·00	1751 ..	185·00	375·00

3692

3691 **Halfcrown.** Young bust; plain (proof only), 1731 *EF* £1000

3692 R. Roses and plumes

1731 ..	25·00	100·00	1734 ..	27·50	110·00	1736 ..	32·50	140·00
1732 ..	25·00	100·00	1735 ..	27·50	110·00			

3693 — R. Roses

1739 ..	37·50	90·00	1741 ..	37·50	90·00

3694 Old bust. R. Roses

1743 ..	35·00	85·00	1745 ..	35·00	85·00

3695 — LIMA below

1745 ..	20·00	60·00	1746 ..	20·00	60·00

3696 — plain

1750 ..	50·00	150·00	1751 ..	80·00	200·00

3701

3697 **Shilling.** Young bust. R. Plumes

1727 ..	37·00	85·00	1731 ..	42·50	100·00

3698 — R. Roses and plumes

1727 ..	25·00	60·00	1729 ..	28·00	70·00	1732 ..	28·00	70·00
1728 ..	35·00	80·00	1731 ..	25·00	60·00			

3699 Shilling. Young bust, larger lettering. ℞. Roses and plumes

	F £	VF £		F £	VF £		F £	VF £
1734 ..	22·00	55·00	1736 ..	22·00	55·00			
1735 ..	22·00	55·00	1737 ..	22·00	55·00			

3700 — plain, 1728 .. .. 45·00 100·00

3701 — ℞. Roses

1739 ..	11·00	42·00	1741 ..	11·00	42·00

3702 Old bust. ℞. Roses

1743 ..	9·00	40·00	1745 ..	9·00	40·00	1747 ..	9·00	40·00

3703 — LIMA below

1745 ..	12·00	42·00	1746/5	25·00	75·00

3704 — plain

1750 ..	12·00	45·00	1751 ..	25·00	75·00	1758 ..	8·00	25·00

3708

3710

3705 Sixpence. Young bust, plain, 1728 .. .. 35·00 80·00

3706 — ℞. Plumes, 1728 .. .. 25·00 60·00

3707 — ℞. Roses and plumes

1728 ..	17·50	50·00	1732 ..	17·50	50·00	1735 ..	32·50	80·00
1731 ..	17·50	50·00	1734 ..	32·50	80·00	1736 ..	22·50	55·00

3708 — ℞. Roses

1739 ..	16·00	45·00	1741 ..	16·00	45·00

3709 — Old bust. ℞. Roses

1743 ..	17·50	45·00	1745 ..	20·00	50·00

3710 — LIMA below

1745 ..	12·50	30·00	1746 ..	12·50	30·00

3711 — plain

1750 ..	12·00	45·00	1757 ..	4·00	10·00
1751 ..	17·00	55·00	1758 ..	4·00	10·00

3712 Fourpence. Young head. ℞. Crowned 4

1729 ..	7·00	15·00	1737 ..	7·00	15·00	1743 ..	7·00	15·00
1731 ..	7·00	15·00	1739 ..	7·00	15·00	1746 ..	6·00	14·00
1732 ..	7·00	15 00	1740 ..	7·00	15·00	1760 ..	7·00	15·00
1735 ..	7·00	15·00						

3713 Threepence. Young head. ℞. Crowned 3

1729 ..	7·50	16·00	1737 ..	7·00	15·00	1743 ..	7·00	15·00
1731 ..	7·50	16·00	1739 ..	7·00	15·00	1746 ..	7·00	15·00
1732 ..	7·50	16·00	1740 ..	7·00	15·00	1760 ..	7·00	15·00
1735 ..	7·50	16·00						

3714 Twopence. Young head. ℞. Crowned 2

1729 ..	3·00	7·00	1737 ..	3·00	7·00	1746 ..	3·00	7·00
1731 ..	3·00	7·00	1739 ..	3·50	8·00	1756 ..	3·00	7·00
1732 ..	3·00	7·00	1740 ..	4·00	9·00	1759 ..	3·00	7·00
1735 ..	3·00	7·00	1743 ..	3·00	7·00	1760 ..	3·00	7·00

3715 Penny. Young head. ℞. Crowned 1

	F	*VF*		*F*	*VF*		*F*	*VF*
	£	£		£	£		£	£
1729 ..	3·00	7·00	1743 ..	2·50	6·00	1755 ..	2·50	6·00
1731 ..	2·50	6·00	1746 ..	2·50	6·00	1756 ..	2·50	6·00
1732 ..	2·50	6·00	1750 ..	2·50	6·00	1757 ..	2·50	6·00
1735 ..	3·00	7·00	1752 ..	2·50	6·00	1758 ..	2·50	6·00
1737 ..	3·00	7·00	1753 ..	2·50	6·00	1759 ..	2·50	6·00
1739 ..	2·50	6·00	1754 ..	2·50	6·00	1760 ..	3·00	7·00
1740 ..	2·50	6·00						

3716

3716 Maundy Set. As last four. Uniform dates

1729 ..	30·00	60·00	1737 ..	28·00	57·50	1743 ..	28·00	57·50
1731 ..	30·00	60·00	1739 ..	28·00	57·50	1746 ..	28·00	57 50
1732 ..	28·00	57·50	1740 ..	28·00	57·50	1760 ..	30·00	60·00
1735 ..	28·00	57·50						

COPPER

3717 Halfpenny. Young bust

1729 ..	4 50	24·00	1733 ..	4·00	22·00	1737 ..	4·00	22·00
1730 ..	4·00	22·00	1734 ..	4·00	22·00	1738 ..	3·50	20·00
1731 ..	4·00	22·00	1735 ..	4·00	22·00	1739 ..	4·00	22·00
1732 ..	4·00	22·00	1736 ..	4·00	22·00			

3718 Old bust, GEORGIUS

1740 ..	4·00	22·00	1743 ..	3·50	20·00	1745 ..	3·50	20·00
1742 ..	4·00	22·00	1744 ..	3·50	20·00			

3719 — GEORGIVS

1746 ..	4·00	22·00	1749 ..	3·50	20·00	1752 ..	3·50	20·00
1747 ..	4·00	22·00	1750 ..	3·50	20·00	1753 ..	3·50	20·00
1748 ..	3·50	20·00	1751 ..	3·50	20·00	1754 ..	3·50	20·00

3720

3722

3720 Farthing. Young bust

1730 ..	5·00	25·00	1733 ..	5·00	25·00	1736 ..	5·00	25·00
1731 ..	5·00	25·00	1734 ..	5·50	30·00	1737 ..	4·00	22·00
1732 ..	5·50	30·00	1735 ..	4·00	22·00	1739 ..	4·00	22·00

3721 Old bust. GEORGIUS

1741 ..	5·50	30·00	1744 ..	5·00	27·50

3722 — GEORGIVS

1746 ..	3·50	18·00	1750 ..	5·00	27·50
1749 ..	3·75	20·00	1754 ..	1·25	9·00

GEORGE III, 1760-1820

During the second half of the 18th century very little silver or copper was minted. In 1797 Matthew Boulton's "cartwheels," the first copper pennies and twopences, demonstrated the improvement that could be effected as a result of the application of steam power to the coining press.

During the Napoleonic Wars bank notes came into general use when the issue of guineas was stopped between 1797 and 1813, but gold 7s. pieces were minted to help relieve the shortage of smaller money. As an emergency measure Spanish "dollars" were put into circulation for a short period after being countermarked, and in 1804 Spanish dollars were overstruck and issued as Bank of England dollars.

The transition to a "token" silver coinage began in 1811 when the Bank of England had 3s. and 1s. 6d. tokens made for general circulation. Private issues of token money in the years 1788-95 and 1811-15 helped to alleviate the shortage of regal coinage. A change over to a gold standard and a regular "token" silver coinage came in 1816 when the Mint, which was moved from its old quarters in the Tower of London to a new site on Tower Hill, began a complete recoinage. The guinea was replaced by a 20s. sovereign, and silver coins were made which had an intrinsic value lower than their face value. Most British silver is still legal tender back to 1816. The St. George design used on the sovereign and crown was the work of Benedetto Pistrucci.

Early coinages

GOLD

3724

3723 Five guineas. Pattern only.
1770 *Extremely rare* — 1773 *Extremely rare* — 1777 *Extremely rare*

3724 Two guineas. Pattern only.
1768 *Extremely rare* — 1773 *Extremely rare* — 1777 *Extremely rare*

	F	*VF*
3725 Guinea. First head, 1761	450·00	950·00

3725

3726

3727

3726 Second head

	F £	*VF* £		*F* £	*VF* £
1763 ..	450·00	950·00	1764 ..	275·00	600·00

3727 Guinea. Third head

	F £	VF £		F £	VF £		F £	VF £
1765 ..	185·00	440·00	1768 ..	165·00	400·00	1771 ..	170·00	375·00
1766 ..	135·00	365·00	1769 ..	165·00	400·00	1772 ..	135·00	365·00
1767 ..	200·00	475·00	1770 ..	200·00	475·00	1773 ..	120·00	350·00

3728 Fourth head

1774 ..	85·00	165·00	1778 ..	125·00	300·00	1783 ..	110·00	215·00
1775 ..	85·00	165·00	1779 ..	90·00	175·00	1784 ..	90·00	175·00
1776 ..	85·00	165·00	1781 ..	100·00	185·00	1785 ..	85·00	165·00
1777 ..	85·00	165·00	1782 ..	95·00	180·00	1786 ..	85·00	165·00

3728

3729

3729 Fifth head, ℞. "Spade" shaped shield

1787 ..	80·00	150·00	1792 ..	85·00	160·00	1797 ..	100·00	190·00
1788 ..	80·00	150·00	1793 ..	80·00	150·00	1798 ..	80·00	150·00
1789 ..	90·00	165·00	1794 ..	80·00	150·00	1799 ..	110·00	205·00
1790 ..	80·00	150·00	1795 ..	105·00	200·00			
1791 ..	80·00	150·00	1796 ..	120·00	225·00			

3730 Sixth head, ℞. Shield in Garter, known as the Military guinea, 1813 *VF* £500 *EF* £1100

3733

3734

3737

3731 Half-guinea. First head

1762 ..	160·00	400·00	1763 ..	275·00	650·00

3732 Second head

1764 ..	125·00	300·00	1768 ..	165·00	375·00	1773 ..	165·00	375·00
1765/4	300·00	725 00	1769 ..	150·00	350·00	1774 ..	325·00	775·00
1766 ..	150·00	350·00	1772	*Extremely rare*				

3733 Third head, (less fine style)

1774 ..	*Extremely rare*		1775 ..	200·00	400·00

3734 Fourth head

1775 ..	75·00	160·00	1779 ..	110·00	225·00	1784 ..	75·00	160·00
1776 ..	75·00	160·00	1781 ..	85·00	170·00	1785 ..	70·00	150·00
1777 ..	70·00	150·00	1783 ..	500·00	1150·00	1786 ..	70·00	150·00
1778 ..	85·00	170·00						

3735 Fifth head, ℞. "Spade" type

1787 ..	60·00	135·00	1792 ..	*Extremely rare*		1797 ..	60·00	135·00
1788 ..	60·00	135·00	1793 ..	60·00	135·00	1798 ..	60·00	135·00
1789 ..	70·00	150·00	1794 ..	70·00	150·00	1800 ..	150·00	400·00
1790 ..	60·00	135·00	1795 ..	90·00	200·00			
1791 ..	70·00	150·00	1796 ..	70·00	150·00			

3736 **Half-guinea.** Sixth head. ℞. Shield in Garter

	F £	VF £		F £	VF £		F £	VF £
1801 ..	60·00	125·00	1802 ..	65·00	135·00	1803 ..	65·00	135·00

3737 Seventh head. Hd. with short hair. ℞. As last

1804 ..	60·00	135·00	1808 ..	65·00	150·00	1811 ..	85·00	175·00
1805 ..	*Extremely rare*		1809 ..	65·00	150·00	1813 ..	75·00	160·00
1806 ..	65·00	150·00	1810 ..	65·00	150·00			

3738 3740 3741

3738 **Third-guinea.** I. First head

1797 ..	30·00	85·00	1799 ..	70·00	175·00	1800 ..	30·00	85·00
1798 ..	30·00	85·00						

3739 II. Similar but date not in legend

1801 ..	35·00	90·00	1802 ..	30·00	85·00	1803 ..	30·00	85·00

3740 III. Second head with short hair

1804 ..	30·00	85·00	1809 ..	35·00	90·00	1811 ..	150·00	400·00
1806 ..	35·00	90·00	1810 ..	30·00	85·00	1813 ..	75·00	170·00
1808 ..	35·00	90·00						

3741 **Quarter-guinea,** 1762 .. .. 55·00 120·00

N.B. For gold of the new Coinage, 1817-20, *see page* 235.

SILVER

3742

		F	VF	EF
3742	**Shilling.** Young bust, known as the "Northumberland" shilling 1763	100·00	225·00	500·00
3743	Older bust, no semée of hearts in the Hanoverian shield, 1787	4·00	10·00	30·00
3744	— — no stop over head, 1787	13·00	28·00	65·00
3745	— — no stops at date, 1787	18·00	35·00	75·00

3746

no hearts

with hearts

	F £	VF £	EF £
3746 — with semée of hearts, 1787	4·00	11·00	32·50
3747 — no stop over head 1798: known as the "Dorrien and Magens" shilling			*FDC* £4,000·00
3748 **Sixpence.** without hearts, 1787	3·00	6·00	15·00
3749 — with hearts, 1787	3·00	6·00	17·00

3750 **Fourpence.** Young bust

	F £	VF £	EF £		F £	VF £	EF £
1763 ..	3·00	8·00	16·00	1776 ..	4·50	9·00	16·00
1765 ..	80·00	200·00	500·00	1780 ..	4·50	9·00	16·00
1766 ..	5·00	10·00	17·00	1784 ..	5·00	10·00	17·00
1770 ..	5·00	10·00	17·00	1786 ..	5·00	10·00	17·00
1772 ..	5·00	10·00	17·00				

3751 — Older bust, R̷. Thin 4 ("Wire Money"), 1792 .. .. 7·00 14·00 30·00

3752 — — R̷. Normal 4

	F £	VF £	EF £		F £	VF £	EF £
1795 ..	3·50	8·00	15·00	1800 ..	3·50	8·00	15·00

3750 3751 3755

3753 **Threepence.** Young bust

	F £	VF £	EF £		F £	VF £	EF £
1762 ..	2·00	4·50	9·00	1772 ..	3·00	6·00	13·00
1763 ..	2·00	4·50	9·00	1780 ..	3·00	6·00	13·00
1765 ..	80·00	200·00	500·00	1784 ..	3·00	7·00	14·00
1766 ..	3·00	6·00	12·00	1786 ..	3·00	6·00	13·00
1770 ..	3·00	6·00	12·00				

3754 — Older bust; R̷. Thin 3 ("Wire Money"), 1792 .. 7·00 14·00 30·00

3755 — — R̷. Normal 3

	F £	VF £	EF £		F £	VF £	EF £
1795 ..	3·50	7·00	13·00	1800 ..	3·50	7·00	13·00

3756 **Twopence.** Young bust

	F £	VF £	EF £		F £	VF £	EF £
1763 ..	2·50	5·00	10·50	1776 ..	2·50	5·00	10·00
1765 ..	60·00	150·00	350·00	1780 ..	2·00	4·50	10·00
1766 ..	2·00	4·50	10·00	1784 ..	2·00	4·50	10·00
1772 ..	2·00	4·50	10·00	1786 ..	2·00	4·50	10·00

3757 — Older bust. R̷. Thin 2 ("Wire Money"), 1792 .. 6·00 13·00 26·00

3758 — — R̷. Normal 2;

	F £	VF £	EF £		F £	VF £	EF £
1795 ..	2·00	4·00	6·00	1800 ..	2·00	4·00	6·00

3759 **Penny.** Young bust

	F £	VF £	EF £		F £	VF £	EF £
1763 ..	2·50	5·00	10·00	1779 ..	2·00	4·50	9·50
1765 ..	*? Exists*			1780 ..	2·50	5·00	10·00
1766 ..	2·00	4·50	9·50	1781 ..	2·00	4·50	9·50
1770 ..	2·00	4·50	9·50	1784 ..	2·00	4·50	9·50
1772 ..	2·00	4·50	9·50	1786 ..	2·00	4·50	9·50
1776 ..	2·50	5·00	10·00				

3760 — Older bust. R̷. Thin 1 ("Wire Money"), 1792 .. 2·50 5·00 8·00

3761 — — R̷. Normal 1

	F £	VF £	EF £		F £	VF £	EF £
1795 ..	1·50	2·50	6·00	1800 ..	1·50	2·50	6·00

3762 Maundy set. Uniform dates

		F	VF	EF			F	VF	EF
		£	£	£			£	£	£
1763	..	26·00	45·00	100·00	1780	..	26·00	45·00	100·00
1766	..	26·00	45·00	100·00	1784	..	26·00	45·00	100·00
1772	..	26·00	45·00	100·00	1786	..	26·00	45·00	100·00

3763 — Older bust. ℞. Thin numerals ("Wire Money"), 1792 60·00 120·00 250·00

3764 — ℞. Normal numerals. Uniform dates

1795	..	26·00	45·00	95·00	1800	..	26·00	45·00	95·00

Emergency issue

3765

3767

3766

		F	VF	EF
3765	**Dollar.** (current for 4s. 9d.). Spanish American 8 *reales* countermarked with head of George III in oval	60·00	125·00	300·00
3766	— — octagonal countermark	100·00	250·00	650·00
3767	**Half-dollar** with similar oval countermark	70·00	160·00	300·00

Bank of England issue

3768

3768 Dollar. (current for 5s.). Laureate bust of king.
℞. Britannia seated l., 1804 .. .. 60·00 100·00 250·00

These dollars were re-struck from Spanish-American 8 *reales* until at least 1811. Dollars that show dates of original coin are worth rather more.

3769 Three shillings. Draped bust in armour. ℞. BANK/TOKEN/ 3 SHILL/date (in oak wreath)

		F	VF	EF			F	VF	EF
		£	£	£			£	£	£
1811	..	10·00	22·50	60·00	1812	..	11·00	25·00	65·00

3770 Three shillings. Laureate head r. ℞. As before but wreath of oak and laurel

1812	..	9·00	20·00	55·00	1815	..	9·00	20·00	55·00
1813	..	9·00	20·00	55·00	1816	..	90·00	175·00	350·00
1814	..	9·00	20·00	55·00					

3771

3772

3771 Eighteen pence. Draped bust in armour

1811	..	9·00	20·00	55·00	1812	..	9·00	20·00	55·00

3772 — Laureate head

1812	..	7·50	18·00	50·00	1815	..	7·50	18·00	50·00
1813	..	7·50	18·00	50·00	1816	..	7·50	18·00	50·00
1814	..	7·50	18·00	50·00					

3773 Ninepence. Similar, 1812 (pattern only) .. .. *FDC* £650

N.B. For the last or "new coinage", 1816-20, *see page* 236.

COPPER

First issue—London

3774

3774 Halfpenny. Cuirassed bust r. ℞. Britannia

1770	..	2·50	12·00	35·00	1773	..	2·50	10·00	30·00
1771	..	2·50	10·00	30·00	1774	..	2·50	12·00	35·00
1772	..	2·50	10·00	30·00	1775	..	3·00	14·00	40·00

3775 Farthing

1771	..	10·00	35·00	85·00	1774	..	3·50	15·00	45·00
1773	..	2·00	9·00	27·50	1775	..	4·00	16·00	50·00

Copper

Second issue—Soho. "Cartwheel" coinage.

3776

		F	VF	EF
3776	**Twopence.** Legends incuse on raised rim 1797 ..	6·00	16·00	90·00
3777	**Penny,** 1797. Similar	5·00	14·00	50·00

Halfpence and farthings of this issue are patterns.

Third issue—Soho.

3778	**Halfpenny.** Draped bust r., 1799	1·00	4·50	18·00
3779	**Farthing,** 1799	1·00	4·50	18·00

3778

3782

Fourth issue—Soho.

3780 Penny. Different bust

	F £	VF £	EF £		F £	VF £	EF £
1806 ..	2·00	9·00	35·00	1807 ..	2·50	10·00	40·00

3781 Halfpenny

1806 ..	1·00	3·00	16·00	1807 ..	1·00	4·00	20·00

3782 Farthing

1806 ..	1·00	3·00	16·00	1807 ..	1·00	4·50	22·00

EIGHTEENTH CENTURY TOKENS

In 1787, the regal copper coinage being very scanty, pennies and half-pennies were struck by the Anglesey Copper Mining Company and there began a fresh token epoch. They present an immense variety of types, persons, buildings, coats of arms, local legends, political events, etc., all drawn upon for subjects of design. They were struck by many firms in most cities and towns in the country and are to be found in good condition. Circulated specimens are so common that they have little value.

For further details of 18th century tokens see *The Provincial Token-Coinage of the Eighteenth Century*, by Dalton and Hamer (reprint 1967, price £25) and Seaby's *British Tokens and their Values* (*out of print*).

		VF	*EF*
Price of commoner pennies	*from*	£7·00	£18·00
Price of commoner halfpennies	..	£3·50	£9·00
— — — farthings	..	£2·50	£7·00

Bury St. Edmunds penny

Lancaster Halfpenny

Issac Newton Farthing

NINETEENTH CENTURY TOKENS

With the issue of the copper coinage of 1797 tokens were made illegal, but the dearth of silver currency was still felt. During the Napoleonic wars there came a small wave of prosperity in the industrial districts and the inevitable need of small change, so in 1811 tokens again made their appearance. On this occasion silver ones were made as well as copper. These, with two exceptions, were suppressed before the last coinage of George III.

For further details of 19th century silver tokens see *The Nineteenth Century Token Coinage* by W. J. Davis (reprint 1979 with valuation sheet, price £18·00) and *Silver Token-Coinage* 1811-1812, by R. Dalton (price £3.50) also Seaby's *British Tokens and Their Values* (*out of print*).

	EF
Price of the commoner shillings	£18·00
— — — sixpences	£10·00

Cheltenham Shilling

Charing Cross Sixpence

	VF	*EF*
Price of the commoner pennies	£2·50	£10·00
— — — halfpennies	£1·50	£6·00
— — — farthings	£3·00	£11·00

Withymoor Scythe Works Penny, 1813

Hull Halfpenny

GEORGE III

Last or new coinage, 1816-20

The year 1816 is a landmark in the history of our coinage. For some years at the beginning of the nineteenth century Mint production was virtually confined to small gold denominations, regular full production being resumed only after the Mint had been moved from the Tower of London to a new site on Tower Hill. Steam powered minting machinery made by Boulton and Watt replaced the old hand operated presses and these produced coins which were technically much superior to the older milled coins.

In 1816 for the first time, British silver coins were produced with an intrinsic value substantially below their face value, the first official token coinage.

Our present "silver" coins are made to the same weight standard and are still legal tender back to 1816 with the exception of the halfcrown. The old guinea was replaced by a sovereign of twenty shillings in 1817, the standard of 22 carat (·916) fineness still being retained.

Engraver's and/or designer's initials:
B. P. (Benedetto Pistrucci)

GOLD

3783

3783* Five pounds, 1820 (Pattern only) .. .. *FDC* £25,000·00

3784 Two pounds, 1820 (Pattern only) .. .. £8000·00

3785 Sovereign. ℞. St. George.

		F	*VF*	*EF*			*F*	*VF*	*EF*
		£	£	£			£	£	£
1817	..	85·00	225·00	650·00	1819	..	*Extremely rare*		
1818	..	110·00	275·00	750·00	1820	..	85·00	225 00	650·00

3785

3786

3786 Half-Sovereign. ℞. Crowned shield.

1817	..	60·00	150·00	450·00	1820	..	70·00	175·00	475·00
1818	..	65·00	165·00	475·00					

*Beware counterfeits.

SILVER

3787

3787 Crown. Laureate head r. ℞. Pistrucci's St. George and dragon within Garter.

		F	VF	EF
		£	£	£
1818, edge	LVIII	10·00	40·00	135·00
— —	LIX	11·00	45·00	145·00
1819 —	LIX	10·00	40·00	125·00
— —	LX	11·00	45·00	145·00
1820 —	LX	10·00	40·00	135·00

3788

3788 Halfcrown. Large or "bull" head.

	F	VF	EF		F	VF	EF
	£	£	£		£	£	£
1816 ..	5·00	20·00	70·00	1817 ..	5·00	20·00	70·00

3789

3789 — Small head.

1817 ..	5·00	20·00	80·00	1819 ..	6·00	25·00	90·00
1818 ..	6·00	25·00	90·00	1820 ..	9·00	30·00	125·00

3790

3791

3790 Shilling. R. Shield in Garter.

		F £	*VF* £	*EF* £			*F* £	*VF* £	*EF* £
1816	..	1·75	6·00	25·00	1819	..	1·75	7·00	30·00
1817	..	2·25	6·00	27·50	1820	..	1·75	7·00	30·00
1818	..	9·00	30·00	95·00					

3791 Sixpence. R. Shield in Garter.

1816	..	1·25	4·75	18·00	1819	..	1·75	6·00	27·50
1817	..	1·75	6·00	25·00	1820	..	1·75	6·00	27·50
1818	..	1·75	7·00	30·00					

3792

3792 Maundy set (4d., 3d., 2d. and 1d.).

			EF £	*FDC* £				*EF* £	*FDC* £
1817	..	..	80·00	110·00	1820	..	..	80·00	110·00
1818	..	..	80·00	110·00					

3793	— **fourpence,** 1817, 1818, 1820 *from*	14·00	23·00
3794	— **threepence,** 1817, 1818, 1820 *from*	14·00	23·00
3795	— **twopence,** 1817, 1818, 1820 *from*	8·00	13·00
3796	— **penny,** 1817, 1818, 1820 *from*	8·00	12·00

GEORGE IV, 1820-30

The Mint resumed the coinage of copper farthings in 1821, and pennies and halfpennies in 1825. A gold two pound piece was first issued for general circulation in 1823.

Engraver's and/or designer's initials:
B. P. (Benedetto Pistrucci)
J. B. M. (Jean Baptiste Merlen)

GOLD

3797

3797 **Five pounds,** 1826 (Proof only). ℞. Shield.. .. .. *FDC* £9000·00

3798

		VF	*EF*
3798	**Two pounds,** 1823. Large bare head. ℞. St. George ..	450·00	1000·00
3799	— 1826. Type as 3797 (Proof only)	*FDC*	£4000·00

3800

3800 **Sovereign.** Laureate head. ℞. St. George.

	F	*VF*	*EF*		*F*	*VF*	*EF*
1821 ..	70·00	200·00	525·00	1824 ..	85·00	225·00	550·00
1822* ..	75·00	210·00	550·00	1825 ..	150·00	375·00	1000·00
1823 ..	175·00	425 00	1100·00				

* Beware counterfeits.

3801

3801 Sovereign. Bare head. R. Crowned shield

		F	*VF*	*EF*			*F*	*VF*	*EF*
		£	£	£			£	£	£
1825	..	75·00	200·00	550·00	1828*	..	650·00	1500·00	3750·00
1826	..	70·00	185·00	525·00	1829	..	80·00	200·00	575·00
— Proof	*FDC* £11·00				1830	..	80·00	200·00	575·00
1827*	..	80·00	175·00	550·00					

3802

3803

3804

3802 Half-sovereign. Laureate head. R. Ornately garnished shield.

1821	..	150·00	350·00	850·00

3803 — As last. R. Plain shield.

1823	..	70·00	200·00	575·00	1825	..	60·00	175·00	525·00
1824	..	65·00	180·00	550·00					

3804 — Bare head. R. Garnished shield.

1826	..	75·00	175·00	500·00	1827	..	75·00	185·00	525·00
— Proof	*FDC* £700				1828	..	65·00	165·00	475·00

*Beware counterfeits.

SILVER

3805

3805 Crown. Laureate head. R. St. George.

1821, edge SECUNDO	12·00	60·00	350·00
1822 — SECUNDO	18·00	80·00	450·00
— — TERTIO	16·00	70·00	375·00

3806

			FDC £
3806	**Crown.** Bare head. ℞. Shield with crest (Proof only), 1826	.. ..	3500·00

3807

3808

3807 Halfcrown. Laureate head. ℞. Garnished shield.

		F £	VF £	EF £			F £	VF £	EF £
1820	..	6·00	27·50	90·00	1823	..	225·00	650·00	1500·00
1821	..	6·00	27·50	90·00					

3808 — Similar. ℞. Shield in Garter and collar.

1823	..	7·00	30·00	95·00	1824	..	10·00	40·00	150·00

3809

3809 — Bare head. ℞. Shield with crest.

1824	..	*Extremely rare*			1826	..	Proof	*FDC* £500	
1825	..	7·00	30·00	100·00	1828	..	12·00	50·00	175·00
1826	..	6·50	27·50	90·00	1829	..	9·00	40·00	160·00

3810

3811

3812

3810 Shilling. Laureate head. ℞. Garnished shield.

	F £	VF £	EF £
1821	4·50	18·00	60·00

3811 — Similar. ℞. Shield in Garter.

	F	VF	EF		F	VF	EF
1823	10·00	45·00	150·00	1825	5·00	20·00	65·00
1824	4·00	17·00	55·00				

3812 — Bare head. ℞. Lion on crown.

	F	VF	EF		F	VF	EF
1825	2·00	9·00	35·00	1827	6·00	30·00	100·00
1826	1·75	8·00	30·00	1829	5·50	25·00	90·00

— Proof *FDC* £225

3813

3814

3815

3813 Sixpence. Laureate head. ℞. Garnished shield.

	F	VF	EF
1821	3·75	15·00	50·00

3814 — Similar. ℞. Shield in Garter.

	F	VF	EF		F	VF	EF
1824	3·75	15·00	50·00	1826	8·00	25·00	90·00
1825	3·00	12·00	45·00				

3815 — Bare head. ℞. Lion on crown.

	F	VF	EF		F	VF	EF
1826	2·00	9·00	37·50	1828	4·50	18·00	60·00
— Proof *FDC* £200				1829	3·50	16·00	55·00
1827	5·50	25·00	90·00				

3816

3816 Maundy Set (4d., 3d., 2d. and 1d.).

	EF £	*FDC* £		*EF* £	*FDC* £
1822	70·00	115·00	1827	65·00	100·00
1823	65·00	100·00	1828	65·00	100·00
1824	70·00	110·00	1829	65·00	100·00
1825	65·00	100·00	1830	65·00	100·00
1826	65·00	100·00			

			EF	*FDC*
3817	**Maundy fourpence,** 1822-30	*from* ..	13·00	21·00
3818	— **threepence,** small head, 1822	..	18·00	30·00
3819	— — normal head, 1823-1830	*from* ..	12·00	20·00
3820	— **twopence,** 1822-30	*from* ..	9·00	12·00
3821	— **penny,** 1822-30	*from* ..	6·50	11·00

COPPER

First issue, 1821-6.

3822

3822 Farthing. Laureate bust, draped.

	F	*VF*	*EF*		*F*	*VF*	*EF*
	£	£	£		£	£	£
1821 ..	·50	3·00	14·00	1825 ..	·50	3·00	14 00
1822 ..	·45	2·75	12·00	1826 ..	1·25	5·00	20·00
1823 ..	·60	3·50	16·00				

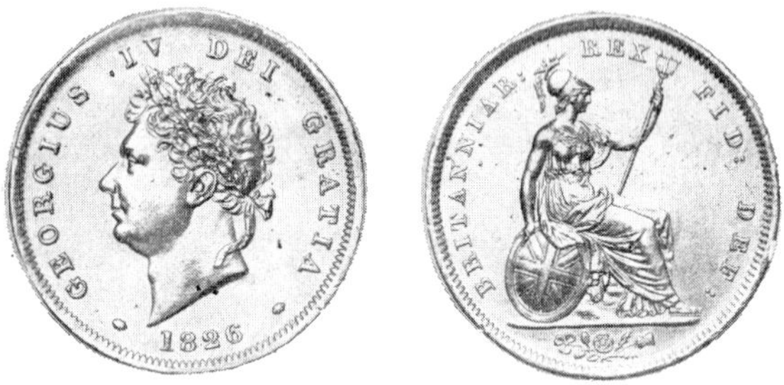

3823

3827

Second Issue, 1825-30.

3823 Penny. Laureate head. ℞. Britannia.

1825 ..	4·00	15·00	45·00	1826	Proof *FDC* £150		
1826 ..	3·00	12·00	35·00	1827 ..	25·00	80·00	600·00

3824 Halfpenny. Similar.

1825 ..	9·00	27·50	75·00	1826	Proof *FDC* £80		
1826 ..	·60	3·50	18·00	1827 ..	1·00	4·50	25·00

3825 Farthing. Similar.

1826 ..	·45	3·00	12·00	1828 ..	·50	3·50	15·00
— Proof *FDC* £90				1829 ..	1·00	5 50	27·50
1827 ..	·60	4·50	22·00	1830 ..	·55	4·00	20·00

3826 Half-farthing (for use in Ceylon). Similar.

1828 ..	2·50	10·00	40·00	1830 ..	2·50	10·00	40·00

3827 Third-farthing (for use in Malta). Similar.

1827	·60	2·50	16·00

WILLIAM IV, 1830-37

In order to prevent confusion between the sixpence and half-sovereign the size of the latter was reduced in 1834, but the smaller gold piece was not acceptable to the public and in the following year it was made to the normal size. In 1836 the silver groat was again issued for general circulation: it is the only British silver coin which has a seated Britannia as the type. Crowns were not struck during this reign for general circulation; but proofs or patterns of this denomination were made and are greatly sought after. Silver threepences and threehalfpence were minted for use in the Colonies.

Engraver's and/or designer's initials:
W. W. (William Wyon)

GOLD

3828

3828 **Two pounds,** 1831 (Proof only) .. .. *FDC* £7000·00

3829 **Sovereign.** ℞. Crowned shield.

	F £	*VF* £	*EF* £
1831 ..	100·00	225·00	625·00
— Proof *FDC* £1200			
1832* ..	90·00	185·00	600·00
1833 ..	100·00	225·00	625·00
1835 ..	100·00	225·00	625·00
1836 ..	100·00	225·00	625·00
1837 ..	95·00	200·00	600·00

* Beware counterfeits.

3829

3830

3831

3830 **Half-sovereign.** Similar; small size.

	F	*VF*	*EF*
1831 .. Proof *FDC* £825			
1834 ..	100·00	225·00	650·00

3831 — large size.

	F	*VF*	*EF*
1835 ..	75·00	175·00	500·00
1836 ..	110·00	250·00	800·00
1837 ..	80·00	200·00	550·00

3832 — Similar, *obv.* struck from 6d. die, 1836 .. .. 900·00

SILVER

3833

3833 Crown. ℞. Shield on mantle, 1831 (Proof only) .. .. .. *FDC* £5000·00

3834

3834 Halfcrown. ℞. Shield on mantle.

		F	VF	EF			F	VF	EF
		£	£	£			£	£	£
1831	Proof	*FDC*	£550		1836	..	9·00	45·00	135·00
1834	..	9·00	40·00	120·00	1837	..	12·00	55·00	175·00
1835	..	14·00	60·00	200·00					

3835

3836

3835 Shilling. ℞. Value in wreath.

1831	Proof	*FDC*	£300		1836	..	4·00	18·00	60·00
1834	..	4·00	18·00	60·00	1837	..	5·00	25·00	80·00
1835	..	5·00	24·00	75·00					

3836 Sixpence. ℞. Value in wreath.

		F	VF	EF			F	VF	EF
		£	£	£			£	£	£
1831	..	2·50	12·00	45·00	1835	..	2·50	12·00	45·00
—	Proof	*FDC*	£175		1836	..	6·00	25·00	100·00
1834	..	2·50	10·00	40·00	1837	..	4·00	20·00	80·00

3837

3837 Groat. ℞. Britannia seated.

		F	VF	EF			F	VF	EF
		£	£	£			£	£	£
1836	..	·50	2·50	14·00	1837	..	·60	2·75	15·00

3838 Threepence (for use in the West Indies). As Maundy threepence but with a dull surface.

1834	..	1·50	9·00	30·00	1836	..	1·00	8·00	28·00
1835	..	1·00	8·00	28·00	1837	..	2·50	10·00	36·00

3839

3839 Three-halfpence (for Colonial use). ℞. Value.

1834	..	·50	2·00	14·00	1836	..	·70	3·00	16·00
1835	..	·55	2·50	15·00	1837	..	4·50	17·50	65·00

3840

3840 Maundy set (4d., 3d., 2d., and 1d.).

			EF	FDC				EF	FDC
			£	£				£	£
1831	..	..	65·00	110·00	1834	..	..	60·00	105·00
—	..	Proof	*FDC* £200		1835	..	..	60·00	105·00
1832	..	..	60·00	105·00	1836	..	..	60·00	105·00
1833	..	..	60·00	105·00	1837	..	..	60·00	105·00

3841	— **fourpence,** 1831-7 *from*	13·00	22·00
3842	— **threepence,** 1831-7 *from*	18·00	26·00
3843	— **twopence,** 1831-7 *from*	9·00	15·00
3844	— **penny,** 1831-7 *from*	8·50	14·00

COPPER

3845

3845 Penny. No initials on truncation.

		F £	VF £	EF £			F £	VF £	EF £
1831	..	5·00	25·00	80·00	1834	..	6·00	30·00	90·00
—	Proof	*FDC* £160			1837	..	10·00	50·00	150·00

3846 — ww on truncation, 1831 .. .. 7·00 35·00 110·00

3847 Halfpenny. As penny.

1831	..	1·00	6·00	25·00	1834	.	1·00	6·50	27·50
—	Proof	*FDC* £80			1837	..	·75	5·50	22·50

3848 Farthing. Similar.

1831	..	·35	2·50	15·00	1835	..	·35	2·25	14·00
—	Proof	*FDC* £90			1836	..	·50	3·00	18·00
1834	..	·35	2·25	14·00	1837	..	·35	2·25	14·00

3848

3849

3849 Half-farthing (for use in Ceylon). Similar.

1837 12·00 35·00 110·00

3850 Third-farthing (for use in Malta). Similar.

1835 .. .. ·65 3·00 16·00

VICTORIA, 1837-1901

In 1849, as a first step towards decimalization, a silver florin ($\frac{1}{10}$th pound) was introduced, but the coins of 1849 omitted the usual *Dei Gratia* and these so-called "Godless", florins were replaced in 1851 by the "Gothic" issue. The halfcrown was temporarily discontinued but was minted again from 1874 onwards. Between 1863 and 1880 reverse dies of the gold and silver coins were numbered in the course of Mint experiments into the wear of dies. The exception being the florin when the die number is on the obverse below the bust.

The gold and silver coins were redesigned for the Queen's Golden Jubilee in 1887. The double-florin which was then issued was abandoned after only four years; the Jubilee sixpence of 1887, known as the "withdrawn" type, was changed to avoid confusion with the half sovereign. Gold and silver was again redesigned in 1893 with an older portrait of the Queen, but the "old head" was not used on the bronze coinage until 1895. The heavy copper penny had been replaced by the lighter bronze "bun" penny in 1860. In 1874-6 and 1881-2 some of the bronze was made by Heaton in Birmingham, and these have a letter H by the date. From 1897 farthings were issued with a dark surface.

Early sovereigns had a shield type reverse, but Pistrucci's St. George design was used again from 1871. In order to increase the output of gold coinage, branches of the Royal Mint were set up in Australia at Sydney and Melbourne, and, later, at Perth, for coining gold of imperial type.

Engraver's and / or designer's initials:

W. W. (William Wyon)
L. C. W. (Leonard Charles Wyon)
J. E. B. (Joseph Boehm)
T. B. (Thomas Brock)

GOLD

NOTE. Over the last few years there has been substantial variation in the bullion price of gold and, as it has fluctuated, it has affected the value of British gold coins, particularly from Victorian issues onwards. The values given here were calculated at a time when the gold price was approximately \$150 per fine oz. Most modern gold below VF condition sells at only a small premium above the quoted daily price for sovereigns.

Young head coinage, 1838-87.

3851

3851 Five pounds, 1839. ℞. "Una and the lion" (proof only) .. *FDC* £14,000·00

3852

3853

3852 **Sovereign,** type I. ℞. Shield.

	F	*VF*	*EF*
	£	£	£
1838	75·00	150·00	425·00
1839	175·00	350·00	1000·00
— Proof *FDC* £1150·00			
1841	1000·00	1750·00	3000·00
1842		75·00	170·00
1843		75·00	170·00
1844		77·50	175·00
1845		77·50	175·00
1846		80·00	185·00
1847		75·00	170·00
1848		85·00	200·00
1849		85·00	200·00
1850		85·00	200·00
1851		77·50	175·00

	VF	*EF*
	£	£
1852	75·00	170·00
1853	75·00	170·00
— Proof *FDC* £2500·00		
1854	77·50	175·00
1855	75·00	170·00
1856	77·50	175·00
1857	75·00	170·00
1858	95·00	225·00
1859	85·00	200·00
1860	85·00	200·00
1861	75·00	170·00
1862	75·00	170·00
1863	75·00	170·00
1872	75·00	170·00

3853 — — die number below wreath.

1863	75·00	160·00
1864	75·50	150·00
1865	80·00	165·00
1866	75·00	150·00
1868	80·00	165·00
1869	75·00	150·00
1870	80·00	170·00
1871	75·00	150·00
1872	75·00	150·00
1873	77·50	165·00
1874	*Extremely rare*	

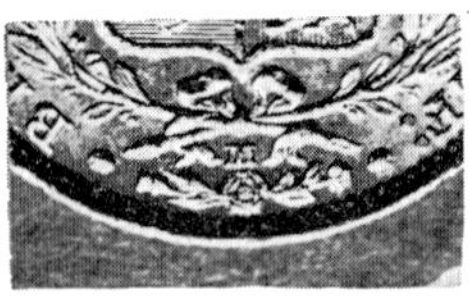

3854

3855

3854 — — M below wreath for Melbourne mint.

1872 M	75·00	165·00
1874 M	75·00	150·00
1875 M	? *None issued*	
1880 M	300·00	1000·00
1881 M	140·00	350·00
1882 M	75·00	165·00
1883 M	150·00	450·00
1884 M	75·00	150·00
1885 M	75·00	150·00
1886 M	*Extremely rare*	
1887 M	*Extremely rare*	

3855 — — S below wreath for Sydney mint.

1871 S	75·00	150·00
1872 S	80·00	165·00
1873 S	75·00	150·00
1875 S	77·50	157·50
1877 S	75·00	150·00
1878 S	75·00	150·00
1879 S	75·00	150·00
1880 S	77·50	157·50
1881 S	80·00	165·00
1882 S	75·00	150·00
1883 S	75·00	150·00
1884 S	75·00	150·00
1885 S	75·00	150·00
1886 S	75·00	150·00
1887 S	77·50	157·50

3856

3856 — Sovereign, type II. ℞. St. George.

	F	VF	EF		F	VF	EF
	£	£	£		£	£	£
1871 ..	..	72·50	95·00	1878 ..	..	85·00	120·00
1872 ..	..	74·00	97·50	1879 ..	80·00	300·00	650·00
1873 ..	..	75·00	100·00	1880 ..	..	72·50	95·00
1874 ..	..	75·00	105·00	1884 ..	..	74·00	97·50
1876 ..	..	72·50	95·00	1885 ..	..	75·00	100·00

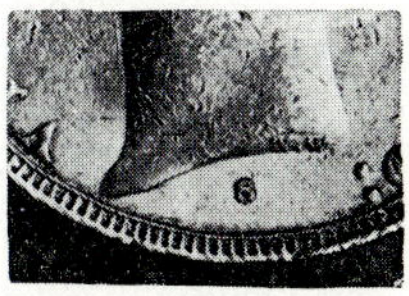

3857 3858

3857 — — M below head for Melbourne mint.

	F	VF	EF		F	VF	EF
1872 M ..	..	75·00	125·00	1880 M ..	..	72·50	90·00
1873 M ..	..	74·00	92·50	1881 M ..	..	72·50	90·00
1874 M ..	..	72·50	90·00	1882 M ..	..	72·50	90·00
1875 M ..	..	72·50	90·00	1883 M ..	..	72·50	90·00
1876 M ..	..	72·50	90·00	1884 M ..	..	72·50	90·00
1877 M ..	..	72·50	90·00	1885 M ..	..	72·50	90·00
1878 M ..	..	72·50	90·00	1886 M ..	..	72·50	90·00
1879 M ..	..	72·50	90·00	1887 M ..	..	72·50	90·00

3858 — — S below head for Sydney mint.

	F	VF	EF		F	VF	EF
1871 S ..	..	75·00	100·00	1881 S ..	..	72·50	95·00
1872 S ..	..	74·00	95·00	1882 S ..	..	72·50	92·50
1873 S ..	..	72·50	90·00	1883 S ..	..	72·50	90·00
1874 S ..	..	72·50	90·00	1884 S ..	..	72·50	90·00
1875 S ..	..	72·50	90·00	1885 S ..	..	72·50	90·00
1876 S ..	..	72·50	90·00	1886 S ..	..	72·50	90·00
1879 S ..	..	75·00	100·00	1887 S ..	..	72·50	90·00
1880 S ..	..	74·00	95·00				

Note. Gold bullion price at time of printing $575 per oz. at $2·40 to the £1 sterling.

Gold

3859

3860

3859 Half-sovereign. ℞. Shield.

		VF £	*EF* £			*VF* £	*EF* £
1838	.. ..	135·00	275·00	1852	.. ..	110·00	210·00
1839	Proof only	*FDC* £750·00		1853	.. ..	75·00	150·00
1841	.. ..	165·00	325·00	—	Proof	*FDC* £1250·00	
1842	.. ..	80·00	150·00	1854	.. ..	*Extremely rare*	
1843	.. ..	165·00	325·00	1855	.. ..	85·00	160·00
1844	.. ..	100·00	175·00	1856	.. ..	85·00	160·00
1845	.. ..	220·00	530·00	1857	.. ..	110·00	210·00
1846	.. ..	110·00	230·00	1858	.. ..	80·00	160·00
1847	.. ..	110·00	230·00	1859	.. ..	80·00	160·00
1848	.. ..	110·00	230·00	1860	.. ..	70·00	150·00
1849	.. ..	100·00	205·00	1861	.. ..	80·00	160·00
1850	.. ..	250·00	550·00	1862	.. ..	*Extremely rare*	
1851	.. ..	100·00	175·00	1863	.. ..	90·00	150·00

3860 — — die number below shield.

1863	.. ..	110·00	230·00	1873	.. ..	70·00	150·00
1864	.. ..	75·00	150·00	1874	.. ..	70·00	150·00
1865	.. ..	75·00	150·00	1875	.. ..	70·00	150·00
1866	.. ..	75·00	150·00	1876	.. ..	70·00	140·00
1867	.. ..	75·00	150·00	1877	.. ..	70·00	140·00
1869	.. ..	75·00	150·00	1878	.. ..	70·00	140·00
1870	.. ..	75·00	150·00	1879	.. ..	85·00	170·00
1871	.. ..	75·00	150·00	1880	.. ..	70·00	150·00
1872	.. ..	75·00	150·00				

3861 — — As 3859 (no die number) but head in slightly lower relief.

1880	.. ..	80·00	170·00	1884	.. ..	70·00	140·00
1883	.. ..	70·00	140·00	1885	.. ..	70·00	140·00

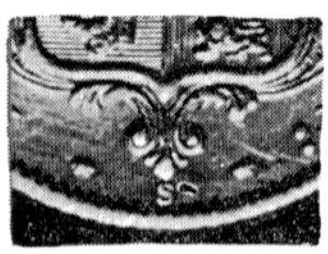

3862

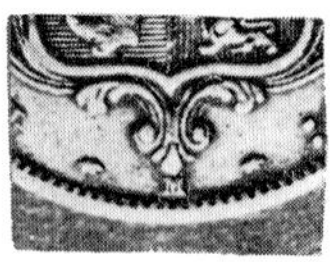

3863

3862 — — S below shield for Sydney mint.

1871 S	.. ..	90·00	180·00	1881 S	.. ..	110·00	210·00
1872 S	.. ..	90·00	180·00	1882 S	.. ..	125·00	230·00
1875 S	.. ..	95·00	190·00	1883 S	.. ..	90·00	180·00
1879 S	.. ..	100·00	210·00	1886 S	.. ..	105·00	210·00
1880 S	.. ..	100·00	210·00	1887 S	.. ..	90 00	180·00

3863 — — M below shield for Melbourne mint.

1873 M	.. ..	100·00	220·00	1884 M	.. ..	130·00	275·00
1877 M	.. ..	100·00	220·00	1885 M	.. ..	240·00	500·00
1881 M	.. ..	145·00	300·00	1886 M	.. ..	115·00	250·00
1882 M	.. ..	105·00	235·00	1887 M	.. ..	115·00	350·00

Gold

Jubilee coinage, 1887-93

3864

3864 Five pounds. ℞. St. George.

	VF £	EF £		VF £	EF £
1887				600·00	975·00
— Proof *FDC* £2250·00					

3865 Two pounds. Similar.

1887				300·00	500·00
— Proof *FDC* £1250·00					

3866 Sovereign. ℞. St. George.

1887	72·50	95·00	1890	72·50	90·00
— Proof *FDC* £600·00			1891	72·50	90·00
1888	72·50	90·00	1892	72·50	90·00
1889	72·50	90·00			

3866

3867

3869

3867 — — M on ground for Melbourne mint.

1887 M	72·50	87·50	1891 M	72·50	87·50
1888 M	72·50	87·50	1892 M	72·50	87·50
1889 M	72·50	87·50	1893 M	72·50	87·50
1890 M	72·50	87·50			

3868 — — S on ground for Sydney mint.

1887 S	75·00	90·00	1891 S	72·50	87·50
1888 S	72·50	87·50	1892 S	72·50	87·50
1889 S	72·50	87·50	1893 S	72·50	87·50
1890 S	72·50	87·50			

3869 Half-sovereign. ℞. Shield.

1887	65·00	85·00	1891	65·00	100·00
— Proof *FDC* £450·00			1892	65·00	85·00
1890	65·00	85·00	1893	70·00	120·00

3870 — — M below shield for Melbourne mint.

1887 M	85·00	150·00	1893 M	85·00	140·00

3871 — — S below shield for Sydney mint.

1887 S	82·50	130·00	1891 S	82·50	130·00
1889 S	85·00	140·00			

Gold

Old head coinage, 1893-1901

3972 Five pounds. ℞. St. George.

1893	750·00	1250·00
— Proof *FDC* £2500		

3873

3873 Two pounds. Similar.

1893	350·00	550·00
— Proof *FDC* £1400		

3874 Sovereign. ℞. St. George.

	VF £	*EF* £		*VF* £	*EF* £
1893	72·50	90·00	1898	72·50	85·00
— Proof *FDC* £650			1899	72·50	85·00
1894	72·50	85·00	1900	72·50	85·00
1895	72·50	85·00	1901	72·50	85·00
1896	72·50	85·00			

3877 3876

3875 Sovereign. ℞. St. George. M on ground for Melbourne mint.

1893 M	72·50	85·00	1898 M	72·50	85·00
1894 M	72·50	85·00	1899 M	72·50	85·00
1895 M	72·50	85·00	1900 M	72·50	85·00
1896 M	72·50	85·00	1901 M	72·50	85·00
1897 M	72·50	85·00			

3876 — — P on ground for Perth mint.

1899 P	75·00	110·00	1901 P	72·50	90·00
1900 P	72·50	90·00			

3877 — — S on ground for Sydney mint.

1893 S	72·50	90·00	1898 S	72·50	90·00
1894 S	72·50	90·00	1899 S	72·50	90·00
1895 S	72·50	90·00	1900 S	72·50	90·00
1896 S	72·50	90·00	1901 S ..	72·50	90·00
1897 S	72·50	90·00			

3878

3878 Half-sovereign. ℞. St. George.

	F	VF	EF
	£	£	£
1893		60·00	80·00
— Proof *FDC* £450			
1894 ..		60·00	80·00
1895		60·00	80·00
1896 ..		60·00	80·00
1897		60·00	80·00
1898		60·00	80·00
1899		60·00	80·00
1900		60·00	80·00
1901		60·00	80·00

3879 — — M on ground for Melbourne mint.

	F	VF	EF
1893 M .. *Extremely rare*			
1896 M		65·00	100·00
1899 M		67·50	110·00
1900 M		62·50	100·00

3880 — — P on ground for Perth mint.

	F	VF	EF
1899 P .. ? proofs only			
1900 P		72·50	115·00

3881 — — S on ground for Sydney mint.

	F	VF	EF
1893 S ..		65·00	100·00
1897 S		65·00	100·00
1900 S		67·50	110·00

SILVER

Young head coinage

3882

3882 Crown. Young head. ℞. Crowned shield.
1839 Proof only *FDC* £3750

	F	VF	EF
	£	£	£
1844 ..	16·50	70·00	500·00
1845 ..	16 00	65·00	475·00
1847 ..	18·00	75·00	550·00

3883

	VF £	EF £	FDC £
3883* **Crown,** "Gothic" type, as illustration; inscribed edge, mdcccxlvii=1847	275·00	500·00	1100·00

— Proof, plain edge *FDC* £1500

* N.B. Beware of recent forgeries.

3884 — mdcccliii=1853. Proof *FDC* £4500

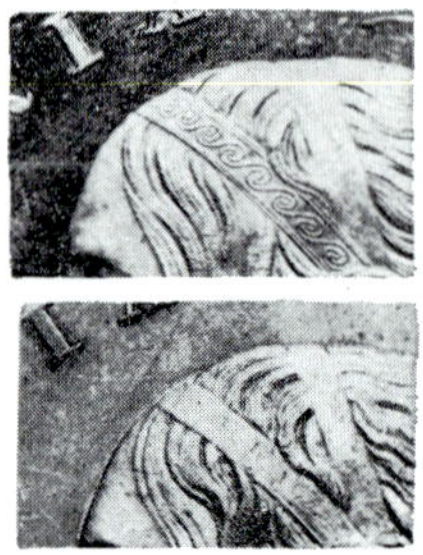

3887

	F £	VF £	EF £
3885 **Halfcrown,** type A¹. Young head with one ornate and and one plain fillet binding hair. ww in relief on truncation, 1839			*Extremely rare*

3886 — Proof *FDC* £450

3887 — type A³. Two plain fillets, ww incuse

			F £	VF £	EF £
1839 .. .. .. *Extremely rare*	1840	..	15·00	60·00	225·00

3888 — type A⁴. Similar but no initials on truncation.

		F £	VF £	EF £			F £	VF £	EF £
1841	..	30·00	100·00	375·00	1846	..	9·00	40·00	145·00
1842	..	10·00	45·00	150·00	1848	..	35·00	125·00	450·00
1843	..	22·00	85·00	300·00	1849	..	15·00	70·00	250·00
1844	..	9·00	40·00	120·00	1850	..	12·00	50·00	180·00
1845	..	9·00	40·00	120·00	1853	Proof	*FDC*	£750	

3889 Halfcrown, type A⁵. As last but inferior workmanship.

		F	VF	EF			F	VF	EF
		£	£	£			£	£	£
1874	..	5·00	20·00	75·00	1881	..	5·00	22·00	75·00
1875	..	5·50	24·00	80·00	1882	..	5·25	24·00	80·00
1876	..	5·75	25·00	85·00	1883	..	5·00	22·00	75·00
1877	..	5·50	24·00	80·00	1884	..	5·00	22·00	75·00
1878	..	5·50	24·00	80·00	1885	..	5·00	22·00	75·00
1879	..	6·00	32·50	110·00	1886	..	5·00	22·00	75·00
1880	..	5·50	24·00	80·00	1887	..	5·00	22·00	75·00

3890

3892

3890 Florin, "Godless" type (i.e. without D.G.) 1849 .. 5·00 22·00 65·00

3891 — "Gothic" type B¹, reads brit:, ww below bust, date at end of obverse legend in gothic numerals (1851 to 1863)

mdcccli ..	*Extremely rare*			mdccclvii ..	5·50	27·00	90·00
mdccclii ..	4·50	25·00	85·00	mdccclviii ..	5·50	27·00	90·00
mdcccliii	4·50	25·00	85·00	mdccclix ..	5·50	27·00	90·00
— Proof	*FDC*	£250		mdccclx ..	6·50	32·50	110·00
mdcccliv ..	200·00	500·00	1250·00	mdccclxii ..	24·00	90·00	300·00
mdccclv ..	5·50	27·00	90·00	mdccclxiii ..	28·00	115·00	375·00
mdccclvi ..	6·50	30·00	100·00				

3892 — — type B²; as last but die number below bust (1864 to 1867)

mdccclxiv	5·50	27·00	90·00	mdccclxvi	6·50	32·50	110·00
mdccclxv ..	6·50	30·00	100·00	mdccclxvii	16·00	70·00	225·00

3893 — — type B³, reads britt:, die number (1868 to 1879)

mdccclxviii	5·50	28·00	100·00	mdccclxxiv	5·00	27·00	90 00
mdccclxix	5·00	27·00	90·00	mdccclxxv	5·00	27·00	90·00
mdccclxx	5·00	27·00	90·00	mdccclxxvi	5·50	28·00	100·00
mdccclxxi	5·00	27·00	90·00	mdccclxxvii	5·50	28·00	100·00
mdccclxxii	4·75	25·00	85·00	mdccclxxix		*Extremely rare*	
mdccclxxiii	4·75	25·00	85·00				

3894 — — type B⁴. As last but with border of 48 arcs and no ww.
1877 mdccclxxvii .. .. *Extremely rare*

3895 — — type B⁵. Similar but 42 arcs, (1867, 1877 and 1878)

mdccclxvii		*Extremely rare*		mdccclxxviii	5·50	27·00	90·00
mdccclxxvii	7·50	35·00	125·00				

3896 — — type B⁵/⁶. As last but no die number. (1877, 1879)
mdccclxxvii *Extremely rare* mdccclxxix *Extremely rare*

3897 — — type B⁶, reads britt:, ; ww; 48 arcs, (1879)
mdccclxxix .. .. 7·50 32·50 125·00

3898 — — type B⁷. As last but no ww, 38 arcs, (1879)
mdccclxxix .. .. 7·50 32·50 125·00

Silver

3899 Florin, "Gothic" type $B^3/^8$. As next but younger portrait (1880)
mdccclxxx .. .. *Extremely rare*

3900 — — type B^8. Similar but 34 arcs, (1880 to 1887)

	F £	*VF* £	*EF* £		*F* £	*VF* £	*EF* £
mdccclxxx	5·50	27·00	90·00	mdccclxxxv	4·50	22·50	80·00
mdccclxxxi	4·50	22·50	80·00	mdccclxxxvi	4·75	25·00	85·00
mdccclxxxiii	4·50	22·50	80·00	mdccclxxxvii	*? exists*		
mdccclxxxiv	4·50	22·50	80·00				

3901 — — type B^9. Similar but 46 arcs.
1887 mdccclxxxvii .. .. 7·50 32·50 125·00

3906

3902 Shilling, type A^1. First head, ww on truncation.

1838 ..	3·50	16·00	60·00	1839 ..	4·00	18·00	65·00

3903 — type A^2. Second head, ww (Proof only), 1839 *FDC* £225·00

3904 — type A^3. Second head, no initials on truncation.

1839 ..	3·00	13·50	50·00	1853 ..	3·25	14·00	55·00
1840 ..	10·00	50·00	150·00	— Proof	*FDC* £350·00		
1841 ..	6·00	28·00	90·00	1854 ..	40·00	125·00	350·00
1842 ..	3·50	16·00	60·00	1855 ..	3·00	13·50	50·00
1843 ..	6·00	28·00	90·00	1856 ..	3·00	13·50	50·00
1844 ..	3·25	14·00	55·00	1857 ..	3·00	13·50	50·00
1845 ..	4·00	18·00	65·00	1858 ..	3·00	13·50	50·00
1846 ..	3·50	16·00	60·00	1859 ..	3·00	13·50	50·00
1848 over 6	24·00	65·00	200·00	1860 ..	5·00	22·00	70·00
1849 ..	3·25	14·00	55·00	1861 ..	5·00	22·00	70·00
1850 ..	100·00	300·00	900·00	1862 ..	9·00	35·00	110·00
1851 ..	24·00	65·00	200·00	1863 ..	9·00	35·00	110·00
1852 ..	3·25	14·00	55·00				

3905 — type A^4. As before but die number above date.

1864 ..	3·25	14·00	55·00	1866 ..	3·00	13·50	50·00
1865 ..	3·00	13·50	50·00	1867 ..	3·25	14·00	55·00

3906 — type A^6. Third head, die number above date.

1867 ..	25·00	65·00	200·00	1874 ..	1·75	9·50	36·00
1868 ..	3·00	13·50	50·00	1875 ..	1·75	9·50	36·00
1869 ..	3·50	16·00	60·00	1876 ..	3·00	13·50	50·00
1870 ..	3·50	16·00	60·00	1877 ..	2·00	10·00	37·50
1871 ..	2·00	10·00	37·50	1878 ..	2·00	10·00	37·50
1872 ..	1·75	9·00	35·00	1879 ..	4·00	18·00	65·00
1873 ..	1·75	9·00	35·00				

3907 — type A^7. Fourth head; no die number.

1879 ..	3·25	14·00	55·00	1884 ..	1·65	7·00	27·50
1880 ..	1·65	7·00	27·50	1885 ..	1·50	5·50	17·50
1881 ..	1·65	7·00	27·50	1886 ..	1·50	5·50	17·50
1882 ..	6·00	28·00	90·00	1887 ..	3·00	13·50	50·00
1883 ..	1·65	7·00	27·50				

Silver

3909

3912

3908 **Sixpence,** type A^1. First head.

		F £	*VF* £	*EF* £
1838	..	1·50	9·00	32·50
1839	..	1·50	9·00	32·50
— Proof	*FDC* £150·00			
1840	..	2·00	10·00	36·00
1841	..	3·00	15·00	47·50
1842	..	1·75	10·00	35·00
1843	..	1·75	10·00	35·00
1844	..	1·50	9·00	32·50
1845	..	1·75	10·00	35·00
1846	..	1·50	9·00	32·50
1848	..	20·00	65·00	175·00
1850	..	1·75	10·00	35·00
1851	..	1·75	10·00	35·00
1852	..	2·00	10·00	36·00
1853	..	1·50	9·00	32·50
— Proof	*FDC* £235·00			
1854	..	32·50	100·00	325·00
1855	..	1·50	9·00	32·50
1856	..	2·00	10·00	35·00
1857	..	2·00	10·00	36·00
1858	..	2·00	10·00	35·00
1859	..	1·50	9·00	32·50
1860	..	2·00	10·00	36·00
1862	..	12·00	40·00	125·00
1863	..	8·00	30·00	90·00
1866	..	20·00	80·00	225·00

3909 — type A^2. First head; die number above date.

1864	..	2·00	10·00	36·00
1865	..	3·00	15·00	47·50
1866	..	2·00	10·00	36·00

3910 — type A^3. Second head; die number above date.

1867	..	3·00	16·00	50·00
1868	..	3·00	16·00	50·00
1869	..	3·75	20·00	60·00
1870	..	3·00	16·00	50·00
1871	..	1·75	10·00	35·00
1872	..	1·75	10·00	35·00
1873	..	1·50	9·00	32·50
1874	..	1·50	9·00	32·50
1875	..	1·50	9·00	32·50
1876	..	3·00	16·00	50·00
1877	..	1·50	9·00	32·50
1878	..	1·50	9·00	32·50
1879	..	3·75	20·00	60·00

3911 — type A^4. Second head; no die number.

1871	..	3·00	16·00	50·00
1877	..	1·75	10·00	35·00
1879	..	1·75	10·00	35·00
1880	..	3·00	16·00	50·00

3912 — type A^5. Third head.

1880	..	1·50	7·00	22·00
1881	..	1·25	6·50	20·00
1882	..	3·75	20·00	60·00
1883	..	1·25	6·50	20·00
1884	..	1·25	6·50	20·00
1885	..	1·25	6·50	20·00
1886	..	1·25	6·50	20·00
1887	..	1·25	5·50	18·00

3913

3914

3915

3913 Groat (4d). ℞. Britannia.

	F	*VF*	*EF*		*F*	*VF*	*EF*
	£	£	£		£	£	£
1838	·50	3·00	16·00	1847/6 (or 8)	12·00	40·00	135·00
1839	·60	4·00	20·00	1848	·75	3·00	18·00
— Proof *FDC* £125				1849	·75	3·00	18·00
1840	·55	3·25	18·00	1851	15·00	60·00	150·00
1841	·90	4·50	24·00	1852	17·50	75·00	200·00
1842	·75	4·00	20·00	1853	22·00	90·00	250·00
1843	·75	4·00	20·00	— Proof *FDC* £250			
1844	·85	4·00	22·00	1854	·75	3·00	18·00
1845	·75	4·00	22·00	1855	·75	3·00	18·00
1846	·75	4·00	20·00				

3914 Threepence. ℞. Crowned 3; as Maundy threepence but with a dull surface.

1838*	·75	4·00	25·00	1864	·60	3·75	22·00
1839*	1·00	6·00	40·00	1865	1·00	6·00	45·00
— Proof (see Maundy)				1866	·75	3·75	22·00
1840*	·75	4·75	35·00	1867	·75	4·50	30·00
1841*	1·00	6·00	42·50	1868	·75	3·75	22·00
1842*	1·25	7·00	50·00	1869*	1·00	6·50	50·00
1843*	·75	3·75	25·00	1870	·75	3·50	20·00
1844*	1·00	6·00	40·00	1871	·75	3·75	27·50
1845	·60	4·00	20·00	1872	·60	3·50	22·00
1846	2·50	10·00	60·00	1873	·50	2·25	16·00
1849	1·25	6·50	50·00	1874	·50	2·25	16·00
1850	·60	3·75	22·00	1875	·45	2·25	16·00
1851	·75	4·50	30·00	1876	·50	2·25	16·00
1853	1·00	6·00	42·50	1877	·45	2·25	16·00
1854	·75	4·75	35·00	1878	·45	2·25	16·00
1855	1·00	6·50	50·00	1879	·45	2·25	16·00
1856	1·00	5·50	45·00	1880	·60	2·75	18·00
1857	1·00	5·50	45·00	1881	·45	2·75	18·00
1858	·75	4·50	30·00	1882	·75	4·75	35·00
1859	·75	3·75	22·00	1883	·40	2·00	14·00
1860	·60	3·75	22·00	1884	·45	2·00	14·00
1861	·60	4·00	24·00	1885	·40	2·00	14·00
1862	·75	4·50	30·00	1886	·40	2·00	14·00
1863	1·00	5·50	45·00	1887	·60	2·00	14·00

* Issued for Colonial use only.

3915 Threehalfpence (For Colonial use). ℞. Value, etc.

1838	·40	2·25	16·00	1842	·60	2·50	18·00
1839	·40	2·00	14·00	1843	·25	1·75	12·00
1840	·85	4·50	30·00	1860	·85	4·50	30·00
1841	·65	2·00	14·00	1862	·85	3·75	25·00

3916

N.B. Overstruck dates are listed only if commoner than the normal date or if no normal date is known.

3916 Maundy set (4d., 3d., 2d. and 1d.).

	EF £	FDC £		EF £	FDC £
1838	40·00	65·00	1862	36·00	60·00
1839	40·00	65·00	1863	36·00	60·00
— Proof *FDC* £175			1864	36·00	60·00
1840	36·00	62·50	1865	36·00	60·00
1841	40·00	65·00	1866	36·00	60·00
1842	36·00	60·00	1867	36·00	60·00
1843	36·00	60·00	1868	36·00	60·00
1844	36·00	60·00	1869	40·00	65·00
1845	36·00	60·00	1870	36·00	60·00
1846	36·00	60·00	1871	36·00	60·00
1847	36·00	60·00	1872	36·00	60·00
1848	36·00	60·00	1873	36·00	60·00
1849	40·00	65·00	1874	35·00	58·00
1850	36·00	60·00	1875	35·00	58·00
1851	36·00	60·00	1876	35·00	58·00
1852	36·00	60·00	1877	35·00	58·00
1853	36·00	60·00	1878	35·00	58·00
— Proof *FDC* £250			1879	35·00	58·00
1854	36·00	60·00	1880	35·00	58·00
1855	40·00	65·00	1881	35·00	58·00
1856	36·00	60·00	1882	35·00	58·00
1857	36·00	60·00	1883	35·00	58·00
1858	36·00	60·00	1884	35·00	58·00
1859	36·00	60·00	1885	35·00	58·00
1860	36·00	60·00	1886	35·00	58·00
1861	36·00	60·00	1887	42·00	70·00

	EF £	FDC £
3917 — fourpence, 1838-1887, *from* ..	6·00	10·00
3918 — threepence, 1838-1887, *from* ..	12·00	20·00
3919 — twopence, 1838-1887, *from* ..	4·00	7·00
3920 — penny, 1838-1887, *from* ..	3·50	6·00

Maundy sets in the original dated cases are worth approximately £5·00 more than the prices quoted.

Jubilee Coinage

3921

3921 Crown. ℞. St. George.

	F £	VF £	EF £		F £	VF £	EF £
1887 ..	10·00	20·00	50·00	1890 ..	12·00	24·00	60·00
— Proof *FDC* £475				1891 ..	12·00	26·00	65·00
1888 ..	12·00	26·00	65·00	1892 ..	14·00	30·00	75·00
1889 ..	10·00	20·00	50·00				

3922

3922 Double-florin (4s.). ℞. Cruciform shields. Roman I in date.

	F £	VF £	EF £
1887	4·50	12·00	27·50

3923 — Similar but Arabic 1 in date.

	F £	VF £	EF £
1887 ..	4·50	12·00	27·50
— Proof *FDC* £250			
1888 ..	6·00	16·00	40·00
1889 ..	5·00	14·00	35·00
1890 ..	6·00	16·00	40·00

3924

3925

3924 Halfcrown. ℞. Shield in collar.

	F £	VF £	EF £
1887 ..	2·00	4·00	16·00
— Proof *FDC* £150			
1888 ..	2·25	8·00	30·00
1889 ..	2·25	8·00	30·00
1890 ..	2·50	12·00	47·50
1891 ..	2·50	12·00	47·50
1892 ..	2·50	12·00	47·50

3925 Florin. ℞. Cruciform shields.

	F £	VF £	EF £
1887 ..	1·50	3·50	14·00
— Proof *FDC* £90			
1888 ..	2·00	5·00	20·00
1889 ..	2·00	6·00	24·00
1890 ..	4·75	22·00	70·00
1891 ..	7·00	35·00	110·00
1892 ..	9·00	42·50	135·00

3926

3927

3926 Shilling. Small head. ℞. Shield in garter.

	F £	VF £	EF £
1887 ..	·75	1·50	4·00
— Proof *FDC* £65·00			
1888 ..	·85	3·00	15·00
1889 ..	12·00	50·00	200·00

3927 — Large head. ℞. As before.

	F £	VF £	EF £		F £	VF £	EF £
1889 ..	1·10	4·00	22·00	1891 ..	1·25	4·50	25·00
1890 ..	1·10	4·00	22·00	1892 ..	1·25	4·50	25·00

3928

3929

3930

3928 Sixpence. ℞. Shield in garter (withdrawn type)

1887	·40	1·00	4·00
— Proof *FDC* £45·00			

3929 — ℞. Value in wreath.

1887 ..	·40	1·10	4·50	1891 ..	·80	3·25	16·00
1888 ..	·65	2·75	14·00	1892 ..	·80	3·25	16·00
1889 ..	·65	2·75	14·00	1893 ..	120·00	300·00	750·00
1890 ..	·70	3·00	15·00				

3930 Groat (for use in British Guiana). ℞. Britannia

1888	2·25	9·00	25·00

3931 Threepence. As Maundy but dull surface.

1887 ..	·50	1·00	4·50	1890 ..	·50	1·50	12·00
— Proof *FDC* £25				1891 ..	·50	1·50	12·00
1888 ..	·75	1·75	14·00	1892 ..	·75	1·75	14·00
1889 ..	·50	1·50	12·00	1893 ..	4·00	22·00	90·00

3932 Maundy set (4d., 3d., 2d. and 1d.).

	EF £	*FDC* £		*EF* £	*FDC* £
1888	42·50	65·00	1891	40·00	62·50
1889	40·00	62·50	1892	40·00	62·50
1890	40·00	62·50			

Maundy sets in the original dated cases are worth approximately £5·00 more than the prices quoted.

3933	— **fourpence,** 1888-1892, *from*	9·00	13·00
3934	— **threepence,** 1888-1892, *from*	11·00	21·00
3935	— **twopence,** 1888-1892, *from*	6·00	10·00
3936	— **penny,** 1888-1892, *from*	6·00	10·00

3932

Silver

Old head coinage

3937

3937 Crown. ℞. St. George. Regnal date on edge.

		F £	VF £	EF £
1893	— LVI	10·00	26·00	95·00
—	— Proof *FDC* £475			
—	— LVII	17·50	55·00	165·00
1894	— LVII	12 00	32·50	110·00
—	— LVIII	12·00	32·50	110·00
1895	— LVIII	11·00	30·00	100·00
—	— LIX	11·00	30·00	100·00
1896	— LIX	18·00	55·00	175·00
—	— LX	11·00	30·00	100·00
1897	— LX	11·00	30·00	100·00
—	— LXI	10·00	26·00	95·00
1898	— LXI	22·00	70·00	250·00
—	— LXII	12·00	32·50	110·00
1899	— LXII	12·00	32·50	110·00
—	— LXIII	12·00	32·50	110·00
1900	— LXIII	11·00	30·00	100·00
—	— LXIV	10·00	26·00	95·00

3938

3938 Halfcrown. ℞. Shield in collar.

	F £	VF £	EF £		F £	VF £	EF £
1893	2·25	10·00	35·00	1897	2·25	10·00	35·00
— Proof *FDC* £150				1898	2·50	12·00	40·00
1894	3·00	14·00	45·00	1899	2·50	12·00	40·00
1895	2·50	12·00	40·00	1900	2·25	10·00	35·00
1896	2·50	12·00	40·00	1901	2·25	10·00	35·00

3939 Florin. ℞. Three shields within Garter.

	F	*VF*	*EF*		*F*	*VF*	*EF*
	£	£	£		£	£	£
1893 ..	2·00	8·00	30·00	1897 ..	2·00	8·00	30·00
— Proof *FDC* £100				1898 ..	2·50	10·00	35·00
1894 ..	2·75	12·00	45·00	1899 ..	2·25	9·00	32·50
1895 ..	2·75	12·00	45·00	1900 ..	2·00	8·00	30·00
1896 ..	2·50	10·00	35·00	1901 ..	2·00	8·00	30·00

3939

3940

3940 Shilling. ℞. Three shields within Garter.

1893 ..	·75	3·50	16·00	1897 ..	·85	3·75	17·50
— Proof *FDC* £90				1898 ..	·85	3 75	17·50
1894 ..	1·10	5·00	22·00	1899 ..	·90	4·00	18·00
1895 ..	1·00	4·50	20·00	1900 ..	·85	3·50	16·00
1896 ..	·85	3·75	17·50	1901 ..	·85	3·50	16·00

3941 Sixpence. ℞. Value in wreath.

1893 ..	·60	2·00	14·00	1897 ..	·70	2·50	16·00
— Proof *FDC* £47·50				1898 ..	·70	2·50	16·00
1894 ..	·85	3·50	18·00	1899 ..	·70	2·50	16·00
1895 ..	·85	3·50	18·00	1900 ..	·60	2·00	14·00
1896 ..	·85	3·75	18·00	1901 ..	·60	2·00	14·00

3942 Threepence. ℞. Crowned 3. As Maundy but dull surface.

1893 ..	·40	·70	5·00	1897 ..	·35	·90	10·00
— Proof *FDC* £32·50				1898 ..	·35	1·00	10·00
1894 ..	·45	1·25	12·00	1899 ..	·35	·90	9·00
1895 ..	·45	1·25	12·00	1900 ..	·35	·90	9·00
1896 ..	·35	1·00	10·00	1901 ..	·35	·90	9·00

3943

3943 Maundy set (4d., 3d., 2d. and 1d.)

	EF	*FDC*		*EF*	*FDC*
	£	£		£	£
1893	32·00	37·50	1897	30·00	45·00
— Proof *FDC* £100			1898	30·00	45·00
1894	30·00	45·00	1899	30·00	45·00
1895	30·00	45·00	1900	30·00	45·00
1896	30·00	45·00	1901	30·00	45·00

3944	**— fourpence,** 1893-1901, *from*	5·00	8·00
3945	**— threepence,** 1893-1901, *from*	10·00	17·00
3946	**— twopence,** 1893-1901, *from*	5·00	6·50
3947	**— penny,** 1893-1901, *from*	5·00	6·50

Maundy sets in the original dated cases are worth approximately £5·00 more than the prices quoted.

COPPER AND BRONZE

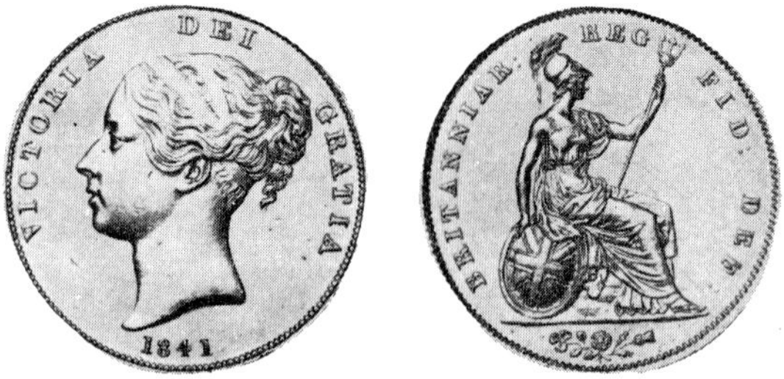

3948

Young head copper coinage, 1838-1860

3948 Penny. R. Britannia.

	F £	VF £	EF £
1839 Bronzed proof	*FDC* £175		
1841	1·25	5·00	22·00
1843	20·00	75·00	250·00
1844	2·75	7·50	30·00
1845	4·50	15·00	55·00
1846	3·50	10·00	40·00
1847	2·75	7·50	30·00
1848	2·75	7·00	28·00
1849	25·00	90·00	275·00
1851	3·50	10·00	40·00
1853	·75	4·00	16·00
— Proof	*FDC* £250		
1854	·75	4·00	16·00
1855	·75	4·00	16·00
1856	6·50	25·00	70·00
1857	·80	4·50	17·50
1858	·75	4·00	16·00
1859	1·25	5·00	20·00
1860*	..	300·00	550·00

3949

3949 Halfpenny. R. Britannia.

	F £	VF £	EF £
1838	·50	2·50	14·00
1839 Bronzed proof	*FDC* £75		
1841	·45	2·25	12·00
1843	2·50	10·00	40·00
1844	·90	3·75	18·00
1845	15·00	50·00	150·00
1846	1·50	5·00	24·00
1847	1·50	5·00	24·00
1848	1·75	6·00	27·50
1851	·90	3·75	18·00
1852	1·50	5·00	22·00
1853	·40	1·75	7·50
— Proof	*FDC* £80		
1854	·40	1·75	7·50
1855	·40	1·75	7·50
1856	1·00	4·50	18·00
1857	·55	2·75	12·00
1858	·50	2·50	14·00
1859	·90	3·75	16·00
1860*	..	..	*Extremely rare*

Copper

3950

3950 Farthing. ℞. Britannia.

		F £	VF £	EF £
1838	..	·60	3·00	14·00
1839	..	·40	2·00	12·00
— Bronzed proof *FDC* £90				
1840	..	·40	2·00	12·00
1841	..	·40	2·00	12·00
1842	..	1·50	6·00	32·50
1843	..	·40	2·00	12·00
1844	..	15·00	40·00	150·00
1845	..	·60	3·00	15·00
1846	..	1·50	6·00	30·00
1847	..	·60	3·00	15·00
1848	..	·60	3·00	15·00
1849	..	7·50	20·00	60·00

		F £	VF £	EF £
1850	..	·60	3·00	15·00
1851	..	3·00	10·00	35·00
1852	..	3·25	11·00	37·50
1853	..	·50	2·50	14·00
— Proof *FDC* £250				
1854	..	·60	3·00	15·00
1855	..	·80	4·00	20·00
1856	..	1·75	6·00	32·50
1857	..	·50	2·50	14·00
1858	..	·50	2·50	14·00
1859	..	5·00	15·00	45·00
1860*	..	..	..	*Extremely rare*

* These 1860 large copper pieces not to be confused with the smaller and commoner bronze issue with date on reverse (nos. 3954, 3956 & 3958).

3951

3952

3953

3951 Half-farthing. ℞. Value.

1839	..	1·50	4·00	14·00
1842	..	1·25	4·00	14·00
1843	..	·15	·50	3·50
1844	..	·15	·50	3·00
1847	..	·90	3·00	10·00
1851	..	1·50	4·00	15·00
1852	..	1·50	4·00	15·00
1853	..	2·00	7·00	27·50
— Proof *FDC* £200				
1854	..	3·50	12·00	35·00
1856	..	3·50	12·00	35·00

3952 Third-farthing (for use in Malta). ℞. Britannia.

1844	.. ..	5·00	15·00	40·00

3953 Quarter-farthing (for use in Ceylon). ℞. Value.

1839	..	3·50	12·00	25·00
1951	..	4·00	14·00	27·50
1852	..	3·50	12·00	25·00
1853	..	4·00	14·00	27·50
— Proof *FDC* £250				

Bronze coinage, "bun head" issue, 1860-1895.

3254

3955

3954 Penny. R. Britannia.

	F £	VF £	EF £
1860	1·00	5·00	18·00
1861	1·00	5·00	18·00
1862	·75	4·50	16·00
1863	·75	4·50	16·00
1864	3·00	35·00	175·00
1865	1·75	10·00	40·00
1866	1·10	6·50	24·00
1867	1·75	10·00	40·00
1868	3·25	20·00	75·00
1869	16·00	75·00	260·00
1870	2·00	13·00	45·00
1871	7·00	40·00	150·00
1872	1·25	7·00	26·00
1873	1·25	7·00	26·00
1874	1·75	10·00	37·50
1875	·85	5·00	18·00
1877	·85	5·00	18·00
1878	1·75	10·00	37·50
1879	·85	5·00	18·00
1880	2·00	12·00	40·00
1881	3·00	13·00	45·00
1883	1·25	7·00	26·00
1884	·65	4·00	15·00
1885	·65	4·00	15·00
1886	·85	5·00	18·00
1887	·65	4·00	15·00
1888	·85	5·00	18·00
1889	·50	3·00	14·00
1890	·50	3·00	14·00
1891	·45	2·75	12·00
1892	·50	3·00	14·00
1893	·50	3·00	14·00
1894	1·00	6·50	25·00

3955 — — H (Ralph Heaton & Sons, Birmingham) below date.

	F £	VF £	EF £
1874 H	1·50	8·00	30·00
1875 H	9·00	50·00	175·00
1876 H	·40	5·00	18·00
1881 H	1·25	7·00	26·00
1882 H	·40	5·00	18·00

3956

3956 Halfpenny. ℞. Britannia.

	F	*VF*	*EF*		*F*	*VF*	*EF*
	£	£	£		£	£	£
1860 ..	·45	2·25	12·00	1878 ..	2·50	10·00	40·00
1861 ..	·45	2·25	12·00	1879 ..	·45	2·50	15·00
1862 ..	·35	1·75	10·00	1880 ..	1·50	6·50	26·00
1863 ..	·80	4·00	20·00	1881 ..	1·25	6·00	24·00
1864 ..	1·50	6·50	26·00	1883 ..	·80	4·50	22·00
1865 ..	2·50	10·00	40·00	1884 ..	·40	2·00	12·00
1866 ..	1·50	6·50	26·00	1885 ..	·40	2·00	12·00
1867 ..	2·50	10·00	40·00	1886 ..	·40	2·00	12·00
1868 ..	1·50	6·00	30·00	1887 ..	·30	1·50	9·00
1869 ..	6·00	25·00	75·00	1888 ..	·40	2·00	12·00
1870 ..	1·50	6·50	26·00	1889 ..	·40	2·00	12·00
1871 ..	7·50	35·00	100·00	1890 ..	·30	1·50	9·00
1872 ..	1·50	6·00	24·00	1891 ..	·30	1·50	9·00
1873 ..	1·75	7·50	30·00	1892 ..	·50	3·50	20·00
1874 ..	5·00	15·00	60·00	1893 ..	·40	2·00	12·00
1875 ..	·55	3·00	18·00	1894 ..	·80	4·50	22·00
1877 ..	·55	3·00	18·00				

3957 — — H below date.

1874 H ..	·90	4·50	22·00	1881 H ..	·50	3·50	20·00
1875 H ..	1·75	7·00	28·00	1882 H ..	·50	3·50	20·00
1876 H ..	·50	3·50	20·00				

3958

3960

3958 Farthing. ℞. Britannia.

1860 ..	·30	1·25	8·00	1880 ..	·50	1·85	12·00
1861 ..	·35	1·40	9·00	1881 ..	·25	1·00	7·00
1862 ..	·40	1·75	10·00	1883 ..	·75	4·00	20·00
1863 ..	12·00	30·00	75·00	1884 ..	·15	·60	3·75
1864 ..	·50	2·25	14·00	1885 ..	·15	·60	3·75
1865 ..	·35	1·40	9·00	1886 ..	·15	·60	3·75
1866 ..	·25	1·10	8·00	1887 ..	·50	1·20	8·00
1867 ..	·45	1·85	12·00	1888 ..	·30	1·00	7·50
1868 ..	·45	1·85	12·00	1890 ..	·30	1·00	7·00
1869 ..	1·00	6·50	20·00	1891 ..	·20	·75	5·00
1872 ..	·50	1·85	12·00	1892 ..	2·50	6·50	20·00
1873 ..	·30	1·25	8·00	1893 ..	·20	·75	5·00
1875 ..	5·00	12·00	35·00	1894 ..	·25	1·00	7·00
1878 ..	·20	·75	5·00	1895 ..	3·50	10·00	30·00
1879 ..	·20	·75	5·00				

3959 — — H below date.

1874 H ..	·40	1·40	10·00	1881 H ..	·50	1·50	10·00
1875 H ..	·20	·75	5·00	1882 H ..	·50	1·50	10·00
1876 H ..	4·00	10·00	30·00				

3960 Third-farthing (for use in Malta). ℞. Value.

1866 ..	·40	1·25	7·50	1881 ..	·50	1·75	9·00
1868 ..	·40	1·50	8·00	1884 ..	·40	1·25	7·50
1876 ..	·50	1·75	9·00	1885 ..	·40	1·25	7·50
1978 ..	·40	1·50	8·00				

Old head issue. 1895-1901

3961

3961 Penny. ℞. Britannia.

	VF £	*EF* £		*VF* £	*EF* £
1895	1·00	6·50	1899	·50	5·00
1896	·50	5·00	1900	·40	3·50
1897	·50	5·00	1901	·30	2·25
1898	1·00	10·00			

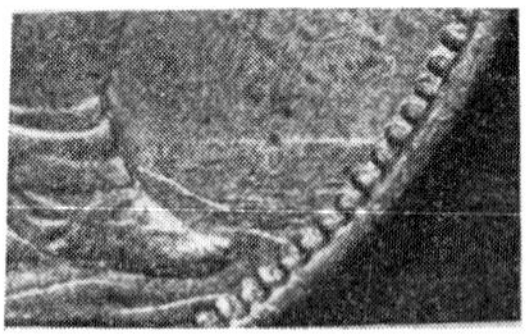

3961 "High tide"

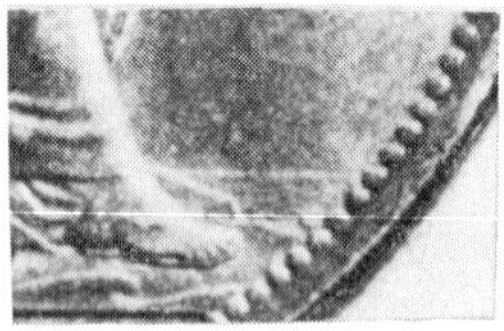

3961A "Low tide"

3961a As last but "Low tide", 1895 . . . . 22·00 75·00

3962 Halfpenny. Type as Penny. ℞. Britannia.

1895	1·25	6·00	1899	·75	4·50
1896	1·00	5·00	1900	·75	3·50
1897	1·00	5·00	1901	·40	2·25
1898	1·10	5·50			

3963 Farthing. ℞. Britannia. Bright finish.

1895	·65	3·75	1897	1·00	5·00
1896	·65	3·75			

3964

3964 — — Dark finish.

1897	·50	3·50	1900	·40	2·75
1898	·60	4·00	1901	·20	1·50
1899	·50	3·50			

EDWARD VII, 1901-10

Crowns, five pound pieces and two pound pieces were only issued in 1902. A branch of the Royal Mint was opened at Ottawa and coined sovereigns of imperial type from 1908.

Unlike the coins in most other proof sets, the proofs issued for the coronation in 1902 have a matt surface in place of the more usual brilliant finish.

Designers' initials:
De S. (G. W. de Saulles)

3965

		VF £	EF £
3965	**Five pounds.** 1902. ℞. St. George	650·00	1025·00
3966	— Proof. 1902. *Matt surface FDC* £1100		
3967	**Two pounds.** 1902. Similar	325·00	525·00
3968	— Proof. 1902. *Matt surface FDC* £1100		

3967

3969

3969 **Sovereign.*** ℞. St. George.

		VF	EF £		EF £
1902	.. Matt proof *FDC* £225			1906	80·00
1902	.. ..		82·50	1907	80·00
1903	.. ..		80·00	1908	80·00
1904	.. ..		80·00	1909	80 00
1905	.. ..		80·00	1910	80·00

3970 — — C on ground for Ottawa mint.

		VF	EF		EF
1908 C	.. ..	500·00	800·00	1910 C	150·00
1909 C	.. ..		135·00		

3971 **Sovereign.** ℞. St. George. M on ground for Melbourne mint.

		EF		EF
1902 M	.. ..	82·50	1907 M	80·00
1903 M	.. ..	80·00	1908 M	80·00
1904 M	.. ..	80·00	1909 M	80·00
1905 M	.. ..	80·00	1910 M	80·00
1906 M	.. ..	80·00		

* The price of common sovereigns in lower grades of condition are closely related to the current gold price; see also note on p. 276.

3972 Sovereign. ℞. St. George. P on ground for Perth mint.

	VF £	EF £		F £	VF £	EF £
1902 P		82·50	1907 P			80·00
1903 P		80·00	1908 P			80·00
1904 P		80·00	1909 P			80·00
1905 P		80·00	1910 P			80·00
1906 P		80·00				

3973 — — S on ground for Sydney mint.

	VF	EF		F	VF	EF
1902 S		82·50	1907 S			80·00
1903 S		80·00	1908 S			80·00
1904 S		80·00	1909 S			80·00
1905 S		80·00	1910 S			80·00
1906 S		80·00				

3974

3974 Half-sovereign. ℞. St. George.

	VF	EF		F	VF	EF
1902 *matt proof FDC* £115			1906		50·00	70·00
1902	50·00	70·00	1907		50·00	70·00
1903	50·00	70·00	1908		50·00	70·00
1904	50·00	70·00	1909		50·00	70·00
1905	50·00	70·00	1910		50·00	70·00

3975 — — M on ground for Melbourne mint.

	VF	EF		F	VF	EF
1906 M	60·00	125·00	1908 M		60·00	125·00
1907 M	60·00	125·00	1909 M		60·00	125·00

3976 — — P on ground for Perth mint.

	VF	EF		F	VF	EF
1904 P	200·00	650·00	1909 P		120·00	325·00
1908 P	160·00	450·00				

3977 — — S on ground for Sydney mint.

	VF	EF		F	VF	EF
1902 S	65·00	150·00	1908 S		60·00	120·00
1903 S	60·00	120·00	1910 S		60·00	120·00
1906 S	60·00	120·00				

SILVER

3978

3978 Crown. ℞. St. George.

	F	VF	EF
1902	30·00	55·00	95·00

3979 — Similar, but *matt proof* *FDC* £150·00

3980 Halfcrown. ℞. Shield in Garter.

3980

		F	VF	EF			F	VF	EF
		£	£	£			£	£	£
1902	..	3·00	14·00	47·50	1906	..	3·75	16·00	70·00
— matt proof		*FDC*	£75		1907	..	3·75	17·50	75·00
1903	..	40·00	135·00	425·00	1908	..	4·75	22·00	100·00
1904	..	20·00	65·00	235·00	1909	..	4·00	18·00	80·00
1905*		80·00	250·00	800·00	1910	..	3·50	15·00	60·00

3981 Florin. ℞. Britannia standing.

		F	VF	EF			F	VF	EF
		£	£	£			£	£	£
1902	..	2·50	9·00	40·00	1906	..	2·75	12·00	50·00
— matt proof		*FDC*	£50		1907	..	4·00	14·00	55·00
1903	..	4·00	14·00	55·00	1908	..	5·50	18·00	65·00
1904	..	5·50	18·00	65·00	1909	..	4·50	15·00	60·00
1905*	..	14·00	45·00	200·00	1910	..	2·50	9·00	40·00

3981

3982

3983

3982 Shilling. ℞. Lion on crown.

1902	..	·90	3·00	16·00	1906	..	1·00	3·50	22·00
— matt proof		*FDC*	£32·50		1907	..	1·75	5·00	27·50
1903	..	3·50	13·50	55·00	1908	..	2·50	9·00	40·00
1904	..	3·00	11·00	45·00	1909	..	2·00	7·00	32·50
1905	..	30·00	90·00	275·00	1910	..	·90	3·00	16·00

3983 Sixpence. ℞. Value in wreath.

1902	..	·75	2·50	15·00	1906	..	1·00	4·00	20·00
— matt proof		*FDC*	£25		1907	..	1·25	4·50	25·00
1903	..	1·75	6·00	27·50	1908	..	1·75	7·00	30·00
1904	..	2·50	9·00	40·00	1909	..	1·25	4·50	25·00
1905	..	1·75	7·00	30·00	1910	..	·75	2·50	15·00

3984 Threepence. As Maundy but dull finish.

	F	VF	EF		F	VF	EF
	£	£	£		£	£	£
1902 ..	·25	·60	3·75	1907 ..	·35	1·25	12·00
1903 ..	·35	1·25	12·00	1908 ..	·35	1·25	12·00
1904 ..	1·75	9·00	35·00	1909 ..	·35	1·25	12·00
1905 ..	1·25	8·00	30·00	1910 ..	·25	1.00	10·00
1906 ..	·90	7·00	25·00				

3985

3985 Maundy set (4d., 3d., 2d. and 1d.).

	EF	FDC		EF	FDC
	£	£		£	£
1902	29·00	42·00	1906 ..	28·00	40·00
— *matt proof*	—	45·00	1907	28·00	40·00
1903	28·00	40·00	1908	28·00	40·00
1904	28·00	40·00	1909	35·00	60·00
1905	28·00	40·00	1910	40·00	65·00

		EF	FDC
3986	— **fourpence,** 1902-10, *from*	5·00	9·00
3987	— **threepence,** 1902-10, *from*	5·00	11·00
3988	— **twopence,** 1902-10, *from*	4·50	8·00
3989	— **penny,** 1902-10, *from*	4·50	8·00

BRONZE

3990

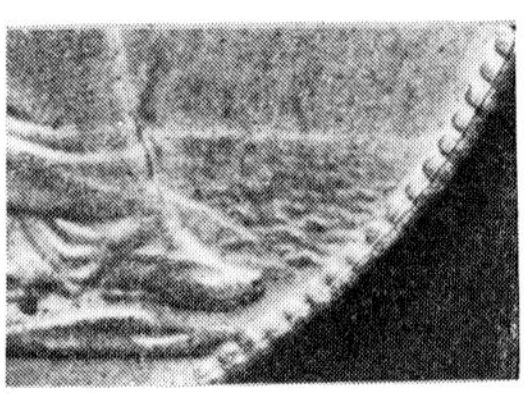

3990 "High tide"

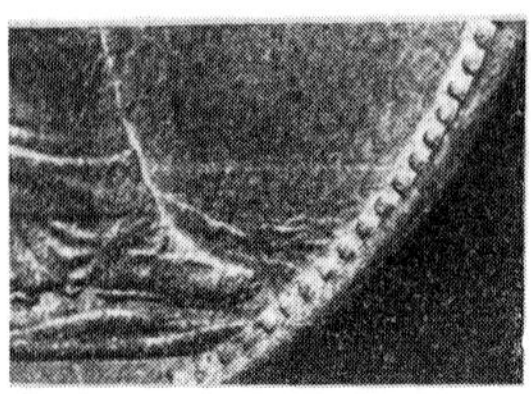

3990A "Low tide"

3990 Penny. ℞. Britannia.

	VF £	EF £		VF £	EF £
1902	1·00	4·50	1907	1·50	9·00
1903	2·00	10·00	1908	1·50	9·00
1904	2·50	14·00	1909	1·50	9·00
1905	2·00	12·00	1910	1·25	7 50
1906	1·50	9·00			

3990a As last but "Low tide", 1902 .. .. 5·00 25·00

3991

3991 Halfpenny. ℞. Britannia.

	VF £	EF £		VF £	EF £
1902	1·00	4·50	1907	1·00	6·00
1903	1·25	7·50	1908	1·00	6·00
1904	2·00	10·00	1909	1·50	9·00
1905	1·50	9·00	1910	1·25	7·50
1906	1·25	7·50			

3991a As last but "Low tide", 1902 .. .. 16·50 45·00

3992

3993

3992 Farthing. Britannia. Dark finish.

1902	·75	3·00	1907	1·00	5·00
1903	·90	5·00	1908	1·00	5·00
1904	1·75	7·00	1909	·90	4·50
1905	1·00	5·00	1910	1·75	7·00
1906	·90	4·50			

3993 Third-farthing (for use in Malta).

1902 ℞. Value .. .. ·50 2·75

GEORGE V, 1910-36

Paper money issued by the Treasury during the first World War replaced gold for internal use after 1915; but the branch mints in Australia and South Africa (the main Commonwealth gold producing countries) continued striking sovereigns until 1930-32. Owing to the steep rise in the price of silver in 1919/20 the issue of standard (·925) silver was discontinued and coins of ·500 silver were minted.

In 1912, 1918 and 1919, some pennies were made under contract by private mints in Birmingham. In 1918, as half-sovereigns were no longer being minted, farthings were again issued with the ordinary bright bronze finish. Crown pieces had not been issued for general circulation but they were struck in small numbers about Christmas time for people to give as presents in the years 1927-36, and in 1935 a special commemorative crown was issued in celebration of the Silver Jubilee.

As George V died in January, it is likely that all coins dated 1936 were struck during the reign of Edward VIII.

Designer's initials:
B. M. (Bertram Mackennal).
P. M. (Percy Metcalfe).
K. G. (Kruger Gray).

GOLD

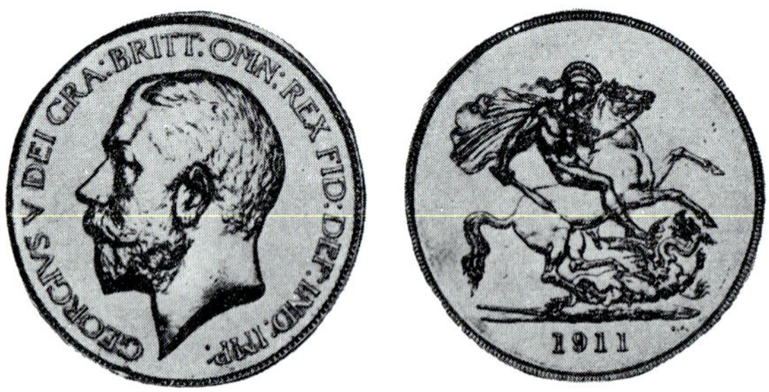

3994

			FDC £
3994	**Five pounds.***	℞. St. George, 1911 (Proof only)	2100·00
3995	**Two pounds.***	℞. St. George, 1911 (Proof only)	925·00

* Forgeries exist.

3996

3996 Sovereign. ℞. St. George.

	EF £		*EF* £
1911	80·00	1915	80·00
— Proof *FDC* £350		1916*	100 00
1912	80·00	1917*	*Extremely rare*
1913	80·00	1925	80·00
1914	80·00		

* Counterfeits exist of these and of most other dates and mints.

3997 Sovereign. R. St. George, C on ground for the Ottawa mint.

	VF £	*EF* £		*VF* £	*EF* £
1911 C		125·00	1917 C		125·00
1913 C	350·00	900·00	1918 C		125·00
1914 C		175·00	1919 C		125·00
1916 C	*Extremely rare*				

3997 3998 4004

3998 — — I on ground for India (Calcutta) mint, 1918 .. .. 95·00

3999 — — M on ground for Melbourne mint.

1911 M		80·00	1920 M	600·00	1000·00
1912 M		80·00	1921 M	*Extremely rare*	
1913 M		80·00	1922 M	*Extremely rare*	
1914 M		80·00	1923 M		100·00
1915 M		82·50	1924 M		100·00
1916 M		85·00	1925 M		82·50
1917 M		82·50	1926 M		95·00
1918 M		82·50	1927 M ? exists.		
1919 M		95·00	1928 M	300·00	625·00

4000 — — — small head.

1929 M	400·00	850·00	1931 M	100·00	225·00
1930 M		110·00			

4001 4002

4001 — — P on ground for Perth mint.

1911 P ..		80·00	1920 P		85·00
1912 P		80·00	1921 P		85·00
1913 P		80·00	1922 P		80·00
1914 P		80·00	1923 P		82·50
1915 P		82·50	1924 P		90·00
1916 P		85·00	1925 P		95·00
1917 P		82·50	1926 P		105·00
1918 P		80·00	1927 P		105 00
1919 P		85·00	1928 P		97 50

4002 — — — small head.

1929 P		85·00	1931 P		82·50
1930 P		85·00			

4003 Sovereign. ℞. St. George. S on ground for Sydney mint.

	VF £	*EF* £		VF £	*EF* £
1911 S		80·00	1919 S		80·00
1912 S		80·00	1920 S	750·00	1500·00
1913 S		80·00	1921 S	500·00	1000·00
1914 S		80·00	1922 S	400·00	850·00
1915 S		82·50	1923 S	750·00	1500·00
1916 S		80·00	1924 S	250·00	500·00
1917 S		80·00	1925 S		82·50
1918 S		80·00	1926 S	900·00	2000·00

4004 — — SA on ground for Pretoria mint.

1923 SA *Extremely rare*			1926 SA ..		80·00
1923 SA *Proof, FDC* £750			1927 SA ..		80·00
1924 SA *Extremely rare*			1928 SA ..		80·00
1925 SA		80·00			

4005 — — — small head.

1929 SA		85·00	1931 SA ..		85·00
1930 SA		85·00	1932 SA ..		90·00

4006

4006 Half-sovereign. ℞. St. George.

— *Proof, FDC* £225			1913	50·00	70·00
1911 ..	50·00	70·00	1914	50·00	70·00
1912	50·00	70·00	1915	50·00	75·00

4007 — — M on ground for Melbourne mint.

1915 M				60·00	95·00

4008 — — P on ground for Perth mint.

1911 P	55·00	90·00	1918 P	300·00	650·00
1915 P	55·00	90·00	1919 P, 1920 P (*Not circulated*)		

4009 — — S on ground for Sydney mint.

1911 S	55·00	85·00	1915 S	55·00	85·00
1912 S	55·00	85·00	1916 S	55·00	85·00
1914 S	55·00	85·00			

4010 — — SA on ground for Pretoria mint.

1923 SA *Proof, FDC* £475			1926 SA ..	50·00	70·00
1925 SA	50·00	72·50			

Note: Gold bullion price at time of printing $575 per oz. at $2·40 to the £1 sterling.

SILVER

First coinage. Sterling silver (·925 fine).

4011 Halfcrown. ℞. Crowned shield in Garter.

4011

	F £	*VF* £	*EF* £		*VF* £	*EF** £
1911 ..	2·75	7·00	35·00	1915	2·50	15·00
— Proof	*FDC* £95			1916	2·50	15·00
1912 ..	3·00	8·00	37·50	1917	2·50	20·00
1913 ..	3·25	9·00	40·00	1918	2·50	15·00
1914 ..	..	2·50	15·00	1919	4·00	22·00

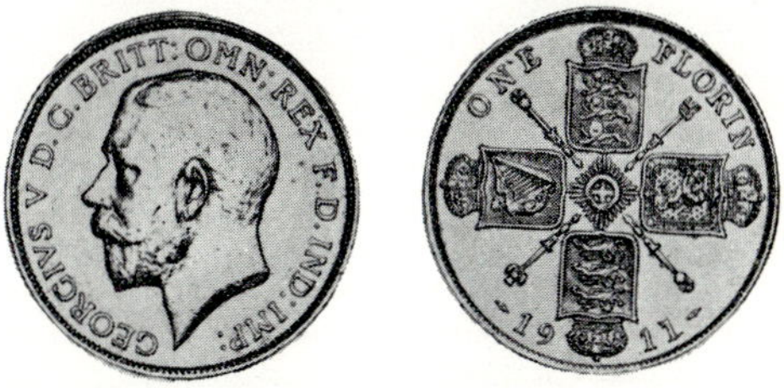

4012

4012 Florin. ℞. Cruciform shields.

1911 ..	1·50	5·00	27·50	1915	2·00	15·00
— Proof	*FDC* £85			1916	2·00	15·00
1912 ..	1·75	5·50	30·00	1917	3·50	22·00
1913 ..	2·25	8·00	37·50	1918	2·00	15·00
1914 ..	..	2·00	15·00	1919	3·50	20·00

4013 Shilling. ℞. Lion on crown, inner circles.

1911 ..	..	1·35	12·00	1915	1·25	9·00
— Proof	*FDC* £50			1916	1·25	9·00
1912 ..	..	2·00	15·00	1917	2·00	14·00
1913 ..	1·00	5·50	30·00	1918	1·25	9·00
1914 ..	..	1·25	7·00	1919	1·75	14·00

* N.B. Prices for strictly *unc.* coins will be considerably higher.

4013

4014

4014 Sixpence. R. Similar.

	VF £	EF £		VF £	EF £
1911	1·50	10·00	1916	1·25	9·00
— Proof *FDC* £35			1917	2·25	16·00
1912	2·25	16·00	1918	1·25	9·00
1913	2·75	20·00	1919	1·50	10·00
1914	1·25	9·00	1920	2·00	15·00
1915	1·25	9·00			

4015 Threepences. As Maundy but dull finish.

	VF £	EF £		VF £	EF £
1911	·50	4·00	1916	·30	3·00
1912	·50	4·00	1917	·30	3·00
1913	·50	4·00	1918	·30	3·00
1914	·50	4·00	1919	·30	3·00
1915	·50	4·00	1920	·50	4·00

4016

4016 Maundy set. (4d., 3d., 2d. and 1d.).

	EF £	FDC £		EF £	FDC £
1911	35·00	47·50	1916	32·00	45·00
— Proof *FDC* £60			1917	32·00	45·00
1912	32·00	45·00	1918	32·00	45·00
1913	32·00	45·00	1919	32·00	45·00
1914	32·00	45·00	1920	32·00	45·00
1915	35·00	47·50			

		EF £	FDC £
4017	**— fourpence,** 1911-1920 *from*	5·00	9·00
4018	**— threepence,** 1911-1920 *from*	8·00	14·00
4019	**— twopence,** 1911-1920 *from*	5·00	8·50
4020	**— penny,** 1911-1920 *from*	7·00	12·00

Second Coinage. Debased silver (·500 fine). Types as before.

4021 Halfcrown.

	VF £	EF £		F £	VF £	EF* £
1920	4·50	25·00	1924	1·00	5·00	35·00
1921	4·50	25·00	1925	3·00	30·00	175·00
1922	4·75	30·00	1926	1·35	7·00	45·00
1923	2·75	20·00				

4022 Florin.

1920	3·50	25·00	1924	·90	5·00	35·00
1921	3·50	25·00	1925	2·75	20·00	150·00
1922	3·00	22·50	1926	·90	5·00	35·00
1923	2·75	18·00				

4023 Shilling.

1920	2·50	18·00	1924	·50	3·00	25·00
1921	2·50	18·00	1925	·75	5·00	40·00
1922	2·50	17·50	1926	·45	2·75	22·00
1923	2·50	18·00				

4024 Sixpence.

	VF £	EF £		VF £	EF* £
1920	1·25	10·00	1923	3·50	25·00
1921	1·25	10·00	1924	1·25	10·00
1922	1·25	11·00	1925	1·75	15·00

4025

4026

4025 — new beading and broader rim.

1925	1·50	12·00	1926	2·00	14·00

4026 Threepence.

1920	·40	3·50	1925	2·00	10·00
1921	·45	3·50	1926	2·50	15·00
1922	·45	3·50			

4027 Maundy set. (4d., 3d., 2d. and 1d.).

	EF	FDC		EF	FDC
1921	33·00	46·00	1925	32·00	45·00
1922	33·00	46·00	1926	32·00	45·00
1923	32·00	45·00	1927	32·00	45·00
1924	32·00	45·00			

		EF	FDC
4028 — **fourpence,** 1921-7	*from*	7·00	10·00
4029 — **threepence,** 1921-7	*from*	9·00	14·00
4030 — **twopence,** 1921-7	*from*	7·00	11·00
4031 — **penny,** 1921-7	*from*	8·00	12·00

* N.B. Prices for strictly *unc.* coins will be considerably higher.

2nd coinage

3rd coinage

Third coinage. As before but **modified effigy,** with details of head more clearly defined. The BM on truncation is nearer to the back of the neck and without stops; beading is more pronounced.

4032 Halfcrown.

1926	10·00	50·00	1927	3·25	20·00

4033 Shilling.

1926	2·75	18·00	1927	3·00	22·00

4034 Sixpence.

1926	1·25	10·00	1927	1·50	11·00

4035 Threepence.

1926	·85	4·00

Fourth coinage. New types, 1927-35.

4036

4036 Crown. ℞. Crown in wreath.

		VF £	*EF* £			*VF* £	*EF* £
1927	Proof only *FDC* £150			1932	.. ..	110·00	225·00
1928	.. ..	80·00	145·00	1933	.. ..	90·00	160·00
1929	.. ..	90·00	160·00	1934	.. ..	500·00	950·00
1930	.. ..	90·00	160·00	1936	.. ..	110·00	250·00
1931	.. ..	100·00	200·00				

4037

4038

4037 Halfcrown. ℞. Shield.

1927	Proof only *FDC* £32·50			1932	.. ..	3·00	25·00
1928	.. ..	1·25	9·00	1933	.. ..	1·50	10·00
1929	.. ..	1·35	9·00	1934	.. ..	3·75	35·00
1930	.. ..	15·00	110·00	1935	.. ..	1·50	10·00
1931	.. ..	1·50	10·00	1936	.. ..	1·00	8·00

4038 Florin. ℞. Cruciform sceptres, shield in each angle.

1927	Proof only *FDC* £50			1932	.. ..	12·00	95·00
1928	.. ..	1·00	8·00	1933	.. ..	1·25	10·00
1929	.. ..	1·00	8·00	1935	.. ..	1·10	9·00
1930	.. ..	1·25	10·00	1936	.. ..	·90	7·50
1931	.. ..	1·10	9·00				

4039

4040

4039 Shilling.. ℞. Lion on crown, no inner circles.

	VF	EF		VF	EF*
	£	£		£	£
1927	1·65	14·00	1932	·80	9·00
— Proof *FDC* £25			1933	·75	8·00
1928	·75	8·00	1934	2·00	16·00
1929	·75	8·00	1935	·75	8·00
1930	2·50	20·00	1936	·60	7·50
1931	·80	9·00			

* N.B. Prices for strictly *unc.* coins will be considerably higher.

4040 Sixpence. ℞. Three oak sprigs with six acorns.

1927 Proof only *FDC* £18·00					
1928	·50	5·00	1930	·65	6·00
1929	·45	4·00			

4041 — — closer milling.

1931	·80	9·00	1934	·75	10·00
1932	·75	10·00	1935	·60	8·00
1933	·60	8·00	1936	·30	4·00

4042

4042 Threepence. ℞. Three oak sprigs with three acorns.

1927 Proof only *FDC* £50					
1928	2·00	12·00	1933		1·20
1930	1·50	10·00	1934		1·20
1931		1·35	1935		1·20
1932		1·25	1936		1·20

4043 Maundy set. As earlier sets.

	EF	FDC		EF	FDC
	£	£		£	£
1928	40·00	50·00	1933	38·00	48·00
1929	38·00	48·00	1934	38·00	48·00
1930	38·00	48·00	1935	40·00	50·00
1931	38·00	48·00	1936	46·00	55·00
1932	38·00	48·00			

4044 — **fourpence,** 1928-1936 *from*	6·00	10·00
4045 — **threepence,** 1928-1936 *from*	7·00	12·00
4046 — **twopence,** 1928-1936 *from*	6·00	9·00
4047 — **penny,** 1928-1936 *from*	8·00	13·00

Silver Jubilee Commemorative issue.

4048

		VF	EF
4048	**Crown,** 1935. R. St. George, incuse lettering on edge ..	5·00	12·00
4049	— Similar. Specimen striking issued in box, ...	*Unc.*	£30
4050	— — Raised lettering on edge, *Proof FDC* £275		

BRONZE

4051

4051 **Penny.** R. Britannia.

	F	VF	EF		F	VF	EF
	£	£	£		£	£	£
1911		·75	4·75	1918		·60	4·75
1912		·65	5·00	1919		·40	4·25
1913		·60	4·75	1920		·35	3·50
1914		·65	5·50	1921		·35	3·50
1915		·75	6·50	1922		1·75	12·00
1916		·60	4·75	1926		2·00	15·00
1917		·50	4·25				

4052 — — H (The Mint, Birmingham, Ltd.) to l. of date.

1912 H		4·00	20·00	1919 H	·90	10·00	80·00
1918 H	1·00	12·00	90·00				

4053 — — KN (King's Norton Metal Co.) to l. of date.

1918 KN	1·75	15·00	125·00	1919 KN	2·25	18·00	150·00

4054 — — modified effigy.

1926	5·50	40·00	300·00	1927		·45	3·00

4055 — — small head.

1928		·25	2·50	1933		*Extremely rare*	
1929		·25	2·50	1934		1·35	10·00
1930		·40	4·00	1935		·20	1·75
1931		·75	5·50	1936			1·25
1932		2·00	14·00				

4055

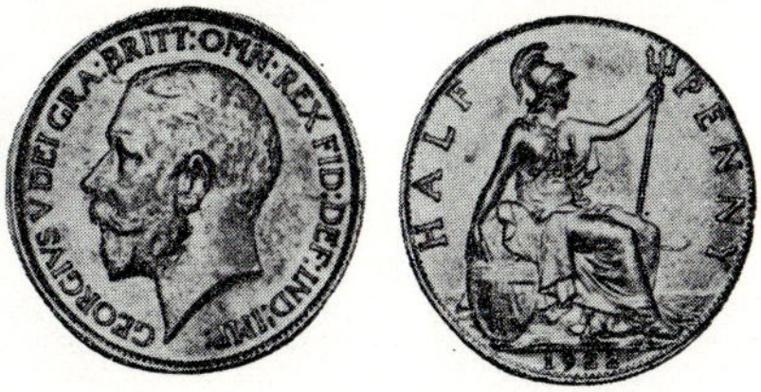

4056

4058

4056 Halfpenny. ℞. Britannia.

	VF £	*EF* £		*VF* £	*EF* £
1911	·60	4·50	1919	·60	4·50
1912	·60	4·50	1920	·60	4·50
1913	·75	5·00	1921	·60	4·50
1914	·75	5·00	1922	1·50	7·50
1915	·75	5·00	1923	·75	6·00
1916	·60	4·50	1924	·75	5·00
1917	·60	4·50	1925	1·00	6·00
1918	·60	4·50			

4057 — — modified effigy.

1925	1·50	8·00	1927	·60	4·50
1926	1·25	7·00			

4058 — — small head.

1928	·30	2·75	1933	·30	2·75
1929	·30	2·75	1934	·50	4·50
1930	·30	2·75	1935	·35	3·00
1931	·30	2·75	1936		1·50
1932	·35	3·25			

4059

4062

4059 Farthing. ℞. Britannia. Dark finish.

1911	·40	2·50	1915	·65	3·75
1912	·25	1·65	1916	·30	2·00
1913	·30	1·75	1917	·15	1·00
1914	·30	1·75	1918		9·00

4060 — — Bright finish, 1918-25 .. .. ·15 1·00

4061 Farthing. ℞. Britannia. Modified effigy.

1926	·15	·90	1932		·45
1927	·15	·90	1933	·15	1·10
1928	·15	·90	1934	·25	1·65
1929	·15	·90	1935	·30	1·90
1930	·20	1·25	1936		·60
1931	·15	·90			

4062 Third-farthing (for use in Malta). ℞. Value.

1913 .. .. ·50 3·00

EDWARD VIII, Jan.-Dec. 1936

Abdicated 10 December. Created Duke of Windsor (1936-1972)

No coins of Edward VIII were issued for currency within the United Kingdom bearing his name and portrait. The mint had commenced work on a new coinage prior to the Abdication, and various patterns were made. No proof sets were issued for sale and only a small number of sets were struck.

Coins bearing Edward's name, but not portrait, were issued for the colonial territories of British East Africa, British West Africa, Fiji and New Guinea. The projected U.K. coins were to include a shilling of essentially "Scottish" type and a nickel brass threepence with twelve sides which might supplement and possibly supersede the inconveniently small silver threepence.

Designer's initials:
H.P. (T. Humphrey Paget)
K.G. (Kruger Gray)

4063

4063 **Proof Set.**

Gold. £5, £2, and £1, 1937 .. .. *not issued*

Silver Crown, Halfcrown, Florin, Scottish shilling, sixpence and threepence, 1937 .. .. *not issued*

Nickel brass. Threepence, 1937	*not issued*
Bronze. Penny, Halfpenny and Farthing, 1937	*not issued*

Pattern.

4064 Nickel brass dodecagonal, threepence, 1937. ℞. Thrift plant of more naturalistic style than the modified proof coin. A small number of these coins were produced for experimental purposes and a few did get into circulation . . . . . . *Extremely rare*

Colonial Issues.

4068 4071

		EF	*Unc.*
4065	**British East Africa.** Bronze 10 cents, 1936	·75	1·75
4066	— — 5 cents, 1936	·75	1·75
4067	**British West Africa.** Cupro-nickel penny, 1936	·75	1·75
4068	— — Halfpenny, 1936	·75	1·75
4069	— — One-tenth penny, 1936	·50	1·25
4070	**Fiji.** Cupro-nickel penny, 1936	1·25	3·25
4071	**New Guinea.** Bronze penny, 1936	1·50	3·50

GEORGE VI, 1936-52

Though they were at first issued concurrently, the twelve-sided nickel-brass threepence superseded the small silver threepence in 1942. Those dated 1943-1944 not issued for U.K. Two different shillings were issued; one, the "Scottish" shilling, has the Scottish lion seated on a crown and was issued as a compliment to the Scottish ancestry of Queen Elizabeth, now Queen Mother. In 1947, as silver was needed to repay the bullion lent by the U.S.A. during the war, silver coins were replaced by coins of the same type and weight made of cupro-nickel. In 1949, after India had attained independence, the title *Indiae Imperator* was dropped from the coinage. Commemorative crown pieces were issued for the Coronation and the 1951 Festival of Britain.

Designer's initials:
K.G. (Kruger Gray)
H.P. (T. Humphrey Paget)
W.P. (Wilson Parker)

GOLD

FDC
£

4074

4074	**Five pounds.** R. St. George, 1937. Proof only	1300·00
4075	**Two pounds.** Similar, 1937. Proof	700·00
4076	**Sovereign.** Similar, 1937. Proof	650·00
4077	**Half-sovereign.** Similar, 1937. Proof	275·00

SILVER

First coinage. Silver, .500 fine, with title IND : IMP

4078

	VF £	EF £
4078 Crown. Coronation commemorative, 1937. R. Arms and supporters	7·50	16·00

4079 — — Proof *FDC* £40·00

4080 4081

4080 Halfcrown. R. Shield.

	EF £	Unc. £		EF £	Unc. £
1937	1·75	7·50	1942	1·00	4·50
— Proof *FDC* £12·00			1943	1·50	6·00
1938	3·75	16·00	1944	1·00	4·00
1939	1·50	6·50	1945	1·00	4·00
1940	1·75	6·00	1946	1·00	4·00
1941	1·35	6·00			

4081 Florin. R. Crowned rose, etc.

	EF £	Unc. £		EF £	Unc. £
1937	1·50	7·00	1942	·70	3·50
— Proof *FDC* £9·00			1943	·70	3·50
1938	4·00	15·00	1944	·70	3·50
1939	1·50	5·50	1945	·70	3·50
1940	1·25	5·00	1946	·70	3·50
1941	1·25	4·50			

4082 4083

4082 Shilling. "English". R. Lion on large crown.

	EF £	Unc. £		EF £	Unc. £
1937	1·75	7·50	1942	1·00	4·00
— Proof *FDC* £7·00			1943	·90	4·00
1938	3·50	15·00	1944	·90	3·75
1939	1·25	5·00	1945	·60	3·00
1940	1·50	5·50	1946	·60	3·00
1941	1·50	5·50			

4083 — "Scottish". R. Lion seated facing on crown, etc.

	EF £	Unc. £		EF £	Unc. £
1937	1·25	6·00	1942	1·25	5·50
— Proof *FDC* £6·50			1943	1·25	5·50
1938	3·75	15·00	1944	1·25	5·00
1939	1·25	5·50	1945	·60	3·00
1940	1·25	5·50	1946	·60	3·00
1941	1·50	6·00			

4084

4085

4084 Sixpence. ℞. GRI crowned.

	VF £	EF £	Unc. £		VF £	EF £	Unc. £
1937	..	·90	3·50	1942	..	·60	2·25
— Proof *FDC* £4·50				1943	..	·60	2·25
1938	..	1·75	7·00	1944	..	·50	2·00
1939	..	1·10	4·25	1945	..	·45	1·75
1940	..	1·25	4·25	1946	..	·50	2·00
1941	..	1·25	4·00				

4085 Threepence. ℞. Shield on rose.

	VF £	EF £	Unc. £		VF £	EF £	Unc. £
1937	·10	·70	2·00	1941	·15	·85	2·75
— Proof *FDC* £4·50				1942*	2·00	9·00	17·50
1938	·10	·70	2·00	1943*	2·25	12·00	20·00
1939	·50	3·00	9·00	1944*	6·00	18·00	30·00
1940	·15	·85	2·75				

*For colonial use only.

4086

4086 Maundy set. Silver, .500 fine. Uniform dates.

	FDC £		*FDC* £
1937	50·00	1942	48·00
— Proof *FDC* £50·00		1943	48·00
1938	48·00	1944	48·00
1939	48·00	1945	48·00
1940	48·00	1946	50·00
1941	48·00		

4087 — fourpence, 1937-1946 *from* .. 8·50

4088 — threepence, 1937-1946 *from* .. 8·50

4089 — twopence, 1937-1946 *from* .. 8·50

4090 — penny, 1937-1946 *from* .. 12·00

Second coinage. Silver, .925 fine, with title IND . IMP (Maundy only).

4091 Maundy set (4d., 3d., 2d. and 1d.). Uniform dates.

1947 .. 50·00 1948 .. 50·00

4092 — fourpence, 1947-48 .. 9·00

4093 — threepence, 1947-48 .. 9·50

4094 — twopence, 1947-48 .. 9·00

4095 — penny, 1947-48 .. 12·00

Third coinage. Silver .925 fine, but omitting IND . IMP. (Maundy only).

4096 Maundy set (4d., 3d., 2d. and 1d.). Uniform dates.

	FDC £		*FDC* £
1949	50·00	1951	50·00
1950	50·00	1952	52·00

The 1952 Maundy was distributed by Queen Elizabeth II.

4097 — **fourpence,** 1949-1952 *from*	9·00
4098 — **threepence,** 1949-1952 *from*	9·00
4099 — **twopence,** 1949-1952 *from*	9·00
4100 — **penny,** 1949-1952 *from*	12·00

CUPRO-NICKEL

Second coinage. Types as first (silver) coinage, IND . IMP.

	EF £	*Unc.* £		*EF* £	*Unc.* £
4101 Halfcrown. ℞. Shield.					
1947	·75	4·00	1948	·75	4·00
4102 Florin. ℞. Crowned rose.					
1947	·65	3·50	1948	·65	3·25
4103 Shilling. "English" type.					
1947	·70	5·00	1948	·50	3·00
4104 — "Scottish" type.					
1947	·65	3·75	1948	·50	3·00
4105 Sixpence. GRI crowned.					
1947	·45	2·50	1948	·35	2·00

Third coinage. Types as before but title IND . IMP . omitted.

4106

4110

4106 Halfcrown.					
1949	1·25	6·50	1951	1·75	8·00
1950	1·45	7·00	— Proof *FDC* £12·00		
— Proof *FDC* £12			1952	*Extremely rare*	
4107 Florin.					
1949	1·50	8·50	1951	1·50	8·50
1950	1·75	8·00	— Proof *FDC* £7·50		
— Proof *FDC* £8·50					
4108 Shilling. "English" type.					
1949	1·25	6·00	1951	1·45	6·50
1950	1·45	6·50	— Proof *FDC* £6·50		
— Proof *FDC* £6·50					
4109 — "Scottish" type.					
1949	2·00	8·00	1951	1·25	7·00
1950	1·25	7·00	— Proof *FDC* £6·50		
— Proof *FDC* £6·50					

Cupro-nickel

4110 Sixpence. As illustration on page 289.

	EF	*Unc.*		*VF*	*EF*	*Unc.*
	£	£		£	£	£
1949	·70	4·00	1951 ..	..	·70	4·00
1950	·70	4·00	— Proof	*FDC* £5·00		
— Proof *FDC* £5·50			1952 ..	2·50	14·00	45·00

Festival of Britain issue.

4111

	EF	*Unc.*
4111 Crown. ℞. St George, 1951 *Proof-like*	3·50	6·50

NICKEL BRASS

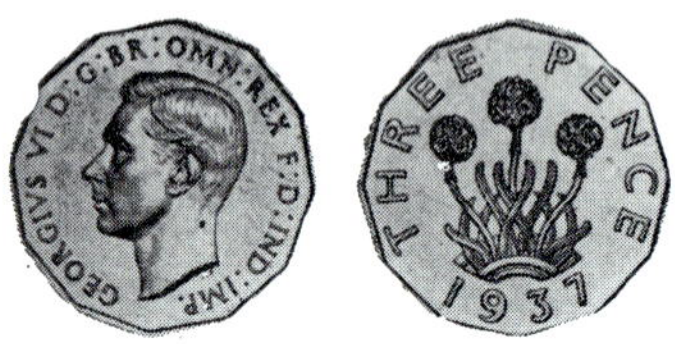

4112

4113

First issue, with title IND . IMP.

4112 Threepence (dodecagonal). ℞. Thrift.

	EF	*Unc.*		*VF*	*EF*	*Unc.*
1937	·45	1·75	1942 ..		·70	2·25
— Proof *FDC* £4·25			1943 ..		·70	2·25
1938	2·50	6·50	1944 ..		·75	3·00
1939	3·75	15·00	1945 ..		1·00	6·00
1940	1·75	5 00	1946 ..	4·00	35·00	125·00
1941	·60	3·50	1948 ..		4·50	15·00

Second issue, omitting IND . IMP.

4113 Threepence.

	VF	*EF*	*Unc.*		*VF*	*EF*	*Unc.*
	£	£	£		£	£	£
1949 ..	5·50	40·00	135·00	1951 ..	1·50	9·00	35·00
1950 ..	1·25	8·00	30·00	— Proof	*FDC* £25		
— Proof	*FDC* £30			1952 ..	·25	·75	4·00

BRONZE

First issue, with title IND . IMP.

4114 Penny ℞. Britannia.

4114

	EF £	Unc. £
1937	·45	2·25
— Proof *FDC* £6·50		
1938	·50	2·25
1939	1·25	5·00
1940	1·75	6·50
1944	1·75	7·00
1945	1·25	5·00
1946	·45	1·75
1947	·35	2·00
1948	·35	1·75

4115 Halfpenny. ℞. Ship.

4115

4116

	EF £	Unc. £
1937	·45	1·75
— Proof *FDC* £4·50		
1938	·55	3·50
1939	1·00	4·50
1940	1·25	6·50
1941	1·10	5·00
1942	·45	1·75
1943	·45	2·00
1944	·50	2·25
1945	·50	2·50
1946	1·75	6·50
1947	·55	3·00
1948	·45	1·75

4116 Farthing. ℞. Wren.

	EF £	Unc. £
1937	·15	1·10
— Proof *FDC* £3·50		
1938	·60	2·50
1939	·15	·65
1940	·25	1·20
1941	·15	·75
1942	·15	·75
1943	·15	·65
1944	·15	·65
1945	·15	·65
1946	·15	·65
1947	·15	·65
1948	·20	·75

Bronze

Second issue, without IND. IMP. Types as before.

4117 Penny.

	VF £	EF £	Unc. £		VF £	EF £	Unc. £
1949 ..	..	·45	1·75	1951 ..	..	12·00	18·00
1950 ..	4·00	10·00	26·00	— Proof	FDC	£16	
— Proof	FDC	£18					

4118

4119

4118 Halfpenny.

1949 ..	..	1·00	5·50	1951 ..	..	1·10	5·00
1950 ..	..	·80	4·50	— Proof	FDC	£4·50	
—	Proof	FDC	£4·50	1952 ..	..	·50	2·50

4119 Farthing.

1949 ..	..	·15	1·25	1951 ..		·15	·70
1950 ..	..	·12	·70	— Proof	FDC	£2·75	
—	Proof	FDC	£4·00	1952 ..	..	·15	·80

The coins dated 1952 were issued during the reign of Elizabeth II.

ELIZABETH II, acc. 1952

The earliest coins of this reign have the title BRITT · OMN, but in 1954 this was omitted from the Queen's titles owing to the changing status of so many Commonwealth territories. The minting of "English" and "Scottish" shillings was continued. A Coronation commemorative crown was issued in 1953, another crown was struck on the occasion of the 1960 British Exhibition in New York and a third was issued in honour of Sir Winston Churchill in 1965. A very small number of proof gold coins were struck in 1953 for the national museum collections, but between 1957 and 1968 gold sovereigns were minted again in quantity for sale in the international bullion market and to counteract the activities of counterfeiters.

Owing to inflation the farthing had now become practically valueless; production of these coins ceased after 1956 and the coins were demonetized at the end of 1960. In 1965 it was decided to change to a decimal system of coinage in the year 1971. As part of the transition to decimal coinage the halfpenny was demonetized in August 1969 and the halfcrown in January 1970. (See also introduction to Decimal Coinage on p. 299).

Designer's initials:
- G. L. (Gilbert Ledward).
- W. P. (Wilson Parker).
- M. G. (Mary Gillick).
- W. G. (William Gardner).
- E. F. (Edgar Fuller).
- C. T. (Cecil Thomas).

Other designers whose initials do not appear on the coins:
- Christopher Ironside.
- Arnold Machin.
- David Wynne.
- Professor Richard Guyatt

PRE DECIMAL ISSUES

GOLD

First coinage, with title BRITT · OMN, 1953. *Proof only.*

4120	**Five pounds.** ℞. St. George.	*None issued for collectors.*
4121	**Two pounds.** Similar	*None issued for collectors.*
4122	**Sovereign.** Similar.	*None issued for collectors.*
4123	**Half-sovereign.** Similar.	*None issued for collectors.*

Second issue, BRITT · OMN omitted.

4125

4124 Sovereign. ℞. St. George.

	Unc.
1957	82·50

4125 — Similar, but coarser graining on edge.

	Unc. £		*Unc.* £
1958	82·50	1965	82·50
1959	82·50	1966	82·50
1962	82·50	1967	82·50
1963	82·50	1968	82·50
1964	82·50		

Note: Gold bullion price at time of printing $575 per oz. at $2·40 to the £1 sterling.

SILVER

The Queen's Maundy are now the only coins struck regularly in silver. The location of the Maundy ceremony is given for each year.

First issue, with title BRITT · OMN.

		FDC
4126	**Maundy set** (4d., 3d., 2d. and 1d.), 1953. *St. Pauls'*	225·00
4127	— fourpence, 1953	40·00
4128	— threepence, 1953	40·00
4129	— twopence, 1953	40·00
4130	— penny, 1953	50·00

Second issue, with BRITT OMN omitted.

4131

4131 Maundy set (4d., 3d., 2d. and 1d.). Uniform dates.

			FDC				FDC
1954	*Westminster*	..	55·00	1963	*Chelmsford*	..	60·00
1955	*Southwark*	..	60·00	1964	*Westminster*	..	55·00
1956	*Westminster*	..	55·00	1965	*Canterbury*	..	60·00
1957	*St. Albans*	..	60·00	1966	*Westminster*	..	55·00
1958	*Westminster*	..	55·00	1967	*Durham*	..	60·00
1959	*Windsor* ..	..	60·00	1968	*Westminster*	..	65·00
1960	*Westminster*	..	55·00	1969	*Selby* ..	..	65·00
1961	*Rochester* ..	..	60·00	1970	*Westminster*	..	65·00
1962	*Westminster*	..	55·00				

See also p. 299.

4132	— **fourpence,** 1954-70, *from*	12·00
4133	— **threepence,** 1954-70, *from*	12·00
4134	— **twopence,** 1954-70, *from*	12·00
4135	— **penny,** 1954-70, *from*	13·00

CUPRO-NICKEL

First issue, 1953, with title BRITT · OMN.

4136

		EF £	Unc. £	Proof FDC £
4136	**Crown.** Queen on horseback. ℞. Crown in centre of cross, shield in each angle, 1953	1·50	3·75	32·50

4137

4138

		EF £	Unc. £	Proof FDC £
4137	**Halfcrown,** with title BRITT · OMN. ℞. Arms 1953	·75	3·25	10·00
4138	**Florin.** ℞. Double rose, 1953	·65	2·75	8·00

4139

4140

4141

		EF £	Unc. £	Proof FDC £
4139	**Shilling.** "English". ℞. Three lions, 1953 ..	·25	·90	4·00
4140	— "Scottish". ℞. Lion rampant in shield, 1953 ..	·30	·90	4·00
4141	**Sixpence.** ℞. Interlaced rose, thistle, shamrock and leek 1953	·25	·70	3·00
4142	Set of 9 uncirculated cu-ni, ni-br and Æ coins (2/6 to ¼d.) in Royal Mint plastic envelope		10·00	

Cupro-nickel

Second issue, similar types but omitting BRITT · OMN.

4143

4144

	EF £	Unc. £
4143 **Crown,** 1960. Bust r. ℞. As 4136	3·50	6·50
— — Similar, from polished dies (New York Exhibition issue) ..	5·50	20·00
4144 — Churchill commemorative, 1965. As illustration. ℞. Bust of Winston Churchill r.		·75
— — Similar, satin-finish. *Specimen*		*Extremely rare*

4145 **Halfcrown.** ℞. As 4137.

	EF £	Unc. £		
1954	2·50	15·00	1961	1·00
1955	·75	4·50	1962	1·00
1956	·90	4·75	1963	1·25
1957	·60	2·25	1964	3·50
1958	2·50	15·00	1965	·95
1959	2·50	15·00	1966	·60
1960	·80	3·50	1967	·60

4146

4146 **Florin.** ℞. As 4138.

1954	6·00	35·00	1961	1·75
1955	·60	2·75	1962	1·10
1956	·60	2·75	1963	·75
1957	4·50	25·00	1964	·60
1958	2·50	12·00	1965	·50
1959	4·50	30·00	1966	·45
1960	·45	2·25	1967	·40

4147 Shilling. "English" type. ℞. As 4139.

	EF £	*Unc.* £		*EF* £	*Unc.* £
1954	·50	2·50	1961		·75
1955	·35	2·00	1962		·50
1956	1·25	7·50	1963		·25
1957	·20	1·50	1964		·30
1958	3·25	18·00	1965		·30
1959	·20	1·00	1966		·30
1960	·20	·90			

4148 Shilling. "Scottish" type. ℞. As 4140.

1954	·35	2·00	1961	·60	6·00
1955	·35	2·00	1962		·90
1956	1·10	7·50	1963		·25
1957	3·25	17·50	1964		·50
1958	·20	·90	1965		·50
1959	2·50	17·50	1966		·30
1960	·25	1·00			

4149 Sixpence. ℞. As 4141.

1954	·40	3·25	1961		3·25
1955	·18	·90	1962		·30
1956	·18	·90	1963		·25
1957	·15	·65	1964		·20
1958	·65	4·00	1965		·15
1959		·35	1966		·15
1960	·55	4·25	1967		·15

NICKEL BRASS

4152

4153

First issue, with title BRITT . OMN.

4152 Threepence (dodecagonal). ℞. Crowned portcullis, 1953 ·65 1·50
— Proof *FDC* £3·50

Second issue, (omitting BRIT. OMN).
4153 Threepence. Similar type.

	EF £	*Unc.* £		*Unc.* £
1954	·90	4·00	1961	·35
1955	1·00	5·00	1962	·30
1956	1·25	5·00	1963	·20
1957	·65	3·50	1964	·20
1958	1·50	6·00	1965	·20
1959	·90	3·50	1966	·15
1960	·75	2·75	1967	·15

BRONZE

First issue, with title BRITT . OMN.

4154

4158

	VF £	EF £	Unc. £	Proof FDC £
4154 Penny. ℞. Britannia (only issued with Royal Mint set in plastic envelope), 1953 ..	·60	1·75	4·50	5·50
4155 Halfpenny. ℞. Ship, 1953 ..		·45	1·75	3·50
4156 Farthing. ℞. Wren, 1953		·25	·75	2·25

Second issue, omitting BRITT . OMN.

4157 Penny. ℞. Britannia (1954-60 *not issued*).

	Unc. £		Unc. £
1954 *Extremely rare*		1964 ..	·15
1961	·60	1965	·15
1962	·20	1966	·15
1963	·20	1967	·15

4158 Halfpenny. ℞. Ship (1961 *not issued*).

	EF	Unc.		Unc.
1954	·70	4·50	1962	·15
1955	·60	4·00	1963	·15
1956	·60	4·25	1964	·15
1957	·25	·75	1965	·15
1958		·40	1966	·15
1959		·25	1967	·15
1960		·25		

4156

4159

4159 Farthing. ℞. Wren.

	Unc. £		EF £	Unc. £
1954	·80	1956 ..	·55	1·75
1955	·75			

DECIMAL COINAGE

In December 1967 a decision to build a new mint at Llantrisant in South Wales was announced. The first phase was completed by December 1968 when H.M. The Queen struck the first coins at the official opening. The second phase was completed during late 1975 at which time all coin production at Tower Hill ceased.

Though the official change-over to a decimal currency did not take place until 15th February 1971, three decimal denominations were circulated prior to this date. The 10 and 5 *new pence*, equivalent to the former florin and shilling, were introduced in 1968 and the seven-sided 50 *new pence* (equal to 10 shillings) was issued during October 1969. The old halfpenny was demonetized on 1st August 1969, and the halfcrown was withdrawn on 1st January 1970.

In 1968 bronze 2, 1 and ½ *new pence* dated 1971 were issued, together with the 1968 10 and 5 *new pence*, as specimens of the new coinage, but these bronze coins were not legalized for current use until 1971.

Britain's accession to the E.E.C. was commemorated by a special 50 pence piece in 1973. A crown-sized 25 pence has been issued to celebrate the Silver Wedding of H.M. The Queen and Prince Philip in 1972, the Queen's Silver Jubilee in 1977 and in 1980 for the 80th birthday of Queen Elizabeth, the Queen Mother.

GOLD

4160

4162

4164

4166

Unc.

4160 **Five pounds.** As illustration, 1980 .. .. .. Proof *FDC* £900

4162 **Two pounds.** As illustration, 1980 .. .. .. Proof *FDC* £475

4164 **Sovereign.** As illustration.

	Unc.		*Unc.*
1974	75·00	1979 .. Proof *FDC* £125	
1976	75·00	1980	75·00
1978	75·00	— Proof *FDC* £115	
1979	75·00		

4166 **Half-sovereign.** As illustration, 1980 .. .. .. Proof *FDC* £70

(For 1980 £5, £2, £1, £½ proof set in case, see PS 31 on p. 303)

SILVER

4170 **Maundy set** (4p, 3p, 2p and 1p). Uniform dates. Types as 4131.

	FDC		*FDC*
1971 (*Tewkesbury Abbey*) ..	60·00	1977 (*Westminster Abbey*) ..	95·00
1972 (*York Minster*)	60·00	1978 (*Carlisle Cathedral*) ..	75·00
1973 (*Westminster Abbey*) ..	60·00	1979 (*Winchester Cathedral*) ..	85·00
1974 (*Salisbury Cathedral*) ..	65·00	1980 (*Worcester Cathedral*) ..	90·00
1975 (*Peterborough Cathedral*) ..	67·50	1981 (*Westminster Abbey*) ..	90·00
1976 (*Hereford Cathedral*) ..	70·00		

4180 — **fourpence,** 1971-81 *from* .. .. 13·00

4181 — **threepence,** 1971-81 *from* .. .. 13·00

4182 — **twopence,** 1971-81 *from* .. .. 13·00

4183 — **penny,** 1971-81 *from* .. .. 15·00

N.B. The Queen's Maundy are now the only coins struck regularly in .925 silver. The place of distribution is shown after each date.

CUPRO-NICKEL

4190

4190 **Fifty new pence** (seven sided). ℞. Britannia r.

	Unc. £		Unc. £
1969	1·75	1978	
1970	3·75	1979	
1976	1·10	1980	
1977	1·10		

4191

4191 Accession to European Economic Community. ℞. Clasped hands, 1973 .. 1·10
— — (Proof in case) .. .. *FDC* 4·00

4200

4200 **Twenty-five new pence** (crown). Silver Wedding Commemorative, 1972 .. ·90
— — (Æ proof in case) .. .. *FDC* 27·50

4201

		Unc.
4201	Silver Jubilee Commemorative, 1977	·60
	— — (Æ proof in case) .. .. *FDC*	18·00
	— — (Cu. ni. proof). Only issued in 1977/Mint set. See PS27 on p. 303	
	— — (Cu. ni. Specimen striking). Issued in Royal Mint folder	£1·75

4202

		Unc.
4202	Queen Mother 80th Birthday commemorative, 1980	·45
	— — (Æ proof in case) .. .. *FDC*	32·50
	— — (Cu. ni. Specimen striking). Issued in Royal Mint folder	1·75

4210

4210 **Ten new pence** R̷. Lion passant guardant l.

	Unc.		*Unc.*
1968	·25	1975	·25
1969	·30	1976	·25
1970	·30	1977	·25
1971	·30	1979	
1973	·25	1980	
1974	·25		

4220

4220 Five new pence. ℞. Crowned thistle.

1968	·15	1977	·15
1969	·18	1978	
1970	·18	1979	
1971	·15	1980	
1975	·15		

BRONZE

4230

4230 Two new pence. ℞. Plumes

	Unc		*Unc*
1971	·07	1978	
1975	·10	1979	
1976	·10	1980	
1977	·10		

4240

4250

4240 One new penny. ℞. Crowned portcullis

	Unc		*Unc*
1971	·07	1977	·10
1973	·10	1978	
1974	·10	1979	
1975	·10	1980	
1976	·10		

4250 Half new penny. ℞. Crown.

1971	·10	1977	·10
1973	·10	1978	
1974	·10	1979	
1975	·10	1980	
1976	·10		

4260 Decimal specimen folder. Contains 1968 10p and 5p and 1971 2p, 1p and ½p. .. .. ·90

PROOF or SPECIMEN SETS

Issued by the Royal Mint in official case from 1887 onwards, but earlier sets were issued privately by the engraver.

All pieces have a finish superior to that of the current coins.

		No. of coins	*FDC £*
PS1	**George IV.** New issue, **1826.** Five pounds to farthing	11	23,000·00
PS2	**William IV.** Coronation, **1831.** Two pounds to farthing	14	15,000·00
PS3	**Victoria,** young head, **1839.** "Una and the Lion" five pounds, and sovereign to farthing	15	26,000·00
PS4	— **1853.** Sovereign to quarter-farthing, including Gothic type crown	16	17,500·00
PS5	Jubilee head. Golden Jubilee, **1887.** Five pounds to threepence ..	11	8,000·00
PS6	— — Crown to threepence	7	1,050·00
PS7	Old head, **1893.** Five pounds to threepence	10	8,500·00
PS8	— — Crown to threepence	6	950·00
PS9	**Edward VII.** Coronation, **1902.** Five pounds to Maundy penny. Matt surface	13	2,100·00
PS10	— — Sovereign to Maundy penny. Matt surface	11	600·00
PS11	**George V.** Coronation, **1911.** Five pounds to Maundy penny ..	12	3,500·00
PS12	— — Sovereign to Maundy penny	10	850·00
PS13	— — Halfcrown to Maundy penny	8	350·00
PS14	New types, **1927.** Crown to threepence	6	300·00
PS15	**George VI.** Coronation, **1937.** Gold. Five pounds to half-sovereign	4	2,250·00
PS16	— — — Silver, etc. Crown to farthing, including Maundy ..	15	120·00
PS17	Mid-Century, **1950.** Halfcrown to farthing	9	55·00
PS18	Festival of Britain, **1951.** Crown to farthing	10	75·00
PS19	**Elizabeth II.** Coronation, **1953.** Crown to farthing	10	55·00
PS20	"Last Sterling" set, **1970.** Halfcrown to halfpenny, plus medallion..	8	15·00
PS21	Decimal coinage set, **1971.** 50 new pence ("Britannia") to ½ penny, plus medallion	6	12·00
PS22	— **1972.** As last, but includes the cu.-ni. Silver Wedding crown ..	7	15·00
PS23	— **1973.** As PS21 but "EEC" 50p.	6	10·00
PS24	— **1974.** As PS21	6	10·00
PS25	— **1975.** As last	6	10·00
PS26	— **1976.** As last	6	10·00
PS27	— **1977.** As PS21 but including the proof Silver Jubilee crown struck in cupro-nickel	7	14·00
PS28	— **1978.** As PS21	6	9·00
PS29	— **1979.** As last	6	9·00
PS30	— **1980.** As last	6	10·50
PS31	— — Five pounds to half sovereign	4	1450·00

Note. The prices given are for absolutely perfect sets with uncleaned, brilliant or matt surfaces. Sets are often seen with one or more coins showing imperfections such as scratches, bumps on the edge, etc. Any flaws will substantially affect the value of a set.

APPENDIX I

A SELECT NUMISMATIC BIBLIOGRAPHY

A list of Seaby publications and other new books are advertised at the end of this catalogue. Listed below are a selection of general books on British numismatics and other works that the specialist collector will need to consult.

General Books:

NORTH, J. J. *English Hammered Coins*, Vol. I, *c. 650-1272*; Vol. II, *1272-1662.*
BROOKE, G. C. *English Coins.* (3rd Ed., 1951).
SUTHERLAND, C. H. V. *English Coinage, 600-1900.*
KENYON, R. Ll. *Gold Coins of England.*
GRUEBER, H. A. *Handbook of the Coins of Great Britain and Ireland.*

Specialist Works:

MACK, R. P. *The Coinage of Ancient Britain.*
ALLEN, D. *The Origins of Coinage in Britain: A Reappraisal.*
DOLLEY, R. H. M. (Ed.). *Anglo-Saxon Coins; studies presented to Sir Frank Stenton.*
KEARY, C. & GREUBER, H. *English Coins in the British Museum: Anglo-Saxon Series.*
BROOKE, G. C. *English Coins in the British Museum: The Norman Kings.*
ALLEN, D. F. *English Coins in the British Museum: The Cross-and-Crosslets ('Tealby') type of Henry II.*
LAWRENCE, L. A. *The Coinage of Edward III from 1351.*
WHITTON, C. A. *The Heavy Coinage of Henry VI.*
BLUNT, C. E. and WHITTON, C. A. *The Coinages of Edward IV and of Henry VI (Restored).*
MORRIESON, LT.-COL. H. W. *The Coinages of Thomas Bushell, 1636-1648.*
SEABY, H. A. *The English Silver Coinage from 1649.*
SPINK & SON, LTD. *The Milled Coinage of England, 1662-1946.*
PECK, C. W. *English Copper, Tin and Bronze Coins in the British Museum, 1558-1958.*

also, just published:

LINECAR, H. W. A. *British Coin Designs and Designers*, 1977.
COPE, G. M. & RAYNER, P. A. *English Milled Coinage 1662-1972.*

and other authoritative papers published in the *Numismatic Chronicle* and *British Numismatic Journal.*

Seaby's Coin & Medal Bulletin

This is a magazine published monthly for all interested in Numismatics. It contains papers, articles and notes on coins and medals; numismatic society meetings; answers to questions; letters to the Editor; cuttings from the press, etc., etc.; also many pages of coins and medals of all kinds offered for sale. These are well catalogued and act as a good guide to help collectors to catalogue and classify their own coins. The subscription price for 12 monthly issues is £7.00 inland (or U.S. $17.00). Cloth bound copies of the Bulletin for 1967--69 available at £7.50 each; 1971, 1974-79 at £6 each; Superior quality binding case to hold twelve *Bulletins* £3.50, the bound copy of the 1980 Bulletin will be available early in 1981 at £7.50 and further volumes should also be available each subsequent year.

APPENDIX II

LATIN LEGENDS ON ENGLISH COINS

A DOMINO FACTUM EST ISTUD ET EST MIRABILE IN OCULIS NOSTRIS. (This is the Lord's doing and it is marvellous in our eyes: *Psalm* 118, 23). First used on "fine" sovereign of Mary.

AMOR POPULI PRAESIDIUM REGIS. (The love of the people is the King's protection). Reverse legend on angels of Charles I.

ANNO REGNI PRIMO, etc. (In the first year of the reign, etc.). Used around the edge of many of the larger milled denominations.

CHRISTO AUSPICE REGNO. (I reign under the auspice of Christ). Used extensively in the reign of Charles I.

CIVIUM INDUSTRIA FLORET CIVITAS. (By the industry of its people the State flourishes). On the 1951 Festival crown of George VI.

CULTORES SUI DEUS PROTEGIT. (God protects His worshippers). On gold double crowns and crowns of Charles I.

DECUS ET TUTAMEN. (An ornament and a safeguard). This inscription on the edge of all early large milled silver was suggested by Evelyn, he having seen it on the vignette in Card. Richelieu's Greek Testament, and of course refers to the device as a means to prevent clipping.

DIRIGE DEUS GRESSUS MEOS. (May the Lord direct my steps). On the "Una" 5 pounds of Queen Victoria.

DOMINE NE IN FURORE TUO ARGUAS ME. (O Lord, rebuke me not in Thine anger: *Psalm* 6, 1). First used on the half-florin of Edward III and then on all half-nobles.

D*omi*N*us* D*eu*S O*mnipotens* REX. (Lord God, Almighty King). (Viking coins).

DUM SPIRO SPERO. (Whilst I live, I hope). On the coins struck at Pontefract Castle during the Civil War after Charles I had been imprisoned.

EXALTABITUR IN GLORIA. (He shall be exalted in glory). On all quarter-nobles.

EXURGAT DEUS ET DISSIPENTUR INIMICI EIUS. (Let God arise and let His enemies be scattered: *Psalm* 68, 1). On the Scottish ducat and early English coins of James I (VI) and was chosen by the King himself.

FACIAM EOS IN GENTEM UNAM. (I will make them one nation: *Ezek.* 37, 22). On unites and laurels of James I.

FLORENT CONCORDIA REGNA. (Through concord kingdoms flourish). On gold unite of Charles I and broad of Charles II.

HANC DEUS DEDIT. (God has given this, *i.e. crown*). On siege-pieces of Pontefract struck in the name of Charles II.

HAS NISI PERITURUS MIHI ADIMAT NEMO. (Let no one remove these [letters] from me under penalty of death). On the edge of crowns and half-crowns of Cromwell.

HENRICUS ROSAS REGNA JACOBUS. (Henry *united* the roses, James the kingdoms). On English and Scottish gold coins of James I (VI).

INIMICOS EJUS INDUAM CONFUSIONE. (As for his enemies I shall clothe them with shame: *Psalm* 103, 19). On shillings of Edward VI struck at Durham House, Strand.

JESUS AUTEM TRANSIENS PER MEDIUM ILLORUM IBAT. (But Jesus, passing through the midst of them, went His way: *Luke* iv. 30). The usual reverse legend on English nobles, ryals and hammered sovereigns before James I; also on the very rare Scotch noble of David II of Scotland and the unique Anglo-Gallic noble of Edward the Black Prince.

LATIN LEGENDS

JUSTITIA THRONUM FIRMAT. (Justice strengthens the throne). On Charles I half-groats and pennies and Scottish twenty-penny pieces.

LUCERNA PEDIBUS MEIS VERBUM EST. (Thy word is a lamp unto my feet: *Psalm* 119, 105). Obverse legend on a rare half-sovereign of Edward VI struck at Durham House, Strand.

MIRABILIA FECIT. (He made marvellously). On the Viking coins of (?) York.

NUMMORUM FAMULUS. (The servant of the coinage). The legend on the edge of the English tin coinage at the end of the seventeenth century.

O CRUX AVE SPES UNICA. (Hail! O Cross, our only hope). On the reverse of all half-angels.

PAX MISSA PER ORBEM. (Peace sent throughout the world). The reverse legend of a pattern farthing of Anne.

PAX QUÆRITUR BELLO. (Peace is sought by war). The reverse legend of the Cromwell broad.

PER CRUCEM TUAM SALVA NOS CHRISTE REDEMPTOR. (By Thy cross, save us, O Christ, our Redeemer). The normal reverse of English angels.

POST MORTEM PATRIS PRO FILIO. (For the son after the death of the father). On seige pieces struck at Pontefract in 1648 (old style) after the execution of Charles I.

POSUI DEUM ADJUTOREM MEUM. (I have made God my Helper: *comp. Psalm* 54, 4). Used on many English and Irish silver coins from Edward III until 1603. Altered to POSUIMUS and NOSTRUM on the coins of Philip and Mary.

PROTECTOR LITERIS LITERÆ NUMMIS CORONA ET SALUS. (A protection to the letters [on the face of the coin], the letters [on the edge] are a garland and a safeguard to the coinage). On the edge of the rare fifty-shilling piece of Cromwell.

QUÆ DEUS CONJUNXIT NEMO SEPARET. (What God hath joined together let no man put asunder: *Matt.* 19, 6). On the larger silver English and Scottish coins of James I after he succeeded to the English throne.

REDDE CUIQUE QUOD SUUM EST. (Render to each that which is his own). On a Henry VIII type groat of Edward VI struck by Sir Martin Bowes at Durham House, Strand.

RELIGIO PROTESTANTIVM LEGES ANGLIÆ LIBERTAS PARLIAMENTI. (The religion of the Protestants, the laws of England, the liberty of the Parliament). This is known as the "Declaration" and refers to Charles I's declaration to the Privy Council at Wellington, 19th Sept., 1642; it is found on many of his coins struck at the provincial mints during the Civil War. Usually abbreviated to REL : PROT : LEG : ANG : LIB : PAR :

ROSA SINE SPINA. (A rose without a thorn). Found on some gold and small coins of Henry VIII and later reigns.

RUTILANS ROSA SINE SPINA. (A dazzling rose without a thorn). As last but on small gold only.

SCUTUM FIDEI PROTEGET EUM *or* EAM. (The shield of faith shall protect him *or* her). On much of the gold of Edward VI and Elizabeth.

TALI DICATA SIGNO MENS FLUCTUARI NEQUIT. (Consecrated by such a sign the mind cannot waver: from a hymn by Prudentius written in the 4th cent., entitled "Hymnus ante Somnum"). Only on the gold "George noble" of Henry VIII.

TIMOR DOMINI FONS VITÆ. (The fear of the Lord is a fountain of life: *Prov.* 14, 27). On many shillings of Edward VI.

TUEATUR UNITA DEUS. (May God guard these united, i.e. kingdoms). On many English, Scottish and Irish coins of James I.

VERITAS TEMPORIS FILIA. (Truth, the daughter of Time). On English and Irish coins of Mary Tudor.

LATIN LEGENDS

Some Royal Titles:

REX ANGL*orum*—King of the English.

REX SAXONUM OCCIDENTALIUM—King of the West Saxons.

DEI GRA*tia* ANGL*iae* ET FRANC*iae* D*omi*N*us* HYB*erniae* ET AQVIT*aniae*—By the Grace of God, King of England and France, Lord of Ireland and Aquitaine.

D*ei* G*ratia* M*agnae* B*ritanniae*, FR*anciae* ET H*iberniae* REX F*idei* D*efensor* BR*unsviciensis* ET L*une-burgensis* D*ux*, S*acri* R*omani* I*mperii* A*rchi*-TH*esaurarius* ET EL*ector* = By the Grace of God, King of Great Britain, France and Ireland, Defender of the Faith, Duke of Brunswick and Lune-burg, High Treasurer and Elector of the Holy Roman Empire.

BRITANNIARUM REX—King of the Britains (i.e. Britain and British territories overseas).

BRITT : OMN : REX : FID : DEF : IND : IMP—King of all the Britains, Defender of the Faith, Emperor of India.

Although not *Latin* legends, the following Norman-French mottos might usefully be added here:

DIEU ET MON DROIT. (God and my right). On halfcrowns of George IV and later monarchs.

HONI SOIT QUI MAL Y PENSE. (Evil to him who evil thinks). The Motto of the Order of the Garter, first used on the Combe Martin halfcrowns of Charles I. It also occurs on the Garter Star in the centre of the reverse of the silver coins of Charles II, but being so small it is usually illegible; it is more prominent on the coinage of George III.

APPENDIX III

MINTMARKS AND OTHER SYMBOLS ON ENGLISH COINS

A MINT-MARK (mm.), a term borrowed from Roman and Greek numismatics where it showed the place of mintage, was generally used on English coins to show (and a religious age preferred a cross for the purpose) where the legend began. Later, this mark, since the dating of coins was not usual, had a periodic significance, changing from time to time. Hence it was of a secret or "privy" nature; other privy marks on a coin might be the code-mark of a particular workshop or workman. Thus a privy mark (including the mm.) might show when a coin was made, or who made it. In the use of precious metals this knowledge was necessary to guard against fraud and counterfeiting.

Mint marks are sometimes termed 'initial marks' as they are normally placed at the commencement of the inscription. Some of the symbols chosen were personal badges of the ruling monarch, such as the rose and sun of York, the boar's head of Richard III, the dragon of Henry Tudor or the thistle of James I; others are heraldic symbols or may allude to the mint master responsible for the coinage, e.g., the mm. bow used on the Durham House coins struck under John Bowes and the WS mark of William Sharrington of Bristol.

A table of mintmarks is given on the next page. Where mintmarks appear in the catalogue they are sometimes referred to only by the reference number, in order to save space, i.e. *mm.* 28 (=mintmark Sun), *mm.* 28/74 (=*mm.*Sun on obverse, *mm.* Coronet on reverse), *mm.* 28/- (=*mm.* Sun on obverse only).

MINTMARKS AND OTHER SYMBOLS

1 Edward III, Cross 1 (Class B+C).
2 ,, broken Cross 1 (Class D).
3 ,, Cross 2 (Class E).
4 ,, Cross 3 (Class G).
5 Cross Potent (Edw. III Treaty).
6 Cross Pattée (Edw. III Post Treaty Rich. III).
7 (a) Plain or Greek Cross.
(b) Cross Moline.
8 Cross Patonce.
9 Cross Fleurée.
10 Cross Calvary (Cross on steps).
11 Long Cross Fitchée.
12 Short ,, ,,
13 Restoration Cross (Hen. VI).
14 Latin Cross.
15 Voided Cross (Henry VI).
16 Saltire Cross.
17 Cross and 4 pellets.
18 Pierced Cross.
19 Pierced Cross & pellet.
20 Pierced Cross & central pellet.
21 Cross Crosslet.
22 Curved Star (rayant).
23 Star.
24 Spur Rowel.
25 Mullet.
26 Pierced Mullet.
27 Eglantine.
28 Sun (Edw. IV)
29 Mullet (Henry V).
30 Pansy.
31 Heraldic Cinquefoil (Edw. IV).
32 Heraldic Cinquefoil (James I).
33 Rose (Edw. IV).
34 Rosette (Edw. IV).
35 Rose (Chas. I).
36 Catherine Wheel.
37 Cross in circle.
38 Halved Sun (6 rays) & Rose.
39 ,, ,, (4 rays) & Rose.
40 Lis-upon-Half-Rose.
41 Lis-upon-Sun & Rose.
42 Lis-Rose dimidiated.
43 Lis-issuant-from-Rose.
44 Trefoil.
45 Slipped Trefoil, James I (1).
46 ,, ,, ,, (2).
47 Quatrefoil.
48 Saltire.
49 Pinecone.
50 Leaf (-mascle, Hen. VI).
51 Leaf (-trefoil, Hen. VI).
52 Arrow.
53 Pheon.
54 A.
55 Annulet.
56 Annulet-with-pellet.
57 Anchor.
58 ,, & B.
59 Flower & B.
60 Bell.
61 Book.
62 Boar's Head, (early Richard III).
63 ,, ,, (later ,,).
64 Boar's Head Charles I.
65 Acorn (a) Hen. VIII (b) Elizabeth.
66 Bow.
67 Br. (Bristol, Chas. I).
68 Cardinal's Hat.
69 Castle (Hen. VIII).
70 Castle with H.
71 Castle (Chas. I).
72 Crescent (a) Henry VIII (b) Elizabeth.
73 Pomegranate. (Mary; Henry VIII's is broader).
74 Coronet.
75 Crown.
76 Crozier (a) Edw. III (b) Hen. VIII.
77 Ermine.
78 Escallop (Hen. VII).
79 ,, (James I).
80 Eye (in legend Edw. IV).
81 Eye (Parliament).
82 Radiate Eye (Hen. VII).
83 Gerb.
84 Grapes.
85 Greyhound's Head.
86 Hand.
87 Harp.
88 Heart.
89 Helmet.
90 Key.
91 Leopard's Head.
92 Lion.
93 Lion rampant.
94 Martlet.
95 Mascle.
96 Negro's Head.
97 Ostrich's Head.
98 P in brackets.
99 Pall.
100 Pear.
101 Plume.
102 ,, Aberystwyth and Bristol.
103 ,, Oxford.
104 ,, Shrewsbury.
105 Lis.
106 Lis.
107 Portcullis.
108 ,, Crowned.
109 Sceptre.
110 Sunburst.
111 Swan.
112 R in brackets.
113 Sword.
114 T (Henry VIII).
115 TC monogram.
116 WS monogram.
117 y or Y.
118 Dragon (Henry VII).
119 (a) Triangle (b) Triangle in Circle.
120 Sun (Parliament).
121 Uncertain mark.
122 Grapple.
123 Tun.
124 Woolpack.
125 Thistle.
126 Figure 6. (Edw. VI).
127 Floriated cross.
128 Lozenge.
129 Billet.
130 Plume. Lundy Is.
131 Two lions.
132 Clasped book.
133 Cross pommee.

N.B. The reign after a mintmark indicates that from which the drawing is taken. A similar mm. may have been used in another reign and will be found in the chronological list at the beginning of each reign.

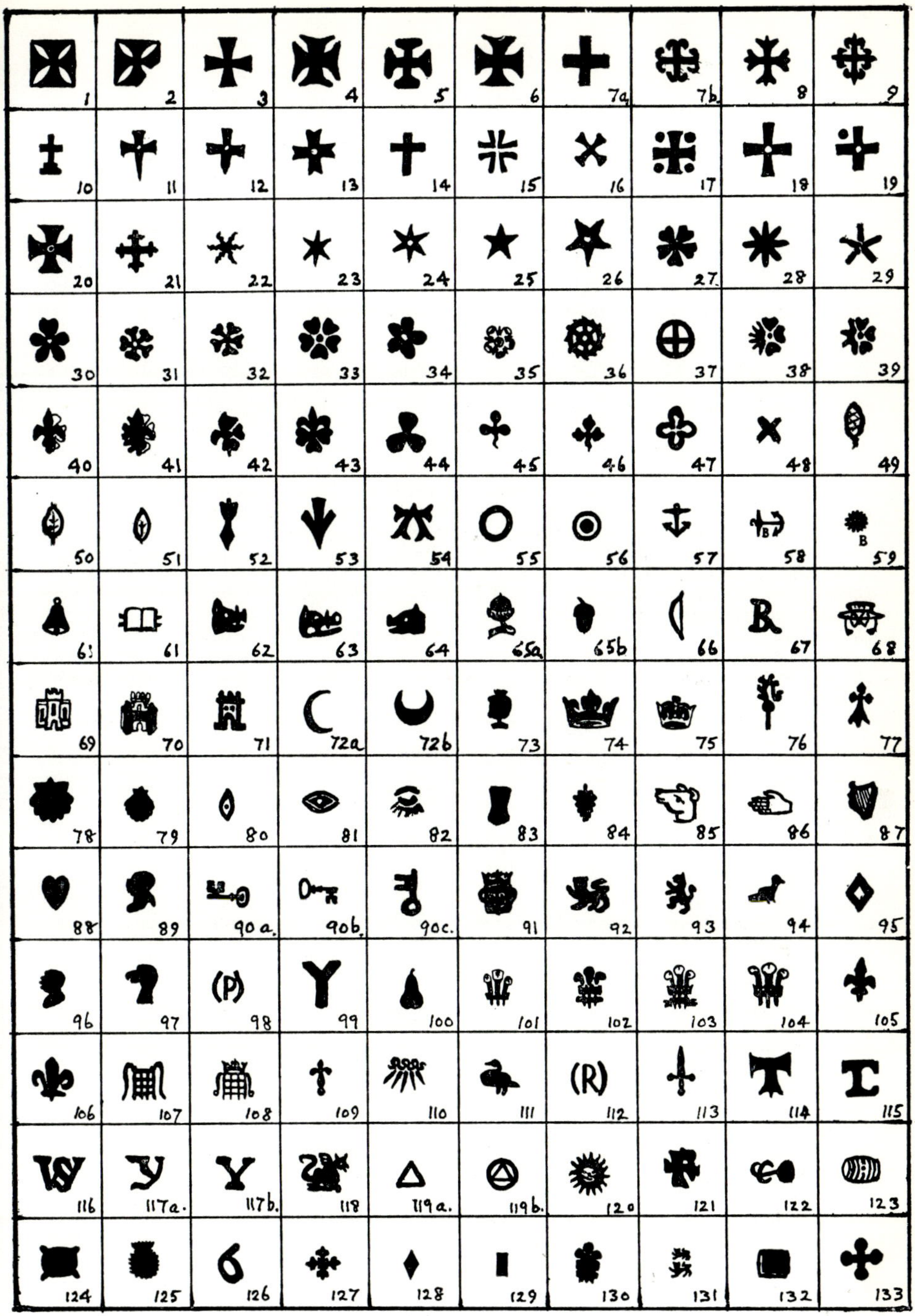

MINTMARKS AND OTHER SYMBOLS

APPENDIX IV

SOME NUMISMATIC CLUBS AND SOCIETIES

There are well over one hundred numismatic societies and clubs in the British Isles, a number of which form a part of the social and cultural activities of scholastic institutions or commercial or industrial concerns.

The two principal learned societies are the Royal Numismatic Society and the British Numismatic Society; both of which publish an annual journal. Listed below are those societies which are affiliated to the British Association of Numismatic Societies (Hon. Sec., K. F. Sugden, Dept. of Numismatics, Manchester Museum, The University, Oxford Rd., Manchester). Enquiries should be made to the secretaries/representatives of the individual societies:

Royal Numismatic Society: Dr. M. J. Price, c/o Dept. of Coins and Medals, British Museum, London, W.C.1.
British Numismatic Society: W. Slayter, 63 West Way, Edgware, Middlesex HA8 9LA.
Andover & District Coin Club: A. C. Raper, 1 Humber Court, River Way, Andover, Hants.
Bath & Bristol Numismatic Society (Bath Branch): R. J. Jeffery, 5 Lincoln Grove, Bowerhill, Melksham, Wilts.
— *(Bristol Branch):* I. P. Layne, 54, Rayens Cross Road, Long Ashton, Bristol.
Bedford Numismatic Society: A. J. Brown, 23, Westdale Walk, Kempston, Beds.
Bexley Coin Club: A. J. Gilbert, 54 Townley Road, Bexleyheath, Kent.
Bideford Numismatic Research Society: E. D. Burt, 11 Stanhope Terrace, Northam Road, Bideford, Devon EX39 3JZ.
Birmingham Numismatic Society: P. J. Leighton, 17 Roughley Drive, Four Oaks, Sutton Coldfield, West Midlands.
Bolton and District Numismatic Society: M. D. Hill, 28 Rayden Crescent, Westhoughton, Bolton, BL5 2ES.
Buckinghamshire Numismatic Society: Dr. P. M. Lewis, 5 Winwood Drive, Quainton, Aylesbury, Bucks.
Cambridgeshire Numistatic Society: M. A. Marsh, Northgate, 63 St. Neots Road, Hardwick, Cambs. CB3 7QH.
Cheltenham Numismatic Society: B. M. Greenaway, Lordswood, The Butts, Lydiard Millicent, Swindon, Wilts.
Chester & District Numismatic Society: K. B. Parry, Draenen Wen, 4 Mayville Avenue, Llay, Wrexham, Clwyd. LL12 0PW.
Colchester Numismatic Society: P. S. Newman, 20, Baden Powell Drive, Colchester, Essex CO3 4SL.
Coventry & District Numismatic Society: L. S. Meer, 192 Canley Road, Earlsdon, Coventry CV5 6AQ.
Crewe & District Coin & Medal Society: B. Edge, 48 Woodside Avenue, Wistaston, Crewe, Cheshire CW2 8AN.
Darlington & District Numismatic Society: D. Evans, 17, Church Close, Newton Aycliffe, Co. Durham.
Derbyshire Numismatic Society: E. W. Danson, 63 Ferrers Way, Darley Abbey, Derby DE3 2BB
Devon & Exeter Numismatic Society: Alan Mills, 13, Clifford Close, Whipton, Exeter, EX1 3JU.
Dunelm (Peterlee) Numismatic Society: R. Fortune, 5 Helford Road, Peterlee, Co. Durham SR8 1ER.
Durham Numismatic Society: J. J. A. Morris, High Farm, Elwick, Hartlepool, Cleveland TS27 3HD.
Essex Numismatic Society: I. R. Buck, 2 Chestnut Grove, Braintree, Essex CM7 7LU.
Glasgow and West of Scotland Numismatic Society: N. G. Brodie, 21, Carrour Gardens, Bishopbriggs, Glasgow G64 3DG.
Harlow Numismatic Society: A. J. Davis, 2, Willowfield, Harlow, Essex, CM13 6RR.
Hayes (Middlesex) & District Coin Club: Dr. J. Lavertine, Hillingdon Hospital, Hillingdon, Middx.
Horncastle & District Coin Club: Mrs. K. F. Smith, 15, Linda Crescent, Louth, Lincs, LN11 9LQ.
Hull & District Numismatic Society: A. Farmer, 65 Hull Road, Anlaby, Hull HU10 6SR.

Ipswich Numismatic Society: Dr. I. T. Holloway, 9, Warrington Road, Ipswich, Suffolk, IP1 3QU.
Isle of Wight Numismatic Society: J. E. Steane, Wentworth, Meadow Drive, Bembridge, Isle of Wight PO35 5XZ.
Kent Numismatic Society: L. Cooper, Keeper's Cottage, Stockbury, Sittingbourne, Kent.
Kingston Numismatic Society: N. Clarkson, 62 Cheshire Gardens, Chessington, Surrey.
Lancashire & Cheshire Numismatic Society: K. Sugden, 19 Bolton Avenue, Cheadle Hulme, Cheshire.
Leicester & District Numismatic Society: P. I. Kelly, 95, Tewkesbury Street, Leicester, LE3 5HR.
Lincolnshire Numismatic Society: D. Goodey, 3 Torrington Street, Grimsby DN32 9QH.
London Numismatic Club: N. Fairhead, 6, Derby Lodge, East End Road, Finchley, London, N3 3QC.
Medway Towns Numismatic Society: E. H. Redfern, Perrydene, Pear Tree Lane, Shorne, Gravesend, Kent.
Merseyside Numismatic Society: A. J. Miller, 33, Picton Avenue, Runcorn, Cheshire, WA7 5DW.
Norfolk & Norwich Numismatic Society: C. J. Laurence-Couzens, Hanover House, 28 Hanover Road, Norwich, NR2 2HD.
Northampton Numismatic Society: P. D. S. Waddell, 22 Jenkinson Road, Towcester, Northants.
North Devon Numismatic Society: I. T. Arnold, 21 Tennacott Heights, Bideford, N. Devon.
North-East Cheshire Numismatic Society: D. L. Dodson, 3 Kennerley's Lane, Wilmslow, Cheshire, SK9 5EQ.
Numismatic Society of Nottingham: S. E. Bell, Redwood, Back Lane, Normanton-on-the-Wolds, Nottingham, NG/12 5NP.
Oxford Numismatic Society: A. S. Adamson, 114 South Avenue, Abingdon, Oxon. OX14 1QS.
Plymouth Numismatic Society: G. W. Stead, 35 Torr Road, Hartley, Plymouth, Devon PL3 5TF.
Preston & District Numismatic Society: J. T. Lennon, 64, Malvern Avenue, Frenchwood, Preston, Lancs.
Reading Coin Club: F. Milward, 189b Oxford Road, Reading, Berks.
Ripon Numismatic Society: F. Wolfenden, c/o Barclays Bank, 17, East Market Place, Ripon.
Romsey Numismatic Society: E. Thomas, 30 Wychwood Grove, Chandler's Ford, Eastleigh, Hants.
Royal Tunbridge Wells & District Numismatic Society: M. Gray, 43, Royal Chase, Tunbridge Wells, Kent.
Rye Coin Club: C. French, 22 Tillingham Avenue, Rye, Sussex.
St. Albans & Hertfordshire Numismatic Society: L. A. Shaw, 30 Coneydale, Welwyn Garden City, Herts. AL8 7RZ.
Scottish Numismatic Society: R. Bain, 14, Craigleigh Hill Gardens, Edinburgh, EH4 2JB.
Scunthorpe Numismatic Society: C. L. Wood, 53, High Street, Yaddlethorpe, Scunthorpe, Lincs.
Sheffield & District Numismatic Society: W. E. Kitson, 187 Crimicar Lane, Sheffield, S. Yorks, S10 4EH.
Southampton & District Numismatic Society: H. J. M. Good, 7 Wood Road, Ashurst, Southampton SO4 2BD.
South Wales & Monmouthshire Numismatic Sociey: A. C. Cox, 32 Exmouth Court, Lynmouth Crescent, Rumney, Cardiff, South Glam. CF3 9AT.
Teeside Numismatic Society: F. Gilbert, The Manor, Ingleby Greenhow, Great Ayton, Teeside.
Torbay & District Numismatic Society: B. S. Warren, 39 Windsor Ave., Newton Abbot, Devon TQ12 4DN.
Tyneside & District Numismatic Society: J. H. Corbett, 105 Clayton Street, Newcastle-on-Tyne, Northumberland.
Waterlooville & District Numismatic Society: H. W. Vinall, 22 Frogmore Lane, Lovedean, Portsmouth PO8 9QL.
Wessex Numismatic Society: D. W. Sadler, 30 Oak Avenue, Christchurch, Dorset.
West Midland Numismatic Society: P. W. Selby, 29 Parkfield Road, Stourbridge, W. Midlands DY8 1HD.
Wickford Numismatic Society: T. S. Wherrett, 59 Brock Hill, Wickford, Essex SS11 7NP
Woking Numismatic Society: J. L. Wetton, 39 Oriental Road, Woking, Surrey.
Worksop Numismatic Society: W. E. Gray, 12 Hamilton Park Road, Cusworth, Doncaster, Yorks.
York Coin & Medal Society: W. Moore, 66 Sutherland Street, York. YO2 1HQ.
Yorkshire Numismatic Society: C. Peel, 162 Acreshall Avenue, Pudsey, W. Yorkshire.

SEABY PUBLICATIONS

THE COINAGE OF ANCIENT BRITAIN

by R. P. Mack

£5·00

$13·00

Completely revised third edition of this standard work of reference to Ancient British Coinage.

200 pages, 33 plates, 19 maps.

ENGLISH COINS

in the British Museum:

Anglo-Saxon Coins

by Charles Keary & Herbert Grueber

£25·00

$65·00

A reprint in 2 volumes of the widely quoted reference work on Anglo-Saxon Coins.

822 pages, 62 plates.

THE ENGLISH SILVER COINAGE FROM 1649

by H. A. Seaby & P. A. Rayner

£4·50

$12·00

The fourth edition of this standard work of reference on English milled silver coinage, giving comparative rarity of all varieties, also patterns and proofs.

238 pages, over 625 illustrations.

Seaby's Standard Catalogue of
British Coins Part 3

COINS AND TOKENS OF IRELAND

Compiled by Peter Seaby

£1·20

$3·25

This is the third part of our Standard Catalogue of British Coins and covers Irish issues from the Viking Age to the present day.

128 pages, over 400 illustrations.

Seaby's Standard Catalogue of
British Coins Part 4

COINS AND TOKENS OF SCOTLAND

Compiled by P. F. Purvey

£2·00

$5·25

A comprehensive listing of all the Scottish coins from David to the Union. The 18th and 19th Century trade tokens, private tokens, advertisement tickets, transport tokens are all listed.

160 pages, approx. 400 illustrations.

MEDIEVAL ANGLO-IRISH COINS

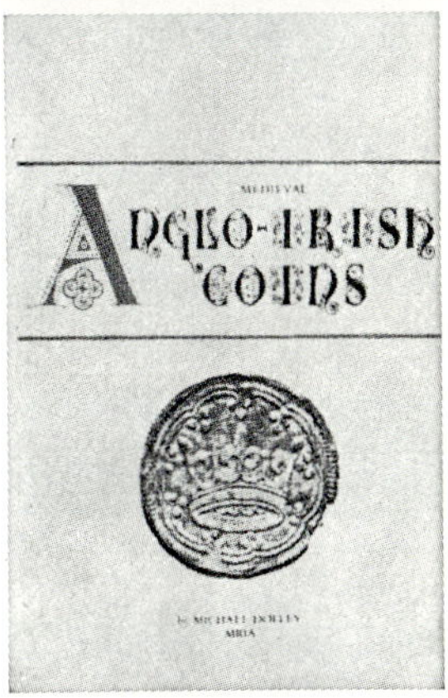

by Michael Dolley

£3·00

$7·00

An authoritative work on medieval Anglo-Irish coins including maps and listings of coin hoards and mints.

90 pages, illustrations in text.

THE PROVINCIAL TOKEN COINAGE OF THE 18th CENTURY

by R. Dalton and S. H. Hamer

£25·00

A reprint of this popular and standard work on the copper tokens of the eighteenth century.

Thousands of tokens listed and illustrated throughout, 565 pages.

THE SILVER TOKEN COINAGE 1811–12

by Richard Dalton

£3·50
$9·00

A reprint of the standard work on silver tokens, first published in 1922.

63 pages, each token is illustrated in text, with additional list of valuations.

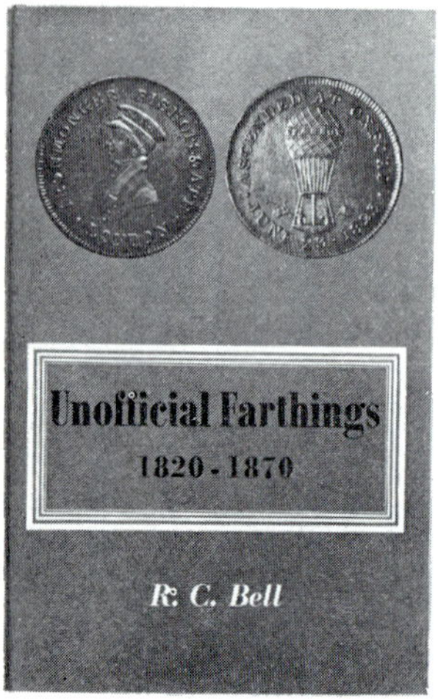

UNOFFICIAL FARTHINGS 1820-1870

by R. C. Bell

£12·00
$27·50

A new publication to stimulate interest in what in the past has been a somewhat neglected area of token collecting.

248 pages, illustrations throughout text, rarity guide.

THE NINETEENTH CENTURY TOKEN COINAGE

by W. J. Davis

£18·00

A new printing of the 1969 Seaby reprint which included an addenda and additional plate of illustrations.

Now offered with a 10 page list of valuations to the section dealing with Overseers', Private Bankers' and Tradesmen's Tokens, 1800-1830 compiled by Robert Sharman.

284 pages, 15 plates.

(*Copies of the valuation list are available separately—price* £1.)

THOMAS SIMON
his life and work 1618-1665

by Alan J. Nathanson

£5·25

$12·00

Thomas Simon's life and work, the creation of dies for coins, medals and seals of England's greatest engraver.

60 pages, 49 illustrations throughout text.

TAVERNS AND TOKENS OF PEPYS' LONDON

by George Berry

£7·50

$16·50

A listing of the tokens of taverns mentioned by Samuel Pepys in his diary, with historical commentary and anecdotes.

144 pages, 4 maps, 20 photos, 77 tokens illustrated.

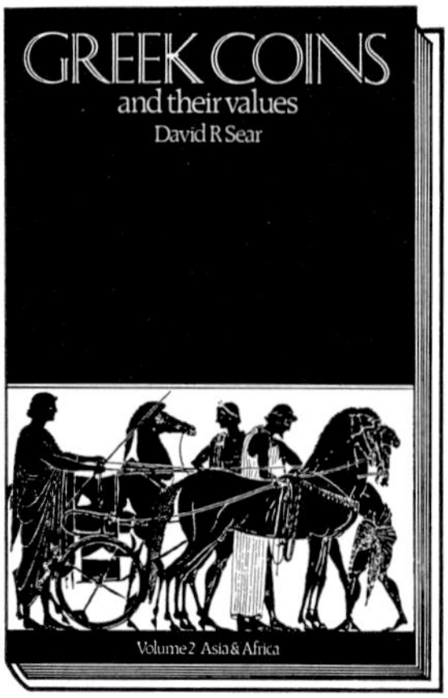

GREEK COINS
and Their Values

by D. R. Sear

Vol I. **Europe**
£12·50 $27·50

Vol II. **Asia & Africa,**
including the Hellenistic Monarchies.
£14·00 $35·00

The most comprehensive priced guide to Greek coins ever published. The average collector should be able to locate all the types he is likely to encounter in one denomination or another. Useful historical notes and illustrated preface. Altogether 7956 coins listed with 3356 photographs of coins in the British Museum.

GREEK COIN TYPES AND THEIR IDENTIFICATION

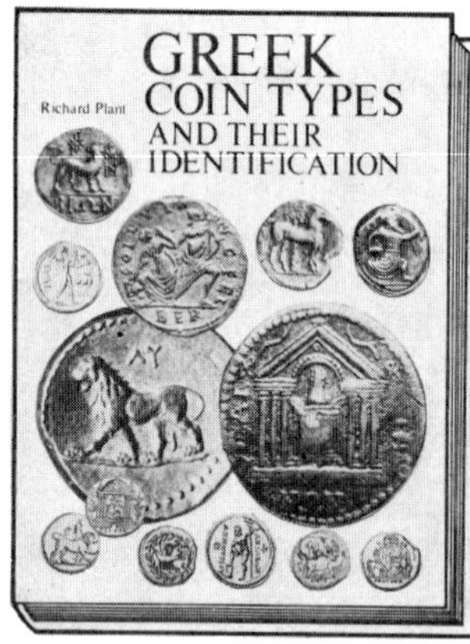

by Richard Plant

£10·00 $24·00

Nearly 3000 Greek coins are listed and illustrated, concentrating on types not immediately identifiable from their inscriptions or subjects represented. Place of issue, date, denomination, metal and size are given. An invaluable aid to the identification of Greek and 'Greek Imperial' coins.

ROMAN COINS
and Their Values

by D. R. Sear

3rd Revised Edition 1981

£10·00 $25·00

A general catalogue of Roman coins, with values, containing biographical and historical details, and descriptions of over 4300 coins.

376 pages, with chronological tables, twelve plates and many half tone illustrations in text.

THE COINAGE OF ROMAN BRITAIN

by Gilbert Askew

£4·75 $12·00

Second edition with new introduction. The most compact listing of the Roman coins relating to the Province of Britannia.

ROMAN SILVER COINS

by H. A. Seaby

New edition revised by D. R. Sear and Robert Loosley

Vol I. Republic to Augustus
£7·50 $16·00

Vol II. Tiberius to Commodus
£12·00 $30·00

The text of the above volumes has been revised to include the latest valuations, new coins and the latest research, and contains new photographic illustrations.
Volumes III & IV in course of revision.
Volumes V & VI in preparation.

A DICTIONARY OF ROMAN COINS

by S. W. Stevenson **£12·00 $30·00**

First published in 1889, this is a reprint of the most comprehensive dictionary of Roman coin types, legends, emperors, etc., ever published in a single volume and contains much information for students of Roman coinage not assembled elsewhere.
929 pages, several hundred illustrations.

BYZANTINE COINS
and Their Values

by D. R. Sear

£7·50

$17·50

An almost complete listing of the main Byzantine coin types known, covering the period from Anastasius 1st (491-518) to the capture of Constantinople by the Turks in 1453.

415 pages, maps, over 600 illustrations throughout text.

BRITISH HISTORICAL MEDALS 1760-1960

by Laurence Brown

Vol. I. The Accession of George III to the death of William IV.

£45·00

The authoritative continuation of *Medallic Illustrations*. Full numismatic description of each piece is given, its designer where known, its size, metal in which specimens are known (together with an indication of their rarity), and locations of specimens in the principal British collections. Full indexes of inscriptions, artists, engravers, medallists, publishers and provenances of illustrated medals. 1755 medals listed, 406 illustrations, 496 pages, cloth bound.

MEDALLIC ILLUSTRATIONS OF THE HISTORY OF GREAT BRITAIN AND IRELAND TO THE DEATH OF GEORGE II

We are pleased to announce the first ever reprint of the plates of this major work on British historical medallions. Not only does it have 183 superb plates but the textual matter which accompanies the illustrations provides adequate information to enable correct identification plus a certain amount of historical data. Reference to the two volumes of text (already reprinted some years ago) are also given.
In addition there are indices covering inscriptions, engravers and artists, engraver's initials and a general subject index.
Size $16\frac{1}{2}$" x $11\frac{1}{2}$". Heavy library binding £100.
Deluxe half-leather limited edition £175

COLLECTING MEDALS AND DECORATIONS

by Alec A. Purves **£7·50 $16·00**

This 3rd edition has been considerably expanded especially in the section on foreign awards. A useful book that can quickly pay for itself. 237 pages, 15 plates, 18 text illustrations.

ARABIC COINS AND HOW TO READ THEM

by Richard Plant **£4·50 $11·00**

A 2nd edition of this popular book with text revised and expanded. 154 pages, numerous line drawings in text.

SEABYSLIDES

COINS IN COLOUR

Each set of thirty 2″ × 2″ (35 mm) slides is accompanied by a brochure giving a brief introduction to the series, a detailed listing of the coins and suggestions for further study and reading. The coins have been especially selected and photographed by P. Frank Purvey.

Each set £12·50 ($30·00) including postage.

GREEK COINS

Greek coins from the 6th Century B.C. to Alexander the Great. (Ref.: SS 1)
The Hellenistic Monarchies — Alexander the Great to Cleopatra VII (Ref.: SS 14)

ROMAN COINS

The Coinage of Republican Rome (Ref.: SS 15)
The Twelve Caesars and other imperial portraits. (Ref.: SS 2)

BYZANTINE COINS

The Byzantine Empire from Constantine the Great to 1453. (Ref.: SS 13)

JEWISH COINS

Coins of Bible Days; 4th Century B.C. to A.D. 135. (Ref.: SS 8)

ENGLISH COINS

Ancient British Coins. (Ref.: SS 16) *In preparation*
English hammered gold coins, Edward III to Charles II. (Ref.: SS 3)
English milled gold coins, Elizabeth I to Elizabeth II. (Ref.: SS 4)
English crown pieces, Edward VI to Elizabeth II. (Ref.: SS 5)
Silver coins of the Tudors and Stuarts. (Ref.: SS 17). *In preparation*
Pattern and trial pieces in the Royal Mint, London. (Ref.: SS 7)

SCOTTISH COINS

Scottish gold coins, Robert III to William III. (Ref.: SS 6)

RENAISSANCE COINS

Renaissance coins and medals. (Ref.: SS 9)

UNITED STATES COINS

United States gold coins. (Ref.: SS 10)
United States coins in silver and copper. (Ref.: SS 11)
United States Commemorative coins in gold and silver. (Ref.: SS 12)

COIN CABINETS

Details on request.

NUMISMATIC ACCESSORIES

Prices of coin accessories exclude postage

COINDEX — An international coin Indexing System

STORAGE BOX

A storage box to hold up to 100 coins in plastic holders, designed to take coloured index cards for identification and easy reference to the coins. Complete with 100 envelopes and coloured cards.
10″ × 2″ × 3″ Price **£5·00**

COINDEX ALBUM

An album featuring colour card indexing, similar to the Coindex Storage box previously described. Holds 10 pages (160 coins), with white card interleaves. Complete with coloured index cards.
12″ × 18″ Price **£9·00**

COIN TICKETS

Round labels made of thin white card — **30p** per 100.

$\frac{7}{8}$″
$\frac{15}{16}$″
1″ full
$1\frac{1}{8}$″
$1\frac{1}{4}$″
$1\frac{5}{16}$″
$1\frac{7}{16}$″
$1\frac{5}{8}$″
$1\frac{7}{8}$″

STORAGE BOXES

Heavyboard, 9″ × $2\frac{1}{2}$″, to hold 2″ × 2″ envelopes.
Price 50p

COIN ENVELOPES

2″ × 2″, white paper, **£1.00** per packet of 100.
2″ × 2″, plastic (transparent), **£2.25** per 100.

MAGNIFYING GLASSES

MG1 ×8 magnifier with 18 mm lens mounted in folding metal case	**£3·50**
MG2 ×10 magnifier, similar	**£6·50**
MG3 ×20 magnifier, similar but 14 mm lens	**£7·50**
MG4 × 10 and ×20 twin lens magnifier in metal case	**£4·00**
MG5 3×, 6×, 9 × Zeiss lens magnifier	**£12·50**